PITT LATIN AMERICAN SERIES **PLAS**

THE
MEXICAN REPUBLIC:
THE
FIRST DECADE
1823–1832

Stanley C. Green

UNIVERSITY OF PITTSBURGH PRESS

To my parents, John and Mary Green, and to my wife Gloria

Published by the University of Pittsburgh Press, Pittsburgh, Pa. 15260
Copyright © 1987, University of Pittsburgh Press
All rights reserved
Feffer and Simons, Inc., London
Manufactured in the United States of America

Library of Congress Cataloging-in-Publication Data

Green, Stanley C.
  The Mexican Republic.

  (Pitt Latin American series)
  Bibliography: p. 289
  Includes index.
  1. Mexico—History—1821–1861.   I. Title.
II. Series.
F1232.G8 1986   972'.04   86-4310
ISBN 0-8229-3817-0

Contents

Illustrations

Acknowledgments

This is the place to remember courtesies that extended beyond professional obligations—which an author-to-be soon realizes is the help that really counts.

The first was Don Worcester of Texas Christian University, whose talent was to quietly set near-impossible expectations of scholarly production. Along the way Bill Timmons and Charles Hale read the manuscript and made valuable suggestions.

In Mexico City, a special interest was taken by José Guzmán and Masae Sugawara at the Archivo General de la Nación. At the Biblioteca Nacional, Alberto A. Lamadrid Lusarreta and his assistant Mr. Castañeda demonstrated high levels of professionalism. The material at the Archivo de Notarías was obtained only through the help of Guillermina Pimentel de Gutiérrez. Personal holdings were made available through the hospitality of José C. Valadés and the family of Salvador Noriega.

At Austin, Don Gibbs and Jane Garner of the Benson Latin American Collection were always ready to spend time in tracking down obscure sources.

Over the years, Laredo State University Presidents Billy Cowart and Manuel Pacheco, and Vice-President Leo Sayavedra provided support. Professor Lem Londos Railsback answered the call for help on more than one occasion. They never lost faith that there really was a book in the making. Laura Rea, in typing most of the manuscript, did far more work than is expected of a typist. Ninfa Molina and Enrique de la Garza also graciously helped with the typing. Mayellen Bresie and her staff at the university library were ever ready to search for ancient books.

The portrait of Agustín de Iturbide on page 10 is taken from Enrique

Olavarría y Ferrari, *Mexico independiente 1821–1855* (Mexico City: Ballescá y Cia., 1888–89). The portrait of Lorenzo de Zavala on page 12 hangs in the Texas State Capitol Building, in Austin. The portraits of Lucas Alamán, Guadalupe Victoria, Nicolás Bravo, Manuel Gómez Pedraza, Vicente Guerrero, and Anastacio Bustamante, on page 12, 49, 156, and 163, may be seen in the Museo Nacional de Historia de México, in Mexico City. The illustrations entitled "View of Guanajuato," "Plaza Mayor, Mexico City," "View of Zacatecas," "Hacendado and Majordomo," and "Tortilla Makers," on pages 26, 27, 28, 60, and 61, are from Carl Nebel, *Voyage Pittoresque et Archaeologique dans la partie la plus intéressante du Mexique* (Paris, c. 1836). "The School Dunce," on page 104, is from José Joachin de Lizardi, *El Periquillo sarniento* (1817). "Grinding Ore at the Salgado Hacienda," on page 129, is from H. G. Ward, *Mexico in 1827* (London: Henry Colburn, 1828). The portrait of Antonio López de Santa Anna, on page 156, is from Manuel Rivera Cambas, *Historia antigua y moderna de Jalapa* (Mexico City: Imprenta Cumplido, 1869–70).

THE MEXICAN REPUBLIC

Introduction

The colony of New Spain ceased to be on September 27, 1821. Colonel Agustín de Iturbide at the head of his Army of Three Guarantees marched into Mexico City, bringing to a successful conclusion the movement begun by Father Hidalgo back in 1810. But he is not revered in Mexican schoolbooks because he was out of step with the sentiments of the age—and his countrymen—and had himself crowned Emperor Agustín I in 1822. It was not a time for princes in the Americas, and Agustín I reigned less than a year. The times and Mexico's new independent status called for institutions of the future, not of the past.

In the early 1820s republican expectations quickened the spirits of Mexico's new citizens. By order of the Guanajuato commanding general, the traditional challenge "Who goes?" was now to be answered by "The Federal Republic." State decrees abolished the traditional address of *don,* and henceforth men were to greet each other with *ciudadano* (citizen). The custom extended to women where *madama* was intended to take the place of *doña.* A new time reckoning was inspired, taking its markings from overthrowing the Spaniards and Iturbide and the creation of the Republic. An 1825 document, for example, might bear the date "4th year of Independence, 3rd of Freedom, and 2nd of the Federation."

In time these affectations were worn away by the weight of tradition. But the story of a land, and men and women who were animated by these noble visions, bear our attention. The republican ethos—this transition from colony to nation-state—lasted some ten years. The social and economic forces that had been contained by the viceregal structures soon molded themselves to republican forms, and by the early 1830s the molds were fixed and the political battles of nineteenth century proper would commence.

3

But while some looked to their own interests, the excitement of independence and republicanism gripped Mexicans at large. It was a new day. The impetus touched almost every part of public life—some lightly and some profoundly—and so the period must be studied in its entirety. Panoramic views of history have been out of date. With the rise of graduate schools and the professionalization of historical writing in the twentieth century, the thrust has been toward monographs. To find comprehensive coverage of this period we have to go back to the gentlemen scholars of the Porfiriato—primarily Olavarría y Ferrari who wrote a massively detailed volume. Or we can go back to the protagonists who left historical apologies, Lucas Alamán, Lorenzo de Zavala, and José María Tornel y Mendívil. In recent years scholars have been chipping away regularly at Mexico's archival stores, and although they are far from finished, their monographs and dissertations—along with public documents of the period—give us reasonably firm footing as we attempt to grasp the whole of Mexican life during the first decade of the Republic.

A history of the Republic's first decade opens in spring 1823. These days marked the end of the reign of Agustín I, and even as he was being escorted out of the country to exile, his opponents began setting up republican institutions to replace the imperial apparatus. The history would carry from the administration of Guadalupe Victoria (1824–1829) when the state-building efforts gave way to partisan politics, to the one-year populist administration of Vicente Guerrero (1829), and finally to the administration of Anastacio Bustamante (1830–1832), when republican forms were bent to the service of Hispanic authoritarianism.

As Mexicans struggled to turn their colony into a republic, the independence ethic gave a coloration to institutions. The common thread of public dynamics was the flux between the weight of the colonial past and the direction called for by nation-state status. While the ideological current of independence generally carried politics toward liberalism, in ecclesiastical matters Mexicans rejected religious toleration for Catholic exclusivity. At the same time, however, state government officials took charge of certain church affairs. In the military the viceregal goal of the professional soldier was compromised to the reality of mass participation carried over from the Revolution. In education the old private schools, convent schools, and colleges of the gentility lived on, but were supplemented by newer institutions inspired by a concern for universal schooling and a modern curriculum. The disturbances of transition were perhaps most clearly seen in economic life. Devotion to free trade was tested as Mexicans learned that access to the outside economic world was not inevitably beneficial.

The first decade of the Republic was an interim period in leadership. The revolutionary heroes had come in from the field but were out of place in the halls of state making, while the era of the politician as caudillo was still to come. During the debates over the new governments, two figures emerged as the standard bearers of the opposing systems, and whose careers embodied the conflict. Lucas Alamán (1792–1853), mining engineer, political prodigy, and publicist, from a very early date assumed the role of spokesman and organizer for those groups who felt that Mexicans would best be served by maintaining order in the tradition of Hispanic authority.

His nemesis was Lorenzo de Zavala (1788–1836), journalist, political organizer of the masses, and investor in the public lands, who came to lead those who felt Mexico's hope lay in following the examples of the world's progressive nations.

Their confrontation previewed the issues that would dominate Mexican history throughout the nineteenth century: the creation of an egalitarian society, the form government should take, church-state conflicts, adjusting European ideologies to the reality of Mexico, land distribution, and economic modernization. The 1820s witnessed the first stage in addressing these issues. Typically the first response was dictated by nineteenth-century liberalism, which meant for traditional Hispanic institutions opening them to modern currents and the new citizens. The results were not all that was hoped for, and the process itself was incomplete, so that by about 1830 both those that wanted to weaken the traditional centers of power and those who wanted to strengthen them were more disposed to use the force of government intervention. The former approach led to the Reform, while the latter led to the search for a foreign prince to recapture the legitimacy lost in 1821.

« 1 »

Mexico at Independence

The viceregal government won the insurrection started in 1810 by Mexico's hero of independence, Father Hidalgo. The royalist troops, directed by viceroys Francisco Javier Venegas (1810–1813), Félix María Calleja (1813–1816), and Juan Ruíz de Apodaca (1816–1821), defeated the rebels in savage fighting—with mostly Mexican soldiers and with little help from Spain. It was a striking testament to Spanish command. By 1817 New Spain had the appearance of a loyal colony once again.

Yet four years later, when Iturbide raised the banner of revolt, hardly anyone could be found to support the Spanish cause. The last viceroy, Francisco Novella, issued a decree to commandeer citizens' horses for use against the rebels in July 1821, and ten days later stated that "not one single individual has voluntarily presented any of the many horses that are to be seen in the city." A few days after this, the Mexico City *ayuntamiento,* or town council, lectured the viceroy when he presumed to ask for help in building a war chest.[1]

How could this be?

The answer is that Spanish officials had won the civil war but had lost the battle for the allegiance of their colonial subjects. Spain had never held the colony by force but by habit and the claim of its right to rule. After all, Spain had brought the colony into being, and provided its institutions and culture and leadership. Spain stood for authority, stability, and above all legitimacy.

There had always been a reservoir of ill will toward Spaniards. Colonial life was clearly managed for their benefit, and events between 1789 and

1821 brought this into relief. The effect of the European wars following the French Revolution was felt with the arrival of foreign ships, forced loans, the scarcity of quicksilver needed for processing silver ore, and especially the calling in of the principal on church loans in 1804. Then in 1807 when Napoleon sequestered the Spanish royal family, the Bourbons, on a French estate and sent French troops to occupy Spain, the colonial system was decapitated.

Throughout Spanish America the occupation led to movements by creoles who claimed to govern for the imprisoned Fernando VII but who in fact led the colonies to independence. In New Spain, events went in another direction. Late on the night of September 15, 1810, Father Miguel Hidalgo y Costilla rang the bells of his Dolores church. To his Indian parishioners that gathered round, he declared in his famous Grito de Dolores that they must strike a blow at bad government—meaning the Spaniards. The Indians that rallied to the call for independence initiated a social revolution. Hidalgo also attracted numbers of mixed bloods *(castas)* and even creoles, and as the insurrection spread to almost every section of the colony, local conditions played a large part in the violence. But the movement remained largely lower-class in composition and anti-European in tone. Hidalgo's army moved from town to town attacking viceregal authorities, but his men did not distinguish between the white faces of creoles and of Spaniards.

As news came in of massacres, creole leaders decided to stand by their Spanish masters and this spelled the balance of power. After Hidalgo's execution in 1811, leadership passed to José María Morelos, who kept the rebellion alive in southern Mexico until he, in turn, was executed in 1815. With the insurgents beaten down on almost all fronts, most of the insurgent leaders, such as Manuel de Mier y Terán and Nicolás Bravo, accepted the pardon of Viceroy Apodaca. The unyielding, like Guadalupe Victoria and Vicente Guerrero, took to their mountain hideouts. From 1817 to 1821 New Spain was relatively calm.

While its troops in the colony continued invincible, at home Spain's tradition of conservative monarchical government was shattered. When French troops streamed into the peninsula, the Spanish people answered with a spontaneous and ferocious resistance that came to be coordinated nationally by the Central Supreme Governing Junta. Staying ahead of advancing French troops, the Central Junta fled to the Isle of León (outside Cádiz) where it convoked a national parliament (Cortes) and then surrendered its authority to a five-man regency.

The Cortes that met from 1810 to 1814 was not representative of Spanish sentiment. Not only did Spanish Americans comprise one-fourth of the membership, but also the vagaries of war and elections had given younger men of the intelligentsia and the bourgeoisie a near-majority. The Cortes took steps to implant a more liberal system. The delegates placed limits on the power of the monarchy, abolished the Inquisition, and did away with prepublication censorship of nonreligious writings. For the colonies the delegates offered a number of reforms: decreeing equal laws for all parts of the empire; making certain concessions to home rule, such as giving smaller towns the right of self-government and creating the provincial deputation (a popularly elected administrative council); and replacing the position of vice-roy with that of supreme political chief, a symbolic demoting of surrogate majesty to obedient functionary.[2] Most of these changes were codified in what was called the Constitution of 1812 or the Cádiz Constitution.

Viceroy Venegas in Mexico City saw these changes, especially the freedom of the press rules, as encouraging the insurrectionists, and in late 1812 his subjects witnessed the novel sight of a viceroy ignoring his superi-ors in Spain. Then when Fernando VII emerged from French internment to claim the Spanish throne in 1814, he closed the Cortes, annulled its laws and constitution, and used his Napoleonic veterans to retard the revolu-tionary process.

New Spain was settling back into political orthodoxy when word came of yet another turn in Spain's politics. An 1820 mutiny led by Colonel Rafael Riego forced Fernando to revalidate the 1812 constitution and call the Cortes back. Delegates of this body, meeting from 1820 to 1822, were prepared to go further down the road of change and reform than their predecessors in 1810–1814. The former delegates, although circumscribing the king with a constitution, had stopped short of a direct confrontation with the established order. But the new Cortes delegates launched a frontal assault on institutions held dear by many Spaniards. Motivated by a spirit of secularism and equality before the law, it was their intention to recon-struct Spanish society in the image of classical liberalism. They legislated against the church's claims to legal apartness, abolishing its *fueros* (immu-nity to civil courts) and monastic orders, and taking steps to limit church property and control over education. The legal privileges of the military (*fueros*) were likewise done away with, and the apparatus of mercantilism was dismantled. The program of the Cortes, although it did not survive in Spain, would be the point of departure for Mexico's legislative reform in the next decade.

In New Spain this most recent change of political course left Spaniards disillusioned and creole leaders jubilant. The overall effect on Spanish au-thority was devastating, for taken together with the other reversals of recent years, it made it hard to believe in a government that changed with the tide.

The first individual to act on this was Colonel Agustín de Iturbide, a thirty-seven-year-old creole with an impressive military record in cam-paigns against the insurgents. Sent out on an expedition against Vicente Guerrero, he instead treated with the rebel chieftain and then issued the Plan of Iguala on February 24, 1821. The plan's first three articles stated that

(1) Mexico was independent, (2) Roman Catholicism was the religion of the nation, and (3) all Mexicans would be united, with no distinctions between Europeans and Americans. It also stated that Fernando VII or another Spanish or European prince would be invited to ocupy the Mexican throne. With his Army of the Three Guarantees, named after the first three articles, Iturbide went from success to success through the spring and summer of 1821. Hidalgo and Morelos failed because they coupled independence and social upheaval. Iturbide, who was reportedly urged on to his mission by clerics who feared a liberal Cortes stirring up the masses, promised independence with no threat to creole society. Whatever his conservative connections, he was now acclaimed by all classes. Spanish authorities, finding their support melting away, allowed Iturbide to march into Mexico City unmolested on September 27, 1821.[3]

By the Treaties of Córdoba, which Iturbide had signed in August with New Spain's first and last supreme political chief, Juan O'Donoju, the Mexican Empire came into being. General governing authority was to pass to a junta that would convoke a Congress, and to a regency that would serve until the monarch was installed. Iturbide had been known to speak disparagingly of the republican way, and he now filled the junta and regency with substantial men of wealth and influence. The nobility of the colony was embraced, while the old insurgents were ignored.

Iturbide had very unrepublican ambitions of his own. Mexico's first independent congress, the Sovereign Constituent Congress, convened on February 24, 1822, and on May 20, the day after a riot in which soldiers and *léperos* (street paupers) demanded his ascension to the throne, Congress agreed to offer Iturbide the crown. Amid much ceremony, he was crowned Agustín I on July 21, 1822.[4]

Iturbide was in the peculiar position of replacing a progressive imperial regime with a reactionary government of rebels. To confound the picture further, Lorenzo de Zavala, who would soon become the prime mover of liberalism, supported Iturbide, as did many of his fellow republicans. And Lucas Alamán, the great conservative leader of early national Mexico, was allied with those who worked to overthrow Iturbide.

THE MAKING OF A MEXICAN LEADERSHIP

Lucas Alamán and Lorenzo de Zavala came of political age in the years between Hidalgo and Iturbide. They had brushed up against the violence of the Revolution, had worked for reform as delegates to the 1820–1822 Cortes, and had come through it with radically different visions of how Mexico should be.

The case can be made that their early lives prefigured their political positions. For his part, Alamán came from a distinguished line. He was born in Guanajuato on October 18, 1792. His father, Juan Vicente Alamán,

Agustín de Iturbide (1783–1824)

had immigrated from Navarre and had acquired wealth in mining, while his mother, the fifth marchioness of San Clemente, could trace her lineage back to one of the champions of Queen Isabela. Through his mother's first marriage to Brigadier Gabriel de Arechederreta, Alamán was half-brother to Juan Bautista Arechederreta, who served as rector of the College of San Juan de Letrán and then as vicar general of convents in the archbishopric of Mexico from 1823 until his death in 1835.[5]

While Alamán was receiving a young gentleman's education—his "first letters" in a private school, then on to classical studies with tutors— Zavala's schooling was carried out on a more modest scale. Lorenzo de Zavala was born at Tecoh (near Mérida) on October 3, 1788, and after his elementary years he became a pensioner at the Tridentine Seminary of Mérida where he studied philosophy and then theology.[6]

From his teachers, especially the famed Pablo Moreno, Zavala acquired the practice of challenging philosophical authorities, and from then on he preferred to frequent the company of dissenting young intellectuals. Without the means to continue his studies at the university level, he had to go to work in 1807, apparently in commerce, and about this time married Josefa Correa y Correa, with whom he had three children. During the revolutionary period he began to meet in the evenings with like-minded young men to talk of political issues.[7]

Zavala and Alamán saw the Revolution from opposite ends. Seventeen-year-old Alamán happened to be in Guanajuato in October 1810 when Hidalgo's Indian army stormed the city. He saw his family's dependents killed, and came close to suffering that fate himself because of his Spanish appearance.[8] He then went to Mexico City where he entered the College of Mining and in January of 1814 embarked for Europe, where he continued his studies of metallurgy and languages.[9]

While Alamán traveled in aristocratic circles, was received and befriended by Europeans of science, learning, and official position—he returned six years later speaking Spanish with a French accent—Zavala received the education of a revolutionary. As one of the leaders of Mérida's Society of San Juan, which favored the reforms of the Cortes, his political agitation, especially his tendency to found critical newspapers, made him obnoxious to the authorities. Since at least 1812 the Inquisition stalked him, and he was finally arrested and incarcerated in the San Juan de Ulúa fortress in the Veracruz harbor. There he studied English and medicine and was inducted into the Scottish rite lodge—from which he was later expelled for revealing Masonic secrets. After his release in 1817 he supported his family as a physician in Mérida.[10]

Alamán's and Zavala's careers came together when they were elected to the 1820–1822 Cortes. Alamán, who was given the responsibility of drafting a colonial proposal for a commonwealth arrangement, emerged as a political prodigy. A pamphlet of character sketches described him as a boy with

Lorenzo de Zavala (1788–1836)   Lucas Alamán (1792–1853)

continental tastes, who "although tiny, knows well where the shoe pinches."[11]

Although it is possible to read this as the story of two young men who grew up to fight the cause of their social class, one can also see the divergent effects of the Enlightenment in the Mexican milieu. Alamán took the path of enlightened despotism, the ideal of a modern rationalized administration imposed by cultivated leaders. The greatest of the Spanish Bourbons, Carlos III (1750–1788), had employed this to help bring about the prosperity New Spain enjoyed in its last years as a colony. After the sack of Guanajuato, Alamán wrote two essays, one an article in the *Diario de México* (1812) defending the Copernican system, the other a eulogy of the imprisoned Fernando VII[12]—an early example of his tendency to be in the vanguard in scientific matters and in the rear guard in political matters.

A number of young men of Alamán's class, whose education put them in touch with progressive currents in Europe, were attracted to these principles. Many of them joined the Scottish rite Masons and worked—notably in the Cortes—to modernize and decentralize Spain's colonial system from above. Before 1821 they were sometimes called "liberals."

The career of Zavala and many of his friends, on the other hand, showed that the Enlightenment could just as easily lead to convictions of popular sovereignty. Although Iturbide's revolution was inspired by conservative instincts, the very act of independence gave currency to a constellation of ideas that included nationalism, federalism, and republicanism.

Zavala came home from the Cortes in time to be elected to Congress in 1822, and there worked to spread these ideas of republicanism. A certain amount of the republican enthusiasm adhered to the person of Agustín I. After all, constitutional monarchy was considered perfectly compatible with a republic. And some of the republicans were generally willing to give the emperor a chance, partly out of respect for him as the author of independence and partly because the alternative might be a government dominated by the Bourbonists, whom the republicans instinctively feared.

The Bourbonists, comprised largely of the aristocratic Scottish rite Masons, were so called because of their devotion to that article of Iturbide's Plan of Ayala promising to bring over a prince of the Bourbon family. They would never accept as ruler a self-anointed commoner. Iturbide's natural support came from ultraconservative circles, the church hierarchy, certain general staff officers, and the *léperos*. Early in his reign, Agustín tried to win over the Spaniards resident in Mexico—unsuccessfully.

Anti-imperial intrigue in 1822 centered in Congress, composed of Iturbidists, Bourbonists, and republicans. On the night of August 26, Iturbide had a number of deputies arrested, and then on October 31 dissolved Congress and replaced it with a picked group, the Instituent Junta.

Agustín I reigned for less than a year, but he presided over a vast region. As New Spain evolved, it had come to be composed of the following territorial divisions:[13]

Kingdom of Nueva España (provinces of México, Tlaxcala, Puebla, Oaxaca, and Michoacán)
Kingdom of Nueva Galicia (provinces of Jalisco or Nueva Galicia, Zacatecas, and Colima)
Government of Nueva Vizcaya (provinces of Durango and Chihuahua)
Government of Yucatán (provinces of Yucatán, Tabasco, and Campeche)
New Kingdom of León (Nuevo León)
Colony of Nuevo Santander
Province of Texas
Province of Coahuila
Province of Sinaloa
Province of Sonora
Province of San José de Nayarit
Province of Vieja (Baja) California
Province of Nueva (Alta) California
Province of Nuevo México

For administrative purposes, these disparate units had been grouped into twelve intendancies by a decree of December 4, 1786. These were:

México	Guanajuato
Puebla	San Luis Potosí
Veracruz	Guadalajara
Mérida	Zacatecas
Oaxaca	Durango
Valladolid	Arizpe (Sonora-Sinaloa)

This was the nation Iturbide laid claim to rule, stretching from the snowy heights of the Rocky Mountains to the subtropical greenery of Chiapas, and he made it even larger. In Guatemala, which had been a captaincy-general under Spain, a Congress was discussing the country's future course. On January 5, 1822, with an army sent by Iturbide in the vicinity, it voted to join Mexico. For the next year and a half, until Guatemala declared its independence (July 1, 1823), Mexico was larger in geographical extent than ever before or since.[14]

Iturbide's downfall dated from the December 6, 1822, Plan of Veracruz which Brigadier Antonio López de Santa Anna issued after he was relieved of his command by the emperor. Santa Anna was put under siege at Veracruz, but the insurgent veterans Vicente Guerrero and Nicolás Bravo took the field in his support, and plottings carried on by Scottish rite Masons spread to the army besieging Veracruz. The final blow came when the principal officers conducting the imperial siege, led by General José Antonio de Echávarri, signed a pact on February 1, the Plan of Casa Mata, which without specifically calling for the emperor's overthrow demanded that a new Congress be assembled.[15]

By February's end, the loyal empire was reduced to Mexico City and its environs, and on March 20 Iturbide delivered his abdication to the reassembled Congress. He was placed under house arrest and Congress selected as his replacement the Supreme Executive Power, an executive of three men with a monthly revolving presidency.[16]

Alamán had arrived in Mexico in March, in time to observe the revolution against Iturbide in full progress. Although he did not hold the rebel leaders in high regard—he met Guadalupe Victoria in Veracruz and thought him a "great fool" *(mentecato)*[17]—they gave him on April 15 the most important office in the cabinet, making him minister for interior and exterior relations.[18] Zavala returned to his seat in Congress. Although he had remained loyal to Agustín I longer than most of his republican friends, defending Iturbide even after the August 26 arrests and taking a prominent role in the Instituent Junta, he had cooperated with the emperor's enemies since late 1822.[19]

With Iturbide in detention, the idea of monarchy was laid to rest and the thoughts of his former subjects turned to creating a government along republican lines. Alamán and Zavala contemplated different versions of the Republic, but very shortly the issue would be decided by new voices on the political scene, voices from the provinces.

AN OVERVIEW OF REGIONS AND CITIES

The Mexico of these years was a disjointed nation. Since even before the arrival of the Spaniards, geography and migrations had made for distinct regions, and although Spanish authority had given a certain cement, the freer atmosphere of republicanism allowed provincial citizens to indulge their particularism. All the regions, however, shared a common thread of life, recovery from the Revolution and adjustment to the new world of independence.

The operative geopolitical regions were the south, where Indian farming cultures dominated the landscape; the central area, traditional fulcrum of Hispanic civilization; north-central Mexico, near enough to fall under the sway of the center but distant enough to nurture dreams of separatism; and the far northern frontier, whose few inhabitants were subject to the raids of nomadic Indians and the relentless tide of Anglo-Saxon expansion.

The South

The states of Yucatán, Oaxaca, Chiapas, and Tabasco made up the south which, compared to central Mexico, was more rural, more Indian, and less dependent on mineral wealth. By virtue of a dense population, a long tradition of high indigenous culture, and relative access to the core areas, Oaxaca was the preeminent southern state. Spaniards had never come in enough strength to overwhelm the native culture, nor to take over the land. By common consent, landownership was spread out wider in Oaxaca than in the more Mexican parts of the Republic, although the Dominicans held many haciendas. For more than a century Oaxacan prosperity had rested on the small cochineal bug, from which the Indians made a scarlet dye. Now, trade in the *grana,* as the cochineal was called, was in a protracted depression, a slump extending back to the 1770s due to declining prices in the world market, a shortage of capital, and competition from Guatemala.[20]

In 1826 José María Murguía y Galardi published a long treatise on Oaxaca's economy in which bleakness was the dominant feature. Landowners, most of whom were Indians, cultivated *grana* to the exclusion of all else, except what maize, beans, haba, and chickpeas *(garbanzos)* were strictly necessary for sustenance. A small number of haciendas were dedicated to cattle and horses. The result was that staples had to be imported, wheat from Puebla, and sugar from the state of Mexico. Artisanry was almost nonexistent: no furniture or farm implements, the weaving profession decimated by imports, and imported Saxon dishware ruling the crockery market. For lighting the natives used goat fat, and for inebriation, curiously enough, pulque was rivaled by brandy *(aguardiente)*.[21] In 1832 the governor noted that some Indians had turned to sugar cane because of the price slump in *grana* and that some cotton was being grown around Tehuantepec and Zoochila.[22]

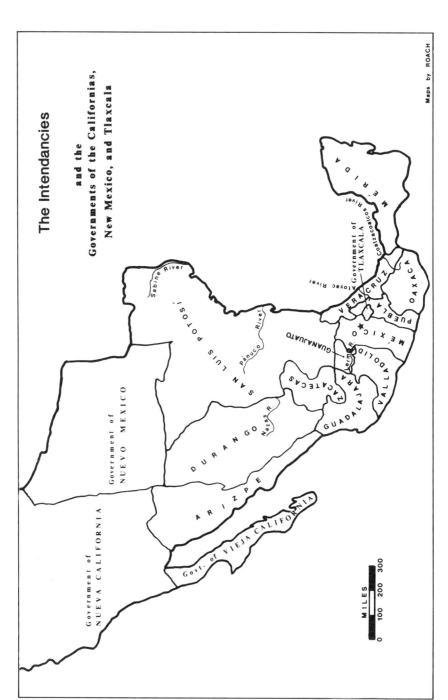

The Intendancies

and the

**Governments of the Californias,
New Mexico, and Tlaxcala**

Government of
NUEVA CALIFORNIA

Government of
NUEVO MEXICO

Sabine River

SAN LUIS POTOSI

Pánuco River

A R I Z P E

Govt. of VIEJA CALIFORNIA

D U R A N G O

Nazas R.

GUADALAJARA

Z A C A T E C A S

GUANAJUATO

VALLADOLID

Lerma R.

MEXICO

PUEBLA

VERA CRUZ

Government of
TLAXCALA

Atoyac River

Coatzacoalcos River

OAXACA

MERIDA

MILES
0   100 200 300

Maps by ROACH

Mexico in the Late Colonial Period

Yucatán, formerly the Intendancy of Mérida, included the present states of Quintana Roo, then almost devoid of population, and Campeche. In the interior the Maya Indians, still speaking their ancestral dialect, lived in economic servitude, a bondage they tried to throw off periodically in savage rebellions. On the coast, the principal cities had maritime economies. The capital, Mérida, lived off trade with Cuba, sending hides, salted meat, henequén, and timber. The city of Campeche, home port for many of Mexico's sailors, faced north, directing a coasting trade with the ports of Veracruz, Alvarado, and Tampico.[23] The Yucatecans, having only occasional contacts with Mexico City, were accustomed to going their own way. They welcomed the free trade declared for the peninsula in 1814. And not finding favor with the independence tariff of November 1821 (with its 25 percent duty and prohibition of imported flour), they had the state government suspend it[24] and suppress the declaration of war with Spain. When pressure from Mexico City forced Yucatán's officials to promulgate the war decree (1825), halting the Cuban trade produced a depression.[25]

In the far south, Chiapas, also contended for by Guatemala, was desired for patriotic reasons, not for its resources. Remote and primitive, it reportedly had not a single stone bridge, the contemporary symbol of minimal civilization, and the road to Tabasco was only a footpath. The Valley of Chiapas held most of the population of 121,322, a majority of whom were Indians, followed by *ladinos* (as mixed bloods were called there), and a few whites. Most Chiapanecos pastured stock on the valley's savannas and slopes, selling the animals and their products to Oaxaca and Central America. Down in the muggy lowlands next to Guatemala, Soconusco's few inhabitants lived off cacao ("the most renowned in the kingdom") and fishing. Tonalá (on the Pacific coast) produced some indigo, Comitán (in the hotlands near Guatemala), distilled brandy, and here and there crude woollens and cottons were woven for local consumption.[26]

On the eastern side of the Sierra de Chiapas, the ocean-bound rivers passed through the state of Tabasco. During the summer months the water washed down in such volume that riverside dwellers had to look for high ground, the pueblos and haciendas became islands, and people could stay in touch only by canoe. Other than subsistence farming, the main economic activity was gathering cacao along river banks or floodplains, and the cultivation of sugar. Of a total of 2,140 rural properties, the state government report for 1831 showed 1,323 cacao haciendas and 605 sugar haciendas. The Tabascans also exported small quantities of coffee, Tabasco pepper, and dyewoods. State officials counted as a "manufacture" the preparation of brandy and the coarse cottons woven by the poor for their own use.[27]

The Center
Out of the core of Mexico—the Valley of Anáhuac and the territory bordering—would be formed the Federal District, five states (Mexico,

Querétaro, Puebla, Veracruz, and Michoacán), and one territory (Tlaxcala). The state of Mexico, richest and most populous (982,418 according to the governor's report of 1828) dominated this area—and at times seemingly the whole Republic. Until forced to disgorge it in 1826, the state had jurisdiction over Mexico City, but even after that date it still surrounded the national capital and reached from Puebla on the east to Acapulco on the Pacific. Its population was varied: predominantly Indian in the many villages surrounding Mexico City, there was much African blood around the Cuautla-Cuernavaca region and Acapulco, and the principal landowners throughout the state tended to be Spanish or creole.

As a provisioner of the Federal District (and Puebla, to a lesser extent), its economy was as diverse as its people. In the prefecture of Mexico, that part ringing Mexico City, two-thirds of the people drew their living from pulque, although the Plains of Apám (to the northwest, near Tulancingo) boasted the best pulque in the Republic. Indians carried their produce from their villages to the capital's markets. The pueblos around Lake Chalco supplied white fish, olive oil, and woods. Grains came from Tula, San Ángel (now a suburb of Mexico City) had a paper factory, and Cuernavaca, exporting its sugar throughout the Republic, was the scene of successful experiments with coffee. Acapulco, once famous for the trade with Asia, was depressed after the termination of that commerce, but was still producing cotton. The state had 777 mines of gold and silver (most near Tulancingo and Taxco), but only a fourth of them were currently active. Toluca, an agricultural district, became the fourth state capital in 1830, after Mexico City (1824–1827), Texcoco briefly, and then Tlalpam (1827–1830).[28]

To the north, formerly a part of the province of México but separated by the 1824 constitution, was the tiny state of Querétaro. The city of Querétaro, though, was one of the larger urban centers by virtue of its population of 35,000. In the late colonial period it had contained numerous tanneries and hatteries and had been a center of woollens. Its woollen industry, now much reduced, was saved from total destitution by a contract for uniforms awarded by the War Department.[29]

To the east of Querétaro was the other textile center, Puebla, long one of the most prosperous areas of New Spain. Although it had no mining to speak of, it had formerly supplied Veracruz, Oaxaca, and even Havana, with wheat, animal products, and its famed craftwares (wool and cotton cloth, animal gear, glassware, and crockery). In recent years foreign imports had put many of its thousands of artisans out of work.[30]

The fabled province of Tlaxcala won statehood in early 1824, lost it on November 24,[31] and remained a territory through the First Federal Republic. It is questionable whether Tlaxcala's meager resources could have supported state apparatus. In an area about thirty miles square lived some 65,000 people, two-thirds of whom were described as Indian laborers. About the only commerce came from pulque haciendas near the plains of

Apám. The capital city, Tlaxcala, located at an elbow of a tributary of the Atoyac, was inundated periodically.[32]

Veracruz, the first link in the Veracruz–Puebla–Mexico City axis, was a port with a state appended. The city of Veracruz, owing its position to Spain's policy of funnelling imports through a single entry point, had profited greatly from the economic boom of the last colonial years, and had not lost its predominance despite the opening of other ports since 1810. Spanish mercantile monopolists gave the city a conservative tone that lasted through the 1820s, while Jalapa, the state capital and entrepot for the state's inland trade (a town of 10,000 in 1830), was more in tune with federalist-republican currents. On the coast the way of life was fishing and shipping. The humid regions—especially Córdoba and Orizaba—permitted the plantation crops of sugar cane and tobacco. Wild-growing vanilla was harvested in places. Elsewhere the traditional devotion to maize, beans, and chile prevailed.[33]

On the other side of Mexico City lay Michoacán, still showing signs of many revolutionary battles. In a humid setting bordering on the subtropical, its numerous haciendas primarily grew maize, plus a little sugar and coffee and indigo for nearby markets. It had one mining area, Tlalpujahua. Almost wholly agricultural and rural, its only real city was Valladolid, soon to be changed to the Mexican-sounding Morelia, and its other settlements were described as "ranch towns."[34]

North Central Mexico

To most Mexicans, living in and around the central plateau, the North was not the faraway region bordering on the United States, but that area enclosed by the states of Jalisco, Zacatecas, Guanajuato, and San Luis Potosí. These states had in common an opposition to Mexico City—making federalism the inevitable northern creed—and a messianic nationalism. Fear of colonial influences from the Spanish-tainted center made this area prone to schemes for a northern confederation. Experiencing now a slow economic upswing after the revolutionary disturbances, the northern states led the agitation to protect native industries from cheap foreign productions. Jalisco and Zacatecas were the usual leaders in these various northern projects, and San Luis Potosí a willing participant. Guanajuato, with its heavy Spanish atmosphere, was somewhat more cautious, but it too was affected by the northern ethos.

The intendancy of Guadalajara, constituted as the state of Jalisco after June 16, 1823, emerged from the revolutionary era with imperialistic ambitions, prepared to challenge the city of Mexico for leadership. Its population in 1826 was reckoned at 656,830, second only to the state of Mexico. Guadalajara, a city of 40,000, was the nerve center of a territory that in the last Spanish years had all the appurtenances of a national capital: a High Court or Audiencia that reached all the way to Texas, a university, theater, colleges, libraries, hospitals, and pious foundations. In the eyes of Jaliscenses it had as much right to leadership as the city of Mexico. Guadalajara's workshops were famous for their leatherware and pottery, and with an agricultural base of maize, beans, and animal products, its merchants had supplied northwest New Spain and even Mexico City to a degree. Mining had become important since the mid-1700s and toward the end of the century Guadalajara became an important source of plain and printed cotton cloth. Now, with the textile industry moribund, the state's main exports were cattle and cattle products.[35] Added to the normal problems of independence, Jalisco feuded with the national government in 1823 and had the region *(partido)* of Colima detached from its jurisdiction. This humid coastal enclave, source of semitropical crops (cotton, tobacco, and chocolate),[36] was made into a territory.

San Luis Potosí and Zacatecas stood along the dividing line of moisture. As one moved northward, farms of maize, beans, chile (and occasional wheat) became rarer and the land was given over to grazing. The state of San Luis Potosí had developed on a mining basis, but many of the northern mines lay abandoned now. The city of San Luis Potosí, by way of compensation, had become a warehousing center for goods, Mexican and imported, many of which came from Tampico and which mule trains then took to Zacatecas, Durango, and up toward Texas. Artificers, finding few buyers for cloth, made hats, boots, earthenware, iron goods, and skin products. On the eastern fringe, where the state reached over into the more verdant Huasteca, Potosinos grew sugar cane and a little rice.[37]

Zacatecas, including what is now Aguascalientes, was a relatively prosperous area, even exporting food products to other states. The city of Zacatecas drew wealth from nearby mines while Aguascalientes, granary for the mining districts, dealt in maize, beans, and chile. The latter also contained one of the few large-scale cloth plants, which employed about 500 workers to make wool cloth for the Querétaro uniform factory. Sheep ranches were concentrated in the northern and eastern parts of Zacatecas near the *ojos de agua,* or water tanks, left by the state's meager rivers when they dried up. It was not an especially populous state, counting only 290,044 people in the 1831 governor's report, but its silver mines, the most productive in the Republic in these years, allowed it to play a leading role in national life.[38]

Guanajuato was once perhaps the king's richest province. All of the colony's major economic activities could be found here. The network of almost coequal towns, Celaya, San Miguel el Grande (now San Miguel Allende), Irapuato, and León, were tied in with mining and known for their fine clothwork and wheat. The city of Guanajuato was a northern center of Spanish culture. But the Bajío (as the basin of the Lerma River was called) had been in the center of the 1810–1811 violence, and fifteen years later travelers were still struck by the large number of burnt-out haciendas. This, combined with the decline of the mines and the deluge of cheap imports, made Guanajuato a depressed area, alleviated partially by the arrival of the English mining companies in 1824–1825. In 1827 the governor complained that the state's only exports were metals. Figures for the maize crop reflected the slowdown: in 1829, 750,000 fanegas were grown in the whole state, while in 1806 the amount had been 500,000 around the capital city alone. Even with the lesser quantities, prices did not hold up, the sale of maize almost ceasing in 1830 and 1831 because of low prices. It was the same story with cloth, whose manufacture had traditionally been spread out in towns and villages. In 1829 cloth prices in the state capital were one-thirteenth those of 1806.[39]

The Far North

On the northern frontier, near the end of Hispanic civilization, men and women had traditionally got by on a combination of mining (except in Texas and California) and stock raising, with sheep predominating in the East and cattle in the West. Indian policy here, in a reverse image of the policy governing the docile southern tribes, had been designed to protect the whites from the Indians. For military reasons the royal government had grouped these thinly populated provinces into two commandancy generals in 1787, the Eastern Interior Provinces (Texas, Coahuila, Nuevo León, and Nuevo Santander or Tamaulipas), and the Western Interior Provinces (New Mexico, Upper and Lower California, Sonora, Sinaloa, and Nueva Vizcaya or Durango-Chihuahua). From 1792 to 1812 there was a single commandancy general.[40]

Revolution and independence had three main results. First was the collapse of mining and commerce. Ranchers could now find fewer buyers for their products. For lack of a buyer in 1822, José Melchor Sánchez Navarro had twenty-one mule loads of wool rotting in a Saltillo warehouse.[41] For the mines, the amount of new capital was generally not sufficient to reach the far North, and the local miners could only comb through the scrap heaps or work the old shafts where water or shoring permitted.

Second, the presidios had deteriorated during the wars, and the "gifts" to Indians became irregular or ceased. This carried terrible consequences for Indian-white relations. Raids by Apache and Comanches demexicanized large portions of a swath running along the Río Bravo (Rio Grande) from Tamaulipas to Chihuahua.

Third, the independence era coincided with the arrival of North Americans. They came as settlers in Texas, as shipborne merchants along the northern Gulf coast (to a lesser extent at the ports of the Californias), and as trappers and merchandise importers by the St. Louis–Santa Fe–El Paso–Chihuahua City route. And everywhere they seeped in as smugglers, their bargain prices undercutting the local craftsmen.

In Texas they crossed the border casually from Louisiana and settled down to farm. Among the first reports received from Texas by the independent government in 1821 were of illegal squatters, believed to number 3,000 by 1823.[42] Texas had been at the tail end of the Spanish empire in North America, and the Tejanos' primitive material equipment showed it. Surveys by the last Spanish governors showed a subsistence economy: no mines, no wheat, no tanneries, no tobacco, not even the house manufacture of crude cloth, just enough maize to survive on (5,000 fanegas a year), and about 20,000 head of stock. With the events after 1810—depredations from fili-busters and the royalist-rebel struggles—Texas's civilization actually slipped back a few notches. The bones of insurgent soldiers killed by General Joaquín Arredondo in 1813 were still to be seen near San Antonio in 1828. In 1821, with a population of about 2,500, the province had only two towns, villages really, San Antonio de Béxar and La Bahía del Espíritu Santo (Goliad), plus a few families living along the Sabine and Red Rivers. Nacogdoches had virtually disappeared. One of the four missions at Béxar was deserted, and the others were deteriorating. At La Bahía, two missions still functioned, but the Indians wandered in and out as they chose. Both places had garrisons, but the soldiers, "unmounted and unclothed," had to forage or thieve for their food.[43] General Manuel de Mier y Terán toured the province in 1828 and found the Mexican settlements little changed. Nacogdoches had come back to life, but North Americans dominated and had partially Americanized the Mexicans living there.[44] So weak was Texas that on May 7, 1824, it was merged with Coahuila, which had a population of about 60,000.[45]

Coahuila lay astride the Sierra Madre Oriental, cut into a small northeast region of Gulf slopelands, and the dry southwestern plains on which grazed thousands of sheep and some cattle. Parras was known for its wines and brandy, and Monclova and Saltillo for their cotton and wool products.[46] Independence and the rise of the Monterrey-Matamoros axis spelled a de-cline for the famous annual fair held in Saltillo.

The oldest of the northern settlements was New Mexico, with a popu-lation during the 1820s of 40,000. Provincial life was centered at Santa Fe and Albuquerque. with 1827 populations of 5,160 and 2,547, respectively. Over the past two centuries, 1,500 miles from the city of Mexico, the New Mexicans had worked out a pastoral life style, tending animals, doing placer mining, raising maize, wheat, vegetables, and tobacco, and wearing homemade cloth. An 1827 census showed 5,000 cattle and 240,000 sheep and goats. To Chihuahua and Sonora they exported wool, sheep, and a little tobacco. A few of the larger landowners sent, on contract, up to 15,000 sheep yearly to Durango (at about nine reales each). The numerous buffalo were hunted for their skins, and in a few experiments, tamed to the plow. Indians came to sell furs, and bought in return vermillion, knives, breads, and awls.[47]

As the northernmost citizens, the New Mexicans were the first to encounter the nomadic merchants from St. Louis, Missouri. The first caravan from St. Louis appeared in 1821, and as news got around of the 50 to 100 percent profit to be made, the Santa Fe trade became a seasonal event. Trains of up to ninety or a hundred wagons arrived in July, and buyers came from as far away as Sonora. Since specie did not suffice to pay for the goods, and its export was taxed, the wagons returned with beaver and nutria pelts. Soon Americans began to seek out the living places of these animals, arriving in bands of thirty or forty armed men and employing New Mexicans as guides. A directive came up from Mexico City in 1824 that the governor was to stop all foreigners from trapping, but this was clearly beyond his resources, and he settled for licensing. Requirements and enforcement varied, so Americans evaded the law whenever possible, and the government inspectors enthusiastically confiscated pelts, which circulated as a general medium of exchange in the absence of money. The trappings went on: in 1827 Governor Manuel Armijo estimated the Americans were taking out 30,000 pesos a year in profits. From Santa Fe the Americans took the next step, down the Rio Grande to El Paso and from there to Chihuahua, where they ran into competition from British goods coming in from western ports.[48] Some were not to be halted. Ambassador Joel Roberts Poinsett wrote that he had seen four American-driven wagons in Mexico City's central plaza, bound for Veracruz.[49]

"The Californias," in the Mexican lexicon of the 1820s, meant a destination for political exiles or a place to send minor criminals for presidio service. A rather cosmopolitan society prevailed, with British and New England ships arriving in growing numbers. Russians were established in their colony at Bodega Bay (near San Francisco). The War Department never carried out an expedition planned to dislodge them, but the Russians did agree not to build any more trading posts in the territory. Lower California, occupying the dry 800-mile peninsula opposite Sonora and Sinaloa, was the less developed of the two, having a Mexicanized population of 10,000–12,000. Its only commerce was in pearls. Each year a half-dozen boats came to the oyster beds and with luck a few thousand dollars' worth of pearls would be found by the divers—some of whom were aided by diving bells brought over by some British companies. The Dominican missions were dilapidated now, and the nominal capital of Loreto had a population of less than 300, while about 2,000 lived in the vicinity of La Paz.[50]

In Upper California (the modern-day state of California), the Mexican presence in the 1820s was expanding from mission-military camp clusters on the coast to an inland network of privately owned ranches and lay communities. Of the population of about 24,000, something over 3,000 were "people of reason" (*gente de razón*) or Hispanic, and about 700 of these were military personnel in the four presidios of San Francisco, Monterrey, Santa Barbara, and San Diego. The rest lived around the three pueblos and twenty missions; San Francisco Solano, the twenty-first and last mission, was founded in 1824. The missions were under the care of

Spanish Franciscans who made no secret of their preference for Spain, but their mission food was needed, so they stayed on. The missions produced about 50,000 fanegas of grain yearly, mostly wheat (reflecting the tastes of Spanish friars), with some maize. Here, as elsewhere in Mexico, it was noted that very few green vegetables were consumed.[51]

Stockraising was the life for the Mexican residents—or Californios. On the vast pastures lived upward of a half million head, mostly cattle, whose carcasses, once stripped of hide and fat, were left to rot. Horses were so plentiful that cattlemen killed wild mares so that they might not eat grasses meant for captive stock. A French traveler, Auguste Duhaut-Cilly, found the Californios excessively devoted to gambling and drink, but commanding such equestrian skill that they roped deer and bear for recreation.[52]

The ranchos, whose day would come after the secularization of the missions in 1833, now numbered only about twenty-five or thirty, and the commerce with the European and New England shippers was dominated by the coastal missions. But word of the profits in hides was getting around, and more Californios, as well as a few foreign merchants and sailors, were beginning to apply for land grants in the interior.[53]

Below the Californias lay Sonora and Sinaloa, strung out a thousand miles along the mainland coast from Tepic in the south to Tucson in the north. These were unbroken regions where wild horses and mules were chased down, branded, and put to the harness or saddle. In Sinaloa the greater amount of rainfall—and the greater distance from the northern Indians—took some of the sting out of life. The 1824 constitution put the two provinces together in the Internal State of the West (Estado de Occidente), a union that would last until 1830, when each became a separate state. Now that the mines were little worked, the main business was wheat (grown near rivers, which were more numerous in Sinaloa), and cattle, for which Sonora was famous. Wheat came in by land from Durango and Sonora to Guaymas, and there, in one of the best harbors on the West Coast, it was embarked for San Blas, Acapulco, and as far as Central and South America. Cattle, when the Indians were peaceful, were slaughtered for their tallow and leather, which were then placed on board ship at Guaymas.[54]

In 1824 Nueva Vizcaya was broken up into the states of Durango and Chihuahua. In Durango many of the storied mines had been abandoned or surrendered to the water, but a few were still worked in primitive fashion. A high percentage of merchandise in Mexico moved on the backs of the famous Durango mules, but sheep far outnumbered mules on the immense ranches. The governor's 1826 report showed 680,573 sheep on the 65 haciendas and 343 ranchos—versus 24,745 mules. Cotton plantations along the Nazas River supplied the weavers of Saltillo, San Luis Potosí, and Zacatecas. Foreign goods entering by way of Mazatlán and San Luis Potosí were leaving the Durango craft workers without employment.[55]

The state of Chihuahua ranged from the moist western foothills of the Sierra Madre Occidental to the dessicated basins of the east. Although the silver mines had occasioned the first settlements and would be partially revived in the 1820s, Chihuahua now was cattle country. Cattle were raised mainly on ranchos, 596 of which were listed in the statistical survey of 1834, along with 111 haciendas. Some stockmen sent horses, mules, and the beeves—as salted meats, animal fats, and on the hoof—as far as Puebla and Mexico City on occasion. Under the Spanish, the state had been a military command center for the North, and local merchants had carried on a regular business supplying the presidios of northwest New Spain, but they lost much of this with the decay of northern defense and the opening of Guaymas and the Santa Fe–Missouri trails. When revolution threw Chihuahuans on their own resources back in 1810–1812, some crude looms had been put into operation, but these too withered under foreign competition after independence.[56]

Nuevo León was spacious and underdeveloped: only five doctors and seven lawyers—but sixty-four clerics—resided in the entire state in 1831. The area presented a panorama of neglect: mining had virtually ceased, and even the cattle, horses, mules, and sheep, still the main commercial activity, were no longer exported as in earlier years. In 1831 the state government valued Nuevo León's main products, in descending order, as sheep, cattle, horses, mules, corn, beans, and piloncillo.[57]

The long state of Tamaulipas did not fall naturally into any one region. Its largest town and the nation's second port, Tampico, was the entry place for goods bound for San Luis Potosí and Zacatecas, which made for connections with north-central Mexico, but parts of the state reached to within 100 miles of San Antonio de Béxar in Texas. It was a stock-raising state, although landowners in the southern part would turn to maize in the 1830s.[58]

Cities

In a vast landscape, where man had little changed natural contours, town and cities loomed as tiny outcroppings. Encircled by high walls, they recalled an earlier, more hazardous age, although watchmen now closed the gates each night not to keep out savage Indians, but to facilitate collecting the sales tax. Civilization was arriving in bits and pieces. Many streets were already stone-paved, provincial homeowners were installing glass in their windows,[59] and downtown lighting was making its appearance—even in provincial Oaxaca City.[60] In Jalapa, 290 houses obtained lighting in 1827 by paying a 3 percent tax on rents.[61] If not exactly the same thing as civic pride, loyalty to one's place of residence was strong, showing up at times in the form of armed feuding between neighboring municipalities over a variety of issues.

After the national capital, the preeminent cities were Guadalajara,

View of Guanajuato

Puebla, and Guanajuato. In recent decades Guadalajara had grown considerably, through Revolution and all, and now offered its 40,000 inhabitants schools, plazas, fountains, a large park, and an impressive commercial sector. Puebla was a fine place to live, with its brisk climate, view of the volcanoes, tiled houses with piped water, wide paved streets, and numerous religious edifices for learning and ministration.[62] Guanajuato, shaken by revolutionary devastation, entered independence with a population of 32,000, down about two-thirds from 1810.[63] But it was the nation's fastest growing city in the 1820s, and soon resumed its accustomed place as the center of culture in the Bajío. Many of the other state capitals were essentially overgrown villages. Monterrey, for example, had only 12,282 inhabitants and a handful of two-story buildings. The bishop had to make a simple parish church serve as the cathedral, and the hospital had one doctor and three interns.[64]

    The port towns of both coasts were growing in population and prosperity, but their pestilential climate made the living miserable, especially during the rainy season. Even lifelong residents found the wet months intolerable, and when the monsoons approached, many families in San Blas and Tampico loaded up their belongings, boarded their windows, and moved to the interior. Veracruz was especially struck with ill fortune.

From afar it was pleasing to the eye, with many of the buildings constructed of white coral. In the evening residents could repair to the flat-
topped roofs to catch the sea breeze, and afterwards, those having beds
protected with netting could sleep without molestation from mosquitoes.
But when the rains came, from about April to October, incoming passengers were advised not to stop over for even a day, for Veracruz was
regularly visited by yellow fever and the black vomit. Then, in 1823, the
Spaniards in the harbor fortress of San Juan de Ulúa opened fire, and the
city became a rubble-strewn ghost town.[65]

The pride of the Republic was the City of Mexico. Although it was not
an economic capital—its manufacturing shops sold little to the provinces
because of transportation costs—it was a great administrative and cultural
center.[66] To those who approached it for the first time, it seemed to emit a
magical aura. As many as sixty domes and twice as many spires could be
counted, many of late colonial construction.[67] From Chapúltepec Hill, a
forested retreat covered with cypresses and shady walks, the outskirts were
seen as a hamlet-dotted plain, marked off with orchards, gardens, and
fields. Surrounding villages traditionally supplied the capital with fruits,
vegetables, unskilled labor, and domestics.[68] Of the famed lakes of the
valley of Anáhuac, Chalco and Xochimilco were still substantial, but Zum-

Plaza Mayor, Mexico City

View of Zacatecas

pango, San Cristóbal, and Texcoco were almost gone, more properly classified as ponds during the dry season. When the rains were heavy, however, there was still no escape for the waters. Decreasing amounts had been spent on drainage since the year 1808,[69] and when the debris-choked trenches at Huehuetoca filled to capacity, the overflow rose through the city's eastern barrios, at times reaching knee-deep levels in the central plaza. In addition, the lakes every year ate away part of the Chalco villagers' lands.[70] Over the lakebeds five causeways *(calzadas)* led the way into the city. Paseo de las Vigas, the causeway from Lakes Xochimilco and Chalco, ran next to a canal on which Indian canoes carried produce up to the Zócalo itself.

As shown on an 1824 map, the municipal gates took in a rough rectangle, two miles wide north and south, and three miles long east and west.[71] The city converged at the Zócalo, the central plaza. Facing it on the east was the national palace, housing the president's apartments, his minister's offices, and soon, the chambers of the Senate, House of Representatives, and Supreme Court—as well as a jail and barracks. On the north was the cathedral, where from dawn to one o'clock, masses were repeated every half hour. On the south was the Mexico City town council building *(ayuntamiento)*. At the Portales, the porticoed shops fronting the Zócalo on the west, were some of the city's main commercial establishments. Taking up some two-thirds of the Zócalo itself was the Parián, a complex of warehouses and kiosks surrounded by wooden walls.

From the Zócalo broad streets led out flanked by two-story buildings—a few had three or four stories—that combined residence with trade. Commonly propertied families lived upstairs and rented out the lower floor for a shop or warehouse. Floors were of brick, although foreigners had begun the fashion of lining them with canvas. The front gates were large enough to admit carriages, with animals stabled in the patio.

Most of the fine houses were located in the Traza, the traditional enclave of Spaniards generally extending south and southwest from the Zócalo. Beyond the Traza lay the neighborhoods, called *colonias* or barrios, normally built around one of the hundred or so lesser plazas.

> Residents endowed each barrio with a distinctive personality. Santa Anna, athwart the great north-south road, was notorious for high-living *arrieros* (mule skinners), and highwaymen frequented its many inns. San Sebastián and El Carmen, relatively close to the center of the city, housed romance-smitten seamstresses, rakish public coachmen and wagoneers, and industrious artisans toiling in the single rooms that served as bedroom and workshops. The eastern barrios of San Lázaro, La Soledad, La Palma, and Manzanares, held the *populacho* and *léperos,* daring rogues who lived from the proceeds of casual labor and petty crime. In the southern barrios of San Pablo, San Antonio Abad, and Salto del Agua, boatmen, impoverished clerks, and women cigar makers worked and played. The inhabitants of the extreme southeastern barrios bordering the trash dumps and the Cementerio de Campo Florida were wretched scavengers who subsisted on offal.[72]

The *ayuntamiento* oversaw basic services for a population of 168,846, a figure originally arrived at by the police department in 1811, but used by the municipal council in 1824 in consideration of the capital's high mortality rate that matched the equally high rate of in-migration. By 1830 population growth strained urban facilities; the *ayuntamiento* members listened to complaints about lack of market space and water shortages. Two aqueducts transmitted the water supply: the Chapúltepec aqueduct, two miles in length, began at the base of that hill; the Tlaxpana aqueduct, six miles in length, originated near the road to Toluca. From the terminus, the water came to consumers either by way of huge jars borne on the backs of the water carriers, or a system of pipes and sluices going to 28 public and 505 private fountains. Sewage passed into drains in the middle of the street, thence to a canal emptying into Lake Texcoco. The streets, wide, paved in stretches, and bordered by sidewalks, were generaly considered adequate, and public coaches, numbering 895 in 1829, waited for hire at various sites. With an eye for the main chance, drivers raised their fares on festival days or at the first sign of rain. Where wagons could not pass, porters, loaded with as much as 300 pounds, made their way on foot. A capital police force, mounted and on foot, patroled the streets, but robberies were common enough that those with nighttime business took care to arm themselves. Weapons also gave protection from the large canine population.[73]

Life on the Mexico City streets can be glimpsed through a pamphlet that somehow came to rest in a volume of the Chamber of Deputies minutes. It described the clothing hung out to dry over the sidewalks, the problem of pedestrians colliding with vendors carrying pig entrails on a stick, and the inner city canals overflowing in times of rains. Water sellers connived with the city water employees to cut the pipes on festival days and thus raise the price of water. Public baths, the sites of illicit meetings of lovers, were a scandal due to a lack of hygiene and the habit of the male attendants viewing ladies as they bathed.[74]

« 2 »

From Monarchy to Federal Republic
1823–1824

CENTRIFUGAL FEDERALISM, 1823

Zavala and Alamán had come home at a moment of national effervescence. All through the land, people were enraptured with a passionate addiction to independence, which became bonded in the public mind with the mystique of a federal republic. Women put patriotic slogans on their shawls, even on their gingerbread. Traditional songs were given patriotic lyrics. The Sixteenth of September became the foremost holiday, at which time celebrating citizens would take to the main square, there to be entertained by parades, fireworks, musicians, dancers, and interminable speeches. When states were established place names of Spanish origin were discarded in favor of the Indian version or of local heroes: Nuevo Santander was replaced by Tamaulipas, Mérida by Yucatán, and Arizpe by Sonora-Sinaloa. In towns the same: San Agustín de las Cuevas would be changed to Tlalpam (later called Tlalpan; 1827), Valladolid to Morelia (1828), and Ciudad Real, Chiapas, to San Cristóbal de las Casas (1828).

Alamán, a lifelong noncombatant with no sympathy whatsoever for social leveling, nevertheless felt obligated to enroll in the militia and spent July 10, 1823, standing around the national palace as a sentinel.[1] Zavala proposed that Congress abolish the titles of marquis and count as unfit for a republic, a measure ratified in 1826.[2]

Out of the wreckage of Iturbide's empire, a republic was being born, and the euphoria of 1823 and 1824 was not diminished by occasional acts of military insurbordination, nor by the shelling of the city of Veracruz from the island of San Juan de Ulúa. This barrage, directed by the last remnant of Spanish might in Mexico, served to unite Mexicans, as did the possibility of invasion by Spain or the Holy Alliance. Mexican pamphleteers frequently printed the name of Fernando VII—who continued to utter threats against unfaithful colonials—upside down as a sign of their contempt.

Overriding all of these concerns now, however, was a contagious enthusiasm for creating not only the apparatus of national and local governments, but also a multitude of other projects—educational, economic, and philanthropic—that were to make a society fit for free men and women. The overwhelming popularity of the new ideology muted political strife among the three political factions, the Iturbidists, the centralists, and the federalists. Iturbide commanded allegiance from a fast diminishing minority, and was strong only among some of the old colonial nobility, certain churchmen and general officers, and the Mexico City *léperos* or street paupers, who insulted officials in the streets. The Mexican aristocrats who had joined the Scottish rite Masons and agitated for reform as "liberals" in the last years of the colony had now become centralists because they favored a centralized republic. Both Iturbidists and centralists, however, were eclipsed by the federalists, a disparate but rapidly growing faction whose antipathy for Spain—and Mexico City as the traditional focus of Spanish influence—led them to espouse liberalism and the cause of the provinces.

Federalism had become the national creed. As a system that promised to gratify growing localist feeling, its very name was coming to command instant allegiance, even from those who had no idea how it worked. In the interim Congress reconvoked in March 1823, and in the Constitutional Congress that met in November 1823, the debate between federalism and centralism was short-lived. The issue was decided almost immediately in favor of semiautonomous states joined in a confederative nation. It was now considered almost un-Mexican to argue as the few centralists did that the states should be subordinated to the central government for the sake of efficiency and orderliness.

Seeing their genteel reformism passed by in the provinces, Alamán and many of his aristocratic friends who had been "liberal" colonials now became conservative citizens. Born to status and comfort, they came to value order and security of property over the Enlightenment ideals that had touched their consciences as young men. Although some of them had risked their position—and their freedom—by sympathizing with the insurgents during the Revolution, what they had really disliked about Spain was the medieval debris in its public administration, which had been largely cut away by the Cortes. Independence was about as far as they wanted to go. Joined by Spanish Mexicans and other traditionally conservative elements, they would end up by harking back to much of the colonial system as the best insurance for a stable Mexico—a strong church to bind the nation's diverse peoples, and a firm, centralized, government administered by men bred to rule. Many of them would actually have preferred a constitutional monarch, if he came with the proper lineage, especially a Bourbon. Alamán himself denied this charge.[3]

Thus the former "liberals" would quickly lose their reformist impulse as the 1820s progressed. They would carry or be given a variety of labels, reflecting the shifting issues: now they were known as "Bourbonists" for their devotion to that part of Iturbide's Three Guarantees proposing to bring over a prince of the Bourbon family; during the 1823 debate over governmental form, "centralists"; from the mid-1820s, Escoceses, for their Scottish rite Masonic affiliation; and toward the end of the decade, *hombres de bien,* for their social respectability.

Not all of them were high-born, but the coterie, evolving as it had, was redolent of social propriety. A prominent family in this group was the Fagoagas, who owed their economic prominence to the Pabellón and Sombrerete mines in Zacatecas, and their current political acceptability to the family's support of the insurgent cause since 1811. Francisco (1788–1851) was the most active politically. Born in Mexico City the son of the first marquis of the Apartado, he embarked on a European tour after completing his studies, served in the 1820 Cortes, and returned to Mexico to be elected first alcalde of the Mexico City town council, and then to Congress in 1822. With his extensive learning, the frank tenor of his voice, and "pair of eyeglasses," Francisco Fagoaga bore himself like the classical gentleman politician—although it was noted that he was capable of asperity.[4] His mother, a Villaurrutia, came from another Spanish-creole family with liberal tendencies. The Villaurrutias were spread through Mexican society in strategic positions. Jacobo de Villaurrutia (1757–1833) had been appointed to the Guatemala high court *(audiencia),* had supported economic societies and newspapers in New Spain, fell under the suspicion of Viceroy Venegas, and would serve as the president of the Mexico State Supreme Court. Colonel Eulogio de Villaurrutia was political chief and commander of the city of Veracruz in 1823.[5]

Occupying center stage among the Bourbonist-centralists in 1823–1824 were Colonel José Mariano Michelena, Fray Servando Teresa de Mier y Noriega, and Manuel de Mier y Terán. The embattled Michelena (1784–1852) came from a Valladolid (now Morelia) family that held coffee and indigo plantations. As a young lieutenant in New Spain's army, he became involved in several proindependence conspiracies from 1806 on. The Spaniards kept him in prison from 1811 to 1813, and then sent him to the peninsula where he served in campaigns against Bonaparte. He worked for the Riego rebellion, was elected to the Cortes, and then returned to Mexico to organize the opposition to Iturbide.[6]

Father Mier (1765–1827) was something of a national monument because of his decades of suffering and writing for the Mexican cause. From Monterrey, he had taken the Franciscan habit and earned Spanish disfavor after a 1794 sermon. He then entered on his vocation as exile, Spanish prisoner, escapee (on a half-dozen occasions), and tireless proselytizer for independence. He conspired against Iturbide and was imprisoned one last time before emerging to take a seat in Congress.[7] His lifelong crusade for republicanism did not dilute his aristocratic pretensions—in Congress he was fond of talking of his titled relations—nor a foppish vanity. Wearing his "gray hair hanging in carefully arranged curls at his neckline and brushed forward to conceal partially a high broad forehead," he donned a purple robe for one speech to Congress.[8]

Mier y Terán (1789–1832) was the quintessential professional officer. After studies in the College of Mining, he served the insurgent cause in southern Mexico, but was drawn into the quarrels among rebel leaders, and in particular had differences with Guadalupe Victoria. His habit of inclining his head downward gave the impression of a "deep thinker," and in fact he was a student of several sciences. During the Revolution he was known for his methodical planning, and in the 1823 Congress for his exactness. Socially he was very reserved, even somewhat aloof, although he was affable enough to court successfully the daughter of Antonio Velasco, a wealthy hacendado.[9]

The federalist leaders in 1823 were more mixed socially than the centralists. Perhaps the dominant voice now was that of the Cortes veteran Miguel Ramos Arizpe (1775–1843). He was a northerner, born in San Nicolás de la Capellanía (Coahuila), and spoke for the North in the Cortes from 1811 to 1814. His schooling had been theological. He took holy orders in 1803 and held various clerical positions, a vocation that did not soften his outbursts of anger—his "comanche transports."[10] After taking a leading role in the first Cortes—and twenty months' incarceration—he was only a substitute delegate in 1821, but still made his presence felt. Iturbide tried to draw him into the official circle, but Ramos Arizpe chose instead to mobilize opposition to the emperor. He spent 1823 organizing the federalists, first in the North and in the capital against the Iturbidists, and then in the Congress against the centralists. He was a marvel of energy in the first years of independence, his short, squat body exuding vitality—his nickname was *toro chicharrón,* the sunburnt bull. Within five years, however, he would quarrel and break away from many of his current federalist allies.[11]

In the Congress the other federalist leaders were Valentín Gómez Farías, Francisco García, and Juan de Dios Cañedo. For most Mexicans, Gómez Farias (1781–1858) was to become the symbol of federalism, a largely deserved reputation, for he held to his political convictions with uncommon tenacity. He was born into a middle-class Guadalajara family, and, after medical studies at the university there, spent the revolutionary years practicing at Aguascalientes. At first an enthusiastic supporter of Iturbide, he was elected to Congress from Zacatecas in 1822 and 1823.[12]

The great orator among the federalists was Juan de Dios Cañedo (1786–1850), whose capacity for eloquent invective made him a figure not to be trifled with in public debate. He was of the Cañedos of Guadalajara, a clan that produced a number of politicians. After studying with the renowned educator, Dr. Francisco Severo Maldonado, he received his lawyer's title in 1809 and then went on to serve in public affairs. At the Cortes in 1821, he sported "eyeglasses of new invention which more often than not present[ed] things to him the opposite of how his countrymen [saw] them."[13] As a leader in most of the Mexican congresses of the 1820s, he would earn universal respect for promoting his party's ideals and opposing its excesses.[14]

An individual who reversed the normal pattern by distinguishing himself first in the national government and then by going on to become a state leader was Francisco García (1786–1841). Born near Jerez, Zacatecas, he studied at the Guadalajara seminary and then worked for several years as a mining engineer. As a young man of twenty-four, he was selected for the Zacatecas town council and then in 1822 and 1823 served in the national Congress.[15]

In an influential book published in 1968, Charles Hale discussed the pathways of Mexican liberalism. The liberals he wrote about were those of the 1820s, 1830s, and 1840s, not to be confused with the cosmopolitan reformers of colonial New Spain. For the postindependence liberals, the basic case example was France, where liberalism had been used to overthrow a feudal regime. The French theoretical liberalism—as opposed to the Anglo-Saxon tradition of building democracy on concrete historical precedents from the top down—came to Mexico via Spain and the Cortes. As at the Cortes, a strong, secular state was axiomatic. Although not autocratic, the state must be powerful enough to wrest sovereignty from feudal groups and secure a reign of law common to all men. Corollaries were that education be secular and "useful rather than theological," and that the Indian be incorporated into the body politic. There were several difficulties in the scheme. The central dilemma was how to have a state sufficiently powerful to carry out the liberal program in a semifeudal society and yet still not tread on "the people."[16] These contradictions were not altogether clear to the nascent liberal class of the 1820s. Although the basic forces of Mexican society were already defining themselves, the liberals of Mexico were few and ideologically unpracticed—not ready yet to strike at the conservative centers of power.

In the spring and summer of 1823 the Bourbonist-centralists held key positions in the Mexico City government. The men selected for the Supreme Executive Power (SEP) represented the groups that brought Iturbide down: Guadalupe Victoria for the old insurgents, Pedro Celestino Negrete for the Spaniards, and Nicolás Bravo for the Bourbonists. They were expected to use their contacts and prestige to conciliate and pacify restive factions in the provinces. Bravo was gone frequently, and Victoria was left in Veracruz for more than a year to oversee operations affecting San Juan de Ulúa, the Spanish-held fortress in the Veracruz harbor and—at the request of the provincial deputation—to keep an eye on Santa Anna.[17] To act in their absence, the Congress on April 1 elected as substitutes Michelena and Miguel Domínguez, selected as recompense for their imprisonment under the viceregal government.[18] Domínguez, sixty-seven years old in 1823, was now politically passive.[19] Vicente Guerrero was added as a substitute on July 3.[20]

The cabinet, offering continuity amid the comings and goings of the Supreme Executive Power, thus assumed a special importance. And in the cabinet Alamán held the premier office as minister of relations. The position had numerous and disparate duties, ranging from diplomacy to immunization, but the most important internal function was to oversee political relations with the provinces. In the immediate aftermath of Iturbide's dethronement, all the ministry portfolios were held by a single man, José Ignacio García Illueca (1780?–1830), who in the following weeks ceded his cabinet functions. Francisco Arrillaga, a Veracruz merchant born in Biscay, became minister of the treasury (Hacienda) on May 2, Pablo de la Llave minister of justice and ecclesiastical affairs on June 6, and José Joaquín de Herrera minister of war and marine on July 12.[21] La Llave (1773–1833), the son of a militia captain, was a noted botanist who received his doctorate at the age of nineteen and then served as director of Madrid's botanical garden.[22] Herrera (1792–1854), like la Llave from the state of Veracruz, had taken a commission under the royalists and had fought against Guerrero.[23]

In the spring of 1823, it was clear the ardent federalism of the provinces was to prevail. In the Supreme Executive Power the federalists could expect acquiescence if not outright support from Guadalupe Victoria, who professed faith in centralism but fraternized with federalists, and Vicente Guerrero, idol of the southern campesinos. In the military a number of general officers displayed federalist preferences.

The federalists' strongholds, though, were the provincial deputations, which became in 1823 the means for expressing a parochialism that viceregal policy had contained but never stifled. They grew out of the provincial juntas that emerged during the Spanish resistance to the French in 1808. The 1812 constitution granted New Spain six of these, now called provincial deputations instead of more autonomous-sounding juntas, and the Cortes created eight more in 1821. Cortes delegates had originally designed them as administrative, not lawmaking, councils, composed of seven elected deputies and presided over by the regions' political chiefs (*jefes políticos*), but they evolved into a legislature in 1823 when they cooperated under the Plan of Casa Mata to oust and then supplant Iturbide's designates.[24]

The restored Congress accepted them as the provinces' voice, but the provincial deputations did not accept Congress. The centralists had used their connections with the town councils to get many of their number elected to the 1822 Congress and there, led by Fagoaga, they now composed a formidable bloc.[25] Their influence reached into the other branches as well. In the Supreme Executive Power there was Bravo, and above all Michelena, who frequently took the lead due to the absence of proprietary members. The cabinet was given a centralist tone by virtue of Alamán's energy and strength of personality.

Congress's immediate order of business, other than finding operating funds—the strong boxes were literally almost empty, with eight pesos[26]— was to close down the Iturbide era, and in this it had the full support of the provincial deputations. Iturbide himself was sent off toward the Gulf coast, consoled by a congressional promise of a 25,000 pesos a year pension if he remained in the Italian peninsula. Along with his wife and eight children, Iturbide was placed on board the British armed merchant ship *Spring*, which sailed for the Mediterranean on May 11. His enemies smiled about the story that he became seasick as soon as he went on board.[27]

Doing away with Iturbide's more objectionable deeds began with expunging mementoes of his royal presence: political prisoners were freed (April 3), construction was halted on palace renovations intended for the princes and princesses, his likeness on coins was replaced with the eagle's outline, and the eagle on the national coat of arms lost its crown.[28] On April 8 Congress annulled the Treaties of Córdoba, invalidated Iturbide's election to the throne as a work of violence, and abrogated the Plan of Iguala itself, declaring the Three Guarantees still in force by the "free will of the nation."[29]

When the deputies turned from liquidating the empire to reconstructing the nation, they ran into a storm. The Plan of Casa Mata had stated that a new congress would be called, and in the provinces it was assumed this meant immediately, but instead the deputies of the reconvoked congress behaved as if they intended to stay in session indefinitely. Specifically, federalists feared the deputies might write a new constitution along centralist lines, and from a distance, it looked like this might happen. On April 12 a committee reported that for the time being new congressional elections should not be held, and that the committee on the constitution should continue its work. In early May this latter committee drew up and presented to Congress a draft of a new constitution—actually federal in nature. A steady stream of emissaries and pronouncements from the provinces finally convinced the deputies it would be wise to make a convocatory summons soon, and on May 21 they declared that a constitutional congress was to meet on November 7.[30]

In spite of the May 21 declaration, congressmen presented sufficient cause for distrust, such as printing and distributing the committee's draft of the constitution (June 9). Thus, provincial deputations from late April openly challenged the central government, especially Congress. By the end of June eleven provinces had formally issued statements of distrust.[31] Normally these took the form of a petition or resolution from the provincial deputation intimating lack of faith in Congress and recognizing Congress as convocatory only, meaning it existed only to convoke its successor.

From the province of Guadalajara came the greatest threat. There were joined two forces feared by the national government: Iturbidism and an exalted federalism. Nationwide, Iturbide's following had dwindled, but one of his most ardent supporters, Luis Quintanar, was now political chief of Guadalajara, a region that had long resented Mexico City's hegemony. Quintanar was loudly defending federalist rights. Contemporary writers commented on the bizarre alliance between the ultraconservative Iturbidists and the liberal federalists,[32] but in truth it came down to both groups happening to have the same enemy—the Bourbonist-centralists.

In decrees of May 9 and May 12, the Guadalajara provincial deputation in effect declared independence from the national government, suspending all decrees from Mexico City. In reply, the Supreme Executive Power on May 24 replaced Quintanar with José Joaquín de Herrera, but the province held its ground. Provincial troops met Herrera at the border and turned him back, and then on June 16 the provincial deputation proclaimed the "Free State of Jalisco."[33]

The distinction between state and province was an important one in 1823, the former inspiring visions of local sovereignty, the latter scorned as a relic of viceregal absolutism. Thus the provincial deputations were eager to clothe themselves in the forms of the new era, to create full-fledged states and legislatures and constitutions. While deputies in Mexico City debated the proper relationships between the nation's center and components, several provincial deputations decided not to wait. State governments were announced for Yucatán on May 30,[34] for Oaxaca on June 2,[35] for Zacatecas on June 18.[36] The other provinces also began moving toward formal statehood, more cautiously, but in any case they already looked upon themselves as the equivalents of states.[37]

Centralists thought at the time that the provinces' breakaway tendencies would end in the dissolution of the Republic. In the early national years it was not certain that the Mexican nation as constituted would endure, for the possibility of creating another nation was especially strong in the North, where residents chafed at domination by a remote capital that seemed unable to care for local needs. In the spring and summer of 1823 there were several such plans and meetings in the northern states, most frequently involving Jalisco, Zacatecas, and San Luis Potosí, usually with an aim to forming a confederation if developments did not go their way in the national capital. For the time being, these impulses were calmed, but they would reappear during future crises.[38]

Santa Anna, hero of the movement to unseat Iturbide and commander of Veracruz, precipitated another crisis when he appeared—with his Veracruz regiment but without orders—in the city of San Luis Potosí to pro-claim a federal republic. Many years later, he admitted that the only thing he knew about a republic at that time derived from what a lawyer in Jalapa had explained to him.[39] Local officials agreed with his federalism, but they had no desire to feed his troops, and there were incidents between the men of the coast, known as *jarochos,* and the San Luis Potosí regiment. On June 5 Santa Anna marched his soldiers to the plaza where they listened to the Plan of San Luis Potosí, the primary object of which was the establishment of a federalist system. After the town council and provincial deputation asked the national government to recall him, General Gabriel Armijo was appointed Santa Anna's replacement, and he began maneuvering around the city. Seeing no support for his Plan, Santa Anna decided to give in and left for Mexico City and a court-martial on July 10.[40]

While the San Luis Potosí situation was still unresolved, the Supreme Executive Power decided something had to be done about Jalisco. First Colima (until now in the jurisdiction of Guadalajara) was separated from the state on June 20. Then on July 4, Bravo and Negrete left Mexico City for Guadalajara with 2,000 troops, artillery, and 200 mules loaded with provisions and ammunition. After an exchange of notes, Bravo, who appar-ently had been directed not to open hostilities, signed an accord at Lagos whereby he withdrew, while Jalisco—and Zacatecas, which had been coop-erating with Jalisco—agreed to pay national taxes and obey Federation decrees, but only those compatible with the federal system and the felicity of the two states.[41] Thus the outcome was still up in the air, and each side bided its time.

Congress, meanwhile, decided to accept the inevitable. On July 11 it widened provincial deputation powers over the provinces' funds and em-ployees, and in a symbolic gesture of July 19 it declared Hidalgo, Morelos, and other insurgent martyrs "benefactors of the fatherland to a heroic degree," ordering pensions for their families, and providing for their re-burial in the cathedral.[42] Morelos's remains were returned in a sumptuous ceremony, arriving at the Villa de Guadalupe on September 15, accompa-nied by three Indian orchestras playing gay waltzes. The bones were then placed in five urns and carried by high officials to the cathedral, escorted by 300 coaches and the capital's garrison. Carlos María de Bustamante, who described the occasion, noticed that Vicente Guerrero wept. Alamán, more cynical, wrote that many of those now paying their respects were the same ones that had had the martyrs shot.[43]

In the fall of 1823, as preparations went ahead for the upcoming Con-stitutional Congress, a reminder came from Veracruz that independence was yet incomplete. Neither Spain's liberal government under the Cortes, nor Fernando VII—after his autocratic powers were restored by French troops in 1823—had renounced their claim on Mexico. Since April 1823 Guadalupe Victoria had been holding conferences with two Spanish en-

voys, Juan Ramón Osés and Santiago de Iríssari, but on the central issue of recognition the Spaniards temporized.[44]

In the Veracruz harbor was a constant signal that Spain had not given up. There the Spanish flag still flew on the island fortress of San Juan de Ulúa where Brigadier Francisco Lemaur commanded about 600 Spanish soldiers and made a show of Spanish sovereignty. He charged duties on all incoming merchandise, forbade the flying of the Mexican flag in the Veracruz plaza, and was collecting the passports of outbound passengers and replacing them with Spanish permits, signed by himself as "Governor of the Plaza of Veracruz, Captain General and Superior Political Chief of the provinces of New Spain." At his orders, Mexicans could not return the salute of foreign ships.[45] In 1823 these imperial pretensions were clearly becoming intolerable.

The confrontation came in September 1823, after several incidents, when Mexican port commander Eulogio Villaurrutia ordered batteries of artillery pieces set up facing the castle. At 2 P.M. on September 25, after the Mexicans refused to dismantle the batteries, Lemaur opened fire.[46] Mexico declared war on October 8, and the Supreme Executive Power decreed all imports from Spain prohibited and ordered all Spanish ships out to sea within twenty-four hours.[47]

While the Mexicans could do little damage to the stout castle walls, the Spanish cannoneers nearly leveled the city. Veracruz almost ceased to exist. Spanish residents took refuge in Ulúa, and most of the Mexican families, rich and poor, moved to other parts. To a British diplomat arriving December 1823, the city looked desolate: buildings half knocked down by artillery, pedestrians replaced by vultures who ambled around, feeding on animal carcasses.[48] Veracruz was officially closed as a port, with the plan of diverting traffic to Alvarado, but the Alvarado harbor was so difficult that some ships preferred to anchor off Sacrificios, war zone or not.[49] Through 1823 and 1824, Mexico remained on the losing end of this war of attrition.

Another issue that came to a head in fall 1823 was that of bandits. Many of these were former revolutionaries, who still mixed in politics with their pillaging. One notorious highwayman was Loreto Cataño, who raided haciendas in the Cuautla area. The most famous, however, was Vicente Gómez, "the castrator" *(el capador)*. He had fought with great ferocity on both sides during the Revolution and now returned to terrorize Puebla and eastern Mexico province, advertising he was doing it all for Iturbide. In April 1824 his band, the "Holy League," killed the whole population of an hacienda on the Plains of Apám, for added sport shooting the women in their private parts. He was finally captured in Puebla in July 1824, sentenced to the Californias, and eventually stabbed to death in a bar in Sonora.[50]

Concern over these bandits—and conspiring Iturbidists—led to the infamous law of September 27, 1823. What was novel about the law was that civilians as well as soldiers could be bound over to a summary court-martial before they had done anything, if four witnesses stated they were dangerous.[51] Widely criticized as an infringement on individual rights, the September 27 law was used sparingly until 1830.

It was a relief for all concerned when the Constitutional Congress was formally convened on November 7. The delegates' most urgent duty was to assure the country at large they were in accord with the universal desire for federalism. Even confirmed centralists agreed, and the deputies decided to create a provisional document, to be known as the Acta Constitutiva, the Constitutive Act, which would serve while they were elaborating the permanent constitution. It was Ramos Arizpe's hour. He offered to draw up an outline of a constitution over the weekend, and a committee was immediately appointed to the purpose. As president of the committee and a powerful speaker, he dominated the sessions. On Monday, he read the outline, for which he had borrowed heavily from the 1812 Spanish Constitution.[52]

The Acta Constitutiva draft, discussed from the last half of November to the end of January and approved with minor changes, stamped the basic political principles and territorial subdivisions of the Mexican Republic. The great issue of governmental form, of course, had been decided back in the spring and summer. In vain the few centralists repeated their arguments: that federalism was a blind imitation of the United States, that governmental costs would burden the states, that federalism would lead to disunity, and that the Mexican people were too immature and too inexperienced for that sophisticated structure. And in vain Padre Mier made his famous hour-long speech (on December 11) for a relatively tight-knit federalism.[53]

Article 5 stated the government would be a "popular, federal representative republic," and even before the voting began Alamán asked for permission to publicize the document. About religion there had been no question. In December a few incautious souls, mainly Zavala and Cañedo, tried to moderate Article 3 of the Acta, which stated that the national religion would be Roman Catholicism "perpetually," but they were voted down.[54]

On January 31 the Acta Constitutiva was promulgated, and on February 3 the delegates took the oath of allegiance.[55] The Federal Republic was now mandated.

THE REPUBLIC CONSOLIDATED, 1824

The Mexican dislike for Spaniards was never far below the political surface. On the evening of January 22, 1824, Mrs. Lobato, wife of the former insurgent General José María Lobato (1785–1830), spied on the front steps General Miguel Barragán. She knew that he had come to arrest her husband for complicity in a recent anti-Spanish conspiracy by Cuernavaca soldiers, and her husband fled to his barracks. There he issued a proclamation for the ousting of Spaniards from Mexico and the removal from the Supreme Executive Power of the presumed Spanish sympathizers Domín-guez and Michelena. With most of the army out of town—the palace guard joined Lobato—the government was a virtual hostage. Lobato, however, hesitated to do violence to the deputies, and after a week-long standoff with Congress agreed to lay down his arms.[56]

The mutiny was a portent for Spaniards, one of several in these months. In December in Querétaro, and then in Cuernavaca in mid-January, troops made demands that measures be taken against Spaniards, and Congress received petitions urging their removal from public positions.[57]

As it turned out, the government was able to contain the anti-Spanish feeling for now, and Lobato's mutiny was the last of those that accompanied the transition from Iturbide to the Republic. In general 1824 was taken up with the more constructive pursuits of nation-building. While the play of forces of the previous year had resolved what type of structure the nation was to have, this year would see the structure elaborated, the Republic given detailed and, purportedly, long-lasting form. It was to be a year of note for the Republic since, on the one hand, certain national concerns would be laid aside, such as the lingering Iturbide threat, and certain milestones would be reached, such as the creation of national and state governments.

The federalist passion and its attendant prejudice against Spaniards took its toll on the executive after the Lobato revolt. One casualty was Negrete (1777–1846), who had come to New Spain as a young naval officer in 1802 and fought against the rebels for ten years. Declaring for Iturbide in June 1821, he was chiefly responsible for the successful siege of Durango, during which he was shot in the jaw.[58] He resigned from the Supreme Executive Power ostensibly because of poor health, but no doubt due to his Spanish birth. The other, Michelena, left for the calmer position of minister to England.[59] In the cabinet Alamán gained an ally when Mier y Terán replaced Herrera as secretary of war on March 12, and an enemy when José Ignacio Esteva replaced the Spaniard Arrillaga as secretary of the treasury on August 9. Alamán and Mier y Terán had tried to keep Esteva out, but Guadalupe Victoria, who had befriended him in Veracruz, prevailed.[60]

Iturbide was still on the minds of government officials. A Dominican friar, José María Marchena, had been sent to Europe to keep watch on him, and he sent letters in late February saying that Iturbide had left Leghorn. In Mexico there were reports of plottings in his favor. The prospect of his return, coupled with the uneasiness over banditry and the Holy Alliance, led to the movement for a supreme director in early 1824. This personage, assumed to be Bravo, would replace the triple executive and presumably be given wide authority to preserve internal security. Congress approved the idea on April 21, but the executive, not wishing to antagonize the federalists' feelings, had the project suspended on May 3.[61]

When Congress was advised that Iturbide had arrived in London, it responded on March 15 by ordering his pension cut off and then decreed on April 16 that all those supporting Iturbide as emperor be considered traitors, and on April 28 that if Iturbide were to return *he* would be considered a traitor. On May 6, in secret session, Congress heard that Iturbide had offered his services to Mexico on the grounds that the Spaniards were about to attempt a reconquest.[62]

Iturbide's followers were strongest in Jalisco, which had kept up its opposition since the Lagos meetings the previous year. Then on March 4 Quintanar appointed Anastacio Bustamante, another Iturbide loyalist, commander of the states' regular and militia troops. Jalisco, it was becoming clear, would have to be neutralized. The government declared Bustamante removed as state commander, arrested Iturbide supporters in Mexico City, and then on the afternoon of May 12 Bravo led a column out of Mexico City bound for Jalisco. When Bravo arrived in Guadalajara, he foreswore any intent to persecute state officials, but nevertheless arrested Quintanar and Bustamante and sent them to Acapulco.[63]

Jalisco was made safe just in time. On July 26 the government newspaper announced to the public that Iturbide had landed in the state of Tamaulipas.[64]

Iturbide's last hours were described by Felipe de la Garza, commander of the Eastern Interior Provinces. Carlos Beneski, an aide to Iturbide, appeared at his headquarters near the port of Soto la Marina and spoke of the English companion he had left on board the brigantine *Spring*. Shortly after Beneski departed, more intelligence arrived, that Beneski and the Englishman (who kept his face covered) had alighted at 5 P.M. on July 15 and requested horses. A witness stated he thought the "disguised one" looked like Iturbide in the frame, and it was noted he mounted the horse with "agility unknown among the English." De la Garza set out after them, caught up, entered their hut, and stood face to face with the former emperor of Mexico. "Here you have me," said Iturbide, "I come from London with my wife and two younger children to offer my services once again to the fatherland."[65] De la Garza informed him he was proscribed and took him to the state capital at Padilla, although he had second thoughts along the way and let Iturbide proceed to the town unescorted. The legislature, however, voted unanimously that the April 28 decree should be followed and the execution was set for July 19. On that morning, Iturbide confessed three times and was taken to the appointed place where he looked about. "Well, men, I'll give the world one last look." He put the blindfold on himself, asked for a glass of water, which he sipped once, gave a short patriotic speech to the assembled soldiery, kissed the crucifix, and was shot.[66]

While Iturbide's landing sent a tremor from the North, summer alarums carried in from the South. Molestation of Spaniards had continued throughout Mexico on a minor scale, and the first atrocity occurred in

Oaxaca. A Spanish sales tax *(alcabala)* collector, Cayetano Machado, was murdered *a machetazos*—slashed apart by a machete. In Oaxaca the powers were the two León brothers: state commander Antonio León (1794–1847), who had received the Oaxaca command for switching to Iturbide after eleven years of service with the royalists,[67] and Manuel León, deputy to the Constitutional Congress, currently on leave without license. With a large following among Indians of the Mixteca—the Leóns were reportedly Indians themselves[68]—they were at the head of a campaign against Spaniards. When a newly appointed military commander arrived, Antonio León told him that he might be "commander of the papers he carried, but not of the troops *(armas)*." The Leóns surrendered in mid-August to Guadalupe Victoria, but were pardoned after Victoria recommended clemency.[69]

Another expedition was required for Tabasco over a dispute between commander José Antonio Rincón and governor Agustín Ruíz de la Peña over who should control certain revenues. The episode marked the appearance of José María Alpuche e Infante, a Tabasco presbyter whom Rincón sent to Mexico City to be tried for sedition.[70] He was absolved and was soon to be one of the most fiery leaders of the federalists.

To the southeast, in Yucatán, Santa Anna had worked himself into a corner again. He had been sent to the Yucatán command, a type of penance on the marches of Mexico, after a court-martial exonerated him for his 1823 San Luis Potosí adventure. When his ship docked at Campeche on May 18, he found he had arrived in the midst of a civil war revolving around the hostilities with Spain and the long-time rivalry between Mérida and Campeche. Merchant families from each place wanted to make their city the commercial capital of the southern Gulf Coast, and the competition was especially sharp in Tabasco. Given the dependence on the Cuban trade of Mérida (the capital), Yucatán had been loath to publish the October 8, 1823, declaration of war on Spain. When the commerce went on, even during the bombardment from San Juan de Ulúa, Guadalupe Victoria closed Veracruz ports to Yucatán. But while Mérida had numerous Spanish families of influence, Campeche had hardly any and traded principally with Mexican ports. Thus after a Campeche junta of civil officials and military officers issued a plan on February 15 acknowledging the war with Spain and removing Spaniards from public positions, an army of several hundred men from Mérida arrived outside the walls of Campeche. Neither side was greatly disposed toward military operations, however, and after a vague statement of conciliation from the city, Mérida's army pulled back. The rancor continued.[71]

When Santa Anna arrived, both sides hoped to win him to their cause. He took Mérida's part in the conflict and decided to suspend his war declaration orders, which the legislature commemorated with a eulogistic poem and by electing him governor (July 5). But his superiors were not satisfied with his explanation for disobeying orders.[72]

Then he thought he saw a way out. Yucatán needed Cuba, and it occurred to him that if a Mexican force landed, the whole island should rally to the liberators, and the commander would become a hero. The troops were reportedly already on the ships when word came that 1,000 Spanish reinforcements had arrived in Cuba. The invasion was called off.[73] On January 15, 1825, the minister of war finally answered Santa Anna's plaintive requests and appointed Ignacio Mora his replacement.[74]

In Congress, meanwhile, discussion began in April on a draft of the constitution. Historians have since sustained a debate over the ideological inspiration of the 1824 constitution. Were the delegates influenced by the French or Spanish or American example? A reading of the minutes of the Constituent Congress leaves an impression of strong American influence. The delegates made almost daily reference to the United States, the principal model for a large-scale republic, and George Washington and Benjamin Franklin were honored names.

On the whole, however, it can be said that the delegates felt most at home following liberal Spanish patterns prescribed by the Cortes. Thus they took Spain's 1812 constitution as a starting point, borrowing from the United States frequently because that republic was a well-known model for federalism—which Spain was not. French ideas suffered from association with the Terror of guillotine days; what French influence there was generally entered via the Spanish constitution of 1812, which latter supplied the delegates not only with "terms, titles, sections, and articles," but frequently with the exact wording of the text.[75]

The constitution officially sanctioned the extent and subdivisions of the Republic. Article 2 stated the nation was to be composed of what had been the viceroyalty of New Spain, the Captaincy General of Yucatán, the Western and Eastern Interior Provinces, and the Californias (Upper and Lower). In December 1823 the delegates had begun delineating the areas of the states and finished the task with the creation of Durango on May 22.[76] The only question marks now were the northern and southern borders.

Jurisdiction over Texas did not seem much of a problem at the time. In 1825 U.S. Ambassador Joel Roberts Poinsett would bring up an old American claim for the province that dated back to the Louisiana Purchase. But Mexican officials were generally less worried about obtaining clear title to Texas than civilizing it. A law of August 18, 1824, that allowed states to provide lands for foreigners, also guaranteed existing colonization contracts. The most important was that of Stephen F. Austin, and Alamán spoke glowingly of the new village of San Felipe de Austin taking shape (near present Houston) in 1825.[77]

When Poinsett, in the midst of 1825 negotiations, was ready to accept Mexican ownership of Texas, Alamán insisted on postponing an agreement until surveyors had marked out the area. Poinsett advised his government to mark time. North Americans, he noted, were filling up the good land, and before long should cause enough trouble so that Mexicans should not

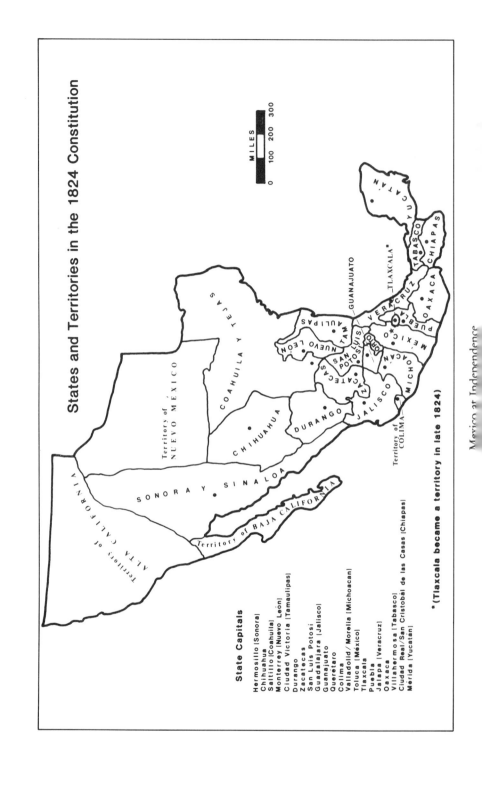

States and Territories in the 1824 Constitution

State Capitals

Hermosillo [Sonora]
Chihuahua
Saltillo [Coahuila]
Monterrey [Nuevo León]
Ciudad Victoria [Tamaulipas]
Durango
Zacatecas
San Luis Potosí
Guadalajara [Jalisco]
Guanajuato
Querétaro
Colima
Valladolid / Morelia [Michoacán]
Toluca [México]
Tlaxcala
Puebla
Jalapa [Veracruz]
Oaxaca
Villahermosa [Tabasco]
Ciudad Real/San Cristóbal de las Casas [Chiapas]
Mérida [Yucatán]

*(Tlaxcala became a territory in late 1824)

MILES

0   100   200   300

Mexico at Independence

be so "averse to part with that portion of their territory as they are at present."[78]

To the south, the question of Chiapas was much more immediate. In the Spanish days, Chiapas had been a part of the Captaincy General of Guatemala, administratively separate from the rest of Mexico. Although Iturbide had sent an army under Vicente Filisola to guarantee Guatemala's inclusion in the empire, the reigning sentiment after Iturbide was that coercion did not befit the new order of fraternal relations. In 1823 the Supreme Executive Power decided to accept the verdict of a congress convoked by Filisola. On July 1, 1823, a Guatemalan assembly had voted for independence, and formal recognition of the United Provinces of Central America came on August 20, 1824.[79]

The next question was where Guatemala ended and where Mexico began. The province of Chiapas was in between. Neither the Mexican congressmen nor the Chiapanecos (residents of Chiapas) were of one voice on where the province belonged. Two governments, the Supreme Provisional Junta and the provincial deputation, claimed to speak for Chiapas, and with conflicting reports coming in, the Mexican government vacillated. Chiapas remained in a state of near civil war in late 1823 and early 1824, but after a provincewide plebiscite, the Mexican group finally prevailed in September 1824. The only holdout was the Soconusco district *(partido)* in southern Chiapas, which declared itself annexed to Guatemala on July 24, 1824. For a while in 1825, war seemed a possibility, with troops from both countries in the *partido,* but Guatemala backed away and Soconusco eventually joined Mexico (1842).[80]

With the plebiscite in Chiapas, Mexico's original nineteen states and four territories were complete. As listed in Article 5 of the constitution, they were:

States

Chiapas	Oajaca
Chihuahua	Puebla de los Ángeles
Coahuila y Tejas	Querétaro
Durango	San Luis Potosí
Estado de Occidente	Tabasco
(Sonora y Sinaloa)	Tamaulipas
Guanajuato	Veracruz
México	Xalisco
Michoacán	Yucatán
Nuevo León	Zacatecas

Territories

Alta California	Colima
Baja California	Santa Fe de Nuevo México

The carving out of additional states and territories would begin shortly after the 1824 constitution was signed. The First Federal Republic would witness the creation of the Federal District on November 18, 1824, the territory of Tlaxcala on November 24, 1824, and the territory of Aguascalientes on May 23, 1835. The Estado de Occidente would be divided into the separate states of Sonora and Sinaloa on October 13, 1830.[81]

The delegates thought they were building a structure for all time. Articles 166 through 169 stated that amendments could not even be considered until 1830, and not acted upon until 1832. In late September the delegates of the Constitutional Congress finished their labors, and they signed the formal copy of the constitution of 1824 on October 4, in a three-and-a-half-hour ceremony. Although the dominant sentiment was jubilation, Father Mier signed in black clothing, explaining this was the funeral of his country.[82] After the signing—the bold hand of Zavala, then president of the Congress, standing out at the top—a congressional delegation carried the constitution to the Supreme Executive Power members for their signatures. President-elect Victoria was visibly shaken, white with emotion, when he signed.[83] The constitution of 1824 was now the law of the land.

The citizens could not know that the constitution was destined to last only eleven years. There was rejoicing, for these were momentous days. On October 4 the nation had its constitution, and five days later the first president was inaugurated. The campaign and election of 1824 augured well for the Republic. Guadalupe Victoria (1789–1843) and Nicolás Bravo (1776–1854), the leading candidates, were natural choices. Victoria was born Miguel Fernández y Félix in Tamazula, Durango. In 1811 the call of the Revolution interrupted his legal studies at the College of San Ildefonso in Mexico City, and he left to serve in Oaxaca and then Veracruz. Although it never shaded into a vendetta against individual Spaniards, the struggle against Spain became his guiding principle, a cause to which he gave the years of his early manhood. He gave up his baptismal name in favor of Guadalupe Victoria, and when armed struggle was no longer possible, he chose to withdraw to the mountains rather than accept a pardon. Believed to be lost, he emerged in 1821 to share in the victory against his old enemy.[84]

Bravo came from a Chilpancingo family that sent a whole clan to war for the insurgents. Nicolás himself fought primarily under Morelos, earning a reputation for moderation in a famous incident involving 300 Spanish prisoners. Just after his victory at Palmar, Bravo received the news his father had been executed by the royalists. The prisoners were called out, expecting a massacre, but instead Bravo set them free. He was a prisoner himself from 1817 to 1820, and then fought against the Spaniards again in 1821.[85] In his personal dealings Bravo was taciturn. He was described in 1826: "Grave and severe his appearance: he laughs when his lips order

Nicolás Bravo (1776–1854)

Guadalupe Victoria (1786–1843)

it; . . . tenacious in his opinions, humane and generous at the bottom of his soul. On campaigns he is serene to the point of coldness. He lives isolated, opening his confidence to few friends."[86]

Bravo and Victoria had much in common: both were tried and true revolutionary heroes, leaders of the resistance to Agustín I and Supreme Executive Power members. They were personally honorable, noble of spirit, and widely respected. Both were republicans with reservations about federalism. Bravo's centralism was better known, but Victoria too made statements favoring a strong central government.[87] There was one report Victoria had proposed to Iturbide a "Mexican" monarchy based on creole and Indian elements.[88] Of the two, Victoria probably had the larger popular following. His legendary sufferings and constancy during the Revolution had become part of national lore. But Bravo's supporters were better placed, thanks to his ties with the Scottish rite lodges and the landowning families of the South.

The campaign, what there was of it, was restrained and decorous.

Neither of the two leading newspapers devoted much coverage to the coming election, nor openly endorsed a candidate, although *El Sol* dwelt at greater length on Bravo's virtues and the *Águila Mexicana* on Victoria's. The contenders, in addition to the restraints imposed by their sense of dignity, were too busy on peacekeeping missions for any obvious seeking of support. Both men, however, knew their duties affected their chances. Bravo's expeditions to Jalisco marked him in the public eye as no great friend to federalism, and a mission to Querétaro in December 1823 to protect Spaniards did not help him either. Victoria, to his good political fortune, had spent most of the previous year and a half in Veracruz guarding the coast against Spaniards.

Through September ballots arrived from the states. According to the constitutional article approved by the Constitutional Congress, each state legislature voted for two candidates on September 1, 1824, the person with the highest number of votes becoming president and the second highest, vice-president. On October 2 Congress opened the ballots: Bravo lost almost all the northern states and Victoria won the presidency, eleven states to six. On October 9 Guadalupe Victoria took office at noon after a dawn artillery salvo and a parade through troop-lined streets.[89]

By the end of 1824, Mexico was a functioning republic. The national government had a constitution and a full complement of personnel, while all of the states had legislatures and most were working on their constitutions. A number of threats had receded: Iturbide was dead and his partisans dispersed, while an invasion by the Holy Alliance or Spain now seemed only a distant possibility.

Politically it was a fast-moving world. In a little more than three years, Mexico had passed from the jurisdiction of a liberal Cortes, to independence under a conservative monarchy, to a federal republic. Alamán shared the bittersweet feelings of his group who in these three years saw their reputations turn around: from admired reformers to reviled opponents of progress. For his part, Alamán refused to accept the inevitable and emerged as a forthright defender of centralism. With his newspaper echo, *El Sol*, he regularly deflated the federalists' pretensions, and even in a federalist framework tried to tilt the workings toward the national government as far as he could. To Congress he reported on the provinces' initiatives in a manner to invite derisive laughter. In one perfunctory note acknowledging receipt of two Mexico state decrees he postscripted a claim to make comments on the decrees, to which the local delegates objected strenuously.[90]

Zavala, on the other hand, had risen with the federalist tide. The death of Iturbide had freed him, and federalists in general, from an unnatural alliance. Elected to the Constitutional Congress, he began to take a larger role during the discussion of the constitution, was elected vice-president of Congress on August 5, and then president on September 6. It was Zavala who gave the congressional speech in response to President-elect Victoria during the ceremonies of October 5.[91]

The emotional wave set off by independence was gathering force. Centralists felt dismayed, but not yet overwhelmed, by the recent reverses, and it was felt the republican process could accommodate the forces that divided Mexicans by class and caste and region. But the federalist leaders were just beginning to sense the full measure of their strength, and within a year would develop the techniques to mobilize new levels of support. They would soon apply the test of liberalism to a wider circle of institutions. In the next two years the basic divisions of society would strain at the framework of Mexico's democracy.

« 3 »

The Mexicans and
Mexican Institutions

The fundamental question at independence was whether political institutions should be tailored to the habits of the people, or whether the institutions should correspond to a political ideal. Events of 1823 answered the question decisively in favor of the latter.

But what manner of people were the Mexicans?

The republican canon presupposed individualism, yet the people of Mexico were in mid-passage toward that status from the caste and corporate groupings of Spain's colonial system. In spite of divisions by region, color, and social rank, however, a sense of nationhood had penetrated. With the exception of the purely Indian communities, the people considered themselves Mexicans.

Along with nationalist feelings went a conviction that independence required new public relationships. There was a predisposition to elevate, or reduce, all classes and races to the rank of citizen. There were exceptions, for some of the civic calls fell on deaf ears, as in the case of Indians, who considered the practices of citizenship a threat to their traditions, and some were not given the chance to belong, as in the case of Spaniards, whose allegiance was suspect.

Nevertheless, the creed of the citizen gave a distinctive coloration to the institutions and social practices of the 1820s.

THE PEOPLE: DEMOGRAPHY AND STRUCTURE

In discussing Mexico's population, one enters a world of extrapolation and qualification. Even the most reliable figures for the last Spanish years reflect an added 20 percent for those who had evaded the census takers, and after independence state officials depended on the *alcaldes,* who because of direct taxes and army quotas had every reason to keep the numbers low. Still, when one compares the several estimates of the late colonial period, and ranges them alongside the state and national *Memorias,* it seems safe to say Mexico had an independence population of about 6.5 million people.[1] (See table 1.) Although most officials agreed that the only segment not growing was that of the Indians, the population was still generally densest in those areas having a large Indian population, such as Guanajuato, Puebla, Mexico, and Oaxaca (in descending order), and thinnest in the almost unoccupied Californias and Texas.[2]

According to official policy, everyone was now to be considered, without distinctions, a citizen. A law of September 17, 1822, stated that no government document was to classify citizens by racial origin.[3] But an Indian or one of the *castas* (as the mixed races or mestizos were then called) in high position would still draw comment, and both Mexicans and visitors still habitually discussed the social structure in terms of bloodlines: *blancos, indios,* and *castas.* Estimates of proportions varied. Navarro y Noriega, whose percentages are the most widely quoted, estimated that the population was 60 percent Indian, 22 percent *casta,* and 18 percent white.[4]

The geographical distribution of these peoples was determined by pre-conquest population patterns and by Spain's economic and political emphases. The highest proportion of Indians was to be found in Mexico, Puebla, Oaxaca, Veracruz, Michoacán, and Yucatán. These were generally the settled, village Indians. As one moved northward to Guanajuato, the uprooted Indians were encountered—*los indios laboríos y vagos*—who migrated to follow their work. Both types were tribute-paying under Spain.[5]

Another group whose place at the bottom of colonial society was certified by their classification as *tributarios,* or tribute-paying, were the *mulatos.* In numbers they were spread throughout the Republic, but in terms of percentage of the population they were most prominent in the lowlands and coasts of central Mexico. They were better off than the Indians economically, and engaged in a wide variety of trades—even as land-owners—but were in the popular mind a vicious class. Slavery was still a legal institution, although the number of slaves had declined to about 3,000 by 1821, since employers found it cheaper to hire free men and avoid the costs of upkeep.[6]

The *castas* were concentrated in the laboring classes of towns, haciendas, ranches, and mines, but it is not accurate to think of the working class as *casta* since in any given place it might be made up of Spaniards or creoles.[7]

Because Spaniards themselves dominated government service, they tended to congregate in the national and provincial capitals, the mining towns, and sugar plantation areas, but they could be found anywhere, even

TABLE 1

Population of Mexico after Independence
(States and Territories)

	Population (or Estimates)	Year of Census	Source
States			
Chiapas	118,775	1831	Chiapas, *Memoria*, 1831, estado 1.
Chihuahua	120,157	1827	Chihuahua, *Memoria*, 1831, p. 18.
Coahuila-Texas	63,154	ca. 1827	Coahuila-Texas, *Nota Estadística*, 1827, p. 8.
Durango	149,421	ca. 1827	Durango, *Memoria*, 1827, estado 2.
Guanajuato	382,829	1825	Guanajuato, *Memoria*, 1826, "Plan que manifiesta el censo general."
Jalisco	547,359	1822	Jalisco, *Memoria*, 1826, estado 2.
México	982,418	ca. 1828	México, *Memoria*, 1828, estado 1.
Michoacán	422,472	ca. 1829	Michoacán, *Memoria*, 1829, estado 1.
Nuevo León	89,792	1826	Report of state government.[a]
Oaxaca	457,504	ca. 1828	Oaxaca, *Memoria*, 1828, p. 6.
Occidente, Estado de (Sonora-Sinaloa)	230,000	ca. 1828	Estado de Occidente, *Nota Estadística*, 1828, p. 77.
Puebla	584,358	ca. 1825	Puebla, *Memoria*, 1826, estado 2.
Querétaro	114,437	1830	Report of Querétaro state government.[a]
San Luis Potosí	298,230	ca. 1829	San Luis Potosí, *Memoria*, 1829, estado 2.
Tabasco	54,499	1831	Tabasco, *Memoria*, 1831, "Detall que manifiesta la población total del Estado en sus tres departamentos."
Tamaulipas	67,434	ca. 1821	De la Torre et al., *Historia general de Tamaulipas*, pp. 108–09.
Veracruz	242,658	ca. 1830	Report of Vice-Governor, 1831.[a]
Yucatán	600,000	1827	Yucatán, *Memoria*, 1827, p. 6.
Zacatecas	290,044	1830	Zacatecas, *Memoria*, 1831, "Plan que manifiesta el censo general del Estado."

	Population (or Estimates)	Year of Census	Source
Territories			
Alta California	27,000	1820s	Report of territorial commissary.[a]
Baja California	10,000– 15,000	1820s	Valdés, *Censo,* and Forbes, *California,* p. 62.
Colima	45,838	1832	Cook and Borah, *Essays in Population History* 1:362.
Federal District	188,793	1823	México, *Memoria,* 1826, p. 10.
Nuevo México	41,458	ca. 1832	Nuevo México, *Ojeada,* 1832, p. 12.
Tlaxcala	66,244	1824	Report of Provincial Deputation, 1824[a]

[a]Cited in Valdés, *Censo actual de la República Mexicana,* 1831.

in wayside villages. Creoles frequented the same locales, but more often lived in smaller towns and in the countryside as owners of haciendas.[8]

Another manner of taking a sight on Mexican social structure is to examine the annual reports of the state governors, the *Memorias,* some of which appended tables listing population by class. From these a picture comes through of a feudal society. Invariably the states had a few hundred storekeepers, a handful of doctors and lawyers, several dozen churchmen, a few score tradesmen or possibly miners, and thousands upon thousands of laborers (*jornaleros* or *labradores*). Poinsett wrote that seven-eighths of the population lived in huts furnished only with a "few coarse mats" and eating only "Indian corn, pepper, and poke."[9]

In the literature of the day one can catch a fleeting glimpse of "the almost mythical *ranchero* class." A few historians, and several travelers, claimed to have discovered in this manager or owner of a medium-sized piece of crop or stock land, a rural middle class. In some of the land tabulations in the annual reports of the governors, ranchos are listed apart from haciendas.[10] The *rancheros'* independence from the greater land barons, however, was not sufficient to allow of long-term survival.

In a few of the larger cities, a class system roughly paralleled the caste schema. This was most apparent in the city of Mexico. The world of the castes could still be seen in the Traza and the Indian *parcialidades* of Santiago Tlatelolco and San Juan Tenochtitlán. The Traza had been officially designated as the Spanish residential area, while the two *parcialidades* had been kept legally separate from the city's regular administration to facilitate religious conversion and labor control. At independence the Traza residents were still noticeably white and possessed the finest houses in the city, and the *parcialidades* were mostly Indian. But outsiders were moving into both places, and the *parcialidades* were absorbed by the Mexico City government. The Indians of Santiago and San Juan worked in construction, shoemaking, carpentry, weaving, and button making.[11] In the emerging class structure they fell into the working class that comprised about 80 percent of the capital's population. Here were the tailors, weavers, peddlers, confectioners, water carriers, plus a host of others who earned a subsistence income or less. They lived near their work in the first-floor apartments that were the first to be inundated during the wet season. They watched so many of their children die—a third of all recorded deaths were of children below the age of three—that migration to the city barely sufficed to cover the population deficit.[12]

Some of the skilled workers, however, had become part of the upper 20 percent of the city, the middle and upper classes. At the top were professionals, financiers, and industrialists, and even merchants. The less affluent of this class shaded into the middle class of successful tradesmen and bureaucrats. They were all, however, distinguished by their quasi-European life style.[13]

Some of the working class drifted into the company of the *léperos*. These were the people of the street, numbered at about 20,000 by Poinsett. He saw them drinking themselves senseless and then sleeping it off outside the pulque shops, begging around the churches, and thrusting their sores and wounds in the faces of passers-by hoping to gain their sympathy.[14] A cross section of occupations and races—many were Spaniards—they lived out their lives in a subculture of common-law marriages and family violence, surviving on an estimated one peso a week, dressing in "filthy blankets and sheets or discarded rags" and haunting the wine and pulque shops. Frederick Shaw wrote their history from the records of the Mexico City Vagrants' Court, established on March 3, 1828, to deal with the growing problem. He described them as part of the underemployed, semiliterate, laboring poor, supplementing their income through begging and crime. When brought before the court, the "meanest among them would claim to have an *oficio* (trade)." Those convicted of a crime would be sent to perform undesirable labor, such as doing chores in a bakery.[15] In their way, they did participate in the history of the day: manipulated by politicians in the cause of Emperor Iturbide and thereafter by the York rite Masons, their criminal excursions shaped the daily habits of all Mexico City residents.

Conditions of life meant small families for Mexicans. Common wisdom then was to calculate five individuals to a family, although local conditions caused fluctuations: a deputy from Oaxaca stated that disease had reduced the average there to 3.5.[16] With the nuclear family predominating, it seems large families were generally the prerogative of the rich. Foreigners noted the many children of their affluent friends—Poinsett paid a call on the Countess of Regla, a young woman of twenty with six children. For others, their children did not live long. Certainly a family with five or six children was looked upon as unusual.[17] Fragmentary studies suggest that girls married in their late teens and boys two to four years later. Illegitimacy was rather common, accounting for 40 to 60 percent of all births in several New Mexico communities in this period.[18] An interesting sidelight is that there are references to intentional miscarriages by Indian girls.[19]

Independence and Mexican Women

The female half of the population is just now becoming visible in the story of early national Mexico. Women surfaced on the public scene only as accompaniments of their men, and little thought was given to bettering their lot at independence. It never seems to have occurred to anyone, except Lizardi, to allow them to vote. Foreigners graded women according to their graces in polite society, and usually found Mexican women wanting, since they smoked tobacco in public, were not conversant in French, and were but little affected by European dress.[20] Alamán offered another perspective when, writing about the revolutionary period, he repeated the old maxim that "in America, the women were worth more than the men." They lacked the defects that historical forces had brought out in the men and made good mothers and wives, their only failing an excessive leniency with their children.[21]

The traditions of Spanish law recognized women's subservient status by extending protections. When marrying, women retained not only their surnames, but also their property, and Lindley noted that Guadalajara's notarial wills showed a faithful division of paternal and maternal lands among male and female heirs.[22] This was little comfort to the average woman, for within the family the prerogatives of the father were not to be breached. In California, Duhaut-Cilly noted that the father ate alone, attended by the whole family. The Vagrants' Court in Mexico City did not consider wife beating punishable if it were provoked by misbehavior; and divorce, although possible, was not a pleasant alternative, since a wife might be incarcerated during the lengthy proceedings while a canonical court investigated the differences.[23]

For a few Mexican women, a passing recompense was their sexual allure, although their capacity to drive men to desperate deeds merely confirmed their decorative-domestic role. The most famous case of romantic scandal involved the Dominican friar Marchena, the individual who spied on Iturbide in Europe. Serving under Nicolás Bravo in 1813–1814, he was overcome by an uncontrollable passion for Bravo's sister, who did not return his interest. After his coming back from Europe in 1825, his love unabated and still spurned, he resolved to kill her husband (Joaquín Rea). When the pharmacist's assistant (Núñez) recruited to supply the poison informed on him, Father Marchena went into hiding and added him as an intended victim. The men contacted to do away with Nuñez finally came to fear Marchena themselves and they killed him in 1826.[24]

For the unmarriageable of the more comfortable classes, the nunnery was an alternative. Even there, however, the nuns were subject to a man's dictates, the supervisor (*mayordomo*) appointed to oversee their accounts. In a study of the archepiscopal convents, Anne Staples drew a picture of these girls who, after taking the vow, were no longer considered part of society. A few orders forbade members to ever again see relatives, while legal secularization, a complicated process requiring Vatican approval, was very rare and few nuns successfully fled the convents. Although life could be dreary in the drafty buildings of the cloister, with no exercise, poor or insufficient food, and repeated penitences, the routine was lightened by small comforts, such as pets, visits from friends, or special treats of pastries or chocolate.[25]

The case of Mexican women brings home the fact that history consists of the images created in our minds by the available documentation. While earlier institutional histories based on newspapers and government records had shown that public life was a man's world, the scholars who have been digging through property records are changing our views. More women than we imagined did not, or could not, fit into the passive, dependent, mold—thanks to their longevity, their inability to attract suitors, or their poverty. Around Guadalajara in the last colonial years, women showed up frequently in the mortgages as purchasers of property, as lenders to merchants and others, as donors to convents and churches, and as heads of large estates. In Mexico City at the time of the Revolution, one out of every four property owners was a woman.[26]

Then, too, in the innumerable villages across the land, women were beyond the reach of the feminine ethic. They were a natural part of the world of work and village life. In the New Mexico censuses, for example, there was no single term for housewife. In Mexico City also, a purely domestic life was not a real option for the women of the poor. They had to work. The tobacco and cloth factories normally hired females, and prostitution was widespread enough in Mexico City that an 1832 pamphlet urged that foreign seamstresses come to teach young girls another profession.[27]

The Nobility

Independence spelled the end of the nobility as such, but titled individuals made the transition with grace. In 1821 about fifty nobles resided in Mexico. Most had been rich and ennobled for a century or so, the "old merchants and miners," while another smaller group dated its arrival from the free trade explosion of the late 1700s. The great external sign of their position was the entail, the legal document that made their property indivisible and ensured that their estate and name would be perpetuated to the greater glory of the family. They were not all opulent, but New Spain had harbored the richest nobles of Spanish America. In 1826 the ex-count of the Valley of Orizaba divided his property, keeping at least twenty-three haciendas, while his son received thirty, plus the famous House of Tiles in Mexico City.[28]

The extent of the nobles' holdings was matched, and more, by the extent of their obligations. The mines or ranches or haciendas were clan enterprises, functioning to maintain the family on a respectable scale, which in the case of a count or a marquis meant they were expected to build chapels, underwrite chantries, lead militias, marry off their daughters in appropriate sumptuousness, and live in a day-to-day style befitting their rank. These unavoidable calls on financial reserves, coupled with the normal insecurity of agricultural and mining activities, led inevitably to large debts and a resultant weakening in families. Newly successful miners and merchants might obtain patents of nobility to take their place, but the process of decline and renewal created an instability in the class. The nobles of New Spain, frequently described as somewhat retiring, thus never became a true political elite.

Although aristocrats owed their ennoblement to royal favor (usually purchased), the great families' fortunes were tied to the economic health of New Spain. Mercantilism and forced loans affected them personally; they remembered that the peninsular nobility looked upon them as less than equals; and so they found no impediment to accepting independence in 1821.[29] The arrival of British investment capital in the 1820s meant a new lease on life for many of the mining families, such as the Reglas, the Fagoagas, the Vivancos, the Sardanetas, and Alamán's mother's family, the Bustos.

Independence made Mexicans unwilling to put up with the more blatant favoritism linked with social status. At a cockfight in 1824, when the steward gave special elevated seats to prominent ladies, the murmurs reached such a pitch that the ladies decided to sit on *petates* like the rest of the women.[30] In such an atmosphere, the nobles, still in ill favor because of their friendliness with Iturbide, were in no position to put up serious resistance to the two issues that most affected them: the abolition of entail and the abolition of titles. Many actually favored the August 7, 1823, law abolishing civil entail, since they needed to sell some of their properties to pay off debts. And there was no appreciable opposition to the abolition of titles when it came in 1826.[31]

After that date, then, nothing was left of the legal appurtenances of nobility. Coats of arms were taken out of public view, formerly indivisible lands might now be sold or parceled out between father and children, and the high and mighty were equal in the eyes of the law to the humblest citizen. The nobles seem to have taken it with even temper, and in all events laws did not alter the family connections or the everyday deference

Hacendado and Majordomo

given the well-born. The public in these years was still likely to address them as the ex-duke and the ex-marquis, and as late as 1835 a Brazilian diplomat wrote that the former nobles still enjoyed their traditional prestige.[32]

The Indians

Whereas the nobles were to be kneaded downward into the Mexican mass, the Indians were to blend upward among the citizenry. The Indians, however, had their own thoughts on the matter, and in spite of well-intentioned policy, the end result was that they were not real Mexicans by their own or virtually anyone else's measure. The peoples to be integrated into national life were described by Zavala, one of their best friends in high place.

> They inhabited and inhabit huts covered with straw or palms, whose extent is normally 15–16 feet in length by 10–12 feet in width, with an oval form. It can be assumed that there are gathered the children, the domestic animals and an altar with the saints or household gods. In the middle there is a fire that serves to heat the water in which they cook the maize, with few exceptions their only food. There are not five among a hundred that have two sets of clothing, which consist of a long shirt of ordinary cloth and pants; their wives or daughters, dressed in the same simplicity or poverty, are unaware of the inclination of their sex to look best in front of others. In the same previously mentioned proportion, there are no proprietors, and they are content with

harvesting thirty five or forty fanegas of maize each year, with which they remain satisfied. When they have earned a small amount of money on some job or task, they use it for a festival to the saint of their preference and consume their miserable earnings in fireworks, masses, foods, and inebriating drinks. The rest of the year they pass in idleness, sleeping many hours a day in the hot lands, or in the pastimes of their taste in the comfortable climes. Two of a hundred would learn to read, but in the present day the situation in this aspect has improved a great deal. In several provinces the curates exercised much domination, and had such authority over the Indians that they ordered them flogged publicly when they failed to pay fees on time or committed some act of disobedience. I have seen many Indians, and their wives, whipped at the doors of the churches for having missed a Sunday or festival mass. And this outrage was authorized by custom in my province! The scourged ones then had the obligation to kiss the hand of the scourger.[33]

This is not to say that they were not very much a part of Mexican life. On the roads, they were seen at their familiar trot, estimated at four miles per hour.[34] Indian women were seen as the markets, seated before mats selling their fruits, vegetables, flowers, and earthenware. And they could be seen as army conscripts.

Still, they preferred to keep to themselves. Observers thought them possessed of a melancholic diffidence, shed only on feast days when they joyously staged the Christians' triumphs over the heathen. Religion com-

Tortilla Makers

manded their devotion, although Mexicans wondered if it was the same Christianity they knew. In Puebla one could buy soap shaped into terrifying animals from Indian mythology as well as the Christian apocalypse.[35] An ancient idol, uncovered many years earlier, was still kept buried in the university courtyard for fear it might awaken the Indians' primeval instincts.[36]

What must be borne in mind when looking at the Indians of the Mexican Republic, Zavala's comments notwithstanding, was their diversity: in physical appearance, complexity of culture, and degree of assimilation. Some had been village agriculturalists for thousands of years, while others, mostly in the far north, ranged about at the band level eating anything edible they came upon. Traveled Mexicans could guess their tribe by facial structure, color, and clothing. Some Indians disdained any contact with the Mexicans, but others, forced out of their villages by need, were rapidly losing their ancestors' ways.

British agent Lionel Hervey was told that the percentage of Indians ranged from four-fifths in Oaxaca and two-thirds in Tabasco and Yucatán, to one-half in Querétaro, México, and Valladolid, and one-third in Jalisco and Guanajuato.[37] Their numbers had been much augmented in the eighteenth century,[38] but around the central plateau, in the Bajío, and in nearby states, opinion of the 1820s was that the Indians were fast disappearing—by assimilation and mortality. A study by the state of Mexico government found that the average Indian family numbered only 3.9 people in the Toluca district—and the living was considered better around Toluca than in the rest of the state. Poverty, the army draft (*sorteo*), and work levies were said to be the causes.[39] The same trend was noted in Guanajuato where they were dying "by the thousands" and must soon disappear as a people if they did not meld with Mexicans.[40] In the south there was no talk of the Indians passing out of existence. There they were holding their own, occupying more than one-half the land in the Valley of Oaxaca in the last colonial years.[41] And on the northern frontier, although their numbers were fewer, mounted Indians would hold off total domination until the latter part of the century.

The official attitude was dominated by a desire to bring the Indians out of their cultural darkness. Among some educated Mexicans there was a sort of sentimental reverence for Aztec grandeur, as a counterweight to Spanish antecedents. Carlos María de Bustamante put in many hours studying Indian manuscripts and monuments. Out of the belief that the Aztecs had stopped off in California on their way south, Governor Echeandía and the Provincial Deputation of Upper California proposed in 1827 renaming the province Moctezuma and commissioning a new coat of arms showing "an Indian with plume, bow, and quiver, in the act of crossing the strait." Mier y Terán gave Nahuatl names like Lipantitlán, Tenoxtitlán, and Anáhuac to new military posts in Texas, and similar names were given to the new Coatzacoalcos colonies.[42] While the aboriginal past was looked to as a vehicle for nationalism, the federalists, and especially the centralists, tended to share the average Mexican's opinion that the Indian was a debased creature. A minority of the federalists saw them as carriers of precious skills, albeit of the arts and crafts type, while the centralists usually consigned them out of hand to the lower ranks of humanity. Alamán considered them inclined to thievery and drunkenness.[43]

In the public documents officials casually dropped comments about the Indians' unfitness for civilized activities. The Oaxaca state government's annual report for 1828 may serve as an example: "The crude Indians' pueblos . . . live . . . and it seems will always live in the grossest ignorance. . . . Their *ayuntamientos* and republics for the lack of these principles are torpid, utterly inept, and crude in the carrying out of their respective attributions."[44] The 1831 Chiapas review of the state pictured them as corrupted by idleness and alcohol following their "almost animal" existence under the Spaniards, needing a law to stimulate them to work.[45]

Independence did make the Indians legally free and equal. The Cortes had issued several decrees to incorporate the Indians into national life, abolishing personal service, dividing communal lands, and forbidding whippings.[46] These laws became national policy, although much evidence indicated that while jurists might have considered Indians equal to whites, few others did. Preparing coastal defenses in 1823, Guadalupe Victoria resorted to an Indian levy, and large numbers died because of the unhealthy climate.[47] Zavala and other Yucatán deputies in 1822 petitioned Congress to carry out in their province the Cortes ban on personal services, and nine years later the state was still passing legislation to halt unpaid services.[48] The Mexico state government in 1828 found it necessary to repeat earlier orders terminating Indians' personal services to parishes. In the 1830s the Tarahumara Indians, 40,000 of whom lived in the Chihuahua Sierra Madre, were still rendering personal services to their priests. And as late as 1845 the town of Los Angeles in Upper California maintained separate cemeteries for Indians and whites.[49]

There was surprisingly little public dialogue on such a large segment of the nation. In the new atmosphere of equality before the law politicians generally thought it unnecessary to single them out for special attention, and some officials were even averse to using the term Indians, calling them instead "so-called Indians" or "those formerly called Indians." What public policy existed was a vague civilizing impulse, a disposition to reaffirm their citizenship—all states accorded them full political rights and the Guanajuato legislature expressly removed their minority status[50]—to decree schools for their villages, and to make them property holders.

In practice, numerous schools for Indians did come into existence. Poinsett wrote that he saw schoolhouses in even the remotest villlages.[51] Additionally, a number of states enacted laws to carry out the Cortes provisions for breaking up tribal lands into individual parcels.[52] Jalisco, where the project was taken seriously, illustrated the complexities involved. Mestizos were not to receive any of the common lands, this taken over from the Cortes, and Indians were not to sell their new property to latifundistas. It turned out that almost all Indians had Spanish or African blood, and officials had to decide exactly who was an Indian. Finally, the Senate ruled that those were Indians whom public opinion considered as such. Another problem involved determining legal ownership, since the Jalisco Indians did not have clear titles. They were the owners simply because they had always occupied the lands.[53]

It soon became apparent Indians had little interest in either becoming citizens or obtaining title to their individual piece of land. They were famously unimpressed with their newfound judicial equality, an irrelevant abstraction at best. They appreciated more the benefits of free trade, exchanging their "leather jerkins" for cheap cotton cloth.[54] As for the common lands, everywhere, according to available documents, they resisted subdividing them. In Michoacán, when some pueblos refused point-blank to do so, the state government had to threaten to send troops.[55] Jalisco eventually (1834) rescinded the division legislation after complaints of violent spoliations and other evils.[56] By 1834, however, the process of alienation had already turned a number of Guadalajara's independent Indian villages into mere barrios. The city's notarial records of the 1820s showed "bill after bill" where the Indians sold the distributed parcels to a variety of buyers.[57]

Although the Indians had little desire to become individual property owners, they were fierce litigants in defending their villages' holdings against either other Indians or Mexicans. The Oaxaca governor cited riots over land cases, the Indians' zeal in defense of their lands such that "no judgment calms them," only force.[58] They did not hesitate to confront even the highest-placed individuals. Bravo lost a case over land in Chichihualco in 1824,[59] and Alamán was taken to court in 1827. A famous case in 1828 involved lands of the hacienda of Atenco (in the Valley of Toluca) disputed by the ex-count of Santiago and nearby Indians. The Mexico state supreme court (Audiencia) decided for the count, but on the day he was to take possession, a multitude of Indians, estimated at between one and five thousand, planted themselves on the land. Exhortations having no effect, troops moved in, the Indians answered with a "cloud of rocks," and the soldiers opened fire. Five Indian bodies were found on the field.[60]

Foreign Visitors

Foreigners were the new ingredient in the population mixture. In 1821 and 1822, as Europeans and Americans read about Iturbide's successful revolution, they recalled the tales of the Indies' glamour and riches, and some of the more enterprising set sail to find out for themselves. They came with schemes that combined profit and progress: schools, river navigation, highways, diving bells, harbor dredging, and mining machinery. The British were the most numerous, more than 500 in the Republic by the end of 1826.[61] Of these the most notable was Francis Baring, connected with the mercantile financial house of Baring Brothers. He invested in mining, purchased the del Cristo hacienda outside Mexico City, and tried to buy up the huge Parras estate of San Miguel de Aguayo.[62] As the source of needed diplomatic patronage and capital, the English were treated as semiofficial guests. Out of gratitude for Great Britain's signing of a treaty, Congress ordered official celebrations to mark the occasion.[63]

The French too were favored in one sense, since as Roman Catholics they were not looked upon with the same suspicion as other "heretical" visitors. On the other hand, they were suspect politically since their king was the patron of the hated Fernando VII. Whereas the British had reputations as peddlers and miners, the French made their mark in the public eye as bearers of culture, as schoolmasters, dancing instructors, and language teachers. In terms of numbers, however, most Frenchmen were really traders and craftsmen. They were found in all parts of the country, even competing with North Americans in the far north.[64]

From the United States came a variety of visitors. Apart from the colonists in Texas, who were a special case, North Americans too were sellers of merchandise. Overshadowed by the British in the central states, they dominated foreign trade in the north. A sprinkling of Germans arrived, for the most part miners.

Mexicans and foreigners had mixed feelings about each other. The newcomers marveled at the exotica, and the more educated collected specimens of never-seen-before flora and fauna and solemnly examined Indian sites and relics. But the country struck them as barbaric. Their first impulse was to pass judgment according to the quality of the inns which at times they had to share with the innkeeper's animals. In Mexico City the principal hotel, The Gran Sociedad, had a coffee salon and casino,[65] but the provincial hotels came furnished with only tables and benches. Foreigners developed affection for individuals, yet hardly any of them respected Mexicans, an attitude they showed soon enough in the books they wrote about their travels. At the mining sites, Englishmen, Cornishmen, and Germans stuck together—in the better jobs—and would not let the Mexicans near the machinery.[66]

Mexicans for their part did not take foreigners into society with ease. Spain's closed-border policy had left a traditional suspicion of outsiders, strongest among the poorer classes. These, urged on by the clergy, might taunt the outsiders with cries of "heretic," and occasionally menace them. Ecclesiastics in general were horrified at the prospect of unbelievers in their midst, frequently blaming them for corrupting Catholic morality, although the *Correo de la Federación Mexicana* claimed that they had raised the level of public morality.[67] At the upper levels, the government, in the belief that Mexico was now a member of the modern family of nations, tried to accommodate them, especially at first.

The Mexican aristocracy too generally made it a point to extend courtesies to visitors of comparable social standing, even marrying their daughters to them. British Consul General Charles T. O'Gorman married Anna Maria Noriega y Vicario in June 1827 and received a dowry of 27,304 pesos. Curiously, the groom's brother George, an agent for London's Goldschmidt and Company, had been expelled earlier for certain financial manipulations.[68] Another prosperous match was made by Thomas Gillow, an Irish clocksmith. He became the agent and then the husband of the marchioness of Sierra Nevada, a considerably older woman.[69]

From an early date, foreigners became conspicuous in public life. Several, mostly Latin Americans, found their way into government service. Vicente Rocafuerte, from Ecuador, acted as secretary and then chargé d'affaires in the London legation (1824–1829), and during the Bustamante administration began an opposition newspaper. The officer corps had a cosmopolitan touch, with Colonel José Antonio Mejía (Cuban), General Arthur Wavell (British), Colonel Carlos Beneski (Polish), and Colonel John Davis Bradburn (American) serving at various times. The navy, needing experienced seamen due to the departure of the Spanish officers, contracted with Captains Charles Thurlow Smith and William Wilson South (both English) and David Porter (American) to command the fleet.

A number of foreigners were drawn into local political questions, diplomats being among the first. The two contenders were the British and the North Americans, the former generally more sympathetic to the Scottish rite centralists and the latter lining up with the York rite federalists. The British—first the commissioners Lionel Hervey, James Morier, and Henry George Ward (1823–1824), then Ward himself (1824–1827), and then Richard Pakenham (1827 on)—discreetly operated from the inside, using their influence with President Guadalupe Victoria, while American Ambassador Joel Roberts Poinsett organized politicians at large. Another foreign type was the crusading journalist, most of whom, as refugees from the Holy Alliance, tried to further the cause of the York rite federalists. Several ran afoul of the authorities and were expelled from the country, the best known being Germán Nicolás Prisette, a French lawyer active in the mutual instruction movement who edited *El Archivista* and then worked with the *Águila Mexicana*. For comments expressed in these newspapers, the government expelled him in 1824. He left the capital strapped to his horse—he was lame—but died before he could be removed from the country.[70] Two years later (August 1826) Marquis O. de A. Santangelo, an Italian, was deported after criticizing the Victoria administration.[71]

There were also spies. Three Frenchmen were arrested and expelled for spying: Lamotte and Schmalz in September 1823,[72] and then Saint Clair in

1825. Thirty-seven-year-old Sylvestre Courtois Saint Clair arrived in spring 1824, after four years in Havana, representing himself as an impoverished gentleman in search of honorable livelihood. With letters of introduction, he gained entry into the homes of the Mexican nobility, but after indiscretions was detained in early June, incarcerated for ten months, and then deported. Apparently sent by the governor of Cuba, Saint Clair received much attention, since his arrest coincided with debates over sending Mexican soldiers to invade Cuba.[73]

At the outset there was much variety in the procedures for registering the arrival and stay of these visitors. Many state officials considered themselves fully competent to decide the question. State constitutions commonly provided for granting of "letters of citizenship," and in their sovereign mood states began issuing passports of their own and even passing on the validity of other states' passports.[74] Laws of June 5, 1826, and March 12, 1828, provided for uniformity. Under the latter, arriving passengers were to have their nationality and profession certified by one of their diplomatic agents and then solicit a security card *(carta de seguridad)* from the Ministry of Relations or state governor.[75] On the question of citizenship, the August 1824 colonization law permitted mass naturalization via the empresario contracts, but on April 14, 1828, Congress made citizenship a matter of individual application. Under this law the applicant was to be a Roman Catholic, of good conduct, and capable of supporting himself.[76] Some states continued to give out citizenship papers into the 1830s.[77]

A February 24, 1822, decree had promised equal rights for all free inhabitants, regardless of country of birth.[78] Nevertheless, the presence of foreign activists, gypsters, and intelligence agents finally moved the government toward stricter controls. A law of December 23, 1824—reportedly inspired by George O'Gorman's schemes—gave to the national government and the governors authority to expel from their jurisdictions foreigners or Mexican citizens. This law was rescinded on May 9, 1826, although for the rest of the decade the states were directed to report to Mexico City on the number and activities of foreigners.[79]

Another side of Mexican apprehension about foreigners was that they would take over all the best lands. The main incident turned on the sale of the Marquisate of San Miguel de Aguayo estate, near Parras, Coahuila, to Francis Baring in 1825. Creditors of the marquis ordered the estate sold, and Baring had already paid 200,000 pesos (of the 800,000-peso purchase price) when José María Covarrubias introduced a bill in the Chamber of Deputies to annul the transaction and prohibit sales to foreigners in the future. Ward wrote in November 1825 that Poinsett was trying to convince Baring to colonize the Parras estate with 400 North American families. The bill, or a version of it, was discussed off and on until 1828, when a law of March 12 made citizenship a prerequisite for the purchase of land.[80]

In general it could be said that foreigners who behaved circumspectly could expect their stay to be reasonably pleasant, secure, and profitable. They might encounter popular repugnance for their Protestantism, but they were also likely to find a certain amount of awe for their European culture, and a genuine graciousness on the part of a great many Mexicans. The tragic story of the Englishman Arthur Short, on the other hand, demonstrated what might take place when one let his feelings override local customs. Short, proprietor of a commercial house at Culiacán, fell in love with María de la Luz Iriarte, daughter of Sonora-Sinaloa governor Francisco Iriarte. Her father had a reputation for eccentricity. He reportedly kept 2 million pesos in his home, and when approached about a contract for one of the mines he owned, scornfully turned down the offer with the comment that he did not need the money. Short married the daughter in 1826 over the family's objections, and Iriarte then claimed that the wedding was illegal and therefore Short had raped his daughter. He submitted the case to Sonora's ecclesiastical tribunal. Although the court ruled the marriage valid, criminal proceedings had been instituted, and after testimony by two "false witnesses," as Short declared, he was imprisoned in 1830. His wife was confined in the Santa Clara convent. Short continued to avail himself of legal and diplomatic appeals, and was on the verge of release in September, 1832, when he was shot and killed during an attempted mass jailbreak by other inmates.[81]

INSTITUTIONS

In parallel with the effort to put citizens on common ground, the test of republicanism was applied to institutions. The progressive writers and nations were studied, and their injunctions given respectful attention. This meant participatory government at all levels, a division of authority between national and state governments, and the separation of power between the executive, legislative, and judiciary. A corollary was a single standard of justice for all, although the need for a strong army and church led to a retention of their legal immunity, their *fuero*. In the case of religion, it was felt that the Cortes delegates had gone far enough, and that the overriding need was to make the church strong enough to meet its pastoral obligations. The governing factor for the army was the atmosphere of an impending Spanish invasion which made the republican ideal of a citizens' army impossible for the moment.

Political Structure

The process of transplanting modern institutions into a traditional Hispanic matrix had a negative and positive side. Suppressed were those institutions considered vehicles of Spanish privilege or oppression. Created were those showing influence of the European and North American experience of the last half-century. The new structures were optimistic, chosen in the expectation that inexperienced Mexicans would rise to the occasion. There were also differences in scale. Linda Jo Arnold, in her study of the bureaucracy of the revolutionary period, listed 390 colonial government employees in the year 1809, while Jalisco alone had about 450 by 1830.[82]

The national political structure created by the constitution of 1824 bore an obvious resemblance to the United States government: an executive, legislative, and judicial branch, an upper and lower chamber of Congress, and a president with a four-year term. The president was to be elected by the state legislatures every fourth September 1, the candidate with the second highest votes becoming vice-president. The Iturbide interlude had rendered Mexicans wary of a too-powerful chief executive, so he could not be reelected immediately, but he would have the power to veto legislation. The Senate was made up of two senators from each state, elected for four-year terms. The Chamber of Deputies had members elected for two years, on the basis of population (1 per 80,000). Unlike the United States practice, if one house passed a bill by a two-thirds vote a second time, the bill would become law unless the other house rejected it by a similar two-thirds vote.

The constitution placed few restrictions on the states, requiring only that governmental powers be divided among an executive, legislative, and judiciary, and prohibiting prepublication censorship and export or import duties. Seventeen of the nineteen states had constitutions by the end of 1826, and Mexico and Coahuila-Texas would finish theirs within a few months.[83] In the states' constitutional congresses, the spirit of republicanism and equality before the law—the latter with some exceptions—also prevailed. The state delegates abolished entailed estates and all hereditary distinctions of title, and freed the slaves; a few states planned for gradual emancipation by declaring that all children of slaves would be born free. The state constitutions placed outside the body politic only vagrants, convicted felons, body servants, individuals with "physical or moral incapacity," and those who by 1835 or 1840 failed to take advantage of schools to learn reading and writing. Michoacán also excluded from the civil process chronic drunkards and professional gamblers.[84] Delegates accepted the prior loyalties and separateness of churchmen and the military by exempting them everywhere from the civil courts, and in cases excluding them from the executive and legislature.

For legislatures and executives, state constitutions merely reshaped the provincial deputation and political chief of the Cortes. Most states chose a unicameral legislature of two years' duration with ten to twenty deputies, while five of the larger states (Durango, Jalisco, Oaxaca, Veracruz, and Yucatán) added an upper chamber with about eight or ten senators. As a link between state capital and the pueblos, states were divided into departments, these into *partidos* or cantons, and these into municipalities. At both the national and state level the pattern of the 1812 Cortes elections was followed. This meant indirect elections with two or three tiers at the levels of municipality or parish, *partido,* and finally the state capital.

Towns and cities in Mexico were governed by a town council *(ayuntamiento),* headed by an *alcalde,* plus about half a dozen councilmen *(regidores).* Since 1813 the number of *ayuntamientos* had multiplied because the 1812 Cadiz constitution had required them in towns with a population of one thousand or more, a provision that was continued with variations by the state governments. The *ayuntamiento* had the duty of protecting the municipality's inhabitants, supervising public markets, keeping up public properties such as jails and roads, providing men for the army, taking the census, and more recently, providing an elementary education. In larger towns a principal obligation was to purchase grain for the municipal granary *(alhóndiga).*

In the flush of independence, Mexicans of all classes stepped forward to participate in local administration. In the larger centers, the town councils might have been instruments of the local oligarchy, but in the pueblos the most average citizens sat—laborers in the state of Puebla, Chamula Indians in Chiapas.[85] Even out-of-the-way villages were captured by the enthusiasm: Jalisco had 134 *ayuntamientos* and México 180 by 1826.[86]

State officials took it upon themselves to educate the rustics in the ways of republicanism. From the capitals were dispatched instructions on how to register voters and how to conduct censuses. State laws and circulars, frequently composed in hortatory style, were continuing lessons in patriotism and citizenship.

The new town council members were not known for administrative finesse, however. Delegates of the México state legislature heard a report from one individual in 1824 who said that the countryside *ayuntamientos* "are formed of persons who are absolutely inept, without political ideas and even without education, who never take interest in public concerns, and who view our political events with indifference as if they were taking place in Italy."[87]

Justice and the Law

In the early days of independence, all was confusion in the realm of law and order and the courts. The law was a mixture of royal *cédulas* accrued from centuries past, reforms by the Cortes, and ad hoc contributions by independent governments. While state and national governments made plans to create new codes, nobody was positive which laws were now valid, although the general rule was to follow Spanish precedent unless specifically replaced. On top of it all, there was a dearth—almost an absence—of trained jurists. States at times had to leave judgeships empty for lack of candidates with legal preparation, and in planning courts for the territories, the minister of justice wrote that not a single lawyer resided in Upper California or New Mexico.[88]

The Constitutional Congress of 1824 set the parameters of justice. Animated by federalism and liberalism, the delegates gave to the states the bulk of criminal and civil law and abolished private courts, notably the merchants' tribunal (Tribunal del Consulado) on October 16, 1824.[89] The miners' court (Tribunal de Minería) would be merged into the national system on May 20, 1826.[90] Out in the *minerales,* or mining camps, however, the miners' deputations continued to rule on local issues. Nationwide, the main exceptions to equality before the law were the military and ecclesiastical *fueros.*

A hierarchy of state and federal courts was established, but "judge" to most Mexicans came in the person of the *alcalde,* who in addition to his *ayuntamiento* duties presided over local judicial matters. The *alcaldes* were notoriously unversed in legal procedure, and there was a general disinclination for vigorous law and order, considered reminiscent of heavy-handed Spanish judges.

The structure of the court system resembled that of the United States, but courtroom procedure stayed close to Hispanic practice. The decision of guilt or innocence lay in the hands of a judge or judges, who rendered a decision after considering presentations by defense lawyers and the prosecutor *(fiscal).* This latter figure, taking depositions and then presenting his findings, had a central role in the process. The Anglo-Saxons' custom of trial by jury was carried into practice in the Federal District and several states. It normally came into use in press cases involving sedition and slander.[91] A Board of Censure *(junta de censura)* would examine writings, pass to the prosecutor those considered libelous or seditious, and he would then take the case before a jury.

To apprehend lawbreakers, a variety of means were employed. Larger towns were creating regular police forces, usually called *gendarmes* or *celadores públicos.* Jalapa had twenty policemen, and Puebla organized forty men for the task in 1824.[92] In some of the medium-sized towns, officials or citizens took turns making nightly *rondas.* In time of stress the army could be called in, and out in the country the civic militia helped, supplemented by landowners' private police forces. The distinction between public and private crime fighter at times blurred. Businessmen subscribed to support merchants' militias, and the Sánchez Navarro haciendas in Coahuila had a resident "police delegate," technically responsible to his civil superiors, but also taking orders from the family.[93]

Those detained for transgressions would be sent to a building slightly renovated for detention purposes, frequently a jail in name only. Mexico City had three principal jails, each a fetid pit exuding odors of human waste that could overpower passers-by. That of the *ayuntamiento* had walls splashed red from squashed bedbugs.[94] Throughout the Republic the jails were often described as ramshackle structures, barely capable of keeping anyone in or out, and the number of escaped convicts was something of a national scandal. In New Mexico the convicts took their leave at night to go dancing, and in the Huasteca jails had straw roofs so that the prisoners either had to agree to stay voluntarily or be placed under guard.[95] Finding ways to feed the convicts was frequently left for the *alcalde* to figure out, further reason for him to keep sentencings down.

It had become the practice since the eighteenth century to send felons off into the regular army (especially to the Acapulco or Veracruz *presidios*), to the Californias, or to work on public projects, a practice that continued in the early national period. In an attempt to make the convicts self-supporting, several states either rented the prisoners out to *obrajes* or kept prison factories, where men and women convicts would weave cloth or make cigars and cigarettes.[96] Jalisco had the island of Mescala where more than 300 convicts (most sentenced for vagrancy and robbery) lived and worked.[97]

Religion

The monarchical structure of the Roman Apostolic Church meshed with Mexico's social and political gradients. In the secular division, authority passed from the bishops down to priests (also called presbyters, composed of archpriests, parish priests or *párrocos,* and penitents) and assisted by the lowest of the secular clerics, the deacons. In the regular division, so called because of each order's *regulum* or rule, each order was committed to a certain calling, such as teaching, missionary work, or caring for the infirm.

Visitors spoke of the heavy religious presence lent by these seculars and regulars in the 1820s, one of the preferred phrases being that Mexicans were "priest-ridden." It was true that clerics occupied a special place in public and private life. They were likely to be the best-educated men in the community, and looked to for advice on matters ranging far beyond spiritual affairs. Their persons were, if not sacred, at least not to be trifled with. A German miner saw a young man half beaten to death by a street crowd after he jostled a priest and failed to abase himself satisfactorily.[98] The devoted competed for the privilege of purchasing a tattered friar's habit so they could be buried in holy raiment.

Over and above the traditional ceremonies that attached to a person's passage through life, such as baptism, marriage, and burial, the church had taken on a presiding function in every important activity. Shopkeepers gave their establishments pious names: Shop of the Deity, Holy Trinity, and so forth. Farm animals, beribboned for the occasion, were blessed by priests, as were soldiers' pennants, even when not going into battle. Church bells marked the passing of each day. When the Mexico City bells announced noon mass or vespers, everyone stopped, and if they did not utter a short prayer, at least they kept a respectful silence. All activity on the streets was brought to a halt at the approach of one of the frequent processions, which normally consisted of the host or a group of icons with a retinue of priests. At times the faithful performed a *morisco,* a mock battle in which the Christians always vanquished the Moslems. During Holy Week, so as not to lighten the mood of Good Friday, no carriages were permitted on Mexico City's streets from 10 A.M. Thursday to 10 A.M. Saturday. After the Saturday morning mass and the burning of effigies of Judas, fireworks were set off. It was said that more powder was consumed by religious celebrants than by the military.[99]

Theology had a distinct Mexican cast. Several regions of the country had their own "virgin," to whom local miracles were ascribed, and standing over all of them were Our Lady of Remedios and Our Lady of Guadalupe. After independence, the creoles' Virgin of Remedios receded, and the "brown virgin" of Guadalupe took on the proportions of a national deity. Each December 12 thousands came to the basilica of Guadalupe north of Mexico City, many crawling from their villages, to celebrate the 1531 appearance there of a dusky Virgin Mary.

Although foreigners might see only a society saturated with superstition, changes from the past generation were clear. Foremost was a new, more secular, tone to society. The Inquisition, with its dreaded methods, was gone since 1817. Mexicans could now hear some officials actually speaking ill of the church, and see criticism even in print. Strangest of all, heretical Protestants were to be seen in the flesh and, by order of the government, were not to be molested.

This new mentality did not emanate from the church. The morals of individual clerics varied—attachments to women were not uncommon and in one spectacular incident Fray Mariano shot Fray Francisco in a monastery dining room over a woman.[100] The church as an institution, however, still set a conservative standard. The bishops, who had taken over censoring duties, were accused by José María Luis Mora of picking up books from dealers that even the Inquisition had let alone.[101] In Querétaro, after monks declaimed against a company of actors in the summer of 1825, the people turned out for two days of street protests and the actors had to leave. To counteract the pernicious effects caused by foreign heretics, the Society for Promoting New Religious Processions was formed in 1825, to which Guadalupe Victoria, Alamán, and the other ministers felt obliged to contribute.[102]

The day-to-day concern of the church, however, was keeping its own house at a functioning level. It was true the church had entered a safer political climate with independence, beyond the liberal wrath of the Cortes. From 1820 to 1822 the Cortes delegates had suppressed monastic and hospital orders while reducing the number of monasteries for mendicant orders and forbidding the acceptance of novitiates. At the same time, the *fuero* was declared invalid for criminal cases.[103] Iturbide's timely success rescued the church from these aggressions, but the transition to nationhood had exacted a price. In the 1820s the church faced the prospect of losing its personnel, from top to bottom.

The trouble began with the bishops, all of whom except one in 1810 were Spanish. Under duress from Fernando VII, the pope refused to recognize the independence of Spain's former colonies, and urged on by the Spanish ambassador, he issued the brief *Etsi iam diu* (dated September 24, 1824), which asked the Spanish American bishops and archbishops to explain to their congregations the virtues of Fernando VII and to invite the faithful to return to Spanish allegiance. In Mexico the brief was printed before governmental permission was given, but it had no visible effect. The following year Pope Leon XII answered in a friendly tone a letter sent by Guadalupe Victoria, but avoided any references to him as president or to Mexico as a nation.[104] Nonrecognition remained in effect, which meant that no new bishops would be named.

When a bishop died, the cathedral chapter *(cabildo eclesiástico)* governed the diocese, but the chapters themselves had been made up of aged and infirm, mostly creole, canons.[105] Only the bishops had the prestige to speak as the voice of the church, and at the end of 1825 seven of Mexico's ten episcopal seats stood vacant. The bishops of Puebla, Yucatán, and Oaxaca remained.[106] The nominal spokesman for the Mexican church was Bishop Antonio Pérez of Puebla, but he had signed a crucial 1814 letter inviting Fernando VII to rule without the Cortes, and more recently was one of Iturbide's ardent supporters.[107]

Without bishops to mobilize resources and make permanent appointments, parishes languished. The 1826 Ministry of Justice and Ecclesiastical Affairs *Memoria* listed 3,523 seculars (including military chaplains), but only 1,240 were actively ministering, the rest being either ill, retired, teaching, in cathedral positions, or serving as chaplains to nuns. This averaged out to about one priest for five thousand people. Since in 1825 only one-fourth as many men became ecclesiastics as had in 1808, the situation could only worsen. The priests were very unevenly distributed, to the general benefit of the central bishoprics. Priests might be sent to the hotlands like Guerrero and Colima only if the bishops promised they would be transferred after two or three years.[108] The Sonora diocese in 1827 had the fewest priests (58), while Puebla had one-fourth of the total (919). Four bishoprics— Mexico, Guadalajara, Puebla, and Michoacán—had over 70 percent of the total number of seculars and regulars. Hacendados were normally obliged to maintain resident priests to minister to their peons, but even the Sánchez Navarros, who owned much of the state of Coahuila, depended on the Monclova priest to meet their needs.[109] Officials from all parts of the nation, possibly excepting Puebla, complained about the shortage. In one instance, the chaplain of Tula resorted to advertising in the newspaper for someone to help him at Easter time.[110]

Similarly, monastic life was on the decline. The 1827 *Memoria* of the

Ministry of Justice and Ecclesiastical Affairs listed 1,918 monks in 1826 representing the five principal orders, the Franciscans, who accounted for more than half the total, Dominicans, Augustinians, Carmelites, and Mercedarians. In addition, there was a scattering of friars from other orders.[111]

Although a large number of friars had given their lives to the insurgent cause (at least 157, as opposed to some 244 seculars),[112] the monasteries were thought of as Spanish lairs, and therefore the object of much official and unofficial resentment. Actually, the monasteries contained relatively few residents of any kind. The Justice and Ecclesiastical Affairs *Memoria* of 1826 showed that an average of thirteen monks lived in each of the 151 monasteries, and at least 39 had fewer than six monks.[113] Unoccupied monasteries met the new public needs for capitols, jails, barracks, and lay schools.

The nuns seem to have weathered the independence crisis better. In central and southern Mexico there were about 2,000 nuns of a variety of orders, whose 58 convents were much fuller than those of the monks. With some of the orders traditionally requiring candidates to be Spanish or creole, the nunneries were also centers of status and conservatism. Their main activities were the pastimes of withdrawal and the education of girls.[114]

Underlying this general picture of clerical attrition were weakening finances. The regular clergy were the great property holders of the church. In 1828 the Minister of Justice and Ecclesiastical Affairs listed the friars as earning 131,846 pesos from 138 haciendas, 205,476 pesos from 1,715 town houses, and 83,558 pesos from loans (the principal of which was 1,962,145). Since rent was usually calculated at 5 percent of value, the haciendas and town houses would have been valued at about 6,746,440 pesos, making the friars' overall property and loan assets worth about 8,700,000 pesos.[115] The nuns had property and capital worth about twice as much, 16,062,215 pesos, which provided an income of 819,874 pesos for the same period.[116] Thus the monks and nuns owned or held liens on about 25 million pesos in property, which made them the largest property owner in Mexico.

In one of the most quoted passages in all of Mexican historiography, Alamán stated that the church owned or controlled about half the property in Mexico. As far as the national capital is concerned, he missed by only three percentage points. Between them, the regular and secular branches owned 47 percent of the total value of Mexico City's property in 1813. The church was in effect landlord to the middle class, as most of these houses were in the middle range of values, between 4,000 and 10,000 pesos. As could be expected, the nuns were the richest, in spite of the fact that the crown called upon them repeatedly during the Revolution for "patriotic loans." The Convento de la Encarnación, for example, had 123 houses in Mexico City worth 1,248,000 pesos.[117] We do not have comparable figures for the whole country, but we do know that indebtedness to the church was widespread, and if we add to these mortgages the *censos enfitéuticos* (the permanent lien payments valued at about 2.5 percent of the property valuation), it might well be that Alamán's estimate was not too far from the mark.

The problem for the church was that in spite of these considerable holdings, the Revolution had lessened the ability of tenants and debtors to make payments. In general, operating income of the secular branch came from four sources: tithes and fees; bequests; payments *(réditos)* on loans; and investments in both urban and rural property. Of these, the mainstay was the tithe, a tax, usually 10 percent, paid in kind on agricultural products which everyone had to pay, including religious corporations.[118] The proceeds of the tithe, or *diezmo,* were traditionally distributed in the following manner:[119]

1/4   to the bishop
1/4   to the cathedral chapter
4/18 to priests' salaries
3/18 to hospitals and churches
2/18 to the royal treasury

Part of the drop in income can be traced to Congress's policy of stimulating agriculture by granting a ten-year tithe moratorium on certain products, notably cotton and wool.[120] But it appears the principal reason, as tithe collectors noted, was that parishioners were less able or less willing to pay.[121] In times of dearness the faithful also donated less, pious bequests having decreased by one-half on the west coast.[122] The working capital of the chaplaincies and pious works foundations (prayers for souls in purgatory, hospitals, charities, etc.) dropped from 44.5 million pesos in 1805 to about 20 million pesos in 1826.[123]

Collection figures confirmed the impressions. When a member of the British commission, James Morier, stopped off in Puebla to pay his respects to Bishop Pérez, he was told that the episcopal revenues there, the most ample in all of New Spain before the Revolution at 130,000 pesos, now amounted to only 30,000 pesos.[124] In a study of the archbishopric of México tithe, Michael Costeloe found the five-year average had fallen from 510,081 pesos for the years 1806–1810 to 277,636 pesos for the years 1824–1828.[125] In Michoacán it was estimated that tithing was down 60 percent. Even when things settled down, people were less inclined to give the church its customary due. Ten years after independence, the Guadalajara bishopric could collect, at best, only half of the amount assessed.[126] The end result was that the income of the seculars, in the opinion of the minister of justice and ecclesiastical affairs in 1826, had declined by one-half in the past fifteen years.[127]

Shortages of funds and personnel were felt most keenly in the missions of the North. The Dominicans and Franciscans were the missionaries to the gentiles, the former in central and southern Mexico, the latter to the north. To train missionaries and oversee the missions, the Franciscans maintained six "apostolic colleges of propaganda."

In this, their next-to-last decade of existence, the northern missions were struggling to survive. The traditional 400-peso annual subsidy—paid to each missionary either by the national government or the Pious Fund of the Californias—was usually not forthcoming now, and there was much uncertainty regarding the status of the many Spanish friars. The Franciscans inherited the expelled Jesuits' northern Sonora missions (the southern ones being secularized), but in spite of state subsidies of 915 pesos a month, there were only eighteen missionaries left in 1827. The Arizona region had lost all of its Franciscans by that date. New Mexico had only about twenty by the late 1820s and a decade later only five. The Tarahumara were being ministered to more and more by seculars, and Texas had only about half a dozen missionaries. Friars were so few in number that openly disloyal Spaniards were kept on for want of replacement.[128]

The Alta California missions appear to have been in the best shape, all things considered. They had an independent endowment, and the Indians were among the least ferocious in the north. Captain Frederick Beechey, British Royal Navy, visited them in 1826 and found that while the degree of prosperity varied considerably from one mission to another, all made a tolerable living selling cattle hides and tallow to European and North American ships—this in addition to the wheat and maize and beans they provided to the soldiers. None was on the verge of succumbing to the wilderness. The fathers, Spanish in the majority, were incensed over the required oath of allegiance to the new government and the order to liberate and give land to Indians of good character. Mortal sickness was on the rise, and desertions were a problem, which diminutions were countered by persuasion and occasional raids among the wild Indians. Decorating the churches were pleasing pictures symbolizing paradise and "all the torments the imagination can fancy" for hell. To guarantee piety, aides checked the huts for malingerers at mass time, and then patrolled the aisles with staffs to keep attention properly directed. Beechey thought the mission residents were at least better off than the unclothed inhabitants of the wilds, but the fathers decided to take no chances. At night they incarcerated all unmarried Indians.[129]

In spite of the relative prosperity of the California missions, they too were subject to the truism that the encounter with mission civilization was fatal for the Indians. The Indian population had already shown a drastic decline from the pre-Spanish level of about 300,000, and demographic studies have shown that the death rate in the missions was leading to extinction. In the famous phrase of A. L. Kroeber, "The brute upshot of missionization, in spite of its kindly flavor and humanitarian root, was only one thing: death."[130]

The Californios, as well as the missionaries, lived off the labor of the Indians. Father Narciso Durán wrote in 1831:

> If there is anything to be done, the Indian has to do it; if he fails to do it nothing will be done. Is anything to be planted? The Indian must do it. Is the wheat to be harvested? Let the Indian come. Are adobes or tiles to be made, a house to be erected, a corral to be built, wood to be hauled, water to be brought for the kitchen? . . . Let the Indian do it.[131]

The decimation of the Indians never made a strong impression on Mexico's civil authorities. But through the first decade of the Republic, it became clear that self-contained communities of an alien people under disaffected Spanish friars did not fit into a republic. The days of the missions were numbered.

Government policy in general toward the church was temperate, given the recent antagonism of the two entities. In general the church, as a graded society in itself, reflected the differing political views of the outer world. The hierarchy did not attempt to conceal its preference for Spain, and the archbishop's cathedral chapter resisted taking down the Spanish coat of arms from the cathedral lamp. Under pressure it finally did so, but then would not put up Mexican insignia nor prepare a mausoleum for rebel martyrs. Archbishop Pedro Fonte retired, ostensibly because of failing health, and then took ship to Spain in February 1823. In spite of repeated requests, he could not be coaxed back—but neither would he resign as archbishop.[132] The general clergy, though, welcomed independence, and cooperated in making their parishes the basic unit in local elections. A total of twenty-five clerics served in the national Congress in the 1820s. There were a few who could not accept the change. During an 1827 service, a Querétaro pastor intoned the routine "Blessed be God, blessed be His Holy Name," but added,

> damned be the governor,
> damned be Victoria,
> damned be Congress, and
> damned be all the powers
> that govern us.[133]

What governmental hostility toward the church existed did not follow a uniform creed. Some public officials were motivated by the Hispanic tradition of regalism (government control of the church for secular ends) and a very few by the creed of classical liberalism (separation of church and state), but both groups felt the Mexican government must keep the church out of the civil sphere. This was not equivalent to a scientific outlook on religion. Without sensing any contradiction, Carlos María de Bustamante could on the one hand use violent invective against the church in 1823 for its maintenance of a paramilitary unit *(regimiento defensor de la fe)*, and on the other hand defend intolerance, and at a later date write impassioned pamphlets to prove the Virgin Mary had physically appeared in New Spain in 1531.[134]

Government statements by the executive and congressmen stressed the need to rebuild in order to meet the needs of the faithful, but the bulk of the Cortes legislation was kept. The expulsion of the hospitalers and mendicants remained in effect, and the national government continued in possession of the properties of the Jesuits, the Inquisition, and of the expelled orders. A movement to bring back the Jesuits began under Iturbide, but it was beaten back by the Fagoaga group in Congress.[135]

Ecclesiastical interference in the economy was an early target. The Mexican emissary to Rome was directed to ask the pope to reduce the number of religious holidays, whose proliferation, according to Ward, had shortened the working year to about 175 days.[136] And the 1824 colonization law said that colonists could not pass their property to "dead hands," meaning the church,[137] a feature frequently included in other land laws of the 1820s. Mexicans did not want to cripple the church, however. Thus the most threatening decrees of the 1820–1822 Cortes, those that had terminated the *fuero* in criminal cases and had ordered the monastic orders to close virtually all their monasteries and to accept no more initiates, never took effect in Mexico. Congress saved the church from devastation on August 7, 1823, by exempting it from the Cortes decree abolishing entail.[138]

The constitution of 1824 was essentially a rather conservative document as regards religion. On the church courts, the *fuero eclesiástico,* it acquiesced, and could hardly do otherwise, since there was no movement to bring clerics under the civil courts. Article 3, stating that the national religion would be Catholic "perpetually," with the practice of all others prohibited, was the cornerstone of religious policy.

The main church-state controversy concerned government patronage. It generated much heat since patronage had come to stand for the state's right to supervise the church, and thus by extension, reform. In the days of Fernando and Isabela, the pope had bestowed the patronage privilege *(patronato real)* upon the Spanish monarchs, which meant they could appoint archbishops, bishops, canons, and so forth, from lists of candidates submitted by the church. At independence, the question was: did patronage stay with Spain's king or did it go with the new nation? In 1822 both sides staked out their positions. The Mexican church claimed the *patronato* had terminated, while Iturbide's officials argued that patronage was inherent in sovereignty. When the Constitutional Congress met, the delegates decided to postpone a confrontation, and declared that Congress would resolve the matter at some future date. In the meantime, the deputies appointed Francisco Pablo Vásquez to go to Rome and work out an agreement. It turned out that no consensus could be reached as to what Mexico's stance should be, and Vásquez had to wait three years for his instructions.[139]

Away from Mexico City, delegates organizing the states gave signs of greater boldness. None challenged Roman Catholic exclusiveness, generally copying Article 3 literally, but Yucatán added to Article 3 this provision: "No foreigner will be persecuted or bothered for his religious belief, provided he respects that of the state."[140]

Jalisco, Mexico, and Tamaulipas included an article in their constitutions that the state would "fix and pay for the expenses" of the church,[141] which in effect, created state churches. In Jalisco the article in question (Article 7) provoked a confrontation. The cathedral chapter refused to take the oath of allegiance to the state constitution, refused to provide the normal mass for the charter's promulgation, and threatened to excommunicate the whole government. While other cathedral chapters joined the remonstrance against Article 7, the state persisted in its claims. Finally Congress, still hoping to win the pope's recognition, gave in to the church and ruled (December 2, 1824) that Article 7 was unconstitutional. On December 18, Congress decreed that until patronage was settled, the states should refrain from doing anything that would decrease ecclesiastical revenue unless the church agreed.[142]

While this closed the issue of a state church for the time being, four state constitutions gave the governor the right of patronage,[143] and it was common for states to exclude certain classes of clerics from participating in government, the main targets being friars and bishops. The state of Mexico had probably the most anticlerical constitution in the Republic. In addition to the state church provision, Article 9 stated that *manos muertos* (or dead hands, as the church was called) could not own real estate, and Article 11 stated that no official appointed by authorities other than the Federation could "exercise his jurisdiction" without consent of the state.[144]

Toleration was not to be allowed to Mexicans, but it could scarcely be denied to foreigners. Protestants, though, had to be on guard. The lower classes often took personal offense at their presence, occasionally threw rocks at them, and asked ingenuously if Protestants really had tails as they had been told. Diplomatic agents pressed for some accommodation. Ward wanted a chaplain attached to the British mission, but Alamán pointed out that the Mexican government would have to protect every Protestant chapel with a ring of troops. No Protestant clergymen ministered, but foreigners did gather in homes for informal services.[145]

The issue of burial could not be postponed even though most Mexicans did not want bodies of heretics defiling sacred ground. Cañedo declared in Congress (1825) that as Mexico had the options of burning, burying, eating, or exporting the bodies, he thought the best solution was interment.[146] After the Anglo-Mexican treaty gave the British burial rights, local authorities would normally set aside a piece of land and funeral services would then be conducted in private.[147]

The religious problem was more a matter of popular prejudice than official intransigence. Few Mexicans in public life were prepared to maintain that Protestants were, in fact, enemies of Christianity. The most common explanation for prohibiting religious freedom was that the masses were not ready. Although an imprudent or unlucky Englishman might run the risk of the *léperos* bullying him, he had a fair chance of finding a sympathetic official to get by legal barriers. President Guadalupe Victoria, for one, decried the church's pretentions to exclusiveness. When Ward was unable to use a church for the wedding of Charles Conrad Lavater, a merchant, and Fermina Susan Agassiz, daughter of a mining official, Guadalupe Victoria lent his influence to get the marriage registered at the "office of provisor" so that it would be valid in Mexico. The marriage was performed by Ward himself, who married several other couples. Toward the end of 1826, a French priest married a Catholic and Protestant (both British), agreeing to take "the whole responsibility of the match in the next world," if the provisor would take the responsibility in this world by registering the union.[148]

Considering the situation, there were not many serious incidents. One did take place before vespers on August 29, 1824. Seth Hayden, a North American shoemaker, was working in his shop when a procession with the consecrated host approached. He knelt on his chair inside the shop, but a soldier nearby felt this was insufficient and ran Hayden through with his sword when he refused to lower himself to the ground. At the funeral, Hayden's friends were insulted and stoned by a large crowd of *léperos*. The government issued a circular that anyone harming a foreigner would be punished, but Hayden's murderer was never found.[149] Another North American who tamed unruly horses was almost killed by a crowd that suspected his power over animals was akin to witchcraft. He was already "stripped of everything that he had about him" when soldiers rescued him.[150]

The days of anticlericalism lay a decade in the future. Neither the church nor state were now ready for battle. The break with Spain had cut Mexicans off from the liberal currents of the Cortes, and now, even those who wanted the government to take a strong stand on the *patronato* did so in the tradition of Bourbon regalism. The right to name bishops carried the implicit obligation to protect the bishops. The church itself was weakened in personnel and divided into prelates and monks who frequently distrusted the new system, and the seculars, who more often cooperated.

In the long run, the church could not help but be harmed by the liberal secular trends that accompanied independence. State officials even now did not hesitate to tread on the church's domain. And the anticlerical program of the Cortes, while dormant now, had a long-range inevitability in a republic.

The Military

The Revolution had left the army a blend of ex-royalists and ex-insurgents—officers and men. Amalgamation began in 1817 when Viceroy Apodaca tried to conciliate the rebels by drawing them into the Spanish army under an amnesty plan. Iturbide's victory completed the graft. For a while Iturbide catered to Spanish officers, but many left the country between 1821 and 1823. The Spanish expulsion of 1827 would complete the army's mexicanization—or remexicanization, since until the arrival of Spanish troops during the Revolution, Mexicans comprised about 95 percent of the ranks.[151]

Since 1762, wars and rumors of wars, plus the threats of hostile Indians, rioters, and bandits, had spawned a variety of military units: urban militias, rural peacekeeping forces, mobile squadrons, provincial militias, and semiautonomous frontier commandancies. With one exception, these diverse military types were now grouped into the regular army and the active militia, the latter consisting of troops more or less indefinitely activated to protect the coasts or do service against the northern Indians.[152] On September 10, 1823, Congress created twenty-four commandancies, roughly one for each state and territory.[153]

The exception was the auxiliary militia, a paramilitary force raised and equipped by landowners, miners, and merchants. Numbered at 5,000–6,000 in 1825 by the secretary of war, these men kept order in their own neighborhoods and provided their own horses and weapons. Their only recompense was obtaining the *fuero militar*.[154]

Events since 1810 brought on several changes in the army, most importantly in size. In 1800 some 30,000 troops (excluding Interior Provinces soldiers) were available in New Spain, about 6,000 of whom were regular soldiers and the rest various types of militia. To deal with the insurgents, the regular army grew to between 35,000 and 40,000,[155] and after independence the Spanish departures were more than matched by additions from the insurgents. In the three to four years before the Spanish invasion of 1829, the army's size was published as about 59,000 men, with some 22,000–23,000 in the permanent army and about 36,000 in the active militia. Of the latter, however, only about 10,000–15,000 were regularly in active service.[156]

The War Ministry figures were all paper men, however, not necessarily the flesh and blood fighting force. During the Spanish invasion in 1829, Poinsett reported that the Mexican government could put only 8,000 soldiers in the field, notwithstanding a supposed figure of 30,000 soldiers, and so more militia had to be called up.[157]

The Revolution had thrown the officer–enlisted man ratio out of balance and had altered the officer corps' ethnic composition. The trend toward topheaviness began when Apodaca took in many self-appointed insurgent officers, and then Iturbide promoted his favorites—and, for a while, Spanish officers.[158] Again in early 1823, during the anti-Iturbide revolution, the rebel leaders created and promoted officers. Generally all of these officers were allowed to keep their rank by the republican government, although some of the empire's more grandiloquent titles were abolished.[159] The War Ministry, with more officers than it could use, left a "multitude" of unattached officers in Mexico City's Deposit *(Depósito)*.[160]

The most eminent officers at the beginning of the republican period were those who had achieved distinction during the Revolution—generally with the insurgents of 1810–1817, although those who fought for Spain until Iturbide were not discredited. The army was no more homogeneous politically than the other institutions, harboring officers of centralist as well as federalist convictions.

The 1823–1824 federalist standard bearers, in addition to Lobato, Guerrero, and the Leóns of Oaxaca, were Juan Álvarez (1790–1868) and José María Tornel y Mendívil (1789–1853). Álvarez, born in Coyuca (state of Mexico), was in the mold of Guerrero. He joined Morelos at the beginning (November 1810) and fought almost constantly, acquiring in the process a large popular following in the Costa Chica (near Acapulco) and disabling wounds in his legs. His main employment in the 1820s was as commander of the port of Acapulco.[161] Tornel was more akin in his tastes to the gentlemen-officers of Europe. He devoted his leisure to aristocratic pastimes, translating Byron and writing plays. Although he had compiled an honorable record as a rebel—once on the verge of execution by the royalists—his route to positions of influence was as personal secretary to the powerful, first to Santa Anna in 1821, and then in 1825 to President Guadalupe Victoria.[162]

The centralists were frequently more enlightened, if not more colorful, then their federalist counterparts. Though the comparison can be overdrawn—since impetuosity was not unknown among them—the centralist generals and colonels tended to be good staff men, students of the science of warfare and military administration. Notable centralist officers were Bravo, Michelena, Mier y Terán, José Morán, and Melchor Múzquiz (1790–1844). The latter, one of the Coahuila dynasty of Muzquizes, was born near Monclova, fought with the insurgents in Michoacán and Veracruz, and went on to serve as Mexico state governor (1824–1827). Notorious for his frugality as a public servant, he would die in poverty.[163] Morán (1790–1844) proceeded in the opposite direction, coming from a poor family of San Juan del Río (Querétaro), rising through the ranks in the royalist army, and finally marrying in 1818 the third marchioness of Vivanco. After service under Iturbide, he would become chief of the general staff from 1824 until 1827.[164]

Among those of debatable or drifting convictions in the first years of the Republic, Santa Anna stands out, but Manuel Gómez Pedraza (1789–1851) also switched sides more than once for his own reasons. As a royalist officer, he fought the insurgents to the end, associated with Bourbonists while a Cortes deputy 1821–1822, and then received a succession of commands from Iturbide. He made his name as an administrator, serving as minister of war from early 1825 through 1828.[165] Felipe de la Garza (ca. 1798–1832), while not a national personage, was a figure of significance in the northeast. A landed proprietor and relative of Ramos Arizpe, he was appointed commanding general of the Eastern Interior Provinces under Iturbide and would serve in the higher echelons of the Tamaulipas military for the next decade.[166]

The new officer, frequently mestizo—hardly ever Indian—thinned out the traditionally all-white Spanish officer caste. At the bottom, the ranks continued multiracial. Mexicans with some African blood (called *pardos*) had earlier served in segregated units, officered by Spaniards,[167] and some units still retained a caste aspect in the 1820s. Yucatán had eight companies of *pardo* riflemen, and the Veracruz veteran infantry had "*pardos* and Negroes."[168] Also it seems that impressment of Indians, especially in time of troubles, became a common practice.[169]

Two factors governed the deployment of army units: the threat of a Spanish invasion, and the presence of warlike Indians. Therefore the far northern states and the Gulf area were the most heavily garrisoned. Yucatán, for example, had some 6,000 troops among regulars and active militia.[170] The northern presidios, theoretically mustering a total of 3,844 men, were considered a special branch. The minister of war admitted that these presidios, the northerners' main line of defense against the *indios bravos,* were in lamentable shape.[171]

The military came through independence with its corporate privileges generally intact. Foremost was the *fuero,* the right of military personnel to be tried in a court of their peers. Because of abuses, the Cortes on August 23, 1820, did away with the military *fuero* in both Spain and the overseas colonies. Iturbide's Plan of Iguala stated that the army would be governed by the Spanish Ordinance of 1768, which gave the *fuero* right back. Many Mexicans questioned the practice, considering it incompatible with a constitutional system, and Congress did limit its workings in slight ways. Reformers, though, were forced to give way since the overriding consideration was the threat of a Spanish invasion, and the *fuero* was considered a necessary inducement to keep the army strong.[172]

As it functioned in the 1820s, officers had both the civil and criminal *fuero* when stationed at their home base, while the common soldier had only the criminal *fuero*. When on campaigns, the common soldiers, and their wives, had both.[173] The *fuero* put soldiers beyond the reach of civil courts, but this was not always a blessing, as military tribunals could be more arbitrary and pitiless than civil courts. If the transgression were political in nature, everything depended upon the War Ministry's political inclinations.

Other military privileges under attack were the military treasury *(tesorería de ejército)*, which allowed officers to collect certain revenues, and baggage transport *(bagages)*, whereby an officer on the move could commandeer any citizen's horses and mules to carry his equipment. The former was abolished by the Cortes, leaving the army dependent on civilian treasury officials. In an 1826 law, Congress abolished the military's right of *bagages*, but the practice continued.[174]

Although the barracks (many of which were ex-monasteries) were considered run-down, the Mexican soldier on the whole was adequately uniformed and armed. The guns were of varying origin, mostly English. From England, Ambassador Michelena sent over equipment from the proceeds of foreign loans, and although much controversy surrounded the price and quality of his purchases—the chief of staff refused to accept some of the uniforms—the Federation now had had enough weapons to be able to pass out guns to the state militias. Artillery men had iron and brass field pieces of varying caliber (16, 18, 24) and quality that could send a ball three miles. Congrew rockets were also in use, but no one was quite sure where they might strike. Powder came from two government factories, one in the pueblo of Santa Fe, the other at Chapúltepec.[175]

Not to be confused with the active militia (the reserve branch of the regular army) were what the Mexicans called the *cívicos* or the civic militia. Sometimes going under the names local militia or national local militia, these were locally organized citizen soldiers used to keep order, but available for national defense if needed.[176]

State constitutions routinely included an article establishing local or civic militias. Immediate control lay with the town councils, overseen by the state government; churchmen, public officials, and the professions generally, were exempt upon payment of a fee; *cívicos* had benefit of the *fuero* only when nationalized.[177] Officials inscribed eligible citizens on the rolls and began organizing Sunday exercises, but it appears the state militias got under way very slowly in the first years.

The phenomenon of independence did not have a uniform effect on institutions. Some were new products of the era, such as the state governments. Some were of royalist origin, whose composition was considerably transformed by the independence experience, such as the army. And some of the institutions, like the church, rather successfully retained their preindependence character.

What was the overall result of this institutional tinkering? By the mid-1820s there could be seen a struggle between two systems, the Hispanic and that inspired by classical liberalism. Ultimately, the determining factor would be whether the institutions would be embraced by the hitherto "inert masses." Mexico's new political institutions were scarcely in place before they were put to the test by a portion of these masses.

« 4 »

The Yorkinos and Mass Politics
1825–1826

THE RISE OF MASONIC POLITICS, 1825–1826

If one were to look through the documents and public papers in search of the high point of the new Republic, the moment might well have been January 1, 1826, when President Victoria addressed the opening session of Congress. He spoke of the recent victory over the Spaniards at San Juan de Ulúa, of progress in international recognition and commerce and education, and of advances in the army and navy and government finance.[1]

Yet as he spoke, there were clear signs that factional lines were hardening, the results of which would shortly undo many of the accomplishments he listed. The federalists had won the battle over governmental form in 1823 and 1824, and in the next two years would take control of many of the state governments. They made use of new types of publications to keep the masses stirred up, and then organized Masonic lodges of the York rite to recruit and organize supporters from these same popular classes. The traditional leading classes, now on the defensive, struck back whenever they could.

By temperament Guadalupe Victoria was incapable of halting the process. His philosophy of governing was to be a chief of state and not a politician, to stand above factional bickerings although not necessarily to mediate them. It was jibed that when his carriage took him for an afternoon ride in the Alameda, he took pains to sit in the exact center.[2] A phlegmatic individual, his were the passive virtues of endurance and constancy, not dispatch. It took a near-crisis to rouse him from his torpor. In fairness to Victoria, it is doubtful that any leader could have reconciled the pressures that were gathering in 1825: the spread of Masonic lodges as vehicles for political warfare, and the rising tide of hatred for Spaniards. Victoria, Guerrero, and the other insurgent heroes that came in from the field had the stature but neither the vision nor the political ability to reconcile these pressures. Ideologues like Alamán and Zavala had organizing talents and a clear picture of what to do, but lacked a following and the inclination to compromise.

Notwithstanding statements in favor of order and harmony that would presuppose centralism, Victoria's abiding hatred for the Spaniards and their fellow travelers made him more comfortable with the federalists, especially his personal secretary Tornel and Treasury Minister Esteva. The president's drift toward the federalists was shown by the departures of centralists from his cabinet. In January 1825, Mier y Terán was removed as war minister on the pretext of leading an expedition to inspect military defenses on the Gulf Coast.[3] He was replaced by Gómez Pedraza, a general of changeable political opinions who from 1825 to 1827 cooperated with the federalists. Ramos Arizpe, after failing election to the 1825 Congress, contrived to be appointed chief deputy (*oficial mayor*) in the Ministry of Justice and Ecclesiastical Affairs, and replaced la Llave as secretary when the latter resigned in December 1825 to become dean of the Valladolid cathedral.[4] Alamán himself resigned on September 27, 1825, after nasty confrontations with federalists in Congress. His replacement was Sebastián Camacho (1791–1847) of Veracruz—lawyer, state legislator, and editor of *El Oriente,* who after retiring from the Relations Ministry in 1827 would serve as governor of Veracruz on several occasions.[5]

Alamán left the government a few weeks before the great victory over the Spanish garrison at the island fortress of San Juan de Ulúa. Since Mexican cannon could not breach the stout castle walls, the War Department early decided on a blockade policy, but this had little success until a fleet was brought into existence.

The Mexican navy had an eight-year life: begun feebly under Iturbide, it was strengthened by purchases in England, reached a high point at San Juan de Ulúa in 1825, then began a slow decline to virtual extinction in 1830. Since the Spaniards had left behind only a few small boats, Iturbide sent Eugenio Cortés to the United States to purchase ships, but he was hampered by lack of funds and once landed in debtors' prison. Although he did manage to send a few small vessels, the true strength of the navy dated from the 1824–1825 purchases which Envoy Plenipotentiary Michelena made in England largely from proceeds of a British loan. By late 1825, Mexico had a respectable fleet in the Gulf, seven gunboats, five schooners, and a brig and pilot boat.

One of the Mexican protagonists in the final victory was General Miguel Barragán (1789–1836). A career military man from San Luis Potosí, he had served under the royalists, was promoted to brigadier under Iturbide, and was now governor and military commander of the state of

Veracruz. Called *petenera* because of his fondness for this national dance, he moved into a ramshackle hut on Mocambo, an island several hundred yards from Ulúa, to direct operations.[6] The other protagonist was José Ignacio Esteva, who was sent to Veracruz in late September 1825 with a million pesos to use against the Spaniards. He began by offering, without success, a 500,000-peso bribe,[7] but about that time the sailors and ships of the new Mexican navy began arriving on the scene.

On the afternoon of October 5, while Esteva was still trying to bribe Ulúa officers, a Spanish relief force of three frigates was sighted approaching the castle. Esteva and Rincón (the port commander) spent the night scouring Veracruz for sailors and supplies, and at 7 A.M. the Mexican fleet set out. By five in the afternoon, the two sides had lined up in battle formation, but darkness fell before either side fired a shot, and in the night a storm dispersed both fleets. The Spanish ships were sighted again on October 11, but the Mexican ships again sailed out to confront them, and they left for good.[8]

The relief expedition had been the last hope for José Coppinger, Ulúa commander since early 1825. His 160 men, weakened by sickness and partial rations, could not even man the watch stations. Only seventy soldiers could stand on their feet in the last days. Coppinger began talks with Barragán on November 14 and signed the surrender four days later. When the news arrived in Mexico City, virtually the entire population turned out on the streets amid pealing church bells, music, and fireworks. In July 1826, the legislature of Veracruz awarded the title "heroic" to the city of Veracruz, and for several years November 18 was marked with celebrations.[9]

While the Ulúa assault preparations were under way, men who had been bound hitherto only by their common distaste for the Spanish system were being organized as York rite Masons—the Yorkinos. Fortunately for the cause of history, the oath of secrecy taken by each initiate was balanced by the fact that the Yorkinos generated mountains of polemical material. Most sources agree that the first formal lodge appeared about 1806.[10] Originally, Masons functioned to combat religious bigotry and to further self-improvement through the study of ideas. Like their European counterparts, Masons in New Spain found that this led easily to political action.

While the early Masons—generally following the Scottish rite organization—were considered subversive and anti-Catholic, by 1825 Escocés Masonry had come to be the bastion of Spaniards and creoles sympathetic to the Spanish system. In addition to the Escoceses, there were a handful of lodges with rather loose affiliations to formal Masonry, among them the Águila Negra, and most important, five lodges, neither influential or active, with nominal ties to York rite Masonry. In the late summer and fall of 1825, some of the more militant federalists thought to invigorate them. U.S. Ambassador Joel Roberts Poinsett, who had occupied high offices in the York rite before arriving in Mexico in May 1825,[11] later recorded that Alpuche, Guerrero, Zavala, Esteva, and Ramos Arizpe asked him to regularize their lodges by obtaining charters.[12] From the New York Grand Lodge he obtained patents for five Mexican lodges, and later presided over the installation of the Grand Lodge of Mexico.[13]

These York rite Masons began recruiting immediately. Whereas the Escoceses maintained the standard of an exclusive gentleman's club, the Yorkinos were less selective. They counted more on numbers, and in practice tended to invite all comers. As a result, the York lodges became a political haven for marginal types, upwardly mobile individuals one remove from poverty. Ward described them alternately as "halfway Subalterns, petty advocates, clerks in the finance department," and as "needy and desperate adventurers," all in all, propertyless, undesirable types.[14] Francisco Ibar, also hostile, called them "butchers, transporters, water-carriers, and ticket-sellers."[15] Pakenham in 1829 echoed the analysis: they were "restless spirits" from the less affluent classes. He added that the army proved to be a convenient matrix, that almost every regiment had a Yorkino lodge, and that a majority of the noncommissioned officers were Yorkinos.[16] General Manuel Rincón lamented how the Yorkinos had spread not only to the "huts of the humble citizen," but had Masonized the whole army. His men had become "*Yorkinos* first, soldiers next."[17]

The political novices, however, did not direct affairs, for the Yorkinos also attracted national figures. In addition to the group that approached Poinsett, there were Tornel, José María Bocanegra, José Ignacio Mejía, Anastacio Bustamante, Ignacio Mora, José Rincón, Michoacán governor José Salgado, and Jalisco governor Prisciliano Sánchez. Most of all, however, the Yorkinos could count on the interminable energies of Zavala and Esteva, who above and beyond their governmental tasks ranged about, organizing lodges. Zavala, after a visit to Guadalajara in mid-1826, could write to Poinsett that he had been successful even among clerics.[18] He was Worshipful Master of Independence Lodge No. 3 and Grand Scribe of Royal Arch Lodge "Liberty" No. 1 (both in Mexico City), and then was Worshipful Master of the Tlalpam Lodge in 1828.[19]

José Ignacio Esteva (d. 1830) was a self-made man. Originally a Veracruz bookseller, according to Morier he owed his rise to Guadalupe Victoria, whose attention he attracted by his energetic actions as intendant. Although uneducated and denigrated because of his dark coloring, he had a clear perception and abundant energy, the latter quality attributed by Carlos María de Bustamante to draughts of opium. He had a singular influence during his first three years in office, thanks to the president's confidence and his good fortune to preside over the revival of trade and customs duties. Selected Grand Master of the Yorkinos, he was accused of transforming the Treasury ministry into a huge Masonic camp.[20]

Uncertainty shrouded the membership of certain national personalities, for in later years when the Yorkinos and Escoceses were remembered for their excesses, it became a stigma to have belonged. Alamán wrote that a friend once showed him Santa Anna's name on the membership rolls of the Yucatán Escoceses,[21] but Santa Anna did not admit it. Guadalupe Victoria, too, might have been an Escocés or a Yorkino, or neither, depending on which source one consults.[22]

The Yorkinos spread like fire in dry grass. Lodges cropped up from Yucatán and Chiapas to California and Texas. Chihuahua City had enough to support three Yorkino newspapers before 1830.[23] A number of Iturbide's old backers joined out of rancor toward the Escoceses, and even Scottish rite Masons themselves defected. Ward estimated the leaders could muster 12,000 in the national capital alone, although he was probably including the street crowds Yorkino leaders could mobilize.[24] An April 1828 list counted 102 lodges, while Zavala calculated 130 lodges, with at least one in every state.[25] British chargé d'affaires Pakenham saw them everywhere in 1829: "There is I believe not a town nor a village throughout the Republic that does not possess one or more Yorkino Lodges, according to its population: the whole under the control and acting according to the orders of the Grand or Directing Lodge in the Capital."[26]

In the Victoria cabinet the Yorkinos made inroads but never dominated completely. Victoria's two right-hand men, Esteva and Tornel, were Yorkino organizers, but Alamán's replacement as secretary of relations, Sebastián Camacho, was a fellow traveler of the Escoceses. After about a year as an Escocés minister of war, Gómez Pedraza dropped his membership in November 1826, and began cooperating, if not actually enrolling with the other side. Ramos Arizpe, however, was moving in the opposite direction, splitting with his old comrades in late 1826, to be forever after hated by them.[27]

In the eyes of many Mexicans, the principal villain in the story of Masonic strife was Joel Roberts Poinsett. A number of Mexican historians have happily blamed him not only for the Yorkinos' abuses, but also for many of the political ills of the decade. Poinsett partially brought it on himself, as he was not averse to taking credit for Mexican events. On August 15, 1827, he wrote to a Charleston friend, Dr. Joseph Johnston: "Most unquestionably had it not been for my foresight and conduct this government would have been overthrown and this country deluged in blood."[28]

Poinsett came to Mexico with good credentials. Of a prominent South Carolina Huguenot family, he had taken the customary grand tour of Europe, and was then in 1810 given a commission by President Madison to report on conditions in South America, where he became immersed in revolutionary politics on the insurgent side. He made an accelerated tour of Mexico in 1822, quickly written up for publication to enhance his chances for an ambassadorship. Thanks to his close ties to Andrew Jackson, he got his chance after Monroe's first two candidates declined, and arrived in

Mexico City in May 1825 a seasoned diplomat, fluent in Spanish and experienced in the Hispanic-American political milieu. Of his skill there was no dispute. His critics saw him as a diabolical puppeteer, cunningly pulling the strings of unsuspecting Mexicans.

His work with the Yorkinos was keyed to his view of U.S. interests. He was eager for the task of promoting the federalist style of democracy, his enthusiasm for the American destiny matched by his abhorrence of aristocratic politics. British diplomats, on the other hand, felt more at home socially with the prominent families and saw little good in a federalism that might complicate trading relations.

When Poinsett came as minister plenipotentiary in 1825, he found that the British already had the ear of the president. The United States had recognized independent Mexico in 1822, two years before Great Britain, but squandered the advantage through a delay in naming an emissary. The news of England's recognition of Mexican independence (December 1824) was announced with great jubilation just before Poinsett's arrival. Mexicans admired North American institutions, but they were more interested in what British recognition might bring: financial help and a restraining influence on Spain and the Holy Alliance. Great Britain's envoy when Poinsett arrived was Henry G. Ward, member of an investigative commission (with Lionel Hervey and James Morier) since late 1823 and appointed chargé d'affaires on May 31, 1825. He would be succeeded in April 1827 by Richard Pakenham.

Poinsett entered into a protracted duel with Ward, each denigrating the other whenever possible and organizing publicized socials to which the other was not invited. At Poinsett's Saint Patrick's Day party, which Ward and his aides did attend on condition that politics not be discussed, Poinsett proposed a toast for Irish civil liberties. Ward then toasted the Irish who did not seek "foreign interference," and the British group stalked out.[29]

The affray did not materially diminish Ward's standing with Victoria, and Poinsett attached himself to the up-and-coming federalists in Congress. He met Zavala within a month of his arrival and formed a committee to preserve the 1824 Constitution from the British. He claimed that his only formal role in the Masons was obtaining the Yorkinos' charters, and helping install the Grand Lodge, and that as soon as the meetings had taken a political turn he withdrew.[30] That was beside the point. Throughout his stay in Mexico he consorted with the Yorkino leaders, and his influence on Zavala and Guerrero in particular was considerable.

The name Poinsett thus became synonymous with political divisiveness. The first official attack came in June 1827 when the Escocés-dominated Veracruz legislature issued a proclamation against him, claiming he was "more dangerous than 20 battalions of the Spanish tyrant." He soon had a defense in print denying any impropriety, and wrote to President Adams that his presence was necessary in Mexico to prevent civil war and preserve civil institutions.[31] While the Yorkinos were on the offensive he was safe from recall, but he had entered a field a diplomat was not to enter, and one day in 1829 his allies would find the price of his association too dear.

Whereas the Escoceses had maintained some interest in Masonic protocol and paraphernalia, the Yorkinos existed for politics. The first test came in the fall 1826 elections which would select several state legislatures, in whole or in part, and the national Chamber of Deputies. Campaigning began in June with the *Águila Mexicana* and *El Sol* trading insults and with agents from both lodges fanning out through the country. The Yorkinos attacked mainly on ideological grounds, calling the other side a nest of Spanish sympathizers. The Escoceses stuck to personalities, their favorite targets Zavala, Tornel, Alpuche, and especially Esteva. Each faction maneuvered to place its men in charge of the polling places, and to distribute as many lists of its candidates as possible.[32]

The most controversial election, and a portent to the Escoceses, took place at Toluca with Lorenzo de Zavala as the main player. Although a senator from his native state of Yucatán, Zavala decided to lobby for the Yorkinos as an elector in the state of Mexico. His first problem was to meet the residence requirement. He was not alone in this, since many state of Mexico politicians lived in Mexico City, and now with the first statewide election since the excision of the Federal District, had to prove property ownership in the state. Tornel, a Yorkino active in the elections, later mused how the Escoceses brushed up old titles from Carlos V or Felipe II, and how some Yorkinos purchased ranches of fifty square *varas* or tried to coax from some notary a paper that would attest to their owning a piece of land, cabin, or hut in the state.[33] Zavala bought a house and land from his brother-in-law in San Agustín de las Cuevas.[34]

Mexico state had the typical election process of three stages. At the second, the electoral junta at San Agustín de las Cuevas on September 6, Zavala was chosen an elector for the state meeting in Toluca, but immediately after the vote electors raised the question of his residence. The deed had never been formalized. A second, secret, vote was held about Zavala's residence, which he lost, but he showed up in Toluca anyway, where the debate began again. Reminding the electors of his sacrifices for Mexico's independence, he wept when he declared that only in Toluca was his honor questioned. In an emotional scene, after applause and shouts of approval, the vote vindicated him.[35] He stayed in the convention and the Yorkinos won a resounding victory.

The Escoceses, however, still controlled the legislature and began an investigation. The Toluca prefect testified that Toluca swarmed with agents of the Yorkinos, that Guerrero had sent numerous letters to electors, that troops were stationed nearby to intimidate voters, and that the gallery crowd shouted obscenities at those not voting with the Yorkinos.[36] On

November 25, Governor Múzquiz promulgated a decree annulling the Toluca elections. The ousted electors then appealed to Congress, which canceled the annulment on January 18—with Zavala, as senator from Yucatán, voting against the Mexico state decree—and the Yorkinos had won the battle. Governor Múzquiz resigned the following March and the legislature chose Zavala as his replacement, followed by celebrations where Zavala's followers aimed their fireworks at the houses of his enemies.[37] Thus the Yorkinos were in possession of the nation's most important state.

Elsewhere the Yorkinos did well too. Noting their strength in the Chamber of Deputies, Ward counted, in addition to their twelve deputies from the state of Mexico, six from Jalisco, eight from Yucatán, and three from Zacatecas. With these, they had "almost a certainty of a majority upon every question."[38]

The Yorkinos fashioned a populist style never before seen in Mexico, their success hinging on their ability to mobilize large numbers of people from the lower strata of society. The lodges themselves had a New World, revolutionary flavor, with names like "Religious Toleration," "Federalism," "Aztec," "Yaqui Indian," "Matamoros," and "Eternal Hatred to Tyrants." In the Águila Negra lodge, a forerunner of the Yorkinos, the members called themselves, not brothers, but Indians. Yorkinos appropriated the Virgin of Guadalupe as their own, in contrast to the Hispanic virgins of the Escoceses, the Virgin of Pilar and the Virgin of Santiago de Galicia.[39]

The Yorkinos' raucous tactics also reflected their plebeian origins. They printed lists of their candidates for their followers to carry into voting areas, a practice used to less effect by the Escoceses. They gathered in public establishments to drink and listen to scurrilous verses about the Escoceses, and on political days in Mexico City they paraded through the streets.[40] When Congress was voting on important legislation, they filled the galleries and menaced the congressmen.

THE PRESS AND POLITICS

The new style could also be seen in the public press. The Yorkinos were the political beneficiaries of a journalistic revolution that had preceded and accompanied the Revolution for Independence. Right after the turn of the century, newspapers and pamphlets—and readers—multiplied considerably.[41] The Cortes' abolition of prepublication censorship was never put into effect because of the Hidalgo Revolution, but Cortes precedents were the basis for Mexico's freedom of the press law of December 13, 1821,[42] which provided for jury trials for publishing infractions.

For independent Mexico the printing press became a symbol of intellectual sovereignty, and for the provinces a symbol of statehood. If the local government was penurious, public subscription drives would be held. In 1823 Bustamante counted nine printing presses in Mexico City.[43] Guadalajara and Veracruz were not far behind, and even distant and impoverished Chiapas and Tabasco were able to make the investment.[44] Government documents were generally the first materials printed, with a newspaper usually following soon after.

The proliferation of presses made for an explosion in the number of newspapers throughout the republic. All of the newspapers vibrated with political excitement. Their pages were filled as much with preachings and teachings as with news. Francisco Severo Maldonado of Guadalajara intended his *Fanal del Imperio Mexicano* to be a schoolbook for the public, reprinting in it important works of Europe's political economists.[45] The *Redactor Municipal* of Mexico City carried statistics, projects for improvement, and in general articles of public edification.

As the national communications center, Mexico City had at least twenty-nine newspapers in the 1820s, including the three best known, *El Sol,* the *Águila Mexicana,* and *El Correo de la Federación Mexicana.* The first, taking its name from the El Sol Scottish rite lodge, stated in its first issue on December 5, 1821, that it expected to be a bearer of light for the public, and it faithfully diffused light from the Bourbonists and Escoceses until its demise in 1833. On the other side was the *Águila Mexicana,* making its appearance on April 15, 1823. It spoke first for the federalists and then for the York rite Masons. In November 1826, the more radical Yorkinos brought out *El Correo de la Federación Mexicana,* and the *Águila Mexicana* began moving toward a more neutral position. Backing up the main three newspapers was a supporting cast. To answer the arguments of the *Correo,* José María Fagoaga and the Scottish rite Masons began *El Observador de la República Mexicana* (June 1827–October 1830) which was in turn countered by *El Amigo del Pueblo* (August 1827–September 1828).[46] In addition, political issues gave birth to single-cause tabloids that tended to expire after a few weeks or a few days.

Both the *Sol* and the *Águila* were closely related to Alamán and Zavala. Alamán never edited the *Sol* apparently, but when it reappeared in June 1823 after being suppressed by Iturbide, it was the most presentable newspaper in Mexico, thanks to the printing press Alamán brought from France. It printed his articles on demand until he left office in 1825. Zavala at first supplied minutes of congressional debates and then (in 1824) edited the *Águila.*[47] He was also a prime mover behind the *Correo.*

With busy politicians as principal contributors and no reportorial staff, the newspapers contained few news stories as such. Most were four-page affairs, with the first two pages normally devoted to documents or the minutes of Congress, and the last two filled in with communications, editorial comment, and business announcements. Politics was the life blood of most newspapers, in finances as well as content. At one real (twelve and a half cents) the newspapers were fairly cheap, and for long-term survival, government aid in the form of subsidy or subscription was almost a prerequisite. While Alamán was secretary of relations, the government received sixty-four subscriptions to *El Sol*. After his resignation, the largesse shifted to the *Águila Mexicana*.[48]

While these newspapers could be read by the partially literate under-classes, more to their taste was the pamphlet. With the poster *(hoja volante)* replaced by the multipage publication in the late 1700s, the pamphlet devel-oped into a true popular literature in the first three decades of the nine-teenth century. The heyday was 1821–1824. A host of writers, including politicians and generals and colonels, turned out tracts as the issues or their patrons inspired them. Some of the more prolific pamphleteers followed the scene of action with portable presses. With a press run of 300–500, they could be purchased for one to three reales, the cost of a dinner.[49]

Coming out frequently in serial form, touching on the most current social and political issues, often written in dialogue form using popular street expressions, and dealing with personalities rather than abstractions, the popular pamphlet was a development unexpected and lamented by the traditional literate minority. In an 1825 note for the Chamber of Deputies, Alamán complained about the tactics: written in a style that had "an im-mense effect on simple people," the pamphlets came off the presses on the day of the mails, so the damage was done before the authorities could act.[50]

The most renowned of these pamphleteers became celebrities: Joaquín Fernández de Lizardi (El Pensador Mexicano, or the Mexican Thinker) and Pablo de Villavicencio (El Payo del Rosario, or the Countryman from El Rosario) for the federalists, and Carlos María de Bustamante and Francisco de Ibar (El Pintor, or the Painter) and Rafael Dávila for the centralists. When Villavicencio was found innocent of breaking press laws, his fol-lowers carried him triumphantly through the streets.[51] But the writers also had to be prepared to endure much public abuse—Lizardi was commonly referred to as "one-eyed" (*el tuerto*), Villavicencio as "the gimp" (*el cojo*), and Bustamante as "the madman" (*el loco*)—and to spend a lot of time in court. In addition to the political dangers inherent in their calling, some of the writers tended to be reckless in their behavior. An 1823 court appear-ance by Lizardi came about after his landlady evicted him. He had re-sponded by leaving a slogan on the wall for his successor: "They were some good women" (*Que eran unas buenas viejas*).[52]

They all had tumultuous lives. Bustamante (1774–1848) was a lawyer and cofounder (with Jacobo de Villaurrutia) of *Diario de México* (1805), the colony's first daily publication. Several times national deputy from Oaxaca in the 1820s and 1830s, he was considered something of an elder statesman because of revolutionary service with the insurgents. Without these creden-tials, his unrestrained outbursts on behalf of the centralists would have placed him in personal danger. His passionate outlook contained a number of mismatched elements, such as an abiding loyalty to Catholic orthodoxy, an interest in aboriginal civilizations and an enduring affection for many of the insurgents. If his congressional status placed him among the reputable statesmen, his writing style, impulsive and colloquial, placed him among the less than respectable pamphleteers. He brought the same manner to his diary and his pamphlet series, *Voz de la Patria,* rarely checking his first impressions and including spicy items about individuals' personal lives.[53]

Lizardi and Villavicencio, speaking for less favored classes, illustrated the dangers of intemperate attacks on the system. Together they were imprisoned at least seven times. The more familiar name is Lizardi (1776–1827), considered the father of the Mexican novel as a result of *El Periquillo Sarniento,* an 1817 comment on creole life. He came from central Mexico—his father was a physician for the College of Tepozotlán—and attended the College of San Ildefonso for a while. Despite his middle-class upbringing, he sympathized with the Revolution and by 1811 was publishing incendiary literature and spending time in prison—his two inseparable occupations. As a writer he was one of the pioneers in bringing issues to the level of the popular classes. With his colorful renderings of street dialogue placed in the mouths of prototype characters—shoemakers, sacristies, alcaldes, men of the country (*payos*), Indians—and couching his commentary in the form of fables, allegories, and maxims, he became the model for propagandists of the masses. His most popular tracts were an 1824–1825 series, *Conversations of the Countryman and the Sacristy,* an acid weekly commentary primarily on the church. His antipathy for the church constituted his most enduring conviction. He denigrated the pope at every turn, and was excommunicated in 1822 for defending Freemasonry. The difficulties of being a public heretic, including the impossibility of finding printers, led him to recant a year and a half later, and the ban was lifted.[54]

As a political thinker, Lizardi was in advance of the age. In addition to the standard federalist issues, he advocated distributing land to the landless (including Indians), limiting the amount of land anyone could own, holding church services in Spanish, and giving to women the right to vote and to sit in Congress. He even wrote a play praising Africans, but the theater manager withdrew his permission for a performance. Lizardi achieved some status toward the end—editorship of the government newspaper in 1825 at 100 pesos a month—but he was soon to be reclaimed by obscurity. He died on June 27, 1827, emaciated by tuberculosis. Against his wishes, his friends placed his remains on public display to refute the rumor that the devil had taken possession of his body. His grave, neglected and forgotten, later became a pigsty.[55]

At times Lizardi had given shelter to a writer even more militant than himself, Pablo de Villavicencio. The Payo had been born of poorer parents than his friend, in El Rosario, Sinaloa,[56] had joined the patriot cause at the age of fourteen, and had received wounds that left him lame. He came to Mexico City in 1822, and took to launching vitriolic attacks against the church, Spaniards, and foreigners in general. Even in the early permissive days he drew the ire of the Victoria administration. In 1825 there appeared on the walls in downtown Mexico City a short anti-Spanish tract by Villavicencio (*Preguntas importantísimas del Payo del Rosario*) criticizing the editors of *El Sol,* among others, and inviting the government to confiscate the property of Spanish emigrés. Alamán immediately ordered it pulled down. Then, on November 19, at 6 P.M., a pamphlet attack on the English issued from the press. The cabinet met within two hours and at 3 A.M. Villavicencio was taken from his home wearing only his bedclothes and escorted to the Acapulco dungeon by nineteen cavalrymen. After two months he was freed when a jury ruled his pamphlet not libelous.[57] The Payo was eventually killed while serving as Zavala's secretary during the 1832 civil war. Zavala fled Toluca and then sent Villavicencio back to fetch some papers, where he was shot.[58]

Little is known of Dávila and Ibar except that they too shared in the journalistic habit of incarceration. Since the beginning of the decade, Dávila had been writing material against the Spaniards, clerical practices, and then, curiously, against the Yorkinos. Ibar sparred with the federalist-Yorkinos early in the decade, but his main effort was a long, serialized, tirade against the 1829 Guerrero administration entitled *Muerte política de la República Mexicana.*[59]

Escoceses looked on these journalistic developments with profound displeasure. Great expectations had been entertained that the printed word would diffuse the "lights of the century" (*las luces del siglo*). To educated Mexicans, publications were to inform in restrained fashion and be respectful of the government's good name, and they thought they saw demagogues perverting the noble purpose. Alamán was an early convert to the position of punishing inflammatory voices he saw inciting the populace, and from 1823 to 1825 was a prime mover in a series of celebrated prosecutions—generally against federalists and generally unsuccessful.[60]

One of the practices that irritated almost all public figures was to hear their name in insulting titles shouted out by Mexico City newsboys. Guadalupe Victoria spoke out several times about this, in September 1827 requesting new legislation to control the problem.[61] Although a law of May 31, 1823, had prohibited pamphlet titles that were "alarming" or at variance with the contents, it was difficult to obtain a conviction.[62] Jurors tended to sympathize more with writers than prosecutors. In an indulgent era, governments were not yet inclined to narrow one of those freedoms felt to be the fruit of independence.

In a little more than a year, the York rite Masons had redrawn the political map. The battle that had been fought between federalists and Bourbonist-centralists now went on as Yorkinos versus Escoceses. For their part, the Escoceses were horrified by the recent elections. They saw themselves menaced by newly elected officials they would not have allowed to step foot in their homes. With their own lodges on the verge of extinction, they themselves took up the cry against "secret societies," and the Senate commenced an investigation in late 1826. But Guadalupe Victoria's government decided not to pursue the issue after equivocal reports came in from the state governors.[63] The Escoceses then tried to create a new group, the Novenarios, so named because each of the nine founders was to recruit nine more members. Attracting eminent names from the Escocés membership, the Novenarios achieved some success in the states of Mexico, Puebla, Veracruz, Guanajuato, and San Luis Potosí,[64] and acquired a door to the public in June 1826 with the newspaper *El Observador de la República Mexicana,* but they were just a ripple on the political stream.

The Yorkinos were not to be halted for now, but winds would shift, and a little more than two years later they would fall from public favor as rapidly as they had risen.

EDUCATION

As befitted men who spent much of their youth pursuing learning, both Alamán and Zavala were enthusiastic promoters of education. Zavala translated European writers, and as Mexico state governor converted the episcopal seminary into a secular institution of higher learning.[65] He was a contributor to the growing movement for reading rooms and public libraries, creating a state library and stocking it with Enlightenment books—though the reading was said to be over the head of most college graduates.[66] Alamán was a founder and first president of the Institute of Sciences, Literature, and the Arts (1825), and one of his first acts as secretary of relations in 1823 had been to send out a circular requesting data on schools with which a committee of specialists was to draw up and forward to Congress a general plan to systematize education.[67] It was symptomatic of the rising expectations and diminished means that neither this plan nor the two that followed it in 1826 and 1827 were ever enacted into law.[68]

Although many projects did not reach fruition, the prevailing attitudes were optimism and enthusiasm for innovation. The energy loosed by cutting colonial ties was perhaps nowhere else as evident as in the field of education. The basic educational policy of the 1820s was to create good citizens through schools. Thus the main effort went into establishing elementary schools, which were to reach out even into the Indian villages. New schools were created, and old schools were looked at with a view to reform. Training for the trades and professions was examined and reorganized, efforts were made to make adults literate, men in the patriotic societies used their membership dues for schooling the poor, and the study of civics was added to the usual homemakers' training of girls.

The educational tradition of the colony had been overwhelmingly ecclesiastical and private. From the age of about five or six to eleven, children had learned their "first letters" (reading, writing, numbers, and Christian doctrine) in either a private school or one of the "pious" schools (*escuelas pías*) maintained by a convent, monastery, or parish. At the other end was the Royal and Pontifical University, founded in 1552 and empowered to grant the degrees of licentiate (*licenciatura*) and doctor in the traditional fields of theology, philosophy, medicine, and law. In between were the colleges, some secular and some under the auspices of the orders, which had originally appeared to offer instruction in Latin as a prerequisite to university studies. After the colleges had expanded from Latin to general liberal arts studies, an intermediate degree, the baccalaureate (*bachillerato*), was offered by them and by the theological seminaries that the bishops had begun organizing in the seventeenth century. Later the colleges began competing with the university by offering higher studies (*estudios mayores*) leading to the licentiate.

New Spain's schools were emerging from orthodoxy. Zavala was possibly overly harsh in this description of late colonial education:

> Primary education was very rare in the small cities, and the schools which were established in the great capitals were directed by the friars and clerics for their own purposes and interests, or by ignorant laymen who taught some principles of arithmetic which prepared one to keep accounts in the commercial houses and how to read and write badly. The catechism of Father Ripaldá, in which were inscribed the axioms of jealous obedience to the pope and the king, was the entire basis of their religion. The children learned from memory those elements of slavery and the fathers, the priests, and the masters constantly inculcated them. In the colleges medieval Latin, canon law, scholastic theology and polemics were taught. With these the students filled their heads with eternal and unintelligible disputes of *grace,* of *half science,* of the *processions of the Trinity,* of physical *premonition,* and other subtleties of school, as useless as proper to make men vain, haughty, and disputers about that which they do not understand.[69]

The momentum for universal education, with secular overtones, began under the late Bourbons, especially Carlos III. Beginning in 1778, the royal government on several occasions ordered monasteries and convents to open free elementary schools.[70] To counteract the university's scholasticism, the crown authorized schools modeled on the spirit of empiricism and staffed largely by laymen: the Academy of Fine Arts of San Carlos, 1785; the Botanical Gardens (also considered an educational institution), 1785; and the Royal Seminary, or College, of Mining, 1792.

The Bourbon educational philosophy was taken over and extended by the Cortes delegates. The 1812 constitution specified that each town was to establish a school to teach basic skills, that there was to be a uniform plan of studies for the kingdom, and that by 1830 only literate individuals could exercise the rights of citizens. The 1820 Cortes elaborated this policy, providing for the state licensing of privately educated teachers, uniform methods, and the establishment of technical schools of veterinary medicine, agriculture, commerce, engineering, and music.[71]

The independence governments grafted these Cortes projects onto the colonial scheme, and generally adopted the Cortes prescription for mass education geared to secular society. Clearly visible in the many school projects of the day were the principles of using the state to regularize education, modernizing pedagogy, and giving the town councils responsibility for elementary education. While the national government did not make any commitment to universal schooling, in the Federal District it did succeed the viceroy as patron of the university and the colleges, approving charters and fee schedules, creating boards to oversee schools, naming most rectors, and rendering financial aid whenever practical. Primary schools in the Federal District remained in the jurisdiction of the Mexico City *ayuntamiento,* and the 1824 constitution placed the state governments in control of their schools.[72]

Congress did not devote a great deal of time to education, out of the conviction that the necessary reforms had already been effected by the Cortes, but a school-decreeing mania took possession of other public bodies. The Mexico City *ayuntamiento* opened three more free elementary schools, in addition to two created in 1786. Twelve of the nineteen state constitutions called for elementary schools in all towns (while generally leaving to the *ayuntamientos* the task of supporting them),[73] and eight states decreed compulsory attendance (excepting hardship cases). The schools, it was expected, would work an almost instant magic on the political system, for all but four states denied political privileges to illiterates, in some cases after a waiting period of ten to fifteen years.[74]

In the national capital there was a variety of elementary schools in the 1820s, the old coexisting with the new: pious schools of convent and monastery, municipal schools, schools for the Indian communities supported by funds of the *parcialidades,* free schools of first letters maintained by several colleges, and the private schools. A survey of 1820 indicated about a hundred elementary schools in Mexico City, with almost 6,000 students (male and female). At the beginning of the independence era the pious schools, which tended to have a much larger average enrollment than the private schools, educated perhaps half of the capital's pupils. About half of the convents and monasteries had a school in operation by the 1820s, but the pious schools had now entered on a period of decline, to be replaced more and more by municipal, and especially the private, schools. In the states the private schools (with smaller individual enrollments) generally educated more pupils than the public institutions.[75]

As one moved toward the north, finding any school at all became less likely. The survey by Alamán's office turned up the fact that San Luis Potosí had almost no elementary schools in 1825, not to speak of colleges. Monterrey showed three elementary teachers in 1824, and the political chief of Sonora reported there was no educational establishment of any kind in his jurisdiction.[76] In California, after exertions by military governor José María Echeandía, there were in existence eleven schools (with 339 pupils) where children of the "people of reason" of the comfortable class received the basic "first letters" instruction, and where Indians were taught to sing the mass, play instruments, and chant Christian doctrine. The Los Angeles *ayuntamiento* incurred the following expenses in beginning its school: primers, 1 peso; blackboard, 2 pesos; earthenware jar for water, 2½ pesos; ink, 1 peso; string for ruling blackboard, ½ peso; inkwell, 3 reales.[77]

At the primary level, the main innovation was the introduction of the mutual instruction method popularized by Joseph Lancaster. Although some teachers had experimented earlier, and there were other types of mutual instruction, the Lancasterian style bid fair to become the dominant philosophy of method. By reputation the system held great promise, for only one supervising instructor, using student monitors to do the actual teaching, could theoretically handle a class of several hundred children. Lancasterians organized the school's daily routine down to the last detail, based on the principle that the student should always be active, and favored positive reinforcement, in the form of recognition and prizes, over harsh discipline.[78]

The Mexican Lancasterian Society, or Company, was founded in August 1822, with the members' monthly dues of two pesos going to support the society's schools. The first, El Sol, opened on September 1, 1822, in the ex-Inquisition building, and within a year had 237 pupils. Shortly afterward, a second school, La Filantropia, was meeting in the convent of the suppressed Bethlemite order. Pupils paid a peso a month if they could afford it; if not they attended free. Foreigners, especially Frenchmen, were active in the movement.[79]

The experiment began optimistically. Prominent citizens proudly signed up, the national government promised help, and the society began to branch out, inaugurating a normal school and sponsoring vaccination programs. The public examinations (*certámenes*) became very ceremonious, that of 1824 presided over by Mexico state governor Múzquiz, and in 1826 President Victoria was in attendance. Although the number of Lancasterian students never exceeded one-fourth of the total student body in the Federal District, the concept was embraced enthusiastically in the states. Affiliate societies were organized to carry out the good work, and almost all states, even New Mexico and Texas, planned mutual instruction schools. Jalisco scored a coup by obtaining the services of Lancaster's son-in-law, Richard M. Jones, to supervise the state school.[80]

The Lancasterian schools became a distinctive landmark on the educational scene, recognizable by the large size of their halls, row upon row of benches, the tables with sand in the front rows for the beginners to practice their letters, the semicircles along the passages used for groups of ten students to study the wall charts, and the lettered board (*telégrafo*) with which the master signaled the monitors.[81]

The common complaint of the Lancasterians, north and south, was the lack of qualified teachers, a complaint universally heard with respect to the public schools too. For the elementary teacher, the first years of independence were a time of transition from the colonial tradition of guild monopoly—with its implications of corporate independence and restricted entry—to the new emphasis on state control and mass education. Teaching was an old and hallowed Mexican profession. The teachers' guild (*gremio*) dated from 1601 and the insignia of "examined teacher" (*maestro examinado*), meaning tested and licensed by the *gremio*, was proudly displayed. But the *gremio*'s decline was evident even before its abolition in 1813, its membership having diminished from thirty-three in 1786 to about ten in the last years of the colony.[82]

In Mexico City the eminent teachers, some of whom kept up the tradition of holding classes dressed in coats with tails, continued to prosper by attracting the children of the aristocracy. Nationwide, however, the problem remained that the number of teachers was not nearly sufficient to meet the needs of an expanded system. Governor Armijo of New Mexico had to insist that applicants at least know how to add and multiply.[83] A number of normal schools were begun, but as a rule they did not prosper. The Lancasterian normal school in Mexico City closed because its student body numbered only five or six.[84] Then, too, a teacher's salary was no great inducement. A figure of 20–25 pesos a month was customary, and even 100 pesos a year was not rare.

Supplies and physical equipment of the schools were spare. Virtually no school buildings were constructed in these years, the children going to class in former convents or chapels or homes. Schools normally had one or two rooms, a noisy one for learning to read, and possibly a quieter room for writing. Equipment usually consisted of benches, charts, and the familiar slate and stone pencil to practice lettering. The Mexico City schools usually had no bathroom facilities, and municipal authorities complained, to no avail, about students relieving themselves on the streets. As for texts, there was no standard for arithmetic, but for spelling there was *La Cartilla ó Silabario* (at a cost of one-half real), and for religion Father Gerónimo Ripalda's *Catecismo y exposición breve de la doctrina cristiana.*[85]

The virtues of education remained those of obedience, memorization, and immobility—although not silence. From the moment a child arrived at about 8 A.M. until he left about 5 P.M., the day was a train of monotonous repetition in an authoritarian atmosphere. The morning inspection of hands and apparel was usually dispensed with, due to the obvious poverty of the children, but there was little physical movement. Going for water or to the bathroom was only permitted with the passboard (*seña*). The Cortes had forbidden whipping in 1813, but it went on. A preferred instrument was

The School Dunce

a paddle, the *palmeta,* with which the instructor slapped the palms of the offender. In vain students would make a cross of two hairs on their hands, in the hopes that the divine symbol would shatter the *palmeta.*[86]

The Cortes had ordered teachers to discuss the Cádiz constitution—favorably only—and the Mexican government prodded schools into adding the teaching of politics. A political catechism circulated in a few states, through which the students were intended to learn republican dogma as they had learned religious dogma. But in general there was as little intellectual change as physical movement.[87] In Mexico City there were murmurings about the "immoral" content in the foreigners' schools, and the *ayuntamiento* ordered their books inspected.[88] The customary way of imparting lessons was choral recitation, the children shouting out the responses in unison. Poinsett described a rural school in San Luis Potosí: a few cowhides on the floor and low benches comprised the furnishings, with ten or twelve kids "all repeating their lessons at the same time as loud as they could bawl."[89]

Most Mexican children, of course, did not learn by this or any other method. Historians calculate that 50 to 60 percent of Mexico City's school-age boys were enrolled in elementary schools,[90] but the percentage was much lower almost everywhere else. The evidence suggests a national figure of between 10 to 20 percent, and not all of those enrolled actually showed up for classes; for example, about half of the Lancasterian students usually did not come to school.[91] Tanck Estrada found that the main single complaint in the archives of the Mexico City *ayuntamiento* was absenteeism: parents displayed little interest in educating their children.[92] The complaint came from everywhere, and the reasons were clear: economics. In Mexico City the family needed the one to one-and-a-half real the child might earn selling "matches, sweets, fruit, or newspapers."[93] In Orizaba (state of Veracruz), the prefect noted that parents kept their children out of school so as to help out in the fields. A state inspector in Zacatecas reported that the school simply adjourned at the coming of the rainy season.[94]

From the elementary schools, the traditional route upward led to one of the seminaries, which supplied most of Mexico's leaders in the Republic's first decade. For those pursuing a career in the professions, the usual steps were a bachelor's degree, and then apprenticeship. The Bourbonist heritage included the beginnings of professional schools. The College of Mining offered courses in mathematics, physics, chemistry, mineralogy, French, and drafting.[95] Aspirants to the law, after the normal degree of "canons and laws," would normally work with a jurist three years before becoming a full-fledged lawyer. The College of Lawyers, founded in 1759, lost its privilege of certifying candidates by a December 1, 1824, decree, which gave this function to the states.[96]

The certifying board for physicians, or Protomedicato, had operated somewhat as a medical guild. It now lost most of its functions, some to local boards of health (*juntas de sanidad superiores y municipales*) that had sprung up during the Revolution, and some through the Cádiz constitution which took away the judicial privilege of investigating crimes against public health. The Protomedicato, to be abolished in 1831, was left only with the right to examine physician candidates. Medical schools, now also beyond the Protomedicato's jurisdiction, were on the increase. There had been a School of Surgery in Mexico City since 1768, and the Mexican Academy of Practical Medicine began by offering a course in surgery in January 1826. Some hospitals offered classes in medicine, although it appears that many of these courses were less than formal. In Puebla's San Pedro Hospital, the surgery course had neither regular hours of instruction, nor books, nor faculty. After four years of standing by, observing, and imitating as best they could, the students emerged prepared "less to succor than to afflict ailing humanity."[97]

If a student aspired to a career in the church hierarchy, the culminating step had always been the National and Pontifical University, although the general regard for ecclesiastical learning had greatly eroded. The doctorate title signified a theologian, and when one writer was praising Dr. Valentín, elected to the 1825–1826 Chamber of Deputies, he hastened to add that he

was not the "rancid scholastic like those that entertain themselves in disput-
ing whether the fruit of the forbidden tree was sapote or apple."[98]

By independence, the university had lost much of its former glory. It
had so far kept some semblance of authority over the colleges, requiring
their students to take university courses and examining them prior to grad-
uation, but the colleges were straining to break away.[99] Unlike the relatively self-sufficient Mexico City colleges, the university depended to a
large extent on the national government. In 1825 it held property and claims
producing about 6,500 pesos annually, while about 8,000 pesos were to
come from public revenues—almost all of which was destined for the
salaries of some twenty-two professors and the library.[100] In the 1820s,
however, remittances were not forthcoming, and classes were canceled.
Rector José Ignacio Grajeda reported in 1828 that some professors had been
absent for two years. By 1830 even Alamán was recommending the university suspend operations.[101]

Most young men now disdained the university as a purveyor of obsolete knowledge and turned instead to the colleges. The most renowned
were in Mexico City.[102] San Juan de Letrán, founded in the time of Viceroy
Mendoza, was the oldest. In the 1820s it had about sixty students and an
annual income of about 10,000 pesos.[103] The College of San Ildefonso
(founded 1573), a former Jesuit school with ninety students, had a budget of
less than 6,000 pesos.[104] In 1828 the College of Santos (Colegio de Santa
María de Todos los Santos, founded 1573) had annual revenues of about
5,000 pesos, eight students, and no faculty. Santos had acquired a reputation as an academic lodge for aristocratic boys, and President Guerrero
finally closed it under his wartime powers in September 1829.[105] San Gregorio, begun in 1575 with the help of Indian caciques for the purpose of
educating Indian boys, had the largest revenues of any college, reaching
25,000 pesos for its fifty Indian students, but its academic reputation was
not good.[106] The fifth and youngest Mexico City college, the San Carlos
Academy of Fine Arts, founded 1783, closed in 1822 for lack of funds but
reopened two years later and by the end of the decade had an enrollment of
300 students.[107]

The 1820s were years of recovery and tentative modernization for the
colleges. The Revolution had lowered the income derived from properties
and they had to rely on temporary faculty, even though the regular professors (*catedráticos*) were not well paid in the first place. Those at San Juan de
Letrán earned the least, 300–400 pesos a year, and those at San Gregorio
the most, about 600 pesos a year.[108] The period witnessed a continuation in
the shift from scholasticism to modern courses such as commerce, agriculture, politics, modern languages, and European history. Mexican history
would have to wait another generation. José María Luis Mora, in an 1823
plan to reform San Ildefonso, wanted the college to get away from memor-

izing rules of Latin grammar, Jesuit style, and to emphasize the national language.[109] His ideas were echoed elsewhere, and there were several instances of course changes, but updating the curriculum was generally secondary to financial security.

Student life was not much fun.[110] In the style of the monks' austere common life, the students studied, prayed, slept, and ate together. In return for an annual fee—150 pesos a year at San Juan de Letrán—the schools supplied pensioners with food, bedding, and uniforms. San Ildefonso's uniforms came in different colors to denote the field of study. At Santos, students wearied of the "mortifications" occasioned by their uniform, which included "cuffed gloves," and petitioned for the privilege of wearing civilian clothing. Meals were taken in common, at San Juan de Letrán described by the rector himself as "inedible." Dinner consisted of a cup of soup, *sopa* (now normally a serving of pasta, then probably of rice), the main dish, bread, and a sweet. Describing this, the rector felt obliged to add that between the serving ladies and the students there was "absolute incommunication."

To keep the students occupied, the day was planned in great detail. At San Ildefonso the following schedule was observed:[111]

6:00	to	7:00	mass and breakfast
7:00	to	8:00	study hour for grammar students and university courses for philosophy students
8:00	to	8:30	lessons (*lecciones*)
8:30	to	9:30	lectures
9:30	to	10:00	review or tutorial (*pasan*)
10:00	to	10:30	lecture
10:30	to	11:00	rest period
11:00	to	12:00	study
12:00	to	12:30	lunch
12:30	to	2:30	rest
2:30	to	3:00	recitations (*toman lecciones*)
3:00	to	4:00	lecture
4:00	to	4:30	review or tutorial (*pasan*)
4:30	to	5:00	lecture
5:00	to	5:30	rest
5:30	to	vespers	review or tutorial in wintertime, study in summertime
vespers	to	7:30	study in wintertime, review or tutorial in summertime
7:30	to	8:00	rosary
8:00	to	8:30	supper
8:30	to	9:00	prepare for bed

Whether the students took all of this seriously is another question. Mora noted they were so accustomed to living with unjust and useless rules that they now resisted even the most well-founded regulations.

Higher education in the states followed, in diluted fashion, Mexico City's pattern. Several state governments now established lay colleges or "scientific establishments" that stressed mathematics, modern languages, and the social and physical sciences. Many of these were in financial straits by the end of the decade.[112]

After the national capital, Puebla and Jalisco were the leading educational centers. The city of Puebla had four colleges. At the seminary, a student could study an Indian language and have access to libraries totaling 19,000 volumes.[113] Jalisco had five institutes of higher learning, although much of the higher learning in the three schools catering to young girls consisted of the domestic sciences. Guadalajara education came under the sway of Prisciliano Sánchez (1783–1826), one of the crusading innovators of the day. Coming from a poor family in Ahuacatlán, he was orphaned at an early age, and at great sacrifice was able to learn Spanish and acquire enough schooling to enter the seminary at Guadalajara. For two and a half months he was in a monastery, but he was marked down in the book of novices as "inconstant." After receiving a degree in law in 1810—friends contributed for the cost of the final examination—he served in several municipal posts in Compostela, was elected to Congress in 1822, to the state legislature in 1824, and to the governorship in 1825. An ardent reformer and unabashed Yorkino, he had been a key figure in the Article 7 controversy and as governor he took aim at the University of Guadalajara. Seeing it an unredeemable clerical stronghold, he had it done away with and replaced with an institute. His successors were inattentive to his creation, however, and the institute had to suspend operations periodically.[114]

These secular colleges did not replace, or even catch up with, the episcopal seminaries that dispensed secondary education in many of the capital cities. Unlike the situation of the pious schools, the seminaries as late as the 1840s still had about twice the colleges' enrollment (averaging 300 versus 150).[115]

The education of girls was neglected, but not forgotten. In the Federal District, what were called "friends'" schools (*amigas*, or *migas*) taught an estimated 1,714 young girls first letters, religion, and domestic skills in 1820.[116] A small number of colleges had curricula that included a sprinkling of academic courses but emphasized preparation for the girls' future role in the home by instructing them in sewing, embroidery, flower making, and Christian doctrine. Changes after independence were not marked. While there was some slight increase in the number of colleges for girls, and a few resident French schoolmistresses opened finishing schools, the sexes were still not mixed, and the proportion of girls to boys attending school was still about two or three to ten.[117] The 1827 plan for the reform of

Federal District and territorial schools was indicative of intentions, if not of current practice. Girls would be taught the normal household tasks, but would also learn the same subjects as the boys, which included principles of arithmetic and "political catechism."[118]

According to progressive educational thinking, Indians were to be among the first beneficiaries of the new schemes. There were no specific acculturation programs, but the many plans to extend elementary schools contained an implicit assumption that Indians were to be Mexicanized.

Indian education had never been entirely lacking, and for some of the Indian boys that had managed to go through a monastery or pueblo school, there was the possibility of attending college, although the general problems of Mexican education were magnified for them. José María de Iturralde, head of the San Juan de Letrán board of directors reported that the few Indians staying there in 1828 slept on a *petate,* were given to eat only a little *atole,* a piece of meat, and some tortillas, and had for clothes only the few their parents had provided. They only received such schooling as would prepare them to aid a priest "submissively" with his congregation.[119]

The accepted solution was to upgrade Indians' schooling by mixing them in with "whites." Mora in 1823 came forth with what he considered the mutually advantageous proposition of merging San Ildefonso and San Gregorio. San Ildefonso's ailing revenues would receive a salutary injection, for which the San Gregorio students would be compensated by mixing with the San Ildefonso students. They would emerge from their state of "abjection," and "odious" caste distinctions would lessen.[120]

San Gregorio, as a sort of national college for Indians, was scorned as an academic center, but its 25,000-peso-a-year income was coveted. Mora's 1823 suggestion was the first of several offers to share the bounty, and from 1828 to 1830 came proposals to do away with San Gregorio altogether, but none of these prospered.[121]

Another tack was to make San Gregorio academically respectable. In October 1824 Congress ratified a decree to improve its facilities and have the governors select as students two worthy Indians a year.[122] Then when rector Juan Francisco Calzada went mad, a government-appointed board entered into a drawn-out battle with area Indians over his replacement, and the board eventually ignored Indian petitions and chose Juan Rodríguez Puebla (July 2, 1829).[123]

The board saw the Rodríguez Puebla appointment as a move to stem the rising Indianism and at the same time improve the quality of education. As board president Pablo de la Llave described it, when the board began its labors San Gregorio was a place in which a few Indians were lodged not very well, and whose instruction was only through an uncared-for elementary school and a "very bad" school of music. Now, he reported—writing in 1830—the *petates* had been replaced by proper bedding, the food was better, and course offerings had been broadened. To attract non-Indians, the board was planning unique courses such as agriculture.[124]

The Indians did not see it this way at all. The appointment of Rodríguez Puebla, who was actually an Indian himself, touched off another train of petitions and counter petitions, signed not only by college students and personnel but by Indian *ayuntamientos* from throughout the Valley of Anáhuac. They considered the board an unfeeling stepfather rather than a protector, and called Rodríguez Puebla a tyrant who persecuted Indian literature, disliked the students, and put them to work sweeping the premises, weeding the garden, and even cleaning the bathrooms. They put forward as their candidate José Calixto Vidal, graduate of San Gregorio, rector and curate of the Seminary College of Tepozotlán, and currently vice-rector of San Gregorio. He was later fired by the board.[125]

Rodríguez Puebla (1798–1848), who would continue as rector up to the time of his death, was one of the most prominent Indians of his day. The son of an Indian water carrier in Mexico City, he attended San Gregorio on a royal scholarship, so poor that when he came he was wearing buckskin pants and shoes of feathers. Among his comrades he took the name *Cuautli* (Eagle). After finishing the course of studies for theology and then law, he served on the supreme court of Durango and as senator from Mexico state.[126] He was an Indian but not an Indianist. The petitioners cited an 1824 speech wherein he said that Indians, due to their vicious condition, could only be educated in an Indian college.[127]

In the swirl of communications surrounding the appointment, one fact stood out. The Indians did not care to mix with the whites and the whites despised the Indians—in the aggregate, if not individually. One group of Indian petitioners wrote that "for the sole reasons that they do not have white skin they are put off, and they are looked at more than with indifference, with derision."[128]

A final judgment on education of the 1820s must place it in the context of the ongoing reforms, begun in the days of the regalism of the later Bourbons and furthered by the liberalism of the Cortes. The intrusion of the state into educational matters continued, but the limits of public management were becoming clear. Benevolent impulses ran head-on into the realities of public finances, the cultural momentum of illiteracy, and a generalized poverty. On occasion, *ayuntamientos* inspected the schools, and the states in prosperous years donated pencils, slates, and reading charts, but these occasional forays into the schoolmaster's domain just about marked the limits of day-to-day involvement. With few exceptions, the amounts budgeted by the Federation and the states for schools approached tokenism, and without funding there was slight control. In the two years after Jalisco's licensing law, only four teachers in the entire state bothered to take out licenses.[129] At the elementary level, responsibility thus lay with the church, traditional keeper of the schools but whose income was increasingly insecure, and with the municipalities, subject to endemic insolvency. At the secondary level, the same forces made the colleges' existence tenuous.

In the final accounting, school life had little changed. The ferment in education had moved state officials across the nation to push the towns and villages into setting up elementary schools, but when the dust had settled, not many of these survived. The net remainder of these efforts was the ideal, if not the reality, of universal education. National and state leaders were learning that the success of schools depended as much on the economy as on political decisions.

« 5 »

Earning a Living

When the Republic was proclaimed, there was much economic distress, but there was at the same time much anticipation. The colonial economy revolved around mining, agriculture, and artisanry, and all had been left depressed by the violence and dislocations of the Revolution. Still, prosperity was expected as a natural consequence of independence, and the Republic was astir with all manner of economic projects.

The themes of economic life in the early 1820s were the transition from the colonial structure of mercantilism and corporate groupings to an independent system with emphasis on private property, and the confrontation with free trade and the international economy. While many of these changes could actually be traced to the last years under Spain, Mexicans found that independence had irrevocably changed the economic rules—often in unexpected ways.

INDEPENDENCE DIRECTIONS

Spain's imperial system had assigned to the colonies the role of raw materials producer. José María Quirós, secretary of the Veracruz merchants' guild (*consulado*), described New Spain's economy in the last colonial years as 60.9 percent agricultural, 26.8 percent industrial, and 12.3 percent extractive.[1] The percentages of Quirós pointed up the fact that the dominion of mercantilism was never complete. Mexicans had built up a widespread network of cottage industries, generally along the lines of artisanry or crude processing of raw materials—flour from horse-powered mills, cloth from hand looms often dispersed in homes, as well as crockery, soap, and hides.

Racial and regional specialities had come to characterize agriculture. Whereas Indian farming tended to be for consumption or to supply neighboring towns with fruits and vegetables, staples generally came from the haciendas. The provinces of the plateau (*altas provincias*) raised grains and swine and sheep for the market, while those nearer the coasts tended toward the plantation crops of sugar, chocolate, tobacco, and pepper. The main areas of commercial agriculture were the Lerma River basin (Bajío), the plains of Toluca, the southern and eastern parts of the Valley of Mexico, the state of Puebla, and the region around Aguascalientes.

Mining was the machine that had driven much of this activity. In production alone—27 to 30 million pesos a year in the flush years about 1800[2]—the mines were the envy of the world. Above and beyond their ores, however, the mines consumed the products of the haciendas: leather hides for bags to carry the ore, animal fats for candles, wood for shoring—and the mineowners developed *haciendas de beneficio* to process the ore.

At independence all of these enterprises were crippled. After a period of unparalleled prosperity in the late eighteenth century, New Spain's economy fell casualty to military events: first of all, the Napoleonic wars, when Spain's financial calls sent a shudder through the credit system and foreigners seized the opportunity to bring in cloth (mainly cotton), to the ruin of Mexican weavers; secondly, the side effects of revolutionary violence, which left prices depressed, specie in short supply, and production reduced virtually everywhere. Quirós in 1817 calculated agricultural output at about one-half the prerevolutionary level.[3]

In spite of the dismal conditions, optimism was widespread in the early 1820s and great achievements were anticipated. Leaders envisioned all manner of experiments, some fanciful, like the subsidized importation of camels, alpacas, and llamas; some of which never got off the ground, like the various plans for a national bank; and some of which turned into successful concerns, like the paper mill in San Angel.[4] They encouraged the patriotic societies as a means to promote economic and intellectual progress, to which public-minded Mexicans responded enthusiastically in all parts.

Part and parcel of progress in the new economic thinking was the need to leave behind the colonial mold. Perhaps *thinking* is an inexact word, for Mexicans embraced the dictates of economic liberalism—a foreign trade free of the constrictions of mercantilism, an economy free to follow natural paths, and private property inviolate from governmental caprice—not only as economic policy but as a psychological necessity growing out of the anti-Spanish imperative.

Some of the first targets were Spanish institutions viewed as a preserve of economic privilege. The professional guilds (the various *gremios*) were abolished by the Cortes back in 1813,[5] reinstated by Fernando VII, and reabolished by the Cortes in 1820. Implicitly they lost their legal privileges in the 1824 constitution, which promised legal equality, but some of the more egregious guilds received special attention after that. Thus the merchant guilds (*consulados*) and their courts, entrusted with regulating commerce, and incidentally, keeping highways and bridges in repair, had always been the preserve of the Spanish merchant princes. The first and greatest, the Mexico City *consulado,* had fought to keep its monopoly intact, but the royal government approved the creation of the Guadalajara and Veracruz *consulados* in 1795. And in 1821 Iturbide approved the Puebla *consulado.* These actions recognized the growing economic strength of the provinces—and prefigured the sectional rivalries of the 1820s. But the *consulados* were institutions of Spaniards and centralism, and so on October 16, 1824, they were stripped of their major functions. Their demise at the state level followed soon after.[6]

So also abolished, on May 20, 1826, was the Mining Tribunal, which had similar supervisory responsibilities with respect to the mining industry. Its functions passed to the states.[7]

Congress tried to stimulate the spread of those products discouraged or prohibited under Spain by decreeing on October 8, 1823, a tax moratorium on new croplands of vineyards and olives—plus coffee and chocolate, which were in general decline.[8] Ports were decreed open to the world as fast as—and at times faster than—customs officials could be sent out.

Recovery from the revolutionary dislocations came slowly, but by mid-decade there was evidence that commerce had revived, and the needs of the new British mining companies fueled a revival of agriculture. One facet that did not recover was credit.

Mexico's economy, however primitive it might be, was a credit economy. Creditors' difficulty in obtaining repayment now matched borrowers' difficulties in obtaining loans. All the normal borrowing sources had dried up. The church was the great lender, at 5 percent annual interest—normally payable forever since the principal was rarely called in—but by independence scarcity of funds was present in all the church's lending arms: monasteries, nunneries, and the Chaplaincy Court (Juzgado de Capellanías).[9] The shortage extended to lay sources such as merchants and the Mining Tribunal. Mexico City businessmen, for example, complained to the town council in 1823 that most of the capital remaining after the Spanish exodus was pledged to service current debts.[10] Even the small borrower was affected, for the national pawn shop, Monte de Piedad, which lent money at a 6.25 percent annual rate—taking in an average of 42,000 pawns a year in the first three decades of independence—was carrying on with considerably less than its normal capital.[11]

There were ineffectual attempts to create more modern institutions of financing. In December 1824, Gómez Farías, Ramos Arizpe, and Carlos María de Bustamante proposed a national bank to foment economic development, and an English firm offered to finance it. But the administration demurred, and the project died.[12] Other development entities that emerged stillborn were the Compañía Mexicana, a quasi-official bank (having among its founders in 1827 a number of prominent figures, including Bravo and Gómez Pedraza), and the Society of Agriculture and Industry in 1828.[13] Richard Lindley, perusing Guadalajara's notarial records for the independence years, noticed the appearance of a new term affixed to the title of business, *y compañía,* denoting a limited-liability joint stock company on the British model, although he considered the relative influence of this innovation meager.[14]

The family or partnership structure continued to be the standard, although in these hard times, family terms could be as harsh as those of any professional lender. José de Arochi, a Guadalajara merchant, had to borrow from his relatives with humiliating restrictions. Among a long list of requirements, he had to promise to live on a peso a day or less, pay no more than six pesos a month rent, "expressly has to dismiss from the store any idle gabbler, and any time his siblings catch him in a lie in matters of commerce, he is to turn over the store without any objection or contest whatsoever even if he is left out in the street."[15] Liquid assets continued in short supply in these years. Even individuals with good credit records and collateral had to pay 3 or 4 percent interest a month.[16]

Transportation projects were also widespread, since the mode of transit, or its lack, had been one of the most obvious constrictions on trade. Rivers tended to be navigable only for short stretches, so the main water transport took place around Mexico City—on the lakes and in the canal to Chalco—and on the eastern coast. A merchant fleet, based in Campeche, supplied the Gulf towns. Statesmen now entertained visions of connecting the Atlantic with the Pacific by way of a canal through the Isthmus of Tehuantepec. A decree of November 4, 1824, invited proposals to build a six-league canal joining the Coatzacoalcos and Chimalapa Rivers, but no serious offers resulted. This decree also aimed at building river commerce as far north as the Rio Bravo (also called the Rio Norte and Rio Grande)— one result of which was a venture by John Davis Bradburn and Stephen M. Staples, who received a concession and were able to send at least one steamship an undetermined distance upriver.[17]

British companies were also interested in 1824 and 1825 in building new highways out of Mexico City.[18] Improvements were made in the Veracruz highway so that coaches could travel large stretches between Veracruz and Mexico City. But all highways became trails in places where freight could move only on the backs of mules. From Veracruz to the capital, the cost was forty pesos per load of 300–400 pounds, and trains of up to 1,000 mules could be seen on the roads. Some of the trips by mining company employees became true odysseys. The Real del Monte Company in 1826 brought in more than fifty heavy-duty British army wagons to carry 350 tons of machinery from Veracruz up to the mines at Real del Monte. The rainy season came early and turned the roads into marshes, forcing them to unload the cargo two or three times a day when the wagons sank in mud up to the axles. The trip took weeks and cost the lives of 100–200 Mexican workers, one-third of the company officers, and half the English workmen. The company afterward went into the freighting business, but the Mexicans in these years preferred to stay with the mule trains.[19]

In the independence era, Mexicans were exhorted to follow Europe's economic lead, but the old ways yielded slowly. European influence could be seen in the consumption of foods such as wheat and barley, and rice was beginning to take hold, but the corn crop dwarfed all others, even in a wheat-producing state like Guanajuato.[20] Dairy products were a novelty in many places, and green vegetables were consumed even less. Although two, and in some places three, crops a year could be obtained, fields were rarely enclosed, manure was little used for fertilizers, and farmers merely abandoned fields periodically instead of rotating crops. Generally, only primitive plows turned the soil over, and in Yucatán plows were hardly used at all because of the stony soil.[21] To cover barley and wheat seeds, a log might be pulled over the furrows, and maize seeds, sown by hand three to five at a time, were covered with the foot. To deseed corn, empty cobs tied together were grated against a full one.[22]

The absence of the sciences of animal husbandry and the mechanical arts had left in use antique practices. Poinsett saw a man raising water from a well by attaching himself to the end of the rope and running the "length of his tether."[23] Alexander Forbes, an Englishman who served England, the United States, and Chile as vice-consul in Tepic, noted that suckling calves were kept around cows as an essential ingredient in the milking process. After the calf began drinking, the milker would "lay hold of one of the teats while the calf [was] still sucking on the others and so by a kind of stealth procure a portion only of the milk."[24] Swine, whose lard was widely used for candles and frying, were kept lean and then fattened up for the slaughter so rapidly the blubber could be peeled off: "They were often so highly fed as to be unable to move. I have seen some unable to get farther up on their haunches, just far enough to reach their food, and when satisfied tumble down again and grunt themselves to sleep."[25]

Toward the end of the decade, a succession of economic reverses would make both federalists and centralists much more flexible in economic policy, but even in the early 1820s adherence to economic liberalism was not without qualification. The tariff demonstrated this. And state officials were ready to improvise if local conditions called for it; several states attempted to prohibit completely foreign goods. Political differences over economic policy—while not as acrimonious as later in the century—could already be seen. What was prominent among the centralists was a set opposition to trifling with private property, policy experiments the federalists sometimes lent themselves to. In 1824 Alamán argued with Zavala in Congress over whether a state government could take over lands an owner was leaving idle, and in 1827 he criticized the Chihuahua legislature for emancipating slaves without compensating their owners.[26]

LABOR

The main fact of life about Mexican labor at this time was its unsettled nature. In the last colonial years, with land prices and population on the increase, labor was becoming cheaper, but the Revolution momentarily deflected these trends. Many workers were uprooted, and as a result hands were frequently needed in the countryside. In towns, however, with the influx of fugitive peons (*peones huídos*) and cheap imports, employment was wanting. Artisans became ambulatory workers, carrying their few tools in a box and seeking work in the street. The terms *carpenter* and *shoemaker* were virtual synonyms for *unemployed*. Some joined the multitude of street vendors, who announced their approach with a distinctive whistle, bell, or rattle.

Many of the medium-sized towns were famed for their craftwares: Silao and León for embroidered saddles, Saltillo for cotton and wool cloth, Tulancingo for rebozos, and Puebla for its imaginatively shaped soaps. Working conditions ranged from the pleasurable, a small shop open to the streetside where the toil was lightened by conversations with customers and passersby, to the horrible. Bakeries, places of heat and dust and the whip, were known to be the worst, and resort had to be made to convict labor.[27]

In the great textile centers of Puebla and Querétaro, the infamous cloth factory of viceregal times, the *obraje*, was declining. Because 25,000 to 30,000 pesos were required to start up an *obraje*, entrepreneurs since the late eighteenth century had been turning to the putting-out system, whereby a merchant or *aviador* supplied the raw material and paid a salary or *jornal*. Even the words *obraje*, as well as *trapiche* (the smaller cloth factory), were falling into disuse. Workers were not locked up now, although it was still the practice that a worker could not change his place of employment unless the new master agreed to take responsibility for any debt.[28] Poinsett remarked in 1822 that the employees in Querétaro's 20 *obrajes* and 300 *trapiches* were mainly former Negro slaves and Indian peons.[29] A public outcry ensued in 1827 over the Cosmo Damián case. He had been sold to an *obraje* in San Ángel at the age of five and worked for five years, among other prisoners there, without any pay.[30] In these days the standard form of cloth production was coming to be the small loom or *telar*, spread out among the homes of the small towns, and even the ranch settlements.

One of the casualties of the era was the child apprentice. Apprenticing had traditionally offered an honorable solution to families with too many sons and not enough income. Boys might be launched on their professions as early as eight years of age. This was a long-term, serious commitment, and if poor parents made arrangements only through an oral understanding, it was a binding contract nevertheless. Now, with the imports and the abolition of the craft guilds (*gremios*), the custom was breaking down. A number of master craftsmen abandoned their charges.[31]

Out on the ranches and haciendas, labor was done through a variety of owner-worker relationships. In Durango and Zacatecas, cowboys and shepherds might be paid by permission to graze their own animals on the owner's lands. In Sonora, Yaquis, Mayos, Opatas, and mulattos did the chores as salaried employees. Sugar planters of Cuernavaca and Cuautla were just ending the transition from African slaves to paid campesinos of Indian and African blood *(zambos)*. In the Bajío and San Luis Potosí, the most common means of obtaining labor was through sharecroppers and tenants.[32]

The common denominator, though, north and south, was debt peonage. The Chiapas governor, noting the need to reform labor regulations, discussed how employers used wage advances to trick Indians into debt.[33] In Oaxaca it was noted that there were not enough laborers because Indians were reluctant to work on the farms, although those that did were hopelessly in debt, owing 200–300 pesos with virtually their entire salary of 4 pesos a month dedicated to repayment.[34]

These workers were not an undifferentiated mass of rural proletariat. On the Sánchez Navarro estates in Coahuila, there were resident peons, household slaves, and temporary workers for the harvest. And among the resident peons there was job specialization, with a different wage level and status for various tasks like shepherding, cow tending, taking care of the ditches, shearing, and lambing. Daily wages for this work—frequently paid in kind or merely noted on the owner's book—remained fairly stable in these years, averaging one-quarter to one-half peso (two to four reales) for a field laborer, and about twice that for a skilled artisan.[35]

In these times, when people still had restless habits following the Revolution, farmers and stockmen talked about the need to bring the men back to the fields and make them obedient workers once again. At times crops were lost for want of harvesters.[36] In response to the landowners' cries, the Puebla legislature passed legislation to force wandering campesinos back to the land.[37] Oaxaca's governor claimed in 1827 that since judges, in the name of "liberty," were not forcing peons to pay back contracted debts, a law was needed to require the Indian "republics" to hand over workers.[38] The legislature produced a decree the same year that would have workers imprisoned if they neither lived up to their labor contracts nor paid back the advanced funds. The employer could lock up debtors for the night, but without shackles.[39] A Coahuila decree of 1828 allowed hacendados to incarcerate insubordinate peons for up to four days, and in 1831 the Tamaulipas legislature said that laborers could be punished "paternally," that is, physically, if they failed in their duties.[40] Generally, a peon fleeing his debt was classified a thief, subject to arrest by peace officers, although in practice it was often the employer's agents who tracked him down.

The legislators did try to build in some protection for the peon. Thus the Oaxaca decree did not make children liable for their fathers' debts, the Coahuila decree mandated fair market prices at the hacienda stores, and both limited indebtedness to the amount of one year's salary. But whatever legal protection the peon had in theory, the economic realities weighted the relationship in favor of the employer. Abuses evidently continued in Coahuila, for the legislature forty years later found it necessary to pass protective legislation again.[41] In the Mexican countryside, however, being a peon was not the worst of all possible worlds, or even the second worst. Some historians have argued that a high debt figure for the hacienda was a good sign for the peons, since it meant that the owner had to offer large sums to attract and keep workers. And a peon at least knew his master had to provide some kind of house and food. Because of this, many landowners avoided peonage, preferring to rely on hired hands or tenants. These could be the true rural proletariat.[42]

There was one class of workers clearly below the peons: slaves. As late as 1800 Humboldt had calculated a slave population of 10,000,[43] but the institution was almost dead by Independence. When Alamán told the Chamber of Deputies on January 2, 1824, that the English were demanding general emancipation as a precondition to diplomatic relations, some deputies laughed, in the opinion that their country had no slaves.[44] There were still a few. Most slaves worked on the sugar plantations of the so-called Tierra Caliente, the subtropical hotlands just south of Mexico City where they were gradually melding into the peon class.[45] The northern states had a few slaves—Zacatecas about fifty, for example, working mainly as household help. In New Mexico territory, the trade in Indian slaves would continue for more than a decade.[46]

Although the constitution of 1824 did not mention slavery, the Constitutional Congress did prohibit the slave trade on July 18, 1824. Some state constitutions abolished slavery outright, and for the September 16 Independence Day festivities it became the custom to buy a few slaves and set them free. In 1825 two were located, with difficulty, and purchased for 450 pesos, but by 1829 none could be found for the occasion. When Guerrero became president in 1829, he took it as his personal mission to liberate his fellow men of color, and used his emergency war powers to proclaim national emancipation on September 15.[47]

In Texas the trend was reversed. Slavery grew and prospered among the North American colonists, and the institution was so strong by 1829 that the political chief suspended the September 15 decree for fear of revolution. The word had been passed among the Texas slaves, however, that southward lay freedom, and by the 1830s there was a sizable colony of fugitive slaves in Matamoros.[48]

We should close this section with a few words on the archtypical Mexican citizen, the peon. Since the Revolution of 1910–1917, the view of the nineteenth-century peon as a miserable, abused creature has been enshrined in the authorized history disseminated through official channels in Mexico. Nevertheless, historians have recently questioned the extent of peonage, especially in the central and northern regions. Harry Cross studied the papers of the Maguey, a 412-square-mile hacienda just west of the city of Zacatecas. The hacienda, raising about 100,000 sheep and goats, and probably some grains and grasses and timber, employed 338 workers in 1825 at an average wage of 4.41 pesos a month. Cross found that only 10 percent of the workers were in debt in the 1820s (somewhat more in the next decade), and the Maguey owners were often *owing* the workers at the end of the year. The prices at the *tienda de raya* or hacienda store were never higher than those elsewhere in the state, the loans were interest-free, and 6 percent of the debtors in 1825 borrowed for reasons of personal investment—such as taking out cloth to manufacture clothing. Thus the Maguey store functioned more as a bank than as a mechanism to ensnare workers. Moreover, the Maguey laborers ate reasonably well. Calculating maize rations and other foods available, median family size, average height and weight—which for the Zacatecas campesinos appears to have been about 64 inches and 122–44 pounds for the men, and about 60 inches and 100–18 pounds for the women—Cross estimated their caloric intake to be higher than that of rural blacks and whites in North Carolina in the 1940s.[49]

The nutrition of the Mexican peon is open to question—for the figures at the Maguey hacienda are an initial effort on the issue—but the bulk of the evidence does not suggest a starving peasantry. And the workday was not taxing, averaging about six hours in farming areas, with a longer day but a more leisurely pace on the stockraising haciendas. On the other hand, reports from all over the Republic speak of workers toiling in servitude under varying degrees of oppression.

What are we to make of these conflicting assertions? Were the Mexican campesinos used and abused, or were they relatively well-fed people of the soil? The research, and the debate, will continue, but if we look at the hacienda hierarchy as a social system, we find that the two conceptions are compatible. Outrageous abuse was not the rule, but on the haciendas and *ranchos,* with complex arrangements of employment, mutual ties of sentiment and loyalty, a mingling of Indian traditions of deference and Hispanic traditions of authority, and above all, economic fear and dependence—in these circumstances, paternal concern and casual exploitation went hand in hand.

When all is said, the documents of the day clearly indicate that throughout the Republic peonage was common, if not inevitable. And there were other types of controlled labor that differed more in form than in substance. A subservient class was being shaped, a class that had existed for centuries but was becoming more and more Mexican and less and less Indian, pulled toward the future by economic changes, but touched only in passing by the vistas of independence. Moreover, a psychology was being developed appropriate to the campesinos' uncertain and dependent station—a psychology that would leave its stamp on the national personality and that did not hold promise for the Republic.

LAND

The Mexican land situation has been described as a timeless struggle between the great land barons and their Indian neighbors—with the hacendados inexorably winning. In actuality the hacendados of the 1820s were yielding land in places, not consuming it, and generally land tenure relations between Indian and Mexican varied considerably across the Republic—from Oaxaca where Indians held on, still dominating the valleys; to the central states where Mexican-Indian land competition was ongoing; to the farms of the Bajío where there was little communal ownership but many Indian migrant workers; up to the far north, where the ranches rambled over hundreds of square miles unimpeded by any independent settlement, but menaced by nomadic Indian warriors.

The situation was not truly polarized either, as evidenced by a third entity that appeared in the governors' reports: the rancho. While in the far north the term signified stockraising, elsewhere rancho meant a piece of property smaller than a hacienda that might have crops as well as a few sheep and cattle. The ranchero class was amorphous, including owners of 300–400 acres, hacienda managers who raised their own crops and animals on the side, tenants who might sublease an entire farm, down to the smallholder who had only a handful of acres. In some areas of Guanajuato the most common agriculturalist was the tenant farmer, and in most states the ranchos outnumbered the haciendas by two to one or more, although the reports do not always indicate which had the highest amount of land.[50]

The life of the middle-class ranchero was as precarious as that of the great hacendado. He was subject to the same pressures, with less to fall back on, so prosperity and position might well not extend beyond a generation. But the class was not on the verge of extinction in these years and the number of rancheros actually continued to grow for several decades.[51]

The land situation in the 1820s was fluid. In an atmosphere where the landholder's position had worsened due to the Revolution—from property destruction, the loss of workers, the collapse of credit—landowning was complicated by a number of new factors. Foremost was the shift from the Spanish system of corporate ownership to a system of private property (excepting the church). The Texas lands were opening up to be disposed of in wholesale lots by impresarios who were granted the land as middlemen to bring in colonists. Most of the Texas lands wound up in the hands of foreigners, and the whole issue of foreign purchase of rural land—in a society unused to seeing outsiders—opened the door to complications. The independence governments also took the first tentative steps toward enlarging the circle of landholders, and some political leaders even now caught a glimpse of more far-reaching agrarian programs.

In the 1820s the hacendados were not thriving. Apart from the inevitable risks of agriculture—the vagaries of prices, weather, and labor—politics had been working against them since 1800. In 1804 the church called in debts to pay a forced loan from the crown. Then came the Revolution and marauding soldiers from both sides. Even in the late 1820s, foreign travelers commented on the large number of burned-out buildings, especially in Guanajuato and Michoacán. The Guanajuato governor's report of February 1830 showed 89 of the state's 148 ore-processing haciendas lying in ruins. By the mid-1820s some recovery could be seen in those regions where the British mining companies moved in and began placing contracts for timber, hides, food, and draft animals. At Fresnillo alone, in the state of Zacatecas, some 500 cattle drove the stamping mill machinery.[52] But independence brought its own set of burdens. Landowners, especially Spaniards, had trouble collecting from tenants who thought that rents had ended along with Spanish rule. Also, it appears that land values had entered a period of decline, partially because there were fewer successful merchants and miners to buy their way into the rural aristocracy. Although population pressures over the past several decades had been pushing land prices upward, the turmoil of the Revolution and independence reversed the trend in many places. There were instances of appreciated land,[53] but a Senate committee reported in 1825 that the selling price of rural property was reduced by as much as two-thirds.[54]

Probably the most serious problem for the hacendado class in the 1820s was debt. During the chaotic revolutionary years the church had called a moratorium on debt payments in most areas (except Puebla), but payment was now expected.[55] Virtually no one seems to have escaped the predicament. In Oaxaca: "No farmer is legitimate proprietor of his land," for it belongs to "Religious Convents of both sexes, to Chaplaincies and Ecclesiastical Patronages, to Colleges, or the Memory of Girls for the Souls of Purgatory."[56] The Tabasco governor in 1826 reported that almost all the farms and ranches in the state had 5 percent debts—to chaplaincies, religious brotherhoods, parishes, and the state.[57] It was the same to the north, in Guanajuato, San Luis Potosí, Chihuahua, and Coahuila.[58] The Zacatecas legislature in 1829 complained that since the nuns and the *clavería* in Guadalajara had made borrowing easy, with the proceeds squandered on vices, "Almost all the state's haciendas, and even urban properties, are burdened with mortgages, that many times exceed the value [of the property]."[59] Proposals appeared in Congress to reduce the debtors' interest payments. Nothing passed, but the Guanajuato hacendados were still trying in 1830.[60]

The weight of the political and economic uncertainties added to the instability of the hacendado class. In the case of five San Luis Potosí haciendas studied by Jan Bazant, the properties were sold about every other generation. Around Guadalajara, lands were hardly ever purchased outright, but ownership changed frequently as a result of foreclosure or marriage.[61] There were a variety of reasons for the turnover of land, from business miscalculations, to the shortage of credit, to weather, to sons who squandered their inheritance. But David Brading, who studied land records of the Bajío, saw the key in the Spanish testamentary tradition: dividing the inheritance among the surviving spouse and all children. A "prolific wife was almost a guarantee that a family would lose its estate."[62]

The hacendados have been pictured by Brading as having virtually no political influence in the final colonial years, not even in the town councils.[63] The assertion relative to the municipal level is open to debate, but the hacendados did not serve conspicuously in Congress, nor did they appear to dominate many state legislatures.

In the far north the great landowners shared some of these same problems, but what set the northerners apart was the scale of their holdings. Here, vast stretches of unclaimed land alternated with ranches measured by the number of days' riding necessary to cross. Ward wrote of traveling from Real de Catorce (near present day Matehuala) to Sombrerete, encountering no sign of human habitation for the first 45 leagues, only "one vast plain" and an occasional hillock. For the next 130 leagues he remained within the confines of three sheep haciendas (Sierra Hermosa, El Mezquite, and La Salada) owned by two men, the Marquis of Jaral and the Count of Pérez Gálvez. Sierra Hermosa was composed of over a million acres of land, and sent to market 30,000 sheep a year from a total herd of about 200,000—not counting goats and horses. The overseer of the estate, with a personal herd of 12,000 goats, qualified as an hacendado in his own right.[64]

There was one landholding that dwarfed even these, the Marquisate of Aguayo. On its 14 million acres, valued at 1,172,383 pesos in an 1815 inventory, lived some 9,000 people in 66 different settlements. When his father the Marquis died in 1818, José María Valdivieso inherited a 576,537-peso debt, and since the estate was entailed could not sell off pieces to clear the obligation. Entail, however, was abolished by the Cortes in 1820, and after debate led by Francisco Manuel Sánchez de Tagle, Congress confirmed the lay part of the abolition (but not the ecclesiastical part) on August 7, 1823. Now the creditors, including de Tagle, determined to foreclose. While the foreclosure process was in the making, English investors—Baring Brothers and Company in the lead, along with Staples and Company—entered the picture with an offer to buy. The transaction went through in September 1825, and the marquisate became the Parras State and Company. But the prospect of foreigners owning half the state of Coahuila alarmed many

Mexicans, and Congress immediately began considering a bill to prohibit foreigners from owning rural property, legislation which finally passed on March 12, 1828. A fresh deal was then made whereby the mortgage holders bought out the marquisate and leased the properties to the British. In 1840 the marquisate was bought by the Sánchez Navarros.[65]

The Sánchez Navarro empire began, as Charles Harris recounted it, with José Miguel Sánchez Navarro, the Monclova curate who bought up property with the profits from merchandising and administering the tithe collection. His family employed familiar methods of the northern ranchers—fighting off Indians with personal armies, controlling workers through debts and pursuing those that fled, and entering into lengthy litigation over foreclosures and use of river waters. With over a million and a half acres by the 1830s, the Sánchez Navarros had become the second largest landowners in the north—soon to be the largest with the Aguayo purchase.[66]

The Sánchez Navarros' commitment to commercial stockraising belied the supposed self-sufficiency of the hacienda. The great landowners tended to specialize in staples—corn, wheat, animals, hides, wool, pulque, and sugar. With the economic disarray of 1810–1821, many haciendas did turn inward, but in the 1820s the owners at least partially recovered. Even long-distance commerce took place: Cuernavaca hacendados sold their sugar in Monterrey, and Durango ranchers their sheep in central Mexico and mules in Oaxaca.[67]

The Guadalajara haciendas studied by Lindley offer a case study. Avoiding one-crop dependence, the proprietors aimed at "flexibility and durability" through a combination of grain, diverse kinds of livestock, and specialized items like cheese and soap. A family had to own property worth 5,000 pesos, plus improvements and stock, to claim a bonafide "hacienda." These hacendados drew their workers, numbering up to 700–800, from the mixed bloods (*castas*) and "displaced Indians" who lived on the hacienda. Although not all these haciendas were profitable in these years, the Porres Barranda estate earned about 12,000 pesos a year and the Villaseñor entail about 14,000 pesos a year.[68]

The makeup of Navajas, a typical Guadalajara hacienda with property valued at 50,000 pesos and chattel goods at 10,000 pesos, was shown in an 1828 inventory:[69]

> a main house (with some 12 rooms and chapel)
> several sheds to manufacture soap and store lime
> 2 or 3 corrals
> 1 carriage house
> 3 granaries (*trojes*) to store maize, wheat, and beans
> 1 shack with thatched roof for the foreman
> 1 well
> 2 threshing floors
> 1 "stone walled plaza with bull pen"

approximately 16 houses for workers

an orchard surrounded by a 13-foot-tall adobe wall (growing apples, peaches, pomegranates, figs, oranges, bananas, grapes, avocado, grapefruit, chirimoya, mamey, tamarind, cherry, apricot, and capulina)

400 head of livestock (horses, mules, burros, oxen, bulls, sheep, goats, hogs)

12 axes, 37 wooden yokes, 9 threshing paddles, 1 copper pump

An article of faith at independence was the exaltation of private ownership of land. Where royalist Spain had fostered corporate holdings of church and Indian communities, the new creed held that individuals would better watch over their own land. There was also a growing recognition that the new nation would be well served if more people entered the landowning class. In the 1820s the term *agrarian reform* was interpreted as handing out titles to vacant lands. There were several national and state programs of one kind or another. Most commonly they followed the Cortes precedent of selling cheaply or giving away empty lands (*terrenos baldíos*) to propertyless workers, with preference to retired soldiers and Indians.[70] Here there was no controversy. Land was available, and any revenue would be welcome. General José Morán on at least two occasions pushed for a plan—never to be carried out—to give land to some of the "turbulent spirits" in the army and turn them into farmers.[71]

The state programs, taken one by one, had mixed results, and the total effect did not make a dent in the general land picture. In the south the projects in Tabasco and Chiapas had little success. Three years after the 1826 law in Chiapas, less than 300 *caballerías* had been sold, even at the low price of three to six pesos per *caballería*.[72] To the north it went better, at least in two states. The Jalisco government claimed to have made 1,000 "petty capitalists" out of impoverished day laborers,[73] and Chihuahua, beginning in 1826, handed out 120,695 acres (27.5 *sitios*) of grazing land until the 1832 Apache raids cut short the program.[74]

A version of this was to pass out lands of suppressed religious orders or defunct missions. This was done in Michoacán, Puebla, and Nuevo León.[75] The Zacatecas legislature proposed to go a step further on December 11, 1829, when it issued a provisional decree for a land bank that had been recommended by Governor Francisco García. Noting the "multitude" of unproductive lands, and that haciendas destined for religious purposes were especially unfruitful, the decree created a state bank that would acquire lands and rent them out perpetually—with landless families of good reputation to be first in line. The catch was that the state would come into possession of these lands by taking over (with compensation) some of the real estate of religious orders and charitable foundations.

Timing of the bank project could not have been worse. The conservative administration of Anastacio Bustamante, which came to power in Mexico City two weeks after the plan's issuance, paid heed to the protests of Guadalajara's cathedral chapter. A Chamber of Deputies committee declared the Zacatecas decree unconstitutional, and the bank died. Thwarted here, the Zacatecas legislature passed a law providing for the state purchase of private holdings. In the next two years the state would pay 169,000 pesos for three haciendas and distribute the plots by lottery.[76]

None of the foregoing addressed the real problem, land concentration, but even in these early years there was some discussion of breaking up the large haciendas. This was suggested—by a small minority—in Congress and in the press in 1822 as part of the discussion on colonization, and then the influential Jalisco writer Francisco Severo Maldonado publicized the idea in 1823.[77] The farthest position taken by a high official came from Durango governor Santiago Baca, who came out openly in 1827 for breaking up the latifundia.[78] Zavala, as Mexico state governor, aroused fears among landowners when he sponsored laws favoring Indian land rights, and he intervened personally in disputes between Indians and hacendados. In his annual report of 1828, he talked about the nation's land situation: three-fifths of the population living in a landless, proletarian state, with a revolution in sight if the situation were not corrected. To put things aright, he proposed to set a limit on the amount of land one person could hold, and to buy lands for the needy through a surtax on absentee landlords.[79] President Guerrero in 1829 promised Indians he would return lands taken by whites,[80] but he never had the opportunity to make his word good. Like so many other reform issues begun hopefully in the first years of independence, the question of agrarian reform receded from center stage as Mexicans were overtaken by violent political strife.

In spite of the many difficulties, the hacendado life had not lost its attraction. Guadalupe Victoria borrowed from the Chaplaincy Court for an hacienda,[81] and more than once Guerrero's friends sought to have Congress award him an estate for his revolutionary sacrifices. Apart from this, Guerrero did acquire in early 1824 Tierra Colorada, a ranch near Tixtla worth about 8,000 pesos that produced cattle, corn, maize, and wheat on a not very profitable basis.[82] Alamán and Zavala also had landowning ambitions. Alamán became the administrator of the Marquisate of Terranova y Monteleone and purchased on his own account a Guanajuato hacienda, while Zavala dealt in land speculation on the Texas frontier.

Zavala won approval in 1829 for a Texas grant along the coast near the Sabine River.[83] He promised to bring in 500 Mexican and foreign families within five years, and although in late 1829 he did enter into an arrangement with Poinsett and Colonel Anthony Butler (Poinsett's successor) to send out colonists, he seems to have taken little interest in the project. In 1830 he visited New York and sold his rights to the Galveston Bay and Texas Land Company, the proceeds of which he lost through an unwise investment in France.[84]

Alamán's ambition was to be a progressive country gentleman, but as in politics his enterprises were victims of unsettled conditions. With the proceeds from the sale of his family home, he purchased the 11,316-acre hacienda of Los Trojes on September 9, 1826. Located near Celaya, Los Trojes was in virtual ruin, and although he took out mortgages to rehabilitate it, he later wrote that Los Trojes brought him nothing but problems.[85]

Meanwhile, on November 24, 1824, Alamán accepted the position of administrator of the Marquisate of the Valley, the estate belonging to the descendants of Hernán Cortés.[86] In 1824 the marquisate was composed of approximately twenty-five houses and the Plaza del Volador in Mexico City, perpetual liens or *censos*—payments in perpetuity, valued at 2.5 percent of value—on forty-seven other houses there, plus property liens and property in Oaxaca, Toluca, Cuernavaca, Coyoacán, Tuxtla, Charo (Michoacán), and Jalapa de Tehuántepec. After deducting expenses and uncollectable claims, the marquisate produced an income of between 25,000 and 30,000 pesos a year.[87] For an annual salary of 2,400 pesos, plus 850 pesos for rent,[88] Alamán's basic responsibility was to extract the maximum profits from the estate and convey them safely to Palermo, residence of the current heir, José María Pignatelli Aragón, duke of Terranova y Monteleone. Alamán also supervised the administration of the Hospital de Jesús, founded by Cortés to minister to the needy.

The hospital budgeted sixteen pesos each year for a service in Cortés's memory, and the very existence of the marquisate was a reminder of Spanish dominance. At independence many tenants resisted paying rents to the estate,[89] and as anti-Spanish feelings grew, the marquisate became an obvious target. Legislation that would have confiscated marquisate property was suggested by state and national governments in 1827. The Monteleone income was equated to tribute to a foreign overlord, a notion Alamán challenged in a long, erudite pamphlet of January 30, 1828.[90]

Alamán was especially worried about Mexico state Governor Zavala, whom he accused of purposely inciting Indians to dispute lands of hacendados. When Zavala, traveling in the vicinity of Cuernavaca, stopped for a meal at the marquisate hacienda of Atlacomulco, Alamán thought some new interference would follow.[91] He feared the worst, since Indians had contested lands with almost every hacienda in the state and now the Tejalpa Indians had suddenly begun to work lands recognized as belonging to the Atlacomulco hacienda "from time immemorial." An agreement was later reached with the villagers which placed the hacienda lands off limits for them.[92]

Alamán and his political friends were able to fight off incursions until 1829. When the Mexico state legislature began discussing a nationalization bill in March, Alamán immediately went into action, sending a petition and copies of his 1828 defense to the legislators. Finally he went to Tlalpam himself to argue the case with Governor Zavala, who stated that he preferred an absentee tax over confiscation. The legislature followed the governor's lead, and on May 7 placed a 1.5 percent tax on the assets of persons residing outside the Republic.[93]

When Zavala became secretary of the treasury in April 1829, he took his tax ideas with him and the Monteleone estate now faced Federation taxes.[94] The Spanish invasion of July 1829 was another calamity for the marquisate. On September 2 Guerrero requisitioned one-third of the income of Monteleone as an "enemy of the state," and the next day Zavala summoned to his office the capital's principal citizens, where Alamán had to lend another 2,000 pesos. The governor of the state of Mexico also put in a claim on the ducal lands, requesting a loan or gift from Atlacomulco, but was met with the reply that the cash was gone.[95]

MINING

The history of Mexican silver in the 1820s—gold made up only about 3 percent of metals production—revolves around the efforts of British companies to bring the mines back to life. The Revolution was catastrophic for most of New Spain's fabled mining districts. Rebels and royalists threw machinery down the shafts and pulled out the shoring when they needed wood. In the north the soldiers were drawn away for guard duty, mercury became scarce, the water level rose. The difficulties scared off investors, and without their money the complex silver-producing structure broke down. Although many miners gave up, a few stayed around to comb through the slag piles or work the upper, drier, sections of the mines, selling ores earlier rejected as too low in silver content.[96]

In the early 1820s the Spanish Cortes and then the Mexican Congress considered measures to revive the industry. The Cortes consolidated various mining taxes into a 3 percent impost and lowered other fees, such as mintage and gold and silver separation, changes accepted in large measure by Iturbide's government.[97] During the 1823–1824 discussions over mining policy, the debates in Congress turned on the role of foreigners. In the closing weeks of the 1823 Congress, Alamán asked the delegates to suspend for ten years the provisions excluding foreigners, pointing out that for rehabilitation no domestic capitalists could be found. In one of its last acts, Congress on October 7, 1823, annulled the restrictive laws and substituted one permitting foreigners to enter into contracts with native mine owners, though forbidding them to register new mines.[98]

It was generally recognized in mining circles that these investors were good for Mexico, but the general fear of foreign profiteering showed itself on occasion in efforts to pass on to the companies certain expenses and taxes. An example of this was the attempt in 1824 to prevent foreign miners from taking advantage of an old Spanish law that allowed entrepreneurs to claim unworked mines.[99] Finance Minister Esteva tried unsuccessfully to reimpose the old mining taxes on the grounds that without them foreigners were getting rich at Mexico's expense.[100]

Getting rich on Mexican silver was, of course, exactly what many

British investors did have on their minds, little knowing that in reality Mexico would be enriched at their expense. New World silver was a long coveted prize. Articles and books on Latin America found an avid public—Humboldt's works passed as scripture—and stories circulated about fabulous fortunes cashed by investors after a three-day speculation.[101]

In the midst of this excitement, brokers had no trouble in marketing shares. Indeed, enthusiastic investors oversubscribed, sending the market price to two or three times the asking amount. By late 1827, 15 million pesos had been invested in Mexico alone.[102] The companies covered almost all of the famous mining areas, although hostile Indians and problems of transportation limited activity in the far north. The largest, the Anglo-Mexican Mining Association, capitalized originally at 1 million pounds, contracted for mines in Guanajuato (including the Valenciana, Mexico's most famous mine), San Luis Potosí, Catorce, and Real Del Monte. The Tlalpujahua Company moved into the Tlalpujahua area of Michoacán. The Catorce Company went farthest north, trying to revive the mines near Matehuala (between San Luis Potosí and Saltillo). The Company of Adventurers in the Mines of Bolaños contracted for, in addition to Bolaños, the famous Veta Madre mines near Zacatecas. The Real del Monte Company went into the Real del Monte mining area near Pachuca. The Mexican Company had contracts in Zacatecas and Oaxaca, and also invested in Veracruz copper diggings.[103] The most far-flung of all was the United Mexican Mining

Grinding Ore at the Salgado Hacienda

Association (UMMA), founded by Lucas Alamán and by September 1825 possessing fifty-six mines in the states of Oaxaca, Mexico, Valladolid, Guanajuato, Zacetecas, and Durango.[104]

No other nation could compete with British capitalists in bidding for the choice Mexican mines, but the Americans and Germans did try some small-scale mining. In the mid-1820s a Mr. Keating (of Baltimore) set up the Tlacoatl Company with three small mines and a capital of 50,000 dollars, one of whose stockholders was American Ambassador Poinsett. The American consul general, James Wilcocks, was involved with the New York Company, which contracted for four mines. The Germany Company of Eberfeld leased some of the marginal mines, and a company known as the German-American Mining Union was in operation in 1831.[105] Some German miners came over to work for the English companies.

In addition there were Mexican-run mines which, although generally smaller in size, were possibly as numerous as the foreigners' mines. The Guanajuato governor reported in 1826 that of the state's 319 mines, 42 were administered by foreign concerns, while 31 were being worked by the owners. An item worthy of note is that the same report listed 202 abandoned mines.[106]

The companies took up most of 1824 and 1825 in organizing and in contracting for mines, the competition for which allowed owners to drive hard bargains. Then began the main part of the companies' labors, getting the mines in produceable shape: bringing in machinery, which required bulding roads, clearing out and reshoring tunnels, renovating the processing haciendas (*haciendas de beneficio*), finding and signing up workmen, and contracting for supplies. The biggest single task was draining the water, which had frequently risen hundreds of feet. The British companies were dependent upon governments for a smooth operation. At the local level, relations were usually cordial, thanks partially—it appears—to considerable bribery of judges, town councils, and mining deputations. The Catorce town council "borrowed" funds from the Catorce Company in order to build a road.[107]

Probably the main argument was with the national government over a March 22, 1822, law—occasioned by the exodus of wealthy Spaniards—that prohibited the export of silver bullion. Mexicans had seven mints to support, most set up during the Revolution when it was impossible to send silver ingots to the Mexico City mint. These generally made miners wait weeks while they rolled and stamped the silver into coins, except in Zacatecas, where customers could receive coins four days after they brought in silver bars. Its 300 employees had been known to turn out 60,000 pesos in twenty-four hours.[108] After much diplomatic pressure, Mexico began permitting bullion export on July 19, 1828 (with a 7 percent tax), but would renew the prohibition on March 9, 1832.[109]

Through the 1820s the mints were coining an increasing quantity of metals, but the export of specie was growing even faster. By 1828 the value of precious metals exported had overtaken the value of metals coined. The value of metals exports (in pesos) for 1820–1829 is given below:[110]

1820	10,104,645
1821	10,023,020
1822	9,338,357
1823	3,391,924
1824	6,503,648
1825	3,714,354
1826	5,925,367
1827	9,669,428
1828	12,367,766
1829	13,010,020

For the British companies, a source of irritation was the mine workers. The miners formed a sort of labor aristocracy, well paid, united in defending their occupational rights, fortified by traditions of the mines, and highly class conscious. The *minerales,* or mining sites, of New Spain had bred a fearless type of man who did not hesitate to descend 1,000 feet on notched logs dressed only in loincloth, sandals, and felt helmet with taper affixed, and clamber back up with 200 pounds of ore in a leather pouch. Rewards were commensurate with the risks. Whereas campesinos toiled for two reales a day, a mine worker could earn four reales (one-half peso) and elite drillers a peso a day—plus the *partido* (one-eighth to one-third of the ore over a certain minimum). A lore had grown up around the mines: famous miners had become immortalized, certain shafts had "psychological" characteristics, and traditional codes were observed. The miners combined a professional militancy with a genuine piety, and an equally genuine dissolution. They crossed themselves with a crucifix before descending, entered the tunnels to the rhythm of a religious chant, placed virgins at crossroads in the underground passages, and gave saints' names to the shafts. At the same time, if they were vouchsafed by these rituals to negotiate the precipitous shafts and unshored passages without injury, after the ore was divided on Saturday they bent their total efforts to drinking, wenching, gambling, and brawling.

From the administrators' point of view, the miners' most aggravating trait was their devotion to the traditional mode of wages. Relatively indifferent to working conditions—semiventilated shafts, sodden working areas—they reacted violently where the *partido* was concerned. Several English companies tried, as had Mexican owners, to abolish the *partido,* and the miners would immediately go on strike, destroy machinery, and attack any workers brought in as replacements.[111] At the Bolaños mines in 1828 the miners burned the house of an official and then gutted the main shaft with fire.[112] Another source of friction was the European workmen, principally Cornishmen and Germans, who generally looked down on Mexican laborers as unfit for any position connected with machinery or responsibility.

In 1827, when the mints were producing at the level of about ten million pesos annually, the minister of finance expressed his satisfaction that mining was recovering adequately.[113] Shareholders of the companies, however, did not agree. The first wave of euphoria ended in June 1826 with a credit scare that drove under some of the smaller companies, including the Catorce and the Mexican Mining Companies. A second critical period occurred in late 1828 and 1829, when companies that had already used up most of their original capital were pushed to the brink of insolvency by political and economic disturbances. Tlalpujahua failed in October 1828.[114]

In the late 1820s, after spending millions to restore the mines, investors tired of the seemingly endless calls for more capital. Real del Monte, for example, had a deficit of 3.5 million pesos by 1830.[115] The companies needed a bonanza to offset the huge outlays, and only the Bolaños Company experienced this good fortune.

Alamán was the initial champion and ultimate victim of these developments. While in France in 1822 he organized what he claimed was the prototype for all Mexican mining companies, Alamán, Vial, and Company, which was moved to London in early 1824 and reorganized as the United Mexican Mining Assocation.[116] The UMMA started out as a medium-sized concern, with a capital of 1.2 million pesos (or 240,000 pounds), 600 shares at 40 pounds each.[117]

As president of the Mexican board of management, Alamán took a leave of absence from the government in September 1824 to travel and contract mines. It was his theory that a large number of undertakings would lead to more successes, but owing to its great extent the UMMA was victimized more than most companies by political and social stress. In March 1828 the commander of the detachment assigned to the UMMA's El Oro mine (near Tlalpujahua) appeared before the manager demanding money. Not satisfied with the reply, the officer returned at the head of his troops and repeated the demand, at which point the manager decided to give him what he wanted.[118] In Sombrerete on the evening of January 12, 1829, about sixty robbers, along with the town rabble, plundered company facilities and the town's better homes, carrying off silver, accounts, books, letters "and in short everything belonging to the company."[119]

Through the first five years, United Mexican made a success of sorts by merely surviving. But the company organizers were overextended and the blame for this was laid largely at Alamán's door, who in turn blamed inaccurate records of the mine owners.[120] By October 1826 expenditures had surpassed 3,300,000 pesos, three times the original capitalization, and Alamán was now writing apologetically that the company had turned the corner and the day of dividends was in sight.[121]

Alamán was doomed to further frustration, a condition he shared with virtually all of the mining administrators. The promotors had not realized the magnitude of the task of restoring the mines and they had unwarranted faith in European techniques. They possessed, after all, the steam engine, more sophisticated methods for processing ore, and accounting techniques to facilitate cost control. With the last they achieved some success, but the technological advantages they brought turned out to have limited application. The Mexican patio process of amalgamation struck Europeans as extremely wasteful, but the smelting processes were not practical for the Mexican ores. There were great hopes for steam engines, two of which could pump out of the shafts 600 gallons of water per minute, many times more than the *malacates,* or water-hoisting machines. But they needed huge quantities of timber, and most mining regions were long since stripped of their forests. The Anglo-Mexican Company planted more than 20,000 trees in Guanajuato, but this was a mere beginning.[122] The revival of Mexican mining would have to wait sixty years.

FOREIGN TRADE AND FOREIGN TRADERS

Mexico entered upon independence to the accompaniment of a revolution in foreign trade. First and foremost, the Spaniards' hold on foreign trade was terminated. Before the Revolution, merchants from the peninsula, with huge facilities in Veracruz, monopolized exporting, importing, and the carrying trade. From the coast they sold to wholesale dealers from the interior, who would then visit the retailers. At independence, many of the Spanish magnates departed, with the result that under Iturbide imports fell by one-half. In the first five years of the Republic, trade figures would reach and surpass preindependence levels, but it was a foreign trade unlike the earlier in almost every respect. The former masters of foreign trade and shipping were replaced, trade routes were splintered and reshaped, and the content of foreign trade was altered. The Spaniards' place was taken not so much by Mexicans—who lacked capital and connections in Europe—as by British (and to a considerably lesser extent the Americans and French), centered mainly in Mexico City and supplying the retailers directly.[123]

Much of the colonial trade had been in Spanish products, 40 percent according to the Veracruz *consulado,* in items such as paper, iron, brandy, and wines.[124] Then came Iturbide's victory. For the year 1823 the Veracruz *consulado* records showed that Spanish products comprised only about one-fourth of the 4 million pesos' worth of goods entering that port.[125] From this point, as a result of the San Juan de Ulúa shelling, the Spanish share declined to virtually nothing.

Spanish shippers also lost out. Within a fortnight of Ulúa's first shot at Veracruz, all Spanish vessels were ordered out and only a handful cleared Mexican ports in the next decade. North Americans continued to move into the breach. Of the 400–500 ships putting in at Mexican ports each year from 1825 to 1828, almost half were North American, followed in numbers by the French, and then by the British (not counting England's New World colonies). The U.S. ships, mostly smaller craft making runs between New Orleans and the Gulf ports, accounted for 40 to 50 percent of the total tonnage. Only the coasting trade was left to Mexicans, who operated principally out of Campeche, where schooners and brigs were constructed for their use.[126] The Mexican government tried various expedients to keep this activity for its nationals, such as tariff differentials and nationality requirements for crews, but the Americans and British were resourceful, even to the point of taking out Mexican papers, and the expedients eventually failed.[127]

The end of Spanish mercantilism meant that trade could follow its natural routes. When the ports of Veracruz and Acapulco lost their monopoly status, there occurred a shift to the north. On the Gulf, the northward movement hurt Veracruz only relatively, for it continued to be the main point of entry, while Tampico and Matamoros became second and third. Independence had less of an impact on the southern ports, which were affected by Spanish raiders and the closing of the Havana trade. On the Pacific side, the changes were more radical. Acapulco, although virtually inaccessible by land during the rainy months of June to November, had formerly derived a modicum of prosperity from commerce with the Orient. But it had lost more than half of its population of 12,000 because of the Revolution and an 1820 earthquake, and recovery came slowly. Ships began putting in at San Blas and Guaymas, and a few at Mazatlán. Overall, the West Coast accounted for only about 7 percent of the national imports. It received the overflow sent up by British dealers in Peru and Chile, and also carried on with the remnants of the Asian trade—mostly in cloth from British colonies in China and India.[128]

Tied in with spreading out of entry points was the rise of the inland cities serving as warehousing centers. San Luis Potosí (supplied via Tampico and Soto la Marina) and Guadalajara (supplied by San Blas) were the two principal distributors for the northeast and northwest, respectively.

Free trade antedated independence. When Spain went to war with England in 1796, the sea lanes could not be kept open—or the colonies supplied—and so neutral ships were licensed to carry Spain's goods to the colonies. But the neutrals inevitably brought in non-Spanish merchandise, and then during the Revolution the Viceroy was forced to open other ports temporarily because of rebel action around Veracruz.[129] The Cortes delegates, recognizing the impossibility of keeping out foreigners and hoping to mollify colonials, declared eight of New Spain's ports open in 1820.[130]

Thus Mexican workmen had already felt the effect of cheap imports, and so the 1821 tariff was not altogether free. Going into effect January 1822, the structure placed heavy taxes on some products and excluded altogether tobacco, hams, bacon, salt, tallow, cotton yarn, ready-made clothing, blankets, lace, skins, worked leather, wood, and bricks.[131] After protests from numerous states, Congress on May 20, 1824 added to the list foods, liquors, woods, hides, worked metal, many fabric cloths, and clay crockery.[132] Exports could go out free, with the exception of vanilla (taxed at 6 percent), and gold and silver objects and coins (taxed from 2 to 3.5 percent).[133]

It was felt at the time that the great virtue of the Mexican tariff was its simplicity. All imports were to pay 25 percent ad valorum—in comparison with the perplexing variety of Spanish taxes. But the 25 percent was levied, not on the easily altered invoice price, but on a list (or schedule) in which each item was assigned a monetary value. In most cases the valuations were carryovers from the Spaniards' inflated prices. And as the goods moved closer to the consumer, other charges came into play.

Total import charges, adjusted to 1821 import valuation, were: 25 percent import duty, computed on the 1821 tariff schedule; 1½ percent *consulado* fee (until late 1823, 2 percent), paid to Veracruz and Mexico City *consulados;* 3⅛ percent *avería* (convoy tax); 18¾ percent internation duty (replacing the *alcabala* of 12 percent); 3 percent levied by states on goods consumed in their areas (law of December 24, 1824).[134] Three months were allowed to pay the import and *consulado* fees.

A new tariff schedule, ratified on November 16, 1827, lowered the valuations on some items but did not appreciably alter the general picture. The most momentous change in import policy took place in May 1829, when cheap cotton cloth was added to the prohibited list.[135]

Foreign businessmen complained about duties that reached 100 percent of invoice prices,[136] and about not being permitted to re-export unsold articles, but the tariff never seemed to stand between them and profits. As Europeans and North Americans moved in to exploit the new markets, a tidal wave of imports resulted, creating a trade deficit, shown below, that was only slowly erased by rising mining production:[137]

	Imports (in pesos)	*Exports* (in pesos)	
1825	19,360,179	4,731,987	–.5
1826	15,450,565	7,648,133	–8
1827	14,889,049	12,171,777	–2
1828	9,947,846	14,488,788	+5

All through Mexico's first decade as a republic, ships brought in more cloth than anything else, 60–75 percent of total imports in 1826–1828,[138] and took out mainly metals. English cloth dominated, then American. After the mid-1820s, the French began to get the edge in some of the finer woollens, such as broadcloth and cashmere.[139] Other imports were foodstuffs, spirits, and paper, but cotton cloth was the most important single item—from a third to half of all imports. Metals, mostly in coin, comprised about 80 percent of exports in these same years.[140] Mexico had little to offer outgoing ships, since British warships normally carried back the metals, and sometimes even cochineal. Outbound vessels, if they did not have a cargo of the traditional exports such as indigo, vanilla, or cochineal, which never took up the slack, loaded up on ballast or dropped down to Campeche or Yucatán to pick up dyewood.[141]

The logistics of free trade strained the capacities of the young nation. Many of the ships coming into the new ports in 1821 and 1822 paid no duties simply because there were no collectors. Esteva wrote at the end of 1824 that the Mazatlán port was composed of six huts, two of mud and four of straw, and one customs officer who was blind.[142] With high duties and 10,000 miles of lightly patrolled coastline, the result was inevitable. References to smuggling in contemporary documents were legion, most indicating complicity by government officials. The practice was nationwide, but contrabandists seemed especially busy in the northern states, where entire cargoes were brought in by sea or overland. Estimates of the smugglers' portion of trade ran from one-third of the total, by Ward, to three-fourths of the total, by David Porter.[143] Methods were as varied as the locale, from merely finding an unguarded stretch of beach, to bringing in prohibited articles ostensibly for one's own use, to making illegal transactions openly in the bay at Veracruz just beyond the reach of the customs house boats.[144] One American was permitted to bring in 15,000 pesos in prohibited goods after he handed out 2,000 pesos in bribes to the chief customs inspector, the military commander, and his soldiers.[145] In 1826 two English merchants found they could have purchased contraband English goods in San Luis Potosí and resold them in Mexico City at a "large profit."[146]

An estimated one million pesos of specie a year were also smuggled out of the country.[147] Congress on March 31, 1831, tried to make it harder on smugglers with a decree that empowered customs inspectors to confiscate any shipment not accompanied by a detailed invoice signed by the Mexican consul at the point of embarcation.[148]

The creature behind these great changes was the businessman from abroad, a very energetic individual. From Nacogdoches to Soconusco, no town was too mean for his attention, whatever its size, and villagers near the trade routes took any visitor to be a peddler and assumed anything he had was for sale. These foreign merchants made Mexico City their headquarters and began leasing the best downtown houses for their offices.[149] By August 1826, the national capital had fourteen English commercial houses, four American commercial houses, three German commercial houses, and "an immense number of Foreign shopkeepers, principally French."[150] Guadalajara, by contrast, had only one foreign "mercantile house" in 1827.[151]

The British houses were the largest, handling about two-thirds of all foreign transactions as of 1826.[152] At the time of the Spanish invasion in 1829, the Federal District had twenty British business houses large enough to qualify for a forced loan by the government.[153] In Guadalajara the British already had a toehold through their revolutionary alliance with resident Panamanians, and although they were slower to move in, before the decade was out they had thoroughly penetrated this region's economy.[154] Even as far north as Matamoros they made their presence felt: this tiny port had fifteen British merchants in 1829.[155]

Frenchmen and Germans drifted in from about the mid-1820s. Although France did not officially recognize Mexican independence until 1830, the size of trade—in France's favor by four or five to one—was considerable even before that, in such products as textiles, hardware, wines, and jewelry. North of Mexico City and Veracruz, U.S. entrepreneurs dominated. Some carried muleloads from town to town, and some set up stores in the northern towns.[156] Reuben Potter, who took a cargo from Matamoros to Monterrey and Saltillo, described the northern commerce. He wrote that thirty to forty mules driven by six to eight muleteers would normally carry the freight of one merchant (foreign or Mexican) and would make fifteen to twenty miles a day. At night the bales and boxes were unloaded and made into a protective wall. At the Saltillo fair he and the other foreign merchants, several of them French, made from 200 to 300 dollars a day.[157]

The foreign merchants were only too successful in their profession. In some states, the amount they sold legally each year (extrapolated from the 3 percent tax on foreign goods) was substantial: 867,000 pesos in Puebla, 1825; 1,122,000 pesos in Jalisco, 1828; 525,000 pesos in Michoacán, 1828; 525,000 pesos in Guanajuato, 1829; 1,232,000 pesos in San Luis Potosí, 1830.[158] By late 1825 the market was saturated, prices plunged, and for about a year British merchants were selling at an average loss of 30 percent.[159] For the consumer, cheap cloth was a godsend. Basil Hall, an English ship's captain traveling on the West Coast (1826), paraphrased a peasant's comment on free trade: "My opinion of the free trade rests on this—formerly I paid 9 dollars for the piece of cloth of which this shirt is made. I now pay 2—that forms my opinion of the free trade."[160]

For Mexican artisans, on the other hand, the competition translated into unemployment and destitution. As early as 1817 Quirós had pointed out the state of ruin to which cotton weavers had been reduced as a result of imported cloth. Local woollens had not suffered as much.[161] Two of the main textile centers, Puebla and Guadalajara, whose weavers had been hurting since 1810, led the outcry in 1822–1823. The protest against foreign profiteering became a common theme in Jalisco publications.[162] In general the Yorkino federalists appeared somewhat readier to break with free trade, because of their political ties with the artisan class.[163] Congress did, in May 1824, exclude a few types of cotton products, but the attachment to free trade was still a key ingredient in the independence ethos.

By the late 1820s, however, Mexicans were in general retreat from free trade. Complaints came from all regions about home industries now in decay. Because of imports, Oaxaca's 500 looms were now 30, and Texcoco had become almost a "deserted" city.[164] Several states, including Jalisco, San Luis Potosí, Chihuahua, and Tamaulipas, enacted special taxes on foreign goods passing through their areas—taxes over and above the permitted 3 percent. The San Luis Potosí law of May 10, 1828, limited the export of specie to once every four months.[165] At the instance of diplomats, the national government would promptly give notice these taxes were unconstitutional, but some of the states ignored the warning.[166] On August 27, 1829, during the Spanish invasion, Congress added another 2 percent tax to the existing 3 percent on foreign merchandise as a war measure.[167]

The movement came to focus on cheap cotton cloth. In 1827 Congress rejected a Puebla petition that "coarse unbleached Cotton Goods" be excluded. Pressure continued, however, and after eighteen deputies signed a petition in January 1829, a bill passed on May 22, 1829, to keep out several imported items, principally low-priced cotton fabric.[168] The exclusion would affect mainly the British,[169] but due to political turns the law's full weight was not to be felt. Treaty obligations required that any law "burdensome to trade" could not go into effect for six months,[170] and at the end of 1829 the executive changed hands. The new administration, with new priorities, would see to the law's repeal in April 1830.

As importers and wholesalers, the foreigners had limited competition from Mexicans, but when they began opening up their own retail businesses, there were enough local storeowners to object. Beginning in 1829, Congress began considering a bill to close all non-Mexican retail shops. In the 1830 session, with petitions from twelve states, the bill passed in the Chamber of Deputies—Alamán used his influence to defeat it in the Senate—and again in 1831 the measure came up. Pakenham was looking into the possibility of having English merchants take out Mexican citizenship when a temporary agreement was reached in London between the British Foreign Office and Manuel Eduardo Gorostiza, the Mexican chargé d'affaires. By this agreement, British subjects would be permitted to sell at the retail level if their families lived with them.[171] The states, meanwhile, did not wait. In that same year (1831), Jalisco, Zacatecas, and Sinaloa, ordered foreigners out of the retail business.[172] Injunctions like these could not prevail in the long run, but they revealed a growing frustration with free trade.

In the mid-1820s it seemed the Mexican economy had recovered from the shock of the Revolution and was beginning to reap the benefits of independence: haciendas and ranchos were producing again, the mines were being refitted, and only the artisans were dissatisfied. But the expectation was short-lived. Much was expected from the outside world—the stimulus of outside trade, financial aid from the British—but with each passing year the lesson was driven home that Mexicans could not meet the world economy on even terms. If mercantilism had been a vehicle to channel profits to the Spaniards, free trade seemed designed to divert them to the British and Americans and French.

The themes of the late 1820s were a turning away from mining and a mounting frustration with the doctrine of free trade. Yet Mexican officials had no program as an alternative. At a personal level, the despair was expressed by a young Mexico City shoemaker, José Hernandez, when he was arrested and taken before the Vagrants' Court:

> You will ask me in what workshop do I work, and I respond that in the workshops of distinction I have not worked because most of them are foreign. And these, when they hire Mexican journeymen, want those that have a decent exterior, and fate has not permitted to me the appearance to work in them; so that all that is left to me is to work along the *rinconeras* [streetcorner craftsmen], and that, Sir, is my situation.[173]

« 6 »

The Yorkinos Triumphant
1827–1828

VENGEANCE AGAINST THE SPANIARDS, 1827

In retrospect, 1827 was a year when the golden age of optimism and high aspirations came to an end. Divisions, which in 1823–1824 might have been expected to be mended in time, were now clearly becoming irreconcilable—and bloody. The guiding principle was the nation's vengeance on the colony, the instinct to expel Spaniards from the body politic once and for all.

The Yorkinos rode high on the issue and in the process extended the nineteenth-century liberalism that the Escoceses had once been instrumental in propagating. Beginning with the tenets of representative government, the rule of law, freedom of the press, and civil supremacy over the church, the Yorkinos were led by their power base among the middle and lower income groups to pursue the logical dictates of liberalism toward majoritarian rule and diminishment of privilege.[1] Their connections with the artisanry, ruined by cheap foreign cloth, led the York rite Masons to depart from the liberal canon of free trade. In the 1820s they were noisier about their patriotism than their more cosmopolitan opponents, primarily because of the international connections of politics. Whereas the Yorkinos were always more alive to any threat from Spaniards, the Escoceses would be quicker to perceive danger from the North Americans, toward whom they felt no ideological debt. The danger from the North Americans had yet to be seen.

Zavala, with his position of governor of the most powerful state in the Republic, his network of confederates in the York rite lodges, and his use of the *Correo de la Federación Mexicana,* was emerging as a central figure among the Yorkinos. Alamán, on the other hand, was in the middle of an active business career, immersed in duties as mining company director, marquisate administrator, and as agent in funds transactions involving various members of the Mexican aristocracy.[2]

His place in politics had been taken by Vice-President Nicolás Bravo, now the leader of the Scottish rite Masons. The Escoceses were able to present only a passive resistance to the 1827 course of events. With second thoughts about their "liberal" positions of the late colonial years, they continued to retrench ideologically, becoming more and more conspicuous as guardians of the system as it was.

The Guadalupe Victoria government, meanwhile, buffeted by the popular outbursts of 1827 and with no clear-cut program of its own, reacted with a passive ambivalence that was coming to be its style. Comments on the absence of leadership were heard more frequently, but Guadalupe Victoria himself never fully gave up on his belief of a balanced government. As some cabinet members were moving toward the Yorkinos, others were moving contrariwise. Along with Victoria's personal secretary Tornel, Esteva still championed the Yorkinos' cause, and Gómez Pedraza cooperated, but the secretary of justice and ecclesiastical affairs, Ramos Arizpe, was becoming progressively disenchanted with his lodge fellows. Secretary of Relations Camacho was an Escocés, although not aggressive about it, and in any case was away in London most of 1827 negotiating a treaty.

The object of everyone's attention, the Spaniards, formed a numerically small but influential component of Mexican society. Alamán numbered them about 70,000 in 1808, but documents related to their expulsion suggest an independence figure close to 10,000. Though found at all levels of society, they had been highly visible in the better circles, as merchants, country gentlemen, military officers, bishops, canons, and monks. This population had turned over considerably in recent years. A number of the 8,000 Spanish soldiers who arrived during the Revolution decided to stay. Known as *capitulados*, they partially replaced the departing Spaniards who were loyal to the king.[3]

Now that the Spaniards had lost their patron the king, they would never again find favor in high political places. Iturbide courted them at first, but his financial measures estranged them, and he began to hold them up as scapegoats to stir up support. His followers blamed his downfall partially on Spanish Mexicans. The brief tenures of Negrete as Supreme Executive Power member and Arrillaga as treasury secretary in 1823 proved the unworkability of a Spaniard giving orders to Mexicans. Some Spanish officers had to give up their commands because Mexicans refused to obey.[4] Only two Spaniards served in Congress between 1824 and March 1828.[5]

Mexico's creole aristocrats had good reasons for breaking politically with Spain, but with personal contacts through intermarriage and joint service in various institutions, creoles frequently defended the Spaniards. What put the situation beyond control was a visceral hatred for the *gachupín* by the middle and lower orders of society. They had grown up knowing that "old Spaniards" boasted about not having been born in Mexico and rarely disguised their contempt for Mexicans. They had seen Spanish brutality visited upon their villages during the Revolution, and Spain's actions since 1821—threats of reconquest and the shelling of Veracruz—kept the resentment at a high pitch. Avidly the public read Villavicencio's fables about the coyote and the hen, where the trusting Mexican befriended the coyote (Spaniard) only to have him open the henhouse for his fellow coyotes and massacre the hens. Mexicans now prepared to even old scores.

Many Spaniards living through all this saw what was in store, sold off their property, and moved away. Many departed during the Revolution, there was an exodus after independence, and more left in late 1823 after the declaration of the Republic.[6] With their property converted into portable wealth—the Monte de Piedad was low on jewelry in 1823 owing to the Spanish demand[7]—they went to New Orleans, Havana, and southern France, as well as Spain. In the process they took out so much money they almost decapitalized Mexico. British diplomats were given figures of 100–150 million pesos for the years 1821 to 1824.[8] Surprisingly, a few peninsulars were still immigrating, some showing up in Gulf ports with U.S. papers (declaration of intention to become citizens). At the beginning of 1827, there were slightly less than 7,000 Spaniards living in Mexico, possibly a third of them *capitulados*.[9]

The year of vengeance against the Spaniards was touched off by a fifty-year-old Spanish member of an institute of the Franciscans known as the *Dieguinos*. Padre Joaquín Arenas thought that he would bring back Spanish rule in Mexico, although he was hardly the person to undertake such an endeavor. He had been sent to Mexico City in chains in 1820 by the Bishop of Durango, and in 1827, by Alamán's report, was the owner of a Mexico City factory making counterfeit money.[10] From all accounts Arenas was a flighty individual, given to unworkable projects, and possessing no family or political connections worthy of note. But by conspiring with equally unpresumptuous acquaintances, he did have the means to inaugurate a wave of hysteria.

It began on the morning of January 19, 1827, when Arenas was ushered into the headquarters of General Ignacio Mora (b. 1773), the officer who had replaced Santa Anna in Yucatán and was now commander of the Federal District and the state of Mexico. Mora, a native of Veracruz, was one of the prerevolutionary officers, beginning his career in 1789 and then serving in the royalist army until 1820, when he was elected to the Cortes.[11] He must have been stunned as this stranger offered him a scarcely believable proposition. Would he be interested in taking part in a revolution to return Mexico to Spanish dominion? Mora listened, asked Arenas to come to his home the following day at 8 A.M., and forthwith informed President Victoria. It was decided that five witnesses of differing political alignments should listen in. They were at the house by 4 A.M., and during this second interview Mora tried to draw out more details. The friar answered vaguely that Fernando VII had selected a "royal commissioner," who was already in Mexico, to take charge of the revolution and that help was expected from generals, canons, and many others. Finally one of the witnesses, Senator Molinos del Campo, could contain himself no longer and burst into the room berating Arenas, who merely replied that he was prepared to be martyred for his religion and his country.[12]

On the basis of Arenas's reputation, the conspiracy at first was considered the product of delirium. Four days after his arrest, a servant at the monastery found a bundle of papers, many in Arenas's hand, proclamations, cryptic notes about a plot, and papers signed by Juan Climaco Velasco. Gradually the case seemed to take on added seriousness. Investigations led to arrests. State governors uncovered purported accomplices. The prosecution later claimed the conspiracy extended from Puebla to Durango.[13] But the type of subversion accumulated in Arenas's dossier was not of a grave nature, generally consisting of reports of suspicious behavior by Spaniards and friars: of five inebriated individuals in San Luis Potosí who shouted *Viva España!*, of Spanish hacendados near Atlixco (Puebla) who had held a mysterious meeting after returning from Mexico City, of a Spanish curate in Michoacán who had guns and powder in his possession.[14] But the arrests went on, eventually totaling about thirty-five.[15]

Many thought the conspiracy extended to the government's inner circles when General Gregorio Arana was arrested on February 4, on the testimony of a detained cleric who called him the leader of the plot. Apprehension was becoming genuine fear. Four deputies proposed executing not only those guilty of sedition, but those who were heard to say phrases like *Viva España, Viva Fernando VII*, or *Viva La Monarquía*. The names of Generals Negrete and Echávarri were mentioned. With reluctance, Guadalupe Victoria ordered their arrest, which was carried out on March 21— Negrete taken from a sickbed.[16]

The detention of Negrete and Echávarri marked the extreme point of fear. After more than a year's incarceration, the state's case being admittedly weak, both were exonerated, but only to fall under the Spanish expulsion law. Echávarri spent his days in the United States as a teacher of Spanish, aided ironically by Iturbide's widow, and Negrete died in Bordeaux, still a Mexican patriot in spite of it all.[17]

A total of six people were executed. Other than Padre Arenas himself, the most celebrated victim was Arana. Tornel, witness at Mora's house and one of the more aggressive Yorkinos at the time, later described Arana's execution of January 5, 1828, how the condemned general grabbed the crucifix and swore that he was dying an innocent man. Spectators desecrated the body anyway.[18]

Arenas never denied his guilt and appeared content with his role as martyr. He did it, he said, to restore the purity of religion after the Masons' heresies. The proceedings were delayed because the church claimed jurisdiction in the case, but this dispute was finally settled and on June 2, 1827, on the road to Chapultepec, a commission from the church officially defrocked him, replacing his habit with black pants, a hood, and a sign on his chest with large letters, "For Treason to the Nation." Unperturbed, Arenas ate a piece of chocolate, smoked a cigar, and walked to the spot of execution in good spirits. After he was shot in the back, his body was delivered to the monks of his order at Tacubaya.[19]

The mysterious royal commissioner Juan Climaco Velasco was never unmasked. For many years the prime candidate was Eugenio Aviraneta, a Spaniard who had fought against the French in the peninsula and then emigrated to France. He came to Veracruz about 1825 on the pretext of settling a bequest by an uncle, made friends with Orizaba political chief Vicente Segura, organized a Lancasterian school, and then began writing for the *Veracruzano Libre* of Veracruz. After taking part in the 1827 publicity battles among the Veracruz Masons, he left for New Orleans and Havana, to return in 1829 briefly as political advisor to the invading Spanish army.[20]

In later years, writers of all political shades agreed that the Arenas threat was nothing more than mutterings of a handful of unrepentant Spaniards. But if the plot itself was trivial, the consequences for Spanish Mexicans were enormous. The rage generated by the plot silenced all but the diehard defenders of the Spaniards. Guadalupe Victoria stated he had hitherto protected them, but was now incensed at their faithlessness and intended to make an example of them. In actuality he never went that far, but neither did he do anything to calm the hysteria. The Yorkinos pointed to Arenas as proof of what they had been saying all along, and the Escoceses lost what little remained of their credibility by claiming the conspiracy was a fabrication. *El Sol,* traditional spokesman for the Spanish-creole aristocracy, also lost favor when it ridiculed the government's investigation. Posters began to appear on streetcorners showing coyotes being hanged.[21]

As news of Arenas spread in early 1827, private citizens and governments began to take actions against Spaniards. The main area of conflict was the port of Veracruz, where the Spaniards had so far managed to retain influence.[22] The legislature and General Miguel Barragán, who combined in his person the governorship and the state military command, were all ardently Escocés, and the local hero, Santa Anna (now in retirement), was their associate. The only noteworthy Yorkino was port commander Colonel José Rincón (1779–1846). He was the elder of two brothers from a Spanish family of the state of Veracruz. While José had fought with the royalists, Manuel Rincón (1784–1849) had been with the insurgents and had received his promotion to brigadier under Iturbide.[23]

In the face of rumors of conspiracies in Veracruz, President Victoria decided to send out Treasury Secretary Esteva as "Commisssary General of the Treasury." Although there was a commissary office in Veracruz to supervise Treasury business—as in each of the states—Esteva was considered a national leader of the Yorkinos. The Veracruz legislature responded with several decrees aimed at discouraging his visit,[24] but Esteva ignored them and came to Veracruz on May 24 to begin his duties. As expected, placards denouncing Bourbonists were reported shortly after his arrival. When the legislature produced a decree ordering him out of the state, Esteva decided to leave quietly, and wrote an exculpatory pamphlet from Perote.[25]

As an epilogue to the matter, in July the Yorkino Rincón sent his troops to smash the presses of the *Veracruzano Libre,* a newspaper backed by former royalist Colonel Pedro Landero and edited by Aviraneta. Barragán then appointed Santa Anna as Rincón's replacement, but Rincón joined his troops and refused to obey orders, and it required a trip by Vicente Guerrero to bring him to obedience. When Guerrero returned to Mexico City—after arresting Santa Anna's brother Manuel for sedition—he left a state still at odds politically with the rest of the nation.[26]

Early in 1827 Congress began considering anti-Spanish legislation, leisurely at first and then with greater concern as news came in from the states of violent acts against Spaniards. A full-scale publicity battle was soon joined. Defending Spaniards was *El Sol,* joined in June by *El Observador,* edited by José María Luis Mora and supported by the Fagoaga family. Leading the attack against the Spaniards was *El Correo de la Federación Mexicana,* generally supported by *El Amigo del Pueblo,* edited by Tornel. The *Águila Mexicana* claimed neutrality. Those arguing for toleration frequently had to work obliquely, since it was becoming not quite safe to side publicy with Spaniards.

The first step was to remove Spaniards from the public employ. This had been proposed off and on since 1824,[27] a general covetousness for their jobs *(empleomanía)* adding to the impetus. Many Spaniards had already been discharged, and in February 1827 Congress began serious discussion of a bill to purge the remainder from the federal bureaucracy, army, and regular clergy—until Spain recognized Mexico's independence. With urgings from state officials, the bill was passed and signed by the president on May 10.[28]

The law was costly—those ejected would continue to receive a part of their salary—and it was not enough. Several states had preceded Congress in removing Spanish civil servants, and even while Congress debated employment, the states began discussing the next step—expulsion. Jalisco, the most strident center of anti-Spanish feeling, took the lead. As early as April, the Jalisco legislature asked the Chamber of Deputies to drive the Spanish from Mexico, and on September 3, 1827, became the first legislature to expel Spaniards from the state. In Guadalajara the populace greeted the news with fireworks and processions. Elsewhere the Jalisco legislation was taken as a model, and within four months every single state had excluded Spaniards from its territory.[29]

The state laws bore down on the type of Spaniards heretofore considered worthy of citizenship: for example, the *capitulados,* and even those marrying and raising families in Mexico (except in three states). The Spanish clergy was reached, by provisions in nine states, that excluded unmarried Spaniards. San Luis Potosí, in an outburst of xenophobia, would decree on February 14, 1828, that Spaniards leaving the state could not take their wives and children with them—a law declared by the Senate unconstitutional.[30] Toward the end of 1827, the Spaniards had no place to go but the Federal District.

Through the summer and fall of 1827, pressure for national legislation was building. From August to December there were provocations in the central states, generally in the form of armed petitions attended by violence against individual Spaniards. Some amounted to large-scale rebellions. The most serious took place on the Pacific coast and in Morelia. In August and September, Lieutenant José María Gallardo roamed through the environs of Acapulco with some two hundred followers, militiamen and civilians, sacking haciendas and killing Spaniards. In October and November first adjutant Ignacio Vásquez laid siege to Morelia with about 700 men.[31]

Neither the War Ministry nor the local commanders were disposed to intervene. Guadalupe Victoria had promised to deal severely with lawbreakers, but in view of the generalized loathing for peninsulars he knew that the army could not be relied upon. Minister of War Gómez Pedraza, fearing that sending army units in pursuit might lead to civil war, limited himself to letters trying to persuade dissidents to lay down their arms. In fact, the government and local commanders virtually had to promise an expulsion law in order to calm the situation.[32]

In the face of such unmistakable signals, the Chamber of Deputies began work on an expulsion bill in late November, which was approved and promulgated as law on December 20. In its final form the national law said that all Spaniards, singling out the surrendered soldiers and regular clergy, would have to leave Mexico within six months. The main exceptions were those with Mexican wives or children, those over sixty years of age, and those with physical impediments. The government could exempt those peninsulars who had lent outstanding service to the Mexican nation. Curiously, expelled public employees would continue to receive their salaries.[33]

The December 20, 1827, law left it to the states to locate and ship out the affected individuals, and thus enforcement turned on governors' attitudes. Federal District Governor Tornel deported large numbers of Spaniards, while nearby in the state of Mexico Lorenzo de Zavala (who had generally not favored the expulsion) gave wholesale exceptions. Veracruz

Spaniards were fortunate also, since Governor Santa Anna, who replaced Barragán in January 1828 and who had Spanish friends and relations, was generous in granting exceptions. In Guanajuato only one Spaniard was recorded expelled, and Zacatecas expelled only 3 percent of its Spanish population. Strangely, Jalisco, the site of the most intense anti-Spanish feeling, expelled very few.[34]

Many "old Spaniards" did not wait, but made ready to move while the legislation was still being debated. Many exiles went to New Orleans, at least as their first stop, and then some possibly on to Philadelphia or Havana. The wealthier ones went to Bordeaux, along with their retinues. Some never made it. In April 1828, pirates of the *Pájaro Verde* murdered twenty-five exiles, their wives, and their children.[35]

The main types affected by the expulsion were the merchants, regular clergy, and rural landowners. British Consul General Charles T. O'Gorman stated in January 1828 that the Spanish expulsion had "completely paralyzed all commerce and caused unexampled scarcity of Specie."[36] Pakenham spoke of a "revolution" in Mexican commerce.[37] The number of regular clergy, which before expulsion was 21.8 percent Spanish, declined from 1826 to 1828 by 325 individuals, at least half of the loss deriving from the 1827 legislation. The northern missions received yet another blow as missionary colleges *(colegios apostólicos)* lost 83 Spaniards. In education the effect was less clear, but the elementary schools seem to have lost many teachers. In the army most Spaniards had already been weeded out, but the navy had relied more heavily on Spanish officers.[38]

The expulsion looked different to various people at the time. To Spaniards the December 20 law was final proof, if they needed any, that the colonials had degenerated into savagery. Poinsett, on the other hand, whose Yorkino friends were leading the persecution, wrote that the disruptions were overstated and temporary.[39] Mexican masses had originally greeted the law as a day of liberation, but as time wore on they wondered if the law was being evaded. In terms of persons immediately affected, the impact was less than anticipated. Minister of Relations Cañedo reported to Congress in January 1829 that 772 Spaniards had been expelled in 1828, but Harold Sims, working from the seventy-one volumes of the Ramo de Expulsión in Mexico's National Archives (including reports not available to Cañedo), came up with a total of 2,293, and more Spaniards left in early 1829 when a second expulsion law was in the making. This was out of 6,000–7,000 resident Spaniards in 1827.[40] In terms of the whole anti-Spanish trend of the 1820s, the cumulative effects were considerable.

It was a time when even experienced leaders could not control events. State of Mexico Governor Zavala had never cultivated moderation, but he was busy with a multitude of new projects in his state—construction of highways and canals, a state mint, cigar and cigarette factories, conversion of the seminary into an educational "institute"[41]—and by most accounts

Zavala did not join in the crusade against the Spaniards. In October he tried to persuade Guerrero to dissociate himself from the anti-Spanish forces, in the knowledge that as a future president he should act like a statesman.[42] Alamán's letters give a glimpse of how it looked from the other side. He thought the government had fallen into the hands of a "Jacobin force" and that society's underside, overcome with a "spirit of rapacity," was marshaling forces for an assault on property. The fall elections meant "affliction for . . . lovers of tranquility and order," and the Chamber of Deputies only ratified what the Yorkino lodges had previously agreed upon.[43]

As 1827 drew on, panic began to take hold of the Escoceses. They watched as the Yorkinos used their new offices to persecute Spaniards and execute General Arana on the barest of evidence, and felt it might be only a matter of time until their turn came. Nicolás Bravo, vice-president and Escocés Grand Master, had not quarreled publicly with the president, but he had asked him to change his cabinet. Bustamante wrote their falling out had dated from 1826 when Bravo showed Guadalupe Victoria a friend's letter critical of the administration.[44] In the fall of 1827 Bravo began to send out letters and hold meetings with supporters, the result of which was agreement that the only solution was armed revolt.[45]

The site chosen for the rebellion was the Tulancingo area, in northeast Mexico state, where Bravo had friends from his 1821 campaigns under Iturbide, and close enough for help to come from Veracruz. This, the second armed revolt against the Republic (Lobato's being the first), was relatively unviolent in its inception and conclusion. It began, not with any great civil disturbances, but with a Plan of Montaño dated from Otumba that circulated in the capital about December 26. It carried the signature of a thirty-one-year-old hacienda manager, Lieutenant Colonel Manuel Montaño who, although he had talked with Bravo, did not even see the Plan before copies had been passed around in Mexico City.[46] The Plan called upon the administration to hand Poinsett his passport within a month, change the cabinet (meaning Gómez Pedraza, primarily, since Esteva was temporarily out of the ministry), and submit legislation to outlaw secret societies.[47]

Bravo joined the rebels belatedly, riding out of Mexico City on New Year's Eve. In his proclamation of January 2, after blasts at the Yorkinos and Poinsett ("who has no god or country"), he predicted the government would defeat the rebels.[48] He had read the situation right. At 4 A.M. on January 7 Governor Barragán wrung from the Veracruz legislature a vote for the Montaño revolution, as the movement came to be called. A few military men declared for it, including Manuel López de Santa Anna, but his more famous brother Antonio rode as far as Huamantla to reconnoiter and, as Colonel Antonio Facio wrote of it, took note of Bravo's military disadvantage and immediately offered his services to the government.[49] No one else answered the call.

Bravo decided to make a stand at Tulancingo, but found only about 600 "armed men" there, while Guerrero was approaching with 2,000.[50] The revolt ended with only one recorded casualty, and with charges of treachery. The issue turned on a letter Guerrero wrote at 7 P.M. on January 6, giving Bravo an eight-hour truce to consider surrender. In Bravo's version, the envelope bore a notation that the letter was being sent at 7 A.M. (January 7). In any case, at about 9 A.M. on January 7 Guerrero's forces entered Tulancingo and captured the unresisting rebel soldiers, who had been ordered not to open fire during the truce.[51] Within days the few other Montaño rebels were rounded up.[52] The rebellion had lasted only two weeks.

When the news of Guerrero's victory arrived in the capital, the Yorkinos gathered at La Sociedad Inn to celebrate. They adjourned to the street for a parade in which the *léperos* joined, all culminating at the plaza outside the national palace where the demonstrators chanted demands that Bravo be decapitated. Some of Bravo's friends called for an amnesty, but Guadalupe Victoria said he would veto it, and a law of April 15 prescribed a six-year exile at half pay for Bravo and the other leaders.[53] On April 20 Bravo and Barragán were sent off in coaches toward the Pacific coast with six months' pay in advance.[54] A pamphlet by Bravo, defending his actions, was dated the same day, wherein expectedly he laid the blame on the Yorkinos and Poinsett, whose chicanery was nodded at by the president.[55] On June 12 a ship carrying Bravo and sixteen other Montañistas left San Blas for South America.[56] Ironically, Bravo's exile would be cut short after a year by a pardon from the man who defeated him at Tulancingo.

In 1827 Mexico's political institutions were young and fragile. The anti-Spanish movement—the virulence of the emotions involved and the categorical demands for action—proved to be too violent a test. The Montaño revolution led by the vice-president against his own government then gave official sanction to the end of working republicanism. From this point on, both sides were ready to abandon the political forum and appeal to arms to defend their positions.

PUBLIC BANKRUPTCY AND THE 1828 ELECTION

While the rule of the law was breaking down during the popular violence against Spaniards, the public revenues of the national government were approaching collapse. The two maladies fed on each other. From 1827 on the government's insolvency was depressing virtually every public activity and was itself compounded by the violent turns politics was taking. The approach to government revenues generally followed the same curve as politics: it began with a passion for republican forms in 1823, forms that were distorted by age-old habits for the next three years, and then in 1827 the new apparatus succumbed to a general breakdown.

The story of government finances can be extracted by those with the fortitude to pore over the reams of published figures, comments on the figures, and comments on the comments. Here it will be sketched in outline only. With independence, a complex system in which governmental funds came from a great diversity of sources—such as royal monopolies (for example, tobacco, playing cards, quicksilver), a head tax (Indian tribute), taxes on internal and overseas commerce, and on metals production, and activities like the post and the lottery—shifted to a system dependent more than anything else on import duties.[57] A decree of August 4, 1824, apportioned the specific revenues between the national and state governments, reserving for the former the export and import duties, properties previously confiscated from the church *(bienes nacionales),* the tobacco and salt monopolies, the national lottery, and the post. The states were left with the others.[58]

Federation Finances

In the flush years before the Hidalgo Revolution, revenues had brought in 18–20 million pesos yearly for the royal coffers, but when Iturbide left in 1823, government finances were at rock bottom: the petty cash boxes were virtually empty, and less than half of the bills were being paid.[59] So disordered were the account books—or nonexistent—it was sometimes necessary to use Humboldt's works for reference. Total collapse was avoided only by the strictest economies and desperate expedients, among them sweeping up the shavings from the mint floor. Moreover, in a move aimed at establishing respectability and at reimbursing Mexicans for forced loans made during the Revolution, Congress accepted responsibility for both the viceregal debt and debts incurred by insurgents—estimated variously at between 44 million and 76 million pesos.[60]

When looking about for financial alternatives, the new public men were ill-disposed toward many royalist revenues that were either regressive or reminiscent of an era of privilege and mercantilism: the sales tax *(alcabala)* and the monopolies of tobacco, salt, and gunpowder. They looked hopefully toward a streamlined system that would replace the antique complexity of Spain's workings with such republican imposts as a direct tax on income.

The income tax, however, failed to produce. When decreed on June 27, 1823, it was hailed as a progressive measure, since all citizens would pay in proportion to their means—the equivalent of three days' pay. But it turned out to be uncollectable as administered by the *ayuntamientos,* less than 35,000 pesos accruing in thirteen months,[61] and the income tax was handed over to the states in 1824. Very soon financial exigency made some of the less palatable revenues inevitable, and by the mid 1820s the monopolies and the *alcabala* became a standard part of the federal budget. There were, however, operational breaks in the general regressiveness of the federal revenue structure, for in times of stress the government always called upon merchants and landowners for gifts or loans. The first loan from the church did not take place until 1832.

It presently became clear that the viceroys' great revenue producers would not carry the weight of government. The national administrations, whose annual expenses by the latter 1820s had stabilized temporarily at approximately 13–14 million pesos,[62] came to depend on three sources of revenue: (a) the states' contingent tax (approximately 1–1.5 million pesos annually); (b) the Federal District customs house, which collected the *alcabala* tax on arriving items of commerce (producing almost a million pesos annually after the national government took it over); and (c) the maritime customs houses (which produced, in normal years, between 6.5 and 8 million pesos a year).[63]

One of the great disappointments was the tobacco monopoly, which was adopted, with distaste, only because of the memories of the 4 million pesos yearly it earned in the 1790s. As the Spaniards had organized it, only the Veracruz farmers around Córdoba and Orizaba could legally grow tobacco and then sell it to the government cigar and cigarette factories, from which it went to government retail stores *(expendios)*. Now the Federation was to purchase tobacco leaf at 3 reales per pound and then sell tobacco to the states either as leaf, at 8 reales per pound, or as cigars and cigarettes.[64] States were to make their profit by setting up their own cigar and cigarette factories, a box containing 12 to 25 cigarettes selling for a half a real.[65] Since the revolutionary disturbances, however, the illegal growers had taken over the market and the Federation found itself with warehouses full of moldering, unsaleable, tobacco, valued at 4.2 million pesos in 1827, and at 8–10 million pesos two years later.[66] On May 23, 1829, Congress finally abolished the monopoly altogether (the abolition to take effect in 1831).[67]

Another source of revenue, of sorts, was the foreign loan. Since the moment of independence, Mexican officials sought to borrow funds from the British.[68] The additional expectation was that a financial commitment would bind that country to the cause of Mexican independence, a crucial factor in 1823–1824 when the Holy Alliance loomed as a menace.

Mexico finally concluded a total of four loans with British banking houses. The two largest were negotiated by Francisco de Borja Migoni, Mexico's agent in London. In February 1824 he concluded a loan with the house of Goldschmidt and Company for 16 million pesos (at 5 percent interest), and another 16 million pesos agreement (at 6 percent interest) was made with Barclay, Herring, Richardson, and Company in August 1824.[69]

The transaction brought momentary relief. Bu the experience was unedifying and ultimately ruinous for all concerned, except Borja Migoni, who arranged with Goldschmidt for special rebates for his associates. Even among the more scrupulous Mexicans, the ready money induced giddiness. Minister Plenipotentiary Michelena was persuaded to advance 10,000 pesos to Thomas Johnson, a follower of Robert Fulton, for an undersea ship that could send new mobile bombs called torpedoes, and the quality of Michelena's military purchases haunted him for years. Later, Secretary of the Mexican Legation Vincente Rocafuerte lent 63,000 pounds sterling on his own authority to the agents of Gran Colombia.[70]

Mexico, meanwhile, paid dearly for the use of the borrowed money. After deductions for sales commissions, initial interest, and amortization (Barclay kept the first two years' payments), Mexico received as disposable income from the Goldschmidt loan only about 6 million pesos, and from the Barclay loan (after diverting several million pesos to pay off earlier loans and obligations), only about 5 million pesos. As of January 1826, Treasury Minister Esteva reported only 2,757,806 pesos were left, while Mexico's debt was 28,437,000 pesos.[71]

British investors competed for the Mexican bonds in early 1825, but by spring of the next year the market had collapsed. Goldschmidt and Company went bankrupt in February 1826 and Barclay failed in August, both carrying down Mexican funds they were holding.[72] By October Minister Ward was writing the Foreign Office of the inadvisability of advancing any more money to Mexico.[73] With the political upheavals of 1827 Esteva found it more and more difficult to keep up the dividend shipments, until finally, in spite of last-minute exertions,[74] the British frigate supposed to carry the October 1827 dividend arrived in England empty. Mexico's credit had come to an end.

In plotting the course of Federation finances in the 1820s one can see a turning point in 1827. It is prudent not to place all one's trust in the Treasury's published accounts, since the totals may not take into account—it is sometimes difficult to say—temporary windfalls such as proceeds from loans, paper assets such as worthless tobacco or uncollectable debts, or current obligations that were simply not paid for the moment. But the *Memorias,* examined together with a number of ancillary documents, make it clear that the Federation's financial health followed an upward path from 1823 to 1827. From 5,409,722 pesos in calendar year 1823, net revenues (excluding loans) rose to a peak of 13,164,644 pesos in the economic year 1825–1826 (July 1 to June 30), and 14,192,132 pesos for the following year.[75] In early 1827 Esteva could speak with pride of the progress during his three-year tenure.[76]

It was his last moment of confidence. By 1829, the customs house income was down by half,[77] and even this was mortgaged. There was hardly any way to significantly reduce expenses, since the War Department was consuming approximately 10 million pesos annually (about 75 percent of the budget in most years),[78] which the continuing state of war with Spain made an inalterable fixture in the budget. Finance ministers from 1828 on had no choice but to resort ever more fequently to loans and "gifts," requested plaintively or imperiously as the circumstances warranted. British Consul General O'Gorman reported in January 1828 the Treasury had been borrowing 20,000 to 30,000 pesos a month to pay the troops and essential civil servants.[79] The practice created a class of traffickers in government notes, called *agiotistas,* who could command highly advantageous terms. A British merchant at Veracruz lent 50,000 pesos in return for a 120,000-peso claim on the customs house.[80] By April 1829 a list that Secretary of Treasury Zavala had printed showed a total of 3,797,065 pesos borrowed in the last twelve months, from both foreign and native lenders.[81]

State and Municipal Finances

Among the state governments, the basic problem derived from the fact that the law of August 4, 1824, which divided revenues between the Federation and state governments, gave the former what were considered the more reliable sources. The states were left with the sales tax (*alcabala*), the retail tobacco trade, some mining taxes, the government's portion of ecclesiastical levies, and the right to impose a 3 percent tax on foreign merchandise consumed within the state.[82]

After a settling-in period of about two years, however, the states' revenues went up, even during the unstable year of 1829. Some states were actually able to make a success out of the "personal contribution" or income tax, especially in areas with heavy Indian populations such as Chiapas, Oaxaca, Tabasco, Yucatán, and parts of Puebla, where it must have struck the payers as the same old Indian tribute (or head tax) under a new name.[83] Elsewhere, though, people evaded the tax. All Mexico could collect in fiscal year 1827–1828 was 5,034 pesos, hardly worth the trouble.[84] In Michoacán the *ayuntamientos* tried lowering the assessments, but this did not save the experiment.[85] By the late 1820s state officials were giving it up as a lost cause.[86] Another attempt at progressive taxation was a land tax in Guanajuato, applicable to rural property, but it too was virtually uncollectable.[87] After the failure of the direct tax experiments, several states fell back on the *alcabala,* unrepublican perhaps, but possessing the virtue of being relatively easy to collect at the city gates. The states often farmed out the tax to collection companies. Most states had various types of *alcabalas,* generally at the 8 to 10 percent level, but ranging from 3 percent on foreign goods to 20 percent on luxury items such as brandy.

In general, state revenue dependence was governed by regional considerations. The Indian areas drew in considerable money from the income tax, and mining areas from metals production. Regions distant from Veracruz—distant enough to make smuggling difficult—found tobacco profitable. What had been the king's portion of the tithe—and salaries of vacant prelacies—provided one-third to one-half of some state budgets.

The unbalancing factor in state budgets was the *contingente,* or contingency tax. This fiscal innovation was an annual sum to be paid to the national government, originally figured, when the amounts were decreed in 1824, on 30 percent of a state's supposed revenue. In actuality it frequently amounted to 40 percent or 50 percent. States fell behind in payments, and the contingency debts reached astronomical heights—as of December 1830, Jalisco owed the national government more than a million pesos.[88]

In the case of municipal governments, they were one step further down the line. As the Federation had preempted most of the lucrative revenues, the states had taken the next best. The cities and towns were left with their traditional resources, what were known as *propios y arbitrios.* The *propios* were the income from the original communal properties, such as commons, springs, and grazing lands *(ejidos).* Through the years, local officials had laid claim to other revenues, the *arbitrios:* public flour mills, license fees (for quasi-public activities such as slaughtering of livestock and the checking of weights and measures), local fines, and in a few cases the direct tax. Budgets varied enormously, even those of state capitals. In 1827 Monterrey spent 250 pesos, and Puebla 30,000 pesos.[89] Overall, the money available was hardly ever sufficient, even for minimal needs.

The failures of government finance contributed in large measure to the decline in public optimism and the slowing of the Republic's momentum. Lack of government money caused the derailment of all sorts of public and semipublic projects. Yet even this situation was being brought into the routine. A document exists in the Santa Inés convent indicating that the national government had already established the policy that civil and military servants did not have to pay their rents to the church if they themselves had not been paid.[90]

GUERRERO'S ROAD TO THE PRESIDENCY

The financial downturn in 1827 had further limited the Guadalupe Victoria government, but his administration had long since lost its authority to manage the Republic. The apparent beneficiary of the past year's developments was Vicente Guerrero, the logical heir to Victoria as president of Mexico. In early 1828 he was at the height of his popularity, fresh from his victory at Tulancingo. When the brig *Guerrero* was sunk by the Spaniards in February, it became a gesture of patriotic faith for Mexicans of all classes to contribute for the construction of a second *Guerrero.*

For the office of vice-president, Zavala and Esteva had been mentioned, but they were too controversial and as a compromise the Yorkinos finally decided to support Anastacio Bustamante.[91] The Guerrero for President campaign began officially with a salute to his birthday (April 4) by the editors of the *Correo de la Federación Mexicana.* The article ended with: "Heaven conserve him until he can occupy the presidential chair."[92]

To arrive at this point, Vicente Guerrero (1782–1831) had traveled a long way, his life demonstrating the possibilities and the limits of revolutionary mobility. He was born in Tixtla (now state of Guerrero) of a "poor farm couple of mixed Spanish, Indian, and probably, Negro ancestry." He apparently had little or no exposure to education. As a young man he could do little more than write his name, and to the end of his life he spoke an Indian tongue better than Spanish. But he possessed a robust constitution and astuteness of judgment, which served him well when he left his occupation of muleteer to join the revolutionaries under Morelos. He never compromised, and was still fighting when most of his comrades-at-arms were either dead or amnestied. His survival in so many battles—499 by his own count—left him physically scarred and fatalistic.[93]

Guerrero came out of the southern mountains a national hero, but the role of statesman-general never quite seemed to fit. In a shifting political world the sure touch of his instincts was insufficient. At times he seemed adrift. He adhered to Iturbide long after other insurgents had become disenchanted, and then stayed somewhat aloof from partisan politics until 1826. He became diffident toward those who had a claim to superior breeding such as Zavala and Poinsett, who exercised a profound influence on him. His prodigious strength could no longer be relied on. A shot had torn into his lungs at Almolonga in 1823 while he was fighting against Iturbide, and now he frequently took leave to visit the Cuernavaca baths. After those years of deprivation he moved into a fine townhouse, made repeated application to the government for financial assistance, indulged himself with costly trinkets—a gold ring, and a golden harp for his daughter—and sought the security and status of landowning.

To the extent that he could, Guerrero kept in touch with his old world. On his daily outings down the Canal de la Viga, he liked to stop and pass a few minutes with the "natives." Forming a sort of retinue, the poor clung to him, a practice he seemed to encourage. His dark, penetrating, eyes, and rugged configuration might have suggested fierceness, but more than one acquaintance noted that his countenance was suffused with expressions of gentleness.[94] It spoke to the nobility of his soul that he was never swept away by the spirit of vengeance now in the political air. While his social betters like Alamán and Zavala unquestioningly used their offices to punish opponents, Guerrero, overwhelmed by political upheavals he scarcely understood, forgave his enemies. Some things in a man were not to be accounted for by upbringing and surroundings.

For the first few months of 1828, Guerrero could have expected to win the presidency unopposed, but there were those of his own group who were having second thoughts. A fissure in the Yorkino front had appeared as far back as mid-1827 when an occasional article appeared in the *Águila Mexicana,* heretofore a reliable enemy of the Escoceses, criticizing excesses of both parties, and then in early 1828 the *Águila* editors announced they

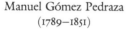

Manuel Gómez Pedraza
(1789–1851)

Antonio López de Santa Anna
(1795–1876)

would henceforth speak for the "impartials." By the beginning of June it was clear the defection of the impartials had evolved into a campaign to halt Guerrero's march to the presidency, and that their candidate would be Manuel Gómez Pedraza.

Minister of War and Marine Gómez Pedraza was the first presidential candidate who was not a war hero. There is disagreement about his place of birth, which his service records fail to clarify. He was born in 1789, in Querétaro or Sota la Marina, of a family of some means. After a youth spent in the pastimes of riding horses up the mountains and racing over the aqueducts, he entered the militia and spent the Revolution fighting against the insurgents. He was elected to the Cortes for 1821–1822, returned to take a command under Iturbide, and then in 1824 became commander of Puebla. From there he moved, after being exonerated of the charge that he had provided inadequate military escort to foreigners who were subsequently assaulted, to the War Ministry. In this office he was considered industrious and self-contained, an energetic administrator and believer in the value of discipline. He was fickle in his politics, however. At the Cortes he had been eager for a Bourbonist prince, but from at least 1824 was siding against the Bourbonists and Escoceses, and now in 1828 he left the Yorkinos.[95]

Alamán pictured the Gómez Pedraza supporters as the former Iturbidists who had turned Yorkino, the "most distinguished" Yorkinos, and the Escocés remnants; and the Guerrero supporters as the old insurgents and the "abject" Yorkists.[96] Taking into account the Alamán idiom, where "abject" was a synonym for "radical," the portrayal is apt. These former were individuals of a progressive bent but who nevertheless were frightened by their first exposure to what the masses had done in the political arena in 1827. Disturbed by the idea of having as president a man of the people like Guerrero, the impartials looked about for an alternative and settled upon Gómez Pedraza as the lesser of the evils. The impartials had a strong base of support in Zacatecas, whose legislature had reportedly sent 20,000 pesos to then Senator Francisco García for use by the *Águila Mexicana*.[97]

The principal organizer behind Gómez Pedraza was the minister of justice and ecclesiastical relations, Ramos Arizpe. He wrote many of the *Águila Mexicana* editorials, and in order to give full time to the campaign resigned from the cabinet on March 7 (to be replaced by Espinosa de los Monteros). Gómez Pedraza was also supported by the other secretaries, by Juan de Dios Cañedo (who had replaced Camacho as secretary of relations, also on March 7), and by Esteva—who had been out of the cabinet for most of 1827, filled in for by Francisco García of Zacatecas, the well-known lawyer Tomás Salgado, and chief deputy José María Pavón.[98] Guadalupe Victoria also gave the appearance of supporting Gómez Pedraza, who by late August could speak confidently of victory.[99]

Although Guerrero saw his position of preeminence evaporate, he could still count on the support of the governors of about half the states, plus Federal District Governor Tornel.[100] Foremost among the Guerrero supporters were Zavala, who in addition to his duties as Mexico state governor directed the publicity campaign through the *Correo de la Federación Mexicana*, and Santa Anna, acting governor of Veracruz.

Santa Anna's public record gave no clue that he would become Guerrero's most fervent supporter in 1828, but his political turns had always been unpredictable. By training and taste Santa Anna (1795–1876) was an army man. His service records indicated he was born in Jalapa and that he entered the military as a cadet in 1810.[101] During the Revolution he served the royalists in various theaters, becoming a colonel in 1821, and then a brigadier general in 1822. It was the military that gave him his basic fund of knowledge and values. Combined with a personality that favored undertakings conducive to personal glory, his early training did not prepare him for a consistent role in ideological battles. Although the Mexican Army at the time was a serviceable vehicle for political ambitions, Santa Anna's pronouncements and actions of the 1820s had been so poorly chosen that he frequently found himself in indefensible situations. He achieved nationwide recognition in December 1822 by defying Iturbide, but was then rescued only when a Masonic plot led to the defection of the army besieging his men at Veracruz. His initiatives in San Luis Potosí, 1823, in Yucatán, 1824–1825, and his vacillation at Tulancingo, 1828, brought further embarrassments.

Thus Santa Anna figured prominently in many of the principal episodes, but in an erratic, impetuous manner—on the side of the federalists in 1823 and as a fellow traveler of the Veracruz Excoceses from 1825 to 1828. The setbacks had not diminished his ambitions, however, nor had they detracted from his ability to recruit a respectable army of admirers in Veracruz. He was a formidable opponent in the field, resourceful and almost impossible to bring to bay. Physically he was an attractive personage, described as somewhat tall, with dark expressive eyes, and a slender but resilient body capable of withstanding the hardships of a campaign.[102]

Santa Anna's attachment to Guerrero, however, came as a surprise since they had had a very unpleasant, and public, exchange of recriminations in 1827 after Guerrero had imprisoned his brother in Veracruz.[103] But then Santa Anna reportedly carried a special dislike for Gómez Pedraza because of a remark made by the minister of war in 1825 when Santa Anna was in Yucatán planning an assault on Cuba. As the story went, Gómez Pedraza had spoken in favor of the adventure since if successful it would be a great achievement, and if not, Mexico might rid itself of an undesirable pest, namely, Santa Anna.[104]

In June the presidential campaign began in earnest. Compared to the 1824 presidential contest, when partisanship was muted, the summer months of 1828 witnessed a campaign unparalleled in viciousness. Debates about centralism versus federalism, or for that matter any discussion of issues, were hardly to be heard now. The two protagonists generally refrained from self-promotion, but the battle went on in the newspapers and pamphlets. The *Águila Mexicana* and *El Sol* announced formally for Gómez Pedraza on August 1 and August 4, respectively, although they had supported him indirectly earlier. Jointly they made light of Guerrero's independence exploits and his reputed 499 battles, pointed to his dissolute habits (especially gambling and philandering), and claimed that a vote for him was a vote for Poinsett.[105] For intemperate slander, however, the *Correo de la Federación Mexicana* had no equal. By August, almost every column inch of its four pages was filled with defamatory editorials, articles, and letters. It pictured Gómez Pedraza as essentially an unrepentant royalist with no fixed loyalties. Friends of the two candidates were given similar attentions.

Two pivotal states where feelings ran especially high were Veracruz and Mexico. In each the governors—Santa Anna and Zavala—were zealous Guerrero supporters, but the legislatures would do the voting, which in the former case was decidedly anti-Guerrero, and in the latter was roughly evenly divided. Santa Anna on more than one occasion advised the legislature that to ignore the people's obvious preference for Guerrero would be to invite a revolution, which he would be obliged to support.[106] In the state of Mexico's capital Tlalpam, a pro-Guerrero mob paraded through the streets on the night of August 23. Zavala kept the crowd under control, but state legislators requested troops to keep the peace, and the Ministry of War acceded. After Zavala vehemently protested their presence, President Victoria ordered them pulled back to Coyoacán.[107]

On September 1 the legislatures voted. By September 18 it was clear that Gómez Pedraza was the winner.[108] In the final counting, he won eleven states, most in the central and north-central region, and Guerrero nine states.[109]

An appeal to arms had been predicted, and even before the election results became known Santa Anna had taken over the castle of Perote in the name of Guerrero. In the city of Veracruz the legislature voted for Gómez Pedraza. Santa Anna sided with the pro-Guerrero Jalapa *ayuntamiento* which voted not to recognize the legislature, and the legislature then removed Santa Anna as governor.[110] A week later he gathered 800 men and marched to Perote Castle, a fortress in the western foothills of the Sierra Madre Oriental, the mountain range separating Puebla and the coast. There he issued a declaration that Gómez Pedraza's election be annulled, for good measure adding an article calling for another Spanish expulsion.[111]

Santa Anna looked like a doomed man. The great outpouring of support he might have expected never came, and although some of Guerrero's old comrades on the Pacific coast—Juan Álvarez, Isidro Montes de Ocá, and Gordiano Bruno—called out their men, virtually all the commanding generals expressed adhesion to the government. Even the *Correo de la Federación Mexicana* editors reproved him, and Guerrero himself remained silent. Congress on September 17 proscribed Santa Anna.[112]

The government's lethargy saved him. Manuel Rincón, known for his "general apathy," commanded a porous siege that allowed Santa Anna to sneak out at night on amorous adventures. Neither could a second army under General José María Calderón force the issue. On the night of October 19 Santa Anna and 626 men evacuated the fortress and, with government troops giving chase, marched to Oaxaca, living off the land by imposing forced loans. In Oaxaca the rebels took over the Santo Domingo monastery and a second siege followed, again with burlesque relief: nightly excursions to pilfer foodstuffs, and Santa Anna reconnoitering enemy positions in feminine dress. One night the rebels stole into a chapel, clothed themselves in the shrouds reserved for the dead, had the call for mass issued and then imposed a loan on the faithful. Still, the encirclement was wearing down the rebels, now numbering only about 250, and an increasingly despondent Santa Anna was trying to negotiate a face-saving surrender when news from the capital changed everything.[113]

The Senate had been moving judicially against Guerrero's other principal supporters. Tornel, Federal District governor, was indicted by the Senate on September 13 for refusing to incarcerate the famous Yorkino street leader Severiano Quesada.[114] When the Senate cited Zavala to testify about his complicity with Santa Anna (October 5), he escaped to the hills of Mexico state.[115] In another move clearly aimed at Guerrero's Yorkino supporters, Congress passed a law on October 25 outlawing secret societies.[116]

Zavala made his way back to Mexico City and spent the month of November secreted in the house of a friend while rumors of revolution spread. On Sunday night (November 30), Gómez Pedraza and President Victoria were debating just this possibility when the report of a cannon settled the issue.[117] It came from the Acordada, an old prison converted to an armory which, Gómez Pedraza and Victoria soon learned, had been taken over by troops sympathizing with Guerrero. For now they were only demanding a law to expel the Spaniards. Within a day Zavala and General Lobato arrived to direct operations, and there followed three days of inconclusive battles and an intermittent artillery duel between the national palace and the Ciudadela, an arsenal occupied by the rebels. On either Tuesday or Wednesday—the sources disagree—Guererro finally joined the revolutionaries.[118]

Guadalupe Victoria, caught with few troops at his disposal, seemed to have lost his nerve. While at one point he told congressmen he would confront Guerrero or Lobato and match swords gladiatorially, at another he reportedly left the palace in disguise to negotiate with Lobato.[119] Gómez Pedraza finally came to the conclusion his cause was lost, and on Wednesday evening strolled out of the palace, walked north as far as the Basilica of Guadalupe, spent the night under a tree, and then borrowed a horse from a friend and took the road for Guadalajara. At the end of December he resigned as president-elect, and on March 2 boarded ship for England.[120]

On Thursday morning (December 4), the word was out that Gómez Pedraza had fled, and palace sentries received orders not to fire on the advancing rebels.[121] Lobato's men had their sights set on the Parián, the complex of shops in the central plaza. Since these were Spanish-owned in the public mind, the contents were considered legitimate spoils of war, although most owners were in reality Mexican. As government officials fled the palace by way of the stables, the mob forced the Parián's doors and began "carrying off the plunder of the inhabitants; . . . the Léperos were stabbing each other in the strife over a piece of linen, a bag of money or a glass."[122]

The pillage went on through the night, reaching stores outside the Parián and even some palace storerooms. Valued at 2 to 3 million pesos,[123] the stolen goods found their way to the Santo Domingo Plaza where the buying and selling went on for several weeks despite an excommunication threat for traffickers in the booty.

As a sequel to the Parián frenzy, those formerly persecuted were now the persecutors. By several accounts, Zavala went berserk temporarily. Colonel Manuel González, a Yorkino who had defected to the other side, was interrogated by Zavala and subsequently executed. Late one night

Zavala and some friends went to the home of Juan Guzmán, the judge who had earlier tried to sequester Zavala's property, with the result that Guzmán was shot in the hand. Although Zavala denied direct responsibility, his vindictiveness was so notorious that Santa Anna wrote from Oaxaca trying to calm him.[124] Certain officials and army officers went into hiding, and *El Sol* was not published for seven months. The *Águila Mexicana* ceased publication forever on December 1.

Slowly order was restored in the capital. Victoria was assured of his position, while reaction in the states pointed up the minority status of the revolution. Officials in Veracruz, Puebla, Querétaro, Jalisco, Zacatecas, and San Luis Potosí—all of which except the latter had voted for Gómez Pedraza—let it be known they were not prepared to accept the verdict of a barracks revolt. Zavala wrote of leading a second revolution. Puebla was considered the center of discontent, but a Christmas Eve coup there, reputedly spurred by the promise of dividing up a silver train, brought this state into line. Troops were dispatched, and in the next few weeks the resisting states decided to come to terms.[125]

At first glance it might have seemed that the events of 1828 constituted a victory for the Yorkinos and the masses. But in truth Guerrero owed the presidency to a mutiny and a failure of will on the part of Guadalupe Victoria. Even the traditional federalist states of Jalisco, Zacatecas, and San Luis Potosí did not come to his aid. Guerrero was to rule as president with only a thin layer of support.

In later years these political depredations would raise no eyebrows, being considered in the nature of things. But the Republic was still young enough now that they caused consternation. Alamán's letters of this period showed how the citizens of means viewed the disorder. In January he wrote to Monteleone to plan for a new administrator in case he should be a victim of the Yorkinos' blood lust.[126] The emigration of Spanish Mexicans "at an astonishing level," he noted, was causing a proportionate degree of misery, and the "country is consuming and ruining itself at full speed."[127] Alamán was called upon for a 900-peso-a-month "voluntary loan" after Perote, and then on December 4 came the greatest horror of all. For Alamán and his friends the looting of the Parián would remain the symbol of the mob, the natural outgrowth of a democracy unrestrained by the civilizing hand of society's men of substance.[128]

« 7 »

Zavala and the Populist Interlude
1829

Zavala, though a fugitive from the law, had in effect nullified the 1828 election and created the presidency of Vicente Guerrero. Was this a sign of anarchy? Or had the promise of the Revolution been realized by the success of a man of the people?

Guerrero was to enter office with serious handicaps, not the least of which was that the government had been virtually bankrupt for more than a year. And because of the patent illegality of his position he had lost the support of many of the traditional federalist leaders, notably of Zacatecas and Jalisco. He could thank Zavala, and to a lesser extent Santa Anna, for his victory, but he had no organized body of support to call upon.

The Mexican campesinos were finally ruled by one of their own, but could he govern?

THE ADMINISTRATION OF GUERRERO, 1829

On January 1, 1829, with the events of the previous month still fresh in everyone's mind, Congress convened. The Chamber of Deputies was newly elected. On the question of selecting a president there was nothing to do but ratify the revolution of the Acordada. Gómez Pedraza was gone from the scene, and Guadalupe Victoria's government did little to obstruct the victorious revolutionaries. Thus on January 12 the Chamber of Deputies officially designated Guerrero president and Anastacio Bustamante (the third highest vote-getter in the fall elections) vice-president.[1]

As the country awaited the new president's scheduled April 1 inauguration, Guadalupe Victoria's term, begun so gloriously four years earlier, creaked to an embarrassing end. His proposition—not to demean the presi-

162

Vicente Guerrero (1783–1831)　　　　Anastacio Bustamante (1780–1853)

dency by engaging in partisan politics—appeared noble and even workable in 1824, but in practice had turned into a posture of passiveness. Lacking a program of his own, he had let factions fight it out, had ended up a captive of the victor, and was held in contempt by both sides.

To clear the floor for the arriving administration, men with the acceptable political shading were appointed to the cabinet. On December 26 Esteban de Moctezuma took over as secretary of war from Guerrero. Esteva retired after delivering his last *Memoria* on the state of the Treasury, to be replaced by Bernardo González Ángulo on January 13. Cañedo, after criticism orchestrated by Zavala, resigned from Relations on January 25 in favor of José María Bocanegra.[2] Only Espinosa de los Monteros in Justice and Ecclesiastical Affairs stayed on.

Standing by was the president-elect. If a man's political intent could be divined from his tastes and friends, Mexicans could well expect a new day in government. Clearly he was not the likes of the customary rulers. Carlos María de Bustamante delighted in anecdotes about his uncultivated mannerisms: his inapt renderings of the Spanish language, *probe* for *pobre* (poor) and *estógamo* for *estómago* (stomach); and his sing-song, Indian-like delivery of block-written speeches. There remained doubt about his race. Bustamante said he was mulatto "on all four sides" despite his fluency in an

Indian tongue and the tale that he had descended from Nezahualcoyotl, King of Texcoco.[3] Whatever his bloodlines, his following among the poorer classes, especially the Indians, was legendary. He was a genuine folk hero. Perhaps the truest assessment came from his fellow Yorkino, Tornel, who saw him crippled, notwithstanding a "singular penetration," by his unlettered condition: "He had little confidence in his ability [*alcances*], he gave in to the slightest impulse, he lived tormented by a fear of doing ill when he tried to do good."[4]

On April 1 Guerrero took the oath of office, in the act becoming heir to immense problems. Not only was his government bankrupt; but also many future revenues had already been spent. The market economy had almost broken down under the dual strains of international competition and political violence. Political vistas were equally depressing. There was no active opposition for now, but Guerrero had earned the undying hatred of the privileged classes. His working-class constituency could support him in a civil war but not in Congress or the state legislatures. The army, for the moment, was quiescent, but a majority of the general officers were known to have sentiments contrary to him.

Guerrero gave a signal of the mood of his presidency at his forty-seventh birthday party held three days after the inauguration. In a gesture to "amalgamate" the classes, he invited people from all levels of society to his country house alongside the Viga Canal.[5] It was an amalgamation he would never have the opportunity to bring about. He would be forced to concentrate first on alleviating the government's poverty, then on repelling the Spanish invasion, and then on political survival. Although during his short stay as president he would impart a tone of populism through his utterances and demeanor, his philosophy would be seen only in the details of desperation measures.

Zavala became secretary of the treasury on April 18. He came to the cabinet in 1829 without resigning the governorship of Mexico state, having persuaded his allies in the legislature to grant him a leave of absence. He dominated his fellow cabinet members—José María Herrera became secretary of justice and ecclesiastical affairs on April 8, and Bocanegra and Moctezuma continued—and the president himself. Zavala was not sanguine about the administration's prospects, writing to Santa Anna on March 4:

> I do not see things as good, because there is neither enlightenment, nor customs, nor wealth, nor a propertied class, and all of the occupations that are habitually healthy have lost their prestige. . . . Our illustrious friend will enter the presidency full of those theories that agitate the heads of those who govern the planners. Guerrero has a well-tuned common sense and a marvelous instinct. This is not enough.[6]

Still, the president and minister of finance complemented each other, Zavala's philosophical radicalism giving shape and rationale to Guerrero's visceral impulses. In the persons of these two, the nativism and populism building since independence had gained access to power—fragile as it turned out to be.

Guerrero's other principal supporter, Santa Anna, was never persuaded to enter the government. Through the spring of 1829 Zavala sent a stream of letters to Santa Anna, who had returned to the Veracruz governorship on January 31, asking him to come to Mexico City as secretary of war. On June 2 his letter rose to eloquence: "Placed in the ministry of hacienda when the republic can not rely on either credit or resources, I placed all of my hopes on the inspirations of genius, which in time of great difficulty comes to the aid of men of resolution. But my tutelary angel has refused to inspire me and only talks of you."[7] The true motive of Zavala's urgings was suspicion. He wrote Santa Anna on several occasions of information received that he had met with individuals planning revolution—reports given no credit whatsoever, Zavala hastened to add. Santa Anna continued to refuse the position with the explanation that the state was in need of him.[8]

The Guerrero era lasted only through 1829, but in that year he presided over significant developments. Any lingering doubts about Mexico's national existence were ended with the defeat of a Spanish expeditionary force. Also the church began to reverse its decade-long decline by the curate appointment law of May 22 and by Guerrero's autumn initiative which led to the designation of new bishops. A major step was taken in the direction of a protective tariff, and Zavala attempted major fiscal innovations by ending the tobacco monopoly and decreeing a progressive income tax for the wealthy.

In the spring of 1829, the nativist-nationalist mood settling over the country produced several legislative proposals aimed at the foreign merchants and Spaniards. The measure to bar foreigners from the retail trade did not pass, but Congress expelled Spaniards a second time and prohibited the importation of cotton cloth.

The law against Spaniards had been considered inevitable in the wake of Santa Anna's Plan of Perote, and Congress dutifully produced a second expulsion decree on March 20. Although very few prominent politicians publicly favored this measure, agitation had not ceased after the December 20, 1827, expulsion.[9] Another anti-Spanish newspaper, *El Cardillo*, appeared with the avowed purpose of exposing seditious Spaniards. Along with their supposed crimes it printed addresses, an open invitation for reprisals. The expulsion bill, introduced in January, had been accompanied by the same pressures as the 1827 legislation: violence in the states against Spanish individuals and threats against congressmen not in agreement, some of whom were afraid to sleep in their own homes.[10]

To make sure that the net was cast wide, the March 20, 1829, law specified that only physically incapacitated Spaniards could remain. Yet though the Yorkinos were determined to cleanse the nation of their former masters, the Spaniards were not without means of defense. There were spectacles of Spaniards trying to demonstrate their maladies to either Congress or the examining board headed by the Protomedicato. Stories circulated about physicians who sold exemptions for a few "ounces of gold." Wives and children plagued Guerrero, as Bustamante wrote, crying, shouting, and grasping his knees in desperation.[11]

In his handling of exemptions Guerrero was generally cautious and legalistic, not wanting to take chances.[12] A rhythm of enforcement had appeared in these laws of passion: a hurried enforcement, followed by a slow working out of the law's complications, during which a Spaniard who had survived so far was likely to find a way to be excepted.

There was the same disparity in how the states handled the law. Speaking of the arrivals from Oaxaca, Veracruz's vice-governor Manuel Argüelles noted that "from that state came the blind, the crippled with crutches, and even some on the point of death, who received their exemption here because they were listened to with justice."[13]

While the wealthy Spaniards had already gone, or could still buy their way out, the weight of the 1829 law fell heaviest on the less well-off merchants and workers, most of whom went to New Orleans. There, without livelihood, they died by the hundreds. About 150 of the survivors signed on with the Spanish expeditionary force when it invaded Mexico in July 1829.[14]

Despite uneven workings of the laws—as well as the voluntary departures occasioned by the expulsions—the expulsions were decimating the Spanish population of Mexico. The December 20, 1827, law had reduced the approximately 6,600 Spaniards to a little over 4,000, and then the March 20, 1829, law left only about 2,000 by the beginning of 1830.[15] It has been estimated that each expelled Spaniard cost the government 38 pesos in travel subsidies, but at times indigent persons remained in the country since officials did not have on hand even these meager amounts. Guerrero was depending on Zavala to find a way out of these difficulties, and the new secretary of the treasury was hardly settled in his new office when he began writing bold proposals for ending the Treasury's yearlong insolvency.

Some of the measures were standard in times of desperation: loan authorizations, selling the tobacco monopoly to tax farmers, and selling confiscated church property (*temporalidades*).[16] But it was a series of decrees requested in May that brought down on Zavala's head denunciations from all sides. A law of May 22 placed a 5 percent tax on incomes of 1,000 pesos or more, 10 percent for those over 10,000 pesos, and a graduated tax in the form of licenses on medium and large businesses in the Federal District and territories—foreigners paid double. A law of the following day placed a surcharge of 5 percent on the income of absentee owners of property in the Federal District and territories.[17]

Zavala's acts, in particular the direct tax of May 22, were greeted by a rising crescendo of disapproval from state and local governments, editorialists, and pamphleteers. *El Sol,* defunct since the Acordada revolution, came out again on July 1, sending most of its invective toward Zavala and Poinsett. *El Sol* attacked Guerrero only by implication at this time, but Francisco Ibar, the professor of painting, serialized a pamphlet (*Muerte política de la república mexicana*) that did not hesitate to revile the president in the most personal terms. He vilified Guerrero for allegedly requesting a two-year advance on his salary, and suggested that Vice-President Bustamante take over the highest office due to the "moral impossibility" of Guerrero doing the job—an eerie prediction of what would actually take place within a year. About Zavala he told the story that, when governor, he had drunkenly threatened a curate who did not peal the bells on his arrival.[18]

In this atmosphere the direct tax was much ignored, and the old plans of a northern confederation were revived. Commenting on these developments on July 25, Poinsett predicted the Republic's "dissolution."[19] Even as Poinsett was drafting this dispatch, his own recall from Mexico was already in motion. Guerrero had already decided Poinsett was expendable, having requested President Andrew Jackson on July 1 that the U.S. ambassador be replaced. Meanwhile the publicity campaign against Poinsett reached its height in the summer and fall. In August, despite competing news from the Spanish invasion, Poinsett could pick up *El Sol* virtually every day and find himself blamed, in letters and articles, for a wide variety of Mexico's ills. On August 8 a congressional resolution for his expulsion narrowly missed (nineteen votes for, twenty-three against),[20] and by the end of the year, petitions for his removal had come from almost every state in central Mexico.[21] Only Zavala in the cabinet and Zavala's *Correo de la Federación Mexicana* had a good word to say about him. When the announcement to Poinsett arrived from the State Department, it was phrased in such a way that he might remain, should he insist, but the intent was obvious. Poinsett took his final leave of Mexican authorities on Christmas Day, and boarded ship in January.[22]

THE SPANISH EXPEDITIONARY FORCE

On August 1 the long-expected news arrived in the capital—a Spanish expeditionary force had landed on the Gulf coast. From July 27 to 29 about 2,800 soldiers, led by Brigadier General Isidro Barradas, waded on to beaches at Cabo Rojo, about 45 miles south of Tampico. Marching north along the coast, they entered Tampico after token resistance by troops under General Felipe de la Garza, Mexican commander of Tamaulipas.[23]

But there the Spaniards settled down and, except for a foray to nearby Altamira to obtain supplies, made no move for the interior. Although the Mexicans never quite realized it, the expeditionary army was not intended as a full-fledged invasion force. One-sided reports and embittered Spanish exiles had persuaded the court at Madrid that the Mexican masses longed for the government of the viceroys.[24] Because of this, horses and artillery had not been embarked—they were to be captured from the Mexicans. Too, prisoners were turned loose without even an oath not to take up arms again. General Garza was temporarily suspect when, after being captured while reconnoitering, he returned to camp within a few hours.[25]

Upon taking Tampico, Barradas announced the Viceroyalty of New Spain was once more, and prohibited commerce with any other ports. All he had to do was hold on, he assumed. He should have suspected something when he marched into a Tampico virtually empty of Mexicans. Along with many of his countrymen, he failed to perceive the depth of ill-will Mexicans felt toward the ex–mother country. In preceding years rumors of a reconquest had been refracted by the political medium, federalists beating the drums against nearby and distant Spaniards, centralists downplaying any possibility of danger. When the attack did come, however, the first thought of each group was to defend the homeland. *El Sol,* for example, was in the forefront of the call to arms. During the crisis, there was not a single movement in favor of Spain. Instead, the Spanish presence gave the tottering Guerrero regime—now the symbol of national existence—a few more months of life.

Patriotism did not preclude using the crisis to strike a passing blow at political adversaries. After Congress was called into special sessions on August 2, charges were brought against Zavala for malfeasance. On the crucial issue of granting war powers to the president (*facultades extraordinarias*), there was bitter resistance for three weeks before the bill finally passed on August 25.[26] Two days after thus suspending the constitution, Congress adjourned, leaving Guerrero in charge of ruling by decree.

Guerrero's supposed abuse of the "extraordinary faculties" would eventually supply the main rationale for deposing him. At the time, however, not the president but Zavala was the man under fire. Under the press of finding operating funds for the armies, he issued a second series of revenue decrees: forced loans, reductions in pensions and salaries, confiscations of Spanish property (or half the property if the Spaniard resided in Mexico), as well as one-third of the property of the duke of Terranova y Monteleone, and then on September 15 a wide variety of license fees on businesses and professions, and special war taxes—even on carriages.[27]

The haphazard response to Zavala's orders was in line with the general state of national defense. Since the invasion had been expected between Veracruz and Campeche, preparations along the northern coast were minimal. In the spring of 1829, when sailors on ships stopping over in Havana brought the first definite news of troops being readied for an assault, the only reaction was to activate a few civic and reserve units.[28] In the northeast, the nearest high commanders were Mier y Terán in Matamoros and Santa Anna, governor and commanding general of the state of Veracruz.

The latter, in an exception to the pattern of unhurried preparations, had already been strengthening the Veracruz defenses. When the news reached him on August 2, he went into a frenzy of activity; impressing men, piling up arms and powder and foodstuffs, and commandeering boats and crews—three American vessels by force when the captain and owners refused to agree to terms.[29] Finally Santa Anna put together a force of about 1,600 men which left for Tampico on August 6 and 7, the cavalry by land and the infantry in a makeshift flotilla of twelve boats.

At the time there were several villages at what is now Tampico. North of the Pánuco River was Tampico proper, in Tamaulipas state. Santa Anna set up his headquarters on August 19 at Pueblo Viejo, south of the Pánuco in the state of Veracruz. Appointed general in chief of the Army of Operations, Santa Anna was almost annihilated at the very beginning when he ferried his men across the Pánuco and attacked a remnant of the Spanish army under Colonel Miguel Salomón. In the middle of the battle the main body of the Spaniards returned and the Mexicans were saved only because Barradas still hoped for a bloodless victory. In the parley Santa Anna listened to statements of peaceful reconciliation and felt obliged to agree that he abhorred the idea of bloodshed. The Mexicans were allowed to cross back to safety, and marched to their boats with flags held up and drums beating time.[30]

Safely on the Pánuco's south side again, Santa Anna waited as Mexican reinforcements filtered in. Mier y Terán arrived and pushed up bulwarks to the north. Barricaded inside Tampico, the Spanish army waited for an uprising among the Mexican people that never came.

Lizardi's prophecy had come true. Writing about the Veracruz coast, he stated that there was no need to fear the Holy Alliance, since "we have a valiant auxiliary army which is the *vómito* [yellow fever]."[31] As the Mexican forces multiplied, demoralization, hunger, and disease set in among the Spanish ranks. Finally, at 1:45 A.M. on September 11, about 900 Mexican soldiers stormed the Spanish parapets, and although the Spaniards threw back eleven assaults, Salomón and Lieutenant Colonel Fulgencio Salas (Barradas' chief of staff) came to the Mexican side that morning with an offer to surrender unconditionally.[32]

At about 10 P.M. on September 21 Vicente Guerrero was in his booth at the theater when a dust-covered courier handed him some papers. The audience looked toward him expectantly, Guerrero stood up, told of the victory at Tampico, and stated he was sending his own general's sash to Santa Anna.[33] Theatergoers congratulated each other, bells pealed, and the city lit up instantaneously. Residents poured out onto the streets, strangers embraced, rockets were set off, and wine merchants and tavern owners gave away bottles to their neighbors.[34]

It was a glorious victory for Mexican arms, and national glory shown brightest on Santa Anna. Until the Spanish invasion presented the opportunity for nonpartisan heroism, he had been the adolescent general, overshadowed by the great insurgents Victoria, Guerrero, and Bravo. Now, when he returned to Veracruz on October 3, the city's most distinguished citizens jostled for the honor of carrying him from the docks to the government palace. Congress declared him "Well-Deserving of the Nation" (*Benemérito de la Patria*) and ordered a medal struck with the inscription "At Tampico he struck down Spanish arrogance."[35] September 11 became a national holiday until in later years Santa Anna's misdeeds made it less popular.

Among the armies, while the winning troops were recounting their exploits, the prisoners were dying off at a rapid rate from disease—especially yellow fever—as well as inadequate housing and diet. Spanish transports were slow in coming, and the meager proceeds from Zavala's war taxes and loans could scarcely feed even Mexican armies. Barradas went to New Orleans on September 21 to arrange for ships—and forthwith deserted rather than face a likely court-martial. Of the total of 3,500 Spanish soldiers put ashore, 1,792 prisoners were finally reembarked between November 9 and December 11.[36] The rest were victims of Fernando VII's Mexican adventure.

It was still considered possible a second wave might come, and for this purpose the Reserve Army had been built up near Jalapa. Commanded by Vice-President Bustamante, it came to include about 3,000 men. Although 500 Spanish soldiers did arrive at Tampico on September 29, they agreed to leave when Mier y Terán informed them of events.[37] The second expeditionary force never came, and Mexican independence was secure. But Guerrero was not. The Reserve Army would soon turn upon its creator.

THE JALAPA REVOLUTION

The storm broke over Guerrero again in late August and September, even before the capitulation of Barradas. With the Spanish army encircled on the beach, the initial shock wore off and partisanship replaced patriotism. Guerrero, the perennial fighter against tyranny and centralism, must have felt bewildered to find himself attacked for these very practices. In Jalisco, the legislature on August 27 raised again the call for a northern confederation.[38] The central issue was whether or not to annul the emergency powers given Guerrero, and in particular Zavala's special taxes, which brought the national government into the states' revenue domain. Increasingly, the states ignored directives from Mexico City. Pakenham reported that not a single state put the September 15 law into effect. An idea of the government's condition that summer can be gathered from the fact that in July some unpaid soldiers wrote Doña Guadalupe Guerrero, the president's wife, asking her for charity.[39]

Then Guerrero lost Zavala, in many ways the voice and brains of the administration. Since summer Zavala's relationship with Santa Anna had turned bitter, partially because Santa Anna wanted his own man to head the Veracruz customs house and partially because Zavala continued to accuse the general of plotting subversion, even during the Spanish invasion. After a critical editorial in the *Correo de la Federación Mexicana*, Santa Anna became openly insulting in a letter to Zavala:

> The accusations against you are many and of much gravity, both as a public and a private individual. They refer to deeds of yours which, true or not, are so degrading and so often repeated that you are left with no prestige at all. As a minister you are accused of monopolies, of illegal disbursements, of usurious loans, etc.; about you as an individual it is told and retold what happened with the young girl related to Tornel, as well as with others.[40]

The Michoacán and Puebla legislatures had petitioned for his removal, and as Zavala himself explained it, the other cabinet members persuaded Guerrero that his departure would placate the administration's opponents.[41] On October 12 Zavala resigned, but his activities as secretary had alienated the state of Mexico legislators, for three days later they declared he could not return as governor, and Zavala was left without a job.[42] Tornel, another key Guerrero supporter, was forced out as Federal District governor, later claiming to be a victim of conspiracies. Santa Anna, who had conferred with Reserve Army commander Bustamante, must have seen what was about to happen and decided to sidestep the issue. In November he resigned his civil and military positions in Veracruz.[43]

Guerrero's detractors attacked him for his dictatorial power, but in truth he was quite circumspect in his actions, taking advantage of the constitution's suspension to take humanitarian steps. He declared an end to slavery (September 15) and issued an amnesty (September 16) for the Montaño revolutionaries. One of Guerrero's most censured decrees, which Zacatecas Governor García refused to promulgate, was that of September 4 which called for punishment for publications subverting independence or federalism.[44] Federal District writers who were arrested for violations, however, received light sentences: Villavicencio was given two months' exile from the capital, Luis Pardiñas a month's labor in a hospital, and Ibar was acquitted—mild punishment in light of what would befall journalists a few months later.[45]

Toward the end, Guerrero tried to pacify his enemies. He acquiesced in Zavala's departure, and then on November 6 revoked the states' portion of the September 15 decree.[46] But none of this could win over the powerful conservative elements who had always hated him and who were now organizing to topple him. His old federalist friends had never approved because he entered the presidency by way of the Acordada revolution, and they now watched as he was reduced to helplessness. In November, with dissatisfaction general throughout the Republic and Reserve Army officers conspiring almost publicly, Guerrero was an easy target.

The first move came from an unlikely place. In Yucatán the commander, Colonel José Segundo Carvajal, had been at odds with Governor José Tiburcio López over state subsidies to the troops. At a November 5 banquet in Campeche (then part of Yucatán), the wine was passed around and officers began giving toasts with an antifederalist tone, someone shouted for centralism, and the whole group marched to the plaza to sign a 3 A.M. centralist pronouncement. Four days later in Mérida, Carvajal deposed Governor López, and the state came under control of the army in the name of centralism.[47]

In Jalapa, the Reserve Army officers found it instructive that in spite of general unrest, the Campeche declaration had been greeted by silence. The lesson to be learned was that they must rebel ostensibly for federalism. Jalapa, meanwhile, had been filling up with officers who were sworn enemies of the Yorkinos, including three—Bravo, Barragán, and Bustamante's private secretary, Colonel José Antonio Facio—who had only recently returned from exile by virtue of Guerrero's clemency.[48] Santa Anna, invited to join the revolution, declined but added thanks for the invitation. General Bustamante himself had still not promised support.

Guerrero saw the revolution coming—it was public knowledge by now—but he had lost control of the situation. He sent orders that the Reserve Army be disbanded, but the staff in Jalapa refused on grounds that the troops had not been paid in two months. Next Guerrero dispatched Zavala with secret orders to send half the army to Perote, but an old friend among the rebels invited him to dine, and in the course of the meal Zavala divulged his intentions. Right after Zavala's visit, Facio and the other leaders took advantage of Bustamante's absence—he was still vacillating—to issue the Plan of Jalapa.[49]

Bustamante accepted the leadership and the Reserve Army started toward Puebla. The Plan of Jalapa only called upon the executive to give up the extraordinary faculties, and did not openly threaten Guerrero, but the crucial fourth article declared for the removal of those public officials against whom public opinion had been expressed.[50] As Puebla governor Patricio Furlong made clear in a December 8 letter to the president, "The object of the Plan is you."[51] Beyond that, the promoters of the Jalapa Plan, known as Jalapistas, intended to restructure public affairs. In another letter, Guerrero was warned:

> These aristocrats, or rather devourers of their fatherland, are only waiting until the extraordinary sessions open to discharge against the present system; . . . they are already making publications ahead of time in the printing shops of the Sol, Galván, Ontiveros, and Balderas. In all of Mexico nothing is heard except in favor of centralism.[52]

With virtually no one willing to stand by the government, the Jalapa revolution became a triumphal march. As more and more government and military units declared for the Jalapa Plan, Guerrero temporized, not knowing whom to trust. He called to his office Esteva (the Federal District provisional governor), but Esteva had already decided the Jalapistas were going to win. He asked Alamán to go to Puebla to confer with Bustamante, and then called off the idea.[53] He called Congress back for special sessions and then renounced the war powers and requested permission to command the army personally. Gathering an army of "1,000 men of every description,"[54] Guerrero left Mexico City, and the Chamber of Deputies—the Senate was abetting the revolution and had disbanded—elected José María Bocanegra provisional president. A lawyer from the Aguascalientes region of Zacatecas, Bocanegra (1787–1862) had served in various positions in the national government, generally in consonance with the Yorkino-federalists, first as deputy from Zacatecas in 1822, then secretary of relations in 1829, and now president—however briefly.[55]

The final blow for Guerrero came on the night of December 22–23, when the capital's seventh infantry regiment, under General Luis Quintanar, began occupying the city's strong points in the name of the Jalapa Plan. The next day the governmental council met and, following constitutional provisions for government interruptions, chose a provisional executive: Alamán, Quintanar, and Supreme Court president Pedro Velez. The revolution's managers wanted an orderly transition to point up the contrast with the Parián looting of a year ago. One *lépero* who tried to force a lock was shot.[56]

Evidence hints at a prominent role for Alamán in the Jalapa movement. On December 21, before Quintanar moved, Esteva sent him a message as leader of the movement and by Alamán's own admission, most of the Jalapa Plan's leaders directed their communications to him personally. When Alamán went to the national palace to take the oath, Quintanar, who had opposed him in Guadalajara in 1823 and 1824, greeted him with "against these evildoers, we are all one."[57]

There was only one dissonant note. Word came from Veracruz that Santa Anna had decided to stand by Guerrero after all. Emerging from his month-long retirement at Manga de Clavo to reclaim his military and political positions, he proclaimed that Guerrero would be removed only over his dead body.[58] It was too late for Guerrero, though. His troops deserted him in Ayacapixtla when they heard the news of the Quintanar coup, and on Christmas Day Guerrero wrote Alamán that he was prepared to abide by the will of Congress, whatever that might be.[59]

Guerrero's capitulation was followed closely by Santa Anna's. On January 2 Alamán had just sent out a circular, warning that the Veracruz general might be maneuvering against the federal system, when fresh dispatches arrived. Santa Anna wrote that since Guerrero, to avoid civil war, had ceded the rights "legally belonging to him," he too would retire. A man's "duty has, like all other things in the world, its limits." Ever flexible,

Santa Anna on January 15 congratulated Alamán on his appointment to the new government: "For my own desires, you would have occupied this position for some time now."[60]

The enduring lesson of 1829 was that liberalism in Mexico was still aborning. The liberal state was based on a premise of free association and free institutions, and Zavala had been working through the 1820s to broaden democracy by opening institutions and organizing the masses. Although the issues were clouded in 1829 by Guerrero's illegitimacy, it was becoming clear that there were distinct limits to parliamentary give-and-take in a state where the centers of power from the colony were still intact. In the future liberals would move toward the next step to use the state to attack privileged classes and institutions at the source of their strength.

INSTITUTIONAL DYNAMICS OF THE 1820s

The difficulty of implanting common political institutions among peoples who still thought of themselves in terms of their own caste, class, or region pointed up the larger question of the relationship between peoples and institutions. What was to be done when there was an imperfect fit between republican institutions and habits from the colony?

The 1820s witnessed a rise and fall of institutionalism. There had been a time when political individuals professed faith in the saving grace of institutions. The belief was current at the onset of independence that Mexico's hope lay in creating enlightened institutions, to which the people would shortly mold their attitudes and customs. In the literature of the day could be noted an abstract, legalist, point of departure, as opposed to the imperatives of reality. Public endeavors frequently began with consultation on salutary principles as enunciated by respected thinkers and practiced by progressive nations. In keeping with this faith, there was a large issuance, not only of the essential political structures, but quasi-public projects: societies, academies, schools, and clubs.

Beginning at Tulancingo, and then with the Acordada and the passing of Guadalupe Victoria's term, the cement of the Republic seemed to give way. Institutions lost their power to enchant. The new political vehicles were clearly malfunctioning, and as for the voluntary associations, they had faded away. Their patrons stopped subscribing and attending meetings. Such was the general dissatisfaction that by 1830 a new government would be able to eviscerate much that had been done since Iturbide and encounter scant opposition—until local politicians felt their vital interests were endangered.

Political and Judicial Institutions

The ebb and flow of institutionalism was most conspicuous in politics, from the auspicious era of 1823–1825 to the disillusionment of 1829. After independence, the central innovations in political life were the multiplication of political institutions and the attempt to bring more people into the process. The centralist thesis—that subalterns out of Mexico City should administer the provinces—had failed to carry the day, and so the states contained the full array of representative government. Differences in scale from late colonial times were obvious. Whereas the viceregal apparatus had maintained a few hundred dependents (including 1,200 revenue collectors),[61] the federal-state establishment was several times that size.[62]

Writers commented on the rush for jobs occasioned by the swelling bureaucracy, for it was an agreeable way to make a living. The schedule was not trying, normal public hours extending from approximately nine o'clock in the morning to one in the afternoon and possibly an evening shift from five to eight to handle the paperwork. If most of the new positions carried only a modest annual salary of 200–400 pesos, there were frequently opportunities for perquisites, especially at the customs houses, *alcabala* stations, and commissaries. A state governor earned 3,000 to 4,000 pesos annually.

Mexicans were infatuated with the republican style, with all its gestures and paraphernalia. To diffuse the new ethic, newspapers printed minutes of Congress and the legislatures and school children were inculcated with the virtues of civic duty. As the legislatures convened and elections were held, however, what developed was not the sober republicanism associated with Switzerland. Such a thing was impossible, given the state of society. Governor Zavala described Mexico state's 200,000 voters in 1833: two-thirds of them could not read, one-half were unclothed, and one-third could not speak the Spanish language.[63]

What did take shape was a vociferous Mexican democracy. In Congress and the legislatures a gallery would routinely shout out preferences and, when one faction or another enlisted a mob, it was not unheard of for legislators to be driven physically from the chambers or governors from their offices. The distinctive element in elections was the list of candidates, printed by each side and then pressed into the voter's hand as he approached the polling place. Apparently the lists, if signed, were counted as ballots. Alamán noted that lists had already been used in the 1812 elections to the Cortes,[64] but in the 1820s the practice was carried even further. Bustamante estimated that 40,000 such lists had been printed for the 1823 election to the Constitutional Congress.[65] One of the most flagrant examples took place in the 1826 Federal District election, where there had been no previous voter registration. "They came up to the voting tables by the thousands and deposited in the urns as many lists as the presses had been able to stamp."[66]

Leadership in the national institutions was unsteady. With the creole nobility as a class having little tradition of political responsibility, topmost leadership in practice generally fell to two groups. The Cortes veterans, the mostly creole reformers of the last Spanish years, were the closest thing to statesmen available. They were joined, to their discomfort at times, by the battlefield insurgents. In the national government the former provided many of the cabinet members and the latter the presidents.

About half a dozen figures achieved the status of national luminary and could move through positions of leadership almost at will between the national and state capitals. State politicians were now in the habit of seeking national personalities to serve as governor, those men whose reputation and connections might bring advantage. Among those who ranged back and forth from duties in the cabinet, Congress, and governorships were Victoria, Guerrero, Francisco García, Gómez Pedraza, José Morán, and Zavala.

A leader's tenure in office tended to be discontinuous and insecure, for the offensive mode of the Revolution lingered. Attacks on a personal level characterized the political scene such that national leaders were subject to speeches and publications impugning their philosophy, ethics, and sexuality. Worse yet, they might expect judicial or legislative vengeance if they were turned out of office. A political change, in particular after 1827, signified imminent personal danger. It would be difficult to name a major political figure who was not formally charged with some type of criminal misconduct.

In Congress and the legislatures, proceedings could be quarrelsome, and there was an occasional fist fight. Zavala's temper carried him to an exchange of blows more than once, but the more frequent comment was that legislators were too little concerned about their duties. Alamán frequently complained about lassitude in the halls of Congress. The problem of absenteeism was such that the presiding officer might have to lock the doors to maintain a quorum.

Legislative institutions were not yet the creature of any one interest group. Although the pattern varied from place to place, scattered descriptions of lawmakers' professions suggest there were more lawyers than anything else in Congress and the legislatures. The other principal groups represented were army officers, merchants, and clerics.[67] Relatively few hacendados were visible on the rolls, but the kind of agrarian and labor law ratified by legislatures indicates their supporters must have been present.

In the relationships between the two levels, the Federation had yet to draw in power from the state governments. Before 1830 the Federation did not calculate to impose its will on the states. All of the states, proud of their new faculties, were chary of pressure from Mexico City, whether the national government was federalist or not.

The most vivid clash concerning federalism took place, with semantic neatness, over the Federal District. Naturally enough, both the government of the Federation and the state of Mexico coveted Mexico City. After two years of discussions, and much opposition from the state, Congress federalized Mexico City on November 18, 1824. The Federal District was to take in an area within a radius of two leagues (5.2 miles) from the main plaza. With about 70 percent of its revenue coming from the metropolis, the state resisted, appealing first to the president, then to the states, and then to the next Congress. But the rest of the country feared domination by a too-powerful state of Mexico and the Federation formally assumed jurisdiction on April 11, 1826. State officials did not give in, and off and on until 1830 demanded that the city be returned. With its conservative core excised, the state of Mexico did a political turnabout. It moved into the federalist camp, and until 1830 vociferously defended states' rights. As for the residents of the national capital, they voted in the Mexico state elections fall 1824, and then were left almost disenfranchised, with no vote in presidential elections, no senators, and only two representatives in the Chamber of Deputies until 1833.[68]

The main strains in the federal relationships were of the inevitable kind, finances and garrisons more than anything else. Often one led straightaway to the other. Over and above the expected squabbles about taxing jurisdictions, contested properties, and tardy transfers of funds, both the contingent tax (*contingente*) and tobacco revenue turned into running sores, giving both federal and state officials the opportunity to blame the other for budget troubles.

The presence of the soldiers, immune to state authority by virtue of their *fuero,* clouded federal relations on several accounts. First, several state commanders were selected as governors in spite of constitutional prohibitions, although it seems frequently the initiative came from local factions. Then there was the matter of unpaid soldiers, which made the Federation's financial embarrassment of more than bureaucratic interest. To meet the military list, commanding officers employed stratagems ranging from begging to extortion. It was not politic to ignore the requests of military commanders, and so state officials usually found it best to pay the troops and then apply to the federal commissary for reimbursement. Added to this was a string of episodes that gave the state commandants a reputation for intimidation when dealing with local authorities.[69]

As serious as fiscal starvation was the absence of formal governing traditions. The erosion of expectations for municipal government can be traced in the governors' annual *memorias*. Village citizens had found out that municipal duties were onerous and usually unremunerated, and as the decade wore on frequently refused to serve. *Ayuntamiento* members, required to follow state guidelines in framing ordinances, were prodded into activity by state officials who became increasingly skeptical about the capacity of local people to manage political affairs. The most frequent complaints were that *alcaldes* and councilmen were illiterate, ignorant of their functions, and remiss in carrying out directives and furnishing reports.

Gradually the state role in municipal government evolved toward stricter control, even in federalist strongholds like Jalisco and Zacatecas. The 1830 San Luis Potosí *Memoria* stated that 719 cases had been filed in the past year against *alcaldes* for malpractice and dereliction of duty.[70] A few states took the positive approach, subsidizing or taking charge of municipal finances.[71] Many more began taking steps to reduce the size of or eliminate the less self-sufficient *ayuntamientos*.[72]

Judicial activity seemed least altered by the institutions of independence. The Supreme Court was negligible in power considerations. It was denied the considerable influence judicial review gave its counterpart in the United States since the Mexican Congress—not the Supreme Court—passed on the constitutionality of state legislation. Throughout the states and territories the hierarchy of regional and state courts gradually came into existence, but these touched very few individuals. Jury trials were introduced for cases concerning publishing violations. As this system worked, a Board of Censure would examine accused publications and send any that were judged subversive or slanderous to a grand jury of nine men, and from there if indicted, to a petit jury of twelve men.[73] These jury trials became so unruly and charged with politics that Congress in October 1828 passed legislation requiring jurors to own a certain amount of property.[74] By 1830 the jury system was generally losing favor in the public mind and in some instances was abolished.[75]

At the bottom, judge to most Mexicans came in the person of the *alcalde,* the head of the *ayuntamiento*. In many places the task of handling the problems of crime and the local clan feuds seems to have surpassed the *alcalde*'s capacities. It was frequently heard that he did not bring the full weight of justice to bear on wrongdoers. The chronically bankrupt towns could rarely provide even minimal police protection, and as a political creature the *alcalde* was open to all kinds of pressure. Since the office rotated, the current occupant found it dangerous to prosecute zealously. Finding ways to feed the town's convicts was frequently left for the *alcalde,* further reason for him to keep sentencings down.

Religious Institutions

Through the 1820s the church continued its decline. Death and desertion continued to diminish the ranks of bishops and canons, and without bishops there were no permanent appointments of curates. The cathedral chapters were at approximately half-strength by 1828,[76] and with the death of Antonio Pérez, bishop of Puebla, on April 26, 1829, the Republic of Mexico was left without a single bishop. Likewise, those that ministered directly to the needs of the faithful, the curates and deacons, were fewer in number each year. In 1830 there were only 3,282 seculars, and about one-half were inactive or ill.[77] The real impact was felt not so much in church-state relations as in the tenor of everyday life. Children were growing up unbaptized and unconfirmed, couples traveled great distances to get married or else made common-law marriages, the dying faced their last moments without spiritual consolation, and cadavers remained unburied for days due to lack of a priest.

To seek a solution to the problem of empty bishoprics, the government dispatched as emissary to Rome Francisco Pablo Vásquez (1769–1847), canon and director of schools of the Puebla cathedral. Born in Atlixco (Puebla) of a family of humble station, Vásquez developed into an academic prodigy, receiving his doctorate in theology at the age of twenty-six. During the Revolution he had demonstrated royalist sympathies.[78] He left in 1825 without instructions since Congress was split between those who wished to respectfully ask the pope to grant patronage, and those who thought Mexico should assert patronage as a basic right of sovereignty. Congressional committees issued several recommendations. After a Senate committee report of February 28, 1826, argued that all religious questions could be decided within Mexico—in effect calling for a national church—the ecclesiastical hierarchy threw its weight behind an earlier, more submissive, Chamber of Deputies report (of February 12, 1825) which was then approved by Congress on October 9, 1827.[79]

Vásquez, meanwhile, had been ordered not to continue on to Rome because of Pope Leo XII's 1824 encyclical extolling the virtues of Fernando VII. He took up residence in Brussels and entered into a reverential correspondence with Vatican officials who wanted him to come to Rome as a private citizen. Vásquez finally decided to go to Rome uninvited, arriving in April 1829, where he settled down to wait until the pope might receive him.[80]

The patronage issue was composed of two elements: the immediate problem of filling the vacancies in the bishoprics, cathedral chapters, and parishes; and recognition by the Vatican of the Mexican government's right to make the appointments. As it became apparent that the Vásquez mission was stalled by Spanish opposition and that Congress would not decree patronage unilaterally, the idea of separating the two elements became more attractive. This appealed to Vicente Guerrero. For all his revolutionary ideas, he was a very pious man and when he became president he sent a circular to the cathedral chapters (September 23, 1829) requesting them to nominate individuals as bishops. He never had the time to carry this through, however, and the decade ended with the Mexican dioceses still without leaders.[81]

In the absence of any patronage agreement, an expedient was to include in church legislation what was called the *exclusiva,* which allowed the president or governor to exclude undesirable candidates in filling any vacancies. The law of May 22, 1829, to appoint curates and sacristans followed this principle. The bishop (or cathedral chapter) would present to the state governor a list of five or more candidates for each position, he could veto three, and the bishop or cathedral chapter would then make the final selection.[82]

The general uncertainty about the church and Rome and Spain led to a number of radical proposals, directed chiefly against those ecclesiastics known to be cool toward republican Mexico. Guadalupe Victoria's cabinet considered limiting the number of novitiates so as to gradually extinguish the monastic orders, with the government falling heir to the regulars' property. In January 1826 the Chamber of Deputies barely rejected (27 to 24) a bill to prohibit anyone under thirty years of age from taking the habit. The following January the deputies defeated a similar bill that would have replaced the cathedral chapters with committees of priests appointed by the state legislatures. A state church was contemplated, as witnessed by the February 28, 1826, Senate committee report, whereby the government would not only appoint prelates but also supervise interior discipline and the ecclesiastical budget. President Victoria and Ecclesiastical Affairs Minister Ramos Arizpe told Ward in 1827 that they and certain congressional leaders were making plans to break completely with Rome, buy off the pope with an annual bribe, and leave him with only "purely spiritual" authority. The tactic now, they explained, was to stall for time. As more bishops died, people would look more and more to the government for religious leadership.[83]

There was never enough general support to carry out these measures, but the public felt very strongly where any links with Spain were concerned. The executive issued a directive making religious orders independent of their superiors in Spain, prohibited any chaplaincy payment to individuals residing in Spain, and banned the custom of tripartite election (rotating selection of monastic heads among Spaniards, creoles, and castes). President Victoria denied the *pase* (circulation permission) for any papal documents that either implied Spanish sovereignty, were countersigned by Spanish officials, or were ultramontanist in nature.[84]

All this while, states had been calling for stronger action from the Federation, and in many cases took it upon themselves to move ahead. Led usually by Jalisco, Mexico state (after Zavala's accession), and Zacatecas, state legislatures deliberated on all of the vital issues, from the *fuero,* to patronage, to church finances. It appears that many of these laws never went into effect or were declared unconstitutional, but they did show that state officials were prepared to act. The church *fuero* was generally considered beyond tampering with since the 1824 constitution sanctioned it, but even so the San Luis Potosí decree of March 28, 1827, provided for a legislature-appointed Superior Ecclesiastical Junta "that would act on all" contentious matters until patronage was settled.[85] In spring 1827, six states reminded Congress it was obligated to protect the church, implying with or without Vatican consent,[86] and the Guanajuato and San Luis Potosí legislatures wanted the states themselves to go ahead and assume patronage, at least temporarily.[87] About half the states (eight) gave the governor the authority to appoint local church personnel.[88]

While a bill to prohibit ecclesiastical entail died in the Chamber of Deputies in 1827, several states enacted limitations on the type of land the church could acquire, in some cases entailed property or pious fund endowments (Mexico state, Yucatán, Durango),[89] in another case land from Indians (Jalisco),[90] and in one case any kind of property at all (San Luis Potosí).[91] Since the states now received the old royal portion of the tithe, six states set up tithing boards which largely took over from the church the job of supervising collection.[92]

Another concern was fees. An Indian woman in Michoacán told Ward her first house had cost her four pesos while the priest charged twenty pesos for her marriage ceremony. In Guanajuato many couples, unable to pay the marriage fee, lived in conjugal sin, and a large part of the debt of the Sánchez Navarro peons came from religious payments.[93] A royal schedule (*arancel*) of 1767 had set down specific charges for marriages, baptisms, burials, and other services, with the amounts fixed according to presumed ability to pay. For a burial Spaniards were to pay five to seventeen pesos, depending on the pomp desired, while Indians were to pay three pesos for an adult and two pesos for a child. In practice, charges varied according to regional tradition, even more so after independence when the *arancel* was no longer considered binding. For example, in southern Mexico tribute had included fees, and with the abolition of tribute the question was left open.[94]

While Congress discussed the question of fees inconclusively in 1827 and 1828,[95] the states again acted. A Zacatecas law of November 29, 1827, responded to complaints from mining areas and haciendas by ordering the church to make its fees uniform, and several other state governments began investigations and persuasive measures.[96] One of Zavala's first acts was to send out a circular threatening fines for certain abuses he had information about: collecting a kind of tribute from Indians under the guise of charging for masses, and in cases even requiring personal services.[97] The church had its own views on the subject. When Jalisco proposed to regulate and reduce the fees for sacraments, a report for the diocese of Guadalajara stated that even at current levels priests had to use their personal funds to maintain the church.[98] Whatever churchmen thought, the idea was spreading that fees were too high.

Another government-inspired reform in the 1820s was the attempt to move burials from inside the churches out into the churchyards. Within the churches, the boards on which the faithful knelt had been left unnailed so that bodies could be lowered into holy ground. Over the years the number of interments had surpassed the capacity of the consecrated soil to absorb the bodies, creating sanitary problems and making floors slippery with the seeping grease.[99] The clerics had no brief against relocating burials, but progress was slow since it took time to ready new ground.

The postindependence era witnessed the end of an institution that seemed synonymous with the Mexican church itself. The missions, as exclusive communities directed by mostly Spanish friars, were now considered relics of a bygone era. Also, most northern missions were already on their last legs by the late 1820s as a result of Indian attacks and the loss of the 300–400 pesos traditionally given to each missionary annually by the government or a pious fund. In Sonora and Arizona the missions, harassed by settlers and called upon for loans by presidio companies, individuals, and the state governments, were on the brink of collapse.[100] In Chihuahua, among the Tarahumara Indians the friars had been replaced by the secular priests as of the 1830s.[101] In New Mexico, where religion was in "pitiful abandon," only five of the nineteen Indian pueblos had Franciscan fathers, and all nineteen showed traces of paganism in the worship of the sun, the moon, and other celestial bodies.[102] In Texas too, the missions were dying, and several had ceased to function. La Bahía still had about fifty Aranama Indians as of 1822, but they no longer worked or attended mass.[103]

In spite of general suspicion toward the missions, local conditions guided policy. In Tamaulipas, where marauding warriors were wiping out settlements, a November 3, 1831, law ordered Indians congregated.[104] The general trend, however, was toward secularization, the basic legislation being the Cortes decree of September 13, 1813, that ordered all missions ten years old or older to be handed over to curates. Enforcement of this law was hastened or retarded by a number of factors, such as the intensity of national and local officials' liberal convictions, the cupidity of neighboring settlers, and the need for the education and food the friars provided.

The surviving missions of Texas were ordered secularized by the national executive on September 15, 1823. San José and San Miguel de Aguayo were soon handed over, and on February 8, 1830, the last two Texas missions, La Bahía and Refugio, passed into secular hands.[105] In Sonora the military commander sent troops at Easter time 1828 to expel the Franciscans from that state's eight missions, but the Bustamante administration in 1830 called the Franciscans back (the few that could be found). In 1841, when the Franciscan College relinquished control of these missions, there were three friars left in Sonora.[106]

The relatively prosperous California missions were a special case. Although the Spanish friars in February 1825 refused to take an oath of allegiance, Governor José María Echeandía needed provisions that only the missionaries could deliver and changed his mind on more than one occasion about removing them. After the secularization law of August 17, 1833, however, secularization was carried through, and the mission lands, long coveted by Californio ranchers, became private cattle ranches.[107]

Thus the missions became regular parishes after the friars, with forlorn resignation, made the required final inventory of each mission's belongings. They did not all leave, though, for here and there some friars lived on with their Indian congregations even after the 1830s.

Military Institutions

During the First Federal Republic, the army possessed a split personality, reflecting its hybrid origins. A part of the officer corps had a personalistic approach to command, after the practices of the insurgent chiefs. Some commanders were more or less permanently attached to their home state, where long years in the region and family connections had made them semi-independent chieftains: Santa Anna in Veracruz, León in Oaxaca, Garza in Tamaulipas, Cortazar in Guanajuato, and Álvarez in the Tierra Caliente of the Pacific coast. These individuals, who looked on their commands as personal property, were to be consulted and courted, but could be transferred only at exceptional times.

Other officers, such as Bravo, Mier y Terán, Morán, and Gómez Pedraza, looked back admiringly to the Spanish days of crisp discipline and subordination. They overlooked the fact that the Spaniards had waged a constant and not very successful struggle to impose order on the military of New Spain, but they correctly saw that the situation had worsened. Under their inspiration, from 1823 to 1827 there was a flurry of decrees and regulations designed to make the army responsible and competent. To coordinate overall planning, a September 5, 1823, decree created the general staff, but this body, reminiscent of an aristocratic tradition, met with opposition. Only those individuals making the army their profession were decreed eligible (March 17, 1826) for military appointments, and illiterate captains were forbidden to attend councils of war (September 14, 1826). A military academy near Perote trained a few officers from 1824 to 1827. When it moved to the ex-convent of the Bethlemites in Mexico City in 1827, it had thirty-two cadets. On August 19, 1826, the War Department, following Colonel José Antonio Facio's experiment in the Fourth Cavalry, decreed Lancasterian schools for every cavalry regiment.[108]

These measures had little apparent impact, however, and in these years the lost ground was not made up. The secretary of war admitted the troops had lost their discipline.[109] One veteran sadly wrote that he had seen more Indians whipped in villages than soldiers in the barracks.[110] Soldiers scandalized the citizenry of Jalapa in 1824 when they brought girlfriends and prostitutes into their quarters, which happened to be in the San Francisco and San Ignacio monasteries.[111] Tampico's British consul, Joseph T. Crawford, noted in 1829 that the invading Spanish troops never got out of line, while the Mexican liberators looted several homes upon retaking the city.[112]

Military politicization went along with the breakdown in discipline. Since soldiers had won independence, some officers thought of themselves as the proper guardians of the new order. Their political participation often took the disarming form of a petition, which really consisted of a list of non-negotiable demands, to be carried out on the spot if the petitioner had sufficient means at his disposal. Officers had their men intimidate voters, and were observed taking their units to vote "in formation as if it were a parade."[113] Some colonels and generals even began newspapers to spread their views, which opponents criticized at their own peril. On more than one occasion, an irritated officer sent his aides to beat up an editor or break up an offending press.

Certain commanders made of their units a political vehicle, but there was no single army program since there was little esprit de corps. Except on the issue of regular pay, the officers agreed with each other politically no more than civilians did.

The War Department's overriding concern was not politics, but the number of troops. Some politicians accepted the general proposition that the Mexican army was too bulky, especially since the Ministry of War and Navy was consuming 75 percent of the Federation's revenues in the late 1820s. Minister of War Gómez Pedraza himself hoped to trim the army's size in 1826, and did succeed in temporarily reducing the active militia to about 10,000 men and the War Ministry's expenses from 18,946,524 pesos in 1825 to projected budgets of approximately 10 million pesos in his annual reports of 1827 and 1828.[114] But the looming Spanish invasion overshadowed all else. Thus the greater fear was that the army, in spite of the swollen rolls, might melt away to nothing.

It stemmed from the method of filling the ranks. Under an August 24, 1824, law, the states were to furnish a total of 16,213 recruits.[115] Each state had a maximum obligation, and as the Federation needed men it called upon the state officials, who in turn notified the *alcaldes*. The methods for actually picking out individuals varied. At first a lottery (*sorteo*) was tried, but experience showed that the mere announcement of an upcoming lottery was sufficient to empty a town instantaneously. Many of those selected preferred to become fugitives, taking their families with them, rather than serve.[116] In the end, those who went into the regular army were whomever the local authorities could lay their hand on, unemployed persons or petty criminals who were sent from jail to jail until reaching camp. State officials were not of a mind to pack off their more industrious subjects. The law in Oaxaca specified that the quota was to be filled first by vagrants and "pernicious" individuals, then bachelors, then unhappily married (*mal casados*), and then widowers without children. In Coahuila-Texas, the legislature directed the governor to give priority, first to vagrants, then disorderly persons, then single men from families that could spare them. And if "entrapment and decoy" were necessary, that would be acceptable. In Tamaulipas, Lyon saw fourteen young men who had been shanghaied at a *fandango,* tied together on their way to camp. Carlos María de Bustamante in January 1825 saw Oaxaca Indian recruits marched through Mexico City chained together. With its large transient population the city of Mexico was a fertile source of draftees, although riots resulted on several occasions when the Federal District governor sent out press gangs to scour the streets and *pulquerías.*[117]

Thus the army resembled a gigantic penal institution. A May 20, 1826, law said that convicted criminals could no longer enter the army as an alternative to jail, and the Secretary of War in 1827 suggested requiring that the states send, not vagrants, but bonafide residents. There is no evidence that he convinced anyone. To a draftee, the fairest solution was simply to go home, which many did at the first opportunity, the favored time being right after receiving clothing. Desertion reached such proportions that congressmen in 1825 and 1826 agitated—vainly—for a tougher law on deserters.[118]

The plain soldier (*soldado raso*) would not find much security in the barracks. Visitors thought pay compared well with European and American standards. Salaries ranged from 6,000 pesos a year for generals on campaign down to 11 pesos a month for privates.[119] After 1827, though, paydays became increasingly irregular, even though soldiers usually received their pay ahead of civilians. Commanders might have to use their personal credit for provisions, or walk into the nearest customs house or commissary and take money by force. It also became fairly common for local officials, more or less willingly, to help. Colonel Mora of the Tampico garrison told the customs house director that he feared his troops, who had not been paid in four months, would go out and pillage if they did not receive a month's pay, and the director decided to cooperate.[120] Santa Anna was less direct. When the Jalapa *ayuntamiento* sent out a committee to greet him on his return from Oaxaca in February 1829, he announced an 8,000-peso voluntary loan. At first the committee members reported back that they could not raise that much. Santa Anna merely asked for a list of those that did and did not contribute, and shortly the total was subscribed, which of course was never paid back.[121]

Common soldiers responded to their plight by selling anything of value, such as uniforms (which had cost about thirty-six pesos),[122] or in the case of Acapulco soldiers, the chains, artillery fittings, and doors from the fortress.[123] In Mexico City there was a brisk traffic in military equipment and munitions in the Baratillo market, taverns, and stores.[124] In Chiapas soldiers had to find outside jobs or even sell firewood.[125] On the marches of Mexico, some soldiers had never enjoyed the experience of drawing pay. California troops were once expected to accept as pay a cargo of cigars, which they might as well have taken since even the salary of their officers was eleven years in arrears.[126] Troops in New Mexico were driven to make "repeated attempts to rob the commissary,"[127] and those in Texas had to hunt down buffalo and deer for food.[128]

The presidios were to be revitalized by the law of March 21, 1826, which created twenty-five new companies in the five northern states and one territory.[129] Each presidio company was to have about 100 men who were to be paid, according to a circular of May 11, 1827, at least twice a year.[130] It appears that any improvements came slowly when they came at all, largely because the 1826 law preceded by only about a year the national budget crisis.

San Francisco's presidio, which Beechey visited in November 1826, showed the results of neglect. He thought it not impressive at all as a center of authority, with its rickety flag staff, "half-accoutered sentinel" guarding shackled prisoners, three rusty field pieces, and trash heaps contested for by dogs, jackals, and vultures. In addition to the nonarrival of the 15-peso-a-month salary, the policy of granting lands after the customary ten-year enlistment was now in doubt, and the soldiers' morale was not high.[131]

To the east, in New Mexico, a similar picture emerged from the territorial papers studied by Daniel Tyler. There the presidio soldier, who averaged about five and a half feet tall, had to swear when signing up for the ten-year term that he had not been impressed. He was to receive food and clothing on the first and fifteenth day of each month and be paid 20 pesos each month, as compared with 125 pesos a month for a captain. Of the three companies allotted New Mexico by the 1826 law, however, only the Santa Fe company was kept near the prescribed strength of 106 men, and only about half of these were normally available for duty.[132] In Texas, the presidio troops were likewise behind in their salaries but they were still obligated to keep up their own equipment, which by ordinance consisted of a carbine, two pistols, a saddle, blanket, spurs, and several horses. In spite of shortages the Texas command was able to bring some relief to the beleaguered communities by using "flying companies" (*compañías volantes*) to carry the war to the Indians themselves.[133]

Trends in the regular army were magnified among the citizen soldiers, the *cívicos*. Reflecting the slide toward federalism, Congress passed new legislation on December 29, 1827, that handed over to the states the job of writing civic militia codes. This law did set down general guidelines: churchmen and government officials were still not required to serve, officers were to be property owners, and the militia was to include at least 1 percent of the state's population. In addition, the Federation promised to distribute 30,000 rifles in "good condition."[134]

Most states produced their own militia codes within a year, which normally provided for cavalry and infantry units, and in some cases artillery. Some states envisaged a plenary force, complete with military bands. While the state government could intervene, the normal procedure was to assign each town a quota, and leave the recruiting and administrative responsibility to the *ayuntamientos*. Men from eighteen to fifty or fifty-five were usually eligible, and those exempted normally paid a fee of about three reales per month. After the exemptions, the civic militia was usually left with a pool of the neighborhood's least substantial men. The militias of the North enrolled Indians, friendly Navajos in New Mexico and Pimas and Opatas in Sonora.[135]

The civic militia's lack of discipline, ragtag appearance, and general unreadiness for battle were notorious. Regular army officers displayed unhidden scorn for the *cívicos*, and citizens came to think of the militia as a home for malingerers and rowdies. Not subject to the discipline ordinances of troops of the line unless nationalized, they resembled more a semi-armed mob than an army. Every state was weapon-short, having enough rifles for only one out of every five or ten soldiers—or, in the case of Tabasco, none at all, only a "handful of bad lances"[136]—until the national government began passing out guns in the latter 1820s. Even then militiamen still relied heavily on lances. Guns were traditionally so rare that the average recruit did not know how to make them work properly.

The original purpose of the civic militia was to keep order (patrol public places, escort prisoners, chase bandits and smugglers), to act as a reserve in case of an invasion from Spain, and in the North to give additional protection from the Indians. But from about 1827 on, protagonists in the armed political squabbles pulled the *cívicos* in. The governors considered the civic militias the bulwark of their states' liberties and resisted any intrusions on their control. A tug-of-war usually ensued whenever the Mexico City government tried to send the units out of state on a national mission.

The size of some states' civic militia put them almost on equal footing with the national army. Several states had forces in the 8,000 to 10,000 range, at least on paper: Jalisco had 11,200 infantry and cavalry in 1828, and Yucatán 17,911 in 1827.[137] After the city of Zacatecas was almost sacked in December 1828, Governor Francisco García took a personal interest in recruiting and provisioning a militia. On December 28, 1830, he claimed over 17,000 troops, although with clothing for only about half the men, and guns for about a third.[138] Even so, it was the best-known militia of the era, and made García a personality to be reckoned with in national politics.

In the late 1820s the Republic's institutions were caught between that equilibrium decreed by the 1824 constitution and the inexorable realities of Mexican society. In government, relationships between the various branches and strata were not yet so lopsided in favor of the national executive. The institution that was momentarily the weakest—the church—still had the greatest claim on the affections of the Mexican masses. As a system of values it still had no real competition among mostly illiterate people whose consciousness was filled with religious imagery. Popular anticlericalism lay in the future. In the military, the efforts at professionalization had come to little, and the general officers were feeling their way toward a stronger political role. With the army as the only organized force in an unstable political world, such a development was inevitable.

In retrospect it was clearly unrealistic to expect people of a folk culture to move in one decade from an autocracy to a Republic. After three centuries of Spanish absolutism, most Mexicans were clan oriented, not community oriented, their attention and allegiance focused inward. Whatever the shortcomings of political decorum, however, the significance of the 1820s experience remained that Mexicans had finally begun their long-delayed journey toward popular government.

« **8** »

The Politics of Control
1830–1831

Guerrero had never flinched before the overwhelming might of Spaniards, but now he had given up without a fight. The old warrior was confused. It seemed that he and his fellows had failed. Federalism, in spite of the political victories of the 1820s, had not been able to bring political peace or prosperity to Mexico. In the eyes of the *gente sensata*, this was the result of a too-free system of politics and society. To them, it was time to discard practices designed for other cultures and look to one's own history, to a time they were now remembering with nostalgia.

It was the basic assumption of the Bustamante administration that Mexicans hungered for peace and stability and that the accident of independence had not altered the age-old customs of obedience. Given the turmoil of the last year and a half, many federalists were prepared to go along.

PERSONNEL AND POLICY

Vice-President Anastacio Bustamante rode in from Puebla on December 31, 1829, and on the following day became chief of state. The first person he named to the cabinet was Alamán, appointed secretary of relations on January 4. Joining him were José Ignacio Espinosa for Justice and Ecclesiastical Affairs, Rafael Mangino for the Treasury, and José Antonio Facio as minister of war.[1]

With Alamán occupying the most powerful position in the ministry, there was no doubt about the direction the administration would take, but the other cabinet members likewise were no friends of federalism. After Alamán, it was Facio who wielded the greatest influence. Facio (1790–1836) was born in Veracruz, but lived in Spain until 1823. A career soldier, he had

189

instructed cadets, campaigned in the cavalry with liberal Spanish officers in the Napoleonic Wars, and attained the rank of colonel. With the French invasion he came home to Mexico, arriving at Veracruz in March 1824, and was given a succession of military assignments: command of the Jalapa canton (1824–1826), command of the Tabasco expedition (fall 1824), and prosecutor (*fiscal*) in the Arenas case. Exiled to the United States for his role in the Montaño rebellion, he returned in early 1829 but was directed to stay in Veracruz six months. From there he was brought onto Bustamante's staff at Jalapa as secretary.[2]

Espinosa and Mangino both had reputations as centralists dating from the 1823 Constitutional Congress. Espinosa was a successful lawyer whom Alamán had recommended to Monteleone as his replacement in 1828 when he was thinking about leaving Mexico.[3] Mangino (1789–1837) came from a family with a tradition of service in the viceregal bureaucracy. Following the footsteps of his father, who was administrator of taxes and customs in Puebla, he worked his way up. Iturbide made him treasurer general of the Army of Three Guarantees, after which he was elected to Congress (1823), and he then returned to the accounting office for the rest of the decade. Mangino's diffidence was famous. In 1822 he was chosen to crown Iturbide, and Carlos María de Bustamante told the story about his worry that the crown, which was heavy and seemed to totter on Iturbide's head, might fall off. "How is it sir? . . . is it placed correctly? . . . are you sure? . . . it won't fall?" he repeated, until finally Iturbide had to reassure him.[4] Although detractors would say that with Mangino the old viceregal spirit of routine had come back to the Treasury, he brought much needed experience with the details of public finance.

The vice-president himself was a thoroughgoing soldier. Bustamante (1780–1853) was born in Jiquilpán, in the Michoacán highlands, to a poor Spanish family, but through the aid of a curate entered the Guadalajara seminary at the age of fifteen and then studied medicine and chemistry at the Colegio de Minería in Mexico City. His proclivity for the military emerged when, while serving in San Luis Potosí as director of the military hospital and Felix Calleja's personal physician, he organized a militia detachment (1808) which was incorporated into the viceregal forces at the outbreak of the Revolution. He saw action with Calleja in the fights against Hidalgo and Morelos, winning a reputation for gallantry and dash. Bustamante reserved his deepest admiration for the martial virtues, and so he took up Iturbide's cause early. Iturbide appointed him Captain General of the Interior Provinces of the East and West, and Bustamante responded with unswerving fidelity, which led to his detention in Guadalajara by Bravo. After his release in December 1824, he was sent north to command the Internal Provinces, where he remained until 1828. In personal dealings he was rather quiet but affable, fond of injecting humor into conversations. He was susceptible to the charms of women. It was said that on the northern frontier "there remained live examples of his cult of love." In appearance Bustamante was roughly soldier-like, of medium height among Mexicans—considered somewhat short by Europeans—and stocky. Because of his liking for great numbers of poached eggs at breakfast he was called "egg-eater."[5]

All in all, Bustamante was a good choice to lead the reaction. For much of the 1820s he had been in the far North fighting Indians and so had not been tainted by the partisan battles. Along the way he had joined the Yorkinos, probably as a gesture against Iturbide's Escocés enemies, but his political reputation was uncertain. As a political leader, though, Bustamante had the disadvantages inherent in his military calling. He was personally likable and his honesty in financial matters was legendary, but he placed no great store in his ability to direct affairs, and for the duration of his term remained somewhat in the background.

It was from Alamán's office that basic policy came. As a type of alter ego for the vice-president, Alamán drafted his addresses to Congress,[6] and constantly invoked Bustamante's name, but privately he marked him a simpleton.[7] In the general administration Alamán's activities extended to other departments. Military commanders wrote to him,[8] their letters suggesting he had a decisive role in army policy, even though Facio superintended day-to-day affairs.

Alamán's great gift was that he had not only a clear image of a desirable Mexican state, but also the will and energy to force public policy in that direction. The Alamán program under Bustamante was the first attempt to proceed toward a comprehensive, coherent set of goals. Up to this point independence governments had essentially reacted, dealing with problems on an ad hoc basis while drawing in desultory fashion from Spanish and North American precedents.

Alamán saw the political path clearly now that the events of the 1820s had put in relief the contradictions of his earlier "liberalism." There was to be no more of the noisy mass electioneering, with its defamatory press, and especially no more Masonic politics. Although the Yorkinos had largely receded from public view, Alamán continued to fulminate against them. In large measure his program amounted to a resurrection of the late colonial regime, with its authoritarian manner, aristocratic tone, and centralism. The traditional institutions of government, church, and military were to be fortified, made efficient, and accountable to the executive. A public peace would be effected by exemplary punishments of common criminals and political troublemakers. At the same time, the administration would seek to inject into society a moral and civilized tone by closing down or at least limiting gambling houses,[9] while patronizing activities of high culture.

In its policy toward foreigners, the Bustamante government joined nationalism and the old colonial suspicion: borders were to be secured against the encroachments of the North Americans, and foreign profitmaking was to be curtailed by creating a native manufacturing industry with up-to-date technology. This was balanced by a covert sympathy for the Spanish. In spite of the administration's repeated protestations that it was carrying out the expulsion law and its frequent warnings that a second invasion was in the making, there was substance to the persistent rumors that Spaniards were reentering the country. There are signed documents showing that Alamán enforced the law, but in questionable cases he came down on the side of leniency. Recent research suggests that he let back in about 500 Spaniards. They were returning primarily from New Orleans, reportedly with U.S. citizenship papers granted for the purpose of relieving that city of beggars. An April 13, 1831, letter from Veracruz spoke of three boatloads of people, in great economic distress, arriving from New Orleans in the past few days.[10]

From a personnel standpoint, the administration combined elements that had been at odds in the Republic's first years. It completed the rapprochement of the old Escocés creole reformers of the colony, like Alamán and Michelena, with Iturbidists like Bustamante, Quintanar, Mangino, Miguel Cervantes, Pedro Otero, and Luis Cortazar. In 1822 they had divided over the question of whether Iturbide or a Spanish prince should sit on the Mexican throne, but both groups had always favored a strong government managed by members of the social elite. Iturbidists and Escoceses had actually moved toward each other at the time of the 1828 election, when they began to style themselves *hombres de bien* or men of substance, a term that would be heard frequently during the Bustamante years.

The wealthier classes were to play a key role in the new scheme of things, with both privileges and responsibilities. Anthony Butler, the American chargé d'affaires who had replaced Poinsett, noted at the outset that the government attracted support from "most of the wealthy, and the whole of the aristocratic hearts of the community."[11]

More was expected than passive acceptance, however. To turn around the Mexican aristocrats' habitual lack of interest in politics, the government newspaper began a campaign to raise their consciousness. Officials looked for active support from the *hombres de bien* and the *gente sensata,* as the administration liked to refer to its backers—in contrast to the opposition, who were the *canalla* and *ladrones.* They were to give their time and money for governmental service, cultural events, textile companies, and private police forces.

Part and parcel of forming a political gentry was election reform. The task was made easier by the fact that many public men shared the Jalapistas' dislike for mass politics as it had taken shape so far. President Guadalupe Victoria had requested a new election law to control disorder, and even the more progressive Yorkinos, including Zavala, were now unsure of universal suffrage.[12] To the general call for making the electorate more responsible, the response was the July 12, 1830, law for the Federal District and territories. Although it was not particularly restrictive in light of later legislation, and it still permitted voting lists, this law did require *algún oficio* (trade) or *industria honesta,* and there was to be voice voting and the recording of the voter's choice.[13] At least two states, Veracruz and Mexico, enacted similar laws.[14] In the state of Mexico the law apparently had the desired effect, for among the twelve individuals elected to Congress in the October 1830 elections, there were included five proprietors, two priests, and a general, miner, and merchant.[15]

CENTRALIZING POWER IN MEXICO CITY

The first few weeks of 1830 were a time for consolidation as trusted Jalapistas, many of them signers of Quintanar's December 23 pact, went out to fill key posts, in particular the states' military commandancies.[16] Melchor Múzquiz, the Jalapa movement's second in command, became inspector general of the army, and later governor of the state of Mexico. Two of the army's most distinguished generals accepted important commands and a third, Santa Anna, was at least momentarily becalmed; Bravo, arriving in Mexico in October 1829, would direct a campaign against rebels in the South, and Mier y Terán, in spite of initial reservations about a government taking over by force, continued as boundary commissioner in Texas and commander of the Eastern Interior Provinces.

It was the best opportunity in a decade for a centralist solution. Since Iturbide, the federalist-Yorkino ideology had been carrying Mexicans farther and farther from the ways of the Spaniards. Now, after the turmoil of the Acordada and the Guerrero administration, the new government opened in an indulgent atmosphere. From almost all corners it could expect at least passive acceptance, even from those who had led the fight for federalism in the past. There was no great outcry from Jalisco and Zacatecas. Leaders there had opposed Guerrero in 1828 anyway. Guerrero himself was at his Tierra Colorada ranch for the first months of 1830, marking time. His old comrade in Acapulco, Juan Álvarez, declared for the Jalapa Plan on January 3 because, according to the Acapulco prefect, of his affection for Bustamante and dislike for Guerrero. Esteva, governor of the Federal District since November, had compromised himself beyond repair during the Jalapa revolt and resigned on January 21 for reasons of health. He would die at the end of July.[17]

Even Zavala was accommodating. On January 3 he wrote a friend that he would advise supporting what was an accomplished fact.[18] Such utterances notwithstanding, Zavala was still one of the most dangerous men in the country, and no one in the executive could rest easy with him at large. Since leaving office in October, he had journeyed to Campeche on an unsuccessful mission for Guerrero, and then had to hide in the mint at the time of Quintanar's December 23 coup. Arrested the next day, he was allowed to proceed to his home after recognizing the new regime. Only two days later, however, an old accusation about exceeding his authority when negotiating loans was revived in the Chamber of Deputies. In March the Senate failed to convict him—after the Chamber voted for indictment—but there were other accusations, and a remark by Alamán that his life might be in danger if he remained. The message was sufficiently clear. On June 2, Zavala boarded ship in Veracruz for an extended visit to the United States, his departure resulting in the shutting down of the *Correo de la Federación Mexicana.*[19]

Congress was the same body that had elected Guerrero in 1829. The senators, many elected before the general takeover by the Yorkinos, would back up the Jalapistas' projects, but the Chamber of Deputies was restive. Some deputies did not wish to tacitly sanction the new government by convening on January 1, but they finally resolved to assemble in hopes of blunting the administration's plans, and elected Alpuche as Chamber president.[20]

In time, new election laws and elections under the guidance of the new leaders would change the personnel, but for the time being the administration used practiced means to extract from Congress desired measures. Unfriendly congressmen were chastened by soldiers and paid bullies shouting threats down from the galleries.[21] Under these conditions, many deputies decided to stay at home, and soon the Chamber was conducting business with only about two-thirds of its members present.[22] Even sporadic resistance disappeared after the fall 1830 elections brought in deputies attuned to executive wishes.[23]

The new administration began immediately to legalize its seizure of power. While legislation to this effect was pushed through Congress in January, government publicity channels began the vilification of Guerrero. In an unsigned five-part pamphlet series, Alamán led the way, making the ex-president appear as a near-imbecile, the greatest criminal in the nation after Guadalupe Victora. Zavala was no better: he supplied himself with fine coaches, gave huge banquets, and kept concubines openly.[24]

On January 14, 1830, Congress ratified the Jalapa Plan, but it remained to legitimize Anastacio Bustamante as chief of state.[25] Guerrero, in a letter to Congress from his retirement in the south, repeated his willingness to abide by its decision.[26] Although the outcome was a foregone conclusion, the proceedings raised an awkward question since to nullify Guerrero's election as president would also logically nullify Bustamante's election as vice-president. *El Sol,* generally following Alamán's anonymous pamphlet, reasoned thus: Gómez Pedraza had renounced his rights to the presidency; Congress had decreed on September 17, 1828, that all those who aided the Perote pronouncement, which Guerrero admittedly had, were traitors; after the Acordada revolt Congress chose an ineligible person, Guerrero, as president; the office, therefore, devolved upon Vice-President Bustamante.[27]

The movement began in the Senate. The Senate committee report on January 14 compared Guerrero to a child, mentally unfit and morally incapable of governing the Republic. The Senate approved this on January 18 (twenty-two votes to three), and although Guerrero's Chamber of Deputies' supporters, led by Quintana Roo, succeeded in expunging the word "morally," a decree was promulgated on February 4 that Guerrero was incapable of governing.[28]

The other potential contender for the presidency, Gómez Pedraza, was living in exile in Paris, and the administration intended to keep him there. After Gómez Pedraza wrote in March 1830 of his intention to return home, Alamán advised him the situation was still sensitive and that he would endanger his life by returning. To soften the blow, the Mexican legation in either France or Colombia was offered, but Gómez Pedraza was not interested. Finally, in August 1830, he set sail for Mexico. He probably thought that since many of the Bustamante men had supported his candidacy in 1828 they could not turn their backs on him now. But it was a long trip for nothing. Facio wrote Veracruz governor Camacho not to let him stay, and Gómez Pedraza was put back on the next New Orleans–bound boat. There he wrote a long self-justifying pamphlet.[29]

Santa Anna was the big question mark in 1830 and 1831. For the time being, he seemed content to bask in the memory of his heroics at Tampico. He had presented to the Veracruz legislature, for lodgment in a place of honor, the suit he had worn during one assault on the Spaniards, although one writer asked that if the legislators thought that highly of the suit, then how much would his underwear (*calzones*) be worth?[30] In March 1830 he wrote to Facio that, happy in the "bosom of his family," he would leave home only in case of a foreign invasion. Although hardly a man to be taken at his word, he did act as if he meant to take the country life seriously. He had just bought 30,000 pesos worth of hacienda land, 6,000 pesos of which came from the dowry of Inés García, whom he had married in early 1829. He passed the time planning sugarcane fields and reading about Napoleon. Although Santa Anna had thought better of fighting for a hopeless cause in December 1829, no one could say when he might take it into his head to make trouble. Trying to keep him happy, the government gratified his appetite for honors. Guanajuato bestowed upon him a bejeweled sword for his services at Tampico, and at the ceremonious presentation on July 15, 1830, Santa Anna toasted Guanajuato and Alamán, who apparently had instigated the award.[31] Thirty-seven years later, when imprisoned in San Juan de Ulúa, Santa Anna gave the sword to his lawyer for services rendered.[32]

If most congressmen did not dare to contest an accomplished coup d'état, a few refused to stay quiet in 1830, either out of loyalty to Guerrero or to their own principles. In the Senate there was Manuel Crescencio Rejón. In the Chamber of Deputies there were José María Alpuche, Anastacio Cerecero, Isidro Rafael Gondra, Juan de Dios Cañedo, and Andrés Quintana Roo. When practicable, distinguished opponents were enticed into the official family. Cañedo, who was challenging the administration's legitimacy in early 1831, was sent on a diplomatic mission to South America. But others saw another face of the government's strategy. Quintana Roo was taken to court for slandering Facio. And the jails contained 200 individuals accused of conspiracy, as *El Atleta* reported on April 20, 1830. Chamber of Deputies President Alpuche was sentenced to five years in exile for a seditious letter to Mier y Terán.[33] While in jail Alpuche feared assassination, but he would live to take revenge.[34]

Anastacio Cerecero, along with his brother Mariano and eight others, was taken into custody on March 24 on the basis of an alleged plot to assassinate the vice-president and members of his cabinet. The court sentenced Cerecero to five years of exile and Gondra, who was implicated, to two years' detainment in a monastery.[35] Senator Rejón was beaten up by two soldiers on his way to lunch after a Senate session of November 3, 1831. Alamán, appearing in Congress to answer charges, stated the soldiers had in all events not infringed upon senatorial immunity since they had attacked Rejón the writer, not Rejón the senator.[36]

It was intended that civil pacification would parallel political pacification. On June 21, 1830, Alamán circulated a directive to several governors citing recent disturbances and urging the governors to collect weapons, excepting only those of citizens who had given proof of their support for "the present order of things."[37] While the government newspaper chanted on the horrors of disrespect for the law, the army made liberal use of the September 27, 1823, law and carried through the most relentless law enforcement since the days of viceregal magistrates. In June 1831, Wilcocks noted that executions occurred almost daily.[38] Two months later Butler wrote Van Buren that the military had executed more than twenty people in the few weeks past. An official explained that the executions formed part of a deliberate policy, since the government felt that leniency encouraged "the opposition."[39]

ARTICLE 4 AND THE STATES

Bringing Congress into line comprised only part of the plan. The six-year waiting period set down by the 1824 constitution had passed, and the present congressmen could consider, although not act upon, amendments offered by the states. The response to the Campeche pronouncement had shown the hour was not yet right for centralism, so the Bustamantistas used the cloak of federalism for their actions while readying the public for a change. *El Sol* editors tried a sideways campaign to make centralism respectable. With lip service to federalism, they spent much time on its failings: federalism was for more mature societies, while Mexico was only in its adolescence; if there were more order and uniformity, criminals could not flee to sanctuaries, and taxation would be more consistent.[40]

On January 19, 1830, Alamán wrote to confidant José María Michelena in Morelia. Things were proceeding well with the Chamber of Deputies, with a thoroughgoing purge in the offing, and it would be well to extend this to the state legislatures.[41] It was easily accomplished, as Alamán recounted in his *Historia de Méjico* twenty years later. Many legislative elections had taken place in unsettled times, amid charges of irregularities. It was "easy to find motives to annul them, and thus it was done with all the appropriate ones."[42] This was not the first time Congress had sat as judge on state elections, but now the practice became an instrument of policy, to bring about compliant legislatures.[43]

Article 4 in the Jalapa Plan offered the mechanism. It declared for the removal of all public officials against whom public opinion had been expressed, and the victorious Jalapistas judged which voices represented true public opinion. Each state required specific treatment, but the procedures used for removing undesirables contained several common elements. Normally the campaign opened with almost daily unfavorable publicity about the target in *Registro Oficial,* the new official newspaper, and *El Sol*—editorial comments and letters from local citizens. State and church units such as *ayuntamientos* or cathedral chapters would issue petitions complaining about the individual or group in question, especially how they came to be elected. Congress would then act, decreeing that said election was faulty and therefore invalid. If the governor or legislature demurred, the army came round to enforce the decree. A key figure in the process was the local military commander, encouraging dissident groups to ask for an Article 4 decree, and standing by to carry out the decree.[44]

In the Gobernación section of the Mexican National Archives, a packet of correspondence has survived showing how one desperate official felt as he saw Article 4 turned toward him. The letters ran between Michoacán governor José Salgado and the minister of relations. Salgado, a well-known Yorkino, had been serving as chief executive since November 9, 1827, when his predecessor refused to promulgate a Spanish expulsion law.[45] Michoacán's military commander at the time was General Juan José Codallos (1790–1831), one of two Codallos generals who were then prominent. Born on the island of Barlovento de Trinidad, in the Antilles, they had both served under the royalists during the Revolution, but Juan José evolved into a Guerrero loyalist, while his brother Felipe (1790–1849) supported the Bustamante administration as Federal District commander.[46]

Salgado had rejected the Jalapa pronouncement and had even moved troops toward Mexico City until Guerrero's sudden flight left him no choice but ignoble retreat. Then on January 4 the state legislature voted not to adhere to the Jalapa Plan, promising to abide by Congress' decision as to who was chief executive. A federal detachment under General

Luis Cortazar was soon on its way to Morelia. It took a while for Salgado to realize he was doomed. On January 5, enclosing the January 4 decree, he mixed veiled threats with a seeming willingness to submit. He pledged himself to maintain order while asking that no "innovation" be made. The militia had been called up, he said, because the state government's enemies had taken advantage of recent upheavals, but it would not be used "except in emergency."[47] By January 18 the movement to unseat him was well under way. On that day he wrote of a widespread conspiracy, centered in the Morelia *ayuntamiento*, to overturn both governor and legislature. The main conspirator was Michelena, who was holding subversive meetings at his home. Salgado asked that Article 4 be ruled inapplicable to popularly elected state officials. Alamán replied simply that Congress had ratified the Jalapa Plan, including Article 4, and it was not Salgado's prerogative to make interpretations. As for Michelena, his military *fuero* gave him immunity to any action by Salgado. If the governor had any complaints, he could go to Cortazar, Michoacán's new commanding general.[48] On March 5 the Morelia *ayuntamiento* announced it would no longer recognize Salgado as governor, and on March 13 Congress declared his election null and void. By that time he had fled Morelia for Zamora in San Luis Potosí state.[49]

San Luis Potosí was another center of discontent. There sitting as governor was Vicente Romero. Later in the year, as a fugitive he was described as a forty-six-year-old Jalisco native, of medium build, although slightly pot-bellied, bald but using a partial wig, and moving his right cheek when he talked. In Iturbide's time Romero had come to San Luis Potosí as a low-echelon bureaucrat and had worked his way up to the governorship in 1828.[50] Now he was turning his state into a sanctuary for pro-Guerrero fugitives and trying to mobilize the northern states to resist the Jalapistas. Under Romero's influence the legislature issued a sheaf of proclamations, all of them highly offensive to the Bustamante administration: on January 13 proposing a defensive confederation of several northern states; on March 15 inviting Congress to move to a safe place where it could deliberate free of coercion; and on March 17 petitioning that the secretaries of relations and war be removed. To back up the plans, *cívicos* were called to the capital—about 2,000 by April.[51]

The Bustamante administration papers immediately unleashed a barrage of criticism against Romero. Facio ordered the state's *cívicos* to Texas, which Romero resisted naturally enough, whereupon Cortazar was sent to San Luis Potosí with 2,000 men. Romero now promised to support the Jalapa Plan, but this did not convince anyone and on June 11 he resigned. The legislature tried to switch to the winning side by joining in the prosecution of the ex-governor—relative to a forced loan during the Spanish invasion—but the legislature came to the same end as Romero.[52]

In marked contrast to preceding administrations, the Bustamantistas moved fast. Through the first half of 1830 the long arm of the central government reached out to the states.

With urgings from Alamán, and with Congress providing legal sanctions and the local commander military pressure—at times the initiative came from the local officials—the states were cleansed of opponents. In the state of Mexico, the legislature was replaced, and the new legislature elected Melchor Múzquiz as governor.[53] In Jalisco unfriendly legislators were removed and Anastacio Cañedo was brought back in as governor after a temporary eviction by the Yorkino leader Juan N. Cumplido.[54] In Puebla the legislature was persuaded to disperse.[55] The Veracruz legislature was voided, although the deposed legislators held a rump session in Coatepec and for a few weeks contending legislatures annulled each other's decrees.[56] In Oaxaca the acting governor resigned and the legislature was dispersed.[57] In Chiapas the legislature was closed and the new legislature selected the state commander as the new governor.[58] In Tabasco the governor was arrested and replaced.[59] In Querétaro the legislature was dissolved.[60] In Durango the legislature was replaced, and prominent Yorkinos, including former governor Baca, were arrested.[61] In Chihuahua anti-Jalapa legislators were removed.[62] In Tamaulipas the governor and legislature were removed.[63]

After the purge, the states that most dependably reflected vibrations from Mexico City were Mexico state, Guanajuato, Querétaro, Puebla, and Oaxaca, and most of the others had generally fallen under the sway of the national capital. If one discounts the far north, where local problems such as Indians took precedence, there were only two notable exceptions, Zacatecas and Yucatán. Zacatecas could hold to an independent course of action because of its large civic militia. At the Jalapa pronouncement García had mobilized these militiamen, and although Zacatecas did later recognize the new government, the legislature proclaimed itself ready to protect the national and state constitutions. For the duration the state would maintain an armed truce with the Bustamante government, and García openly gave refuge to Romero of San Luis Potosí.[64]

Yucatán, in the curious position of splitting off from the rest of Mexico in the name of centralism, continued to rebuff the reconciliation offers extended by a centralist administration. The Bustamante officials took a benign attitude toward Yucatán's independence, sending emissaries and letters exhorting the state to rejoin the Republic. The man in charge there, José Segundo Carbajal, tried to effect a sort of union on his own terms, convoking a General Assembly which declared that the national and state constitutions were in effect but that Yucatán might veto any national decrees. Carvajal even tried, unsuccessfully, to have the state's deputies admitted to Congress in 1831.[65]

MILITARISM AND THE MILITARY

One of the most persistent charges levied against the Bustamante officials was that they used the army to carry out their centralist ambitions. Soldiers now let civilians know that support for Guerrero would not be tolerated. In Puebla troops set up an effigy of the former president and affixed to it a deck of cards, a gamecock, and some verses:

> I became unworthy of my fatherland
> Because its ruin I did cause
> But am I the one who is guilty
> Or is the one the rite of Yorkino?
> I was born a little black chicken
> Knowing nothing of reading and writing
> And President I finally came to be
> By the Plan of the Acordada.

The soldiers then set fire to Guerrero and retired to a nearby cantina.[66]

On the other side, Alamán inveighed privately as well as publicly, and without duplicity it should be added, against military high-handedness. Alamán and his opponents were talking about different phenomena. What administration opponents wrote against with such passion was the commandants' practice of systematically coercing public officials, and court-martialing and executing civilians for political offenses.

What Alamán detested was any spontaneous political stirring by the officer corps. In his 1830 *Memoria* he listed the basic faults of Mexican politics, and high on the list was abuse of the right of petition. Here he was actually striking out at military pronouncements masquerading as petitions—the petition carried out on the spot by force. In the 1832 *Memoria* he noted the government was preparing a bill that would distinguish between the right of petition and that of legislative initiative, the former a guaranteed right, the latter limited in all except purely personal cases to bona fide legislators.[67] The 1832 civil war cut short this proposal, but for two and a half years the administration went a long way toward integrating army officers into the political scheme.

There was a negative and a positive side to the new standard. Personalistic politics were now to be beyond the pale. No more were generals and colonels, aroused by one or another issue, to jump into the political fray with their troops. They also had new responsibilities: in addition to supervising local politics on cue, they were now to disseminate propaganda, build roads, and cooperate in industrial and agricultural projects.[68]

In practice, the Bustamante men, living in the shadow of illegitimacy and facing at least some armed opposition, frequently had no choice but to cater to the general officers. In early 1830, when there were not enough revenues to satisfy all obligations, military salaries were given high priority.[69] At about the same time the official newspaper revealed more than a hundred promotions at the level of noncommissioned and company command levels, most of which probably had political motivation.[70] Indeed, *El Fénix de la Libertad* reported that the number of generals grew from thirty to fifty-one, enough, quipped the correspondent, for an army of a half million.[71]

The Mexican National Archives' collection of correspondence of the commanding officers illustrated the near impossibility of keeping them in check. They complained about the *cívicos,* about the interference of independent inspectors, about legal impediments to chastising criminals, and about tax collectors wishing to make "levies extensive even to me." These letters also demonstrated Alamán's enormous capacity for administrative detail. Once he questioned the Celaya commander about the fate of a certain thief.[72]

One of the pivotal commanders was Luis de Cortazar y Rábago (1796–1840), commanding general of Guanajuato. Although a typical rough-hewn soldier in many ways, Cortazar was a nephew of the Count of Rábago and had married Manuela Cevallos y Monterde, the countess of Presa de Jalpa. He had fought for the royalists, then declared for Iturbide early and won several victories. He was called upon by the emperor to dissolve Congress in 1822, a task he executed with remorseless celerity. In the 1820s he had not been closely associated with any political group nationally, but by this time had emerged as something of a regional arbiter thanks to his command, influential relations, and personal landholdings.[73]

Another government aim was, once again, to professionalize the troops. Facio, with his long service in the peninsula, was military through and through. He enjoyed reviewing the Second and Third Cavalry regiments, commanded by Mariano Arista and Gabriel Durán.[74] It was his stated policy to bring back the smart discipline absent since independence, but time was short for any marked success.

Beyond the reach of Facio were the *cívicos.* The Bustamante officials look upon them as rabble, remembering them as key players in episodes like the anti-Spanish terrorism of 1827 and the Acordada mutiny. More than anything else, they could stand in the way of administration plans. Controlling the civic militia was made somewhat easier since by the early 1830s the federalists had become skeptical too. Although the *cívicos* had a democratic appeal, federalists could stand for only so much disorder for the sake of leveling. Even Lizardi had written that they looked like "troops of boys on the day of San Juan. You've seen them. They elect their leaders and they obey them while they feel like it, and when they don't, they boot them out and change."[75] The official press began an attack almost immediately, and soon, apparently at the behest of the central government, several militias were neutralized. In Puebla the *cívicos* were disarmed, in Tamaulipas disarmed and disbanded, and in Mexico state disarmed and replaced with private forces. In Michoacán, pro-Salgado officers refusing to sign an Article 4 petition were purged, and the Oaxaca militia was tampered with.[76]

For the future, Alamán planned to reconstitute the *cívicos* to harmonize with his vision of society. He proposed a tripartite division: heads of families and small proprietors would compose the "fixed" detachments stationed in population centers; these would coordinate their activities with the haciendas' mounted patrols; a third group, those lacking the qualifications of the first two, would serve only in emergencies. Smaller pueblos would lose their militias altogether.[77] The *cívicos* gave little trouble throughout 1830 and 1831, but Congress failed to reorganize them and in 1832 they were built up again—principally by Zacatecas—for the civil war.

The Bustamante administration had the distinction of presiding over the demise of the first Mexican navy. The Ulúa Spaniards had been the spur for a navy program, and after they surrendered, interest began to wane. Following the same curve as the army, there were early attempts to professionalize: a naval academy, established at Tlacotalpám in January 1825, and the employment of first British and then American officers to instill European discipline. But the academy languished, as the main instructor had to look for operating funds as well as teach spherical trigonometry. And the foreign officer experiment ended when fleet commander Commodore David Porter, having lost a son and a nephew in Mexico and having failed to re-educate the sailors, resigned on September 20, 1829. After 1826, on the downward slope of its existence, the navy had the same troubles as the army in filling the ranks and obtaining operating funds. Makeshift crews, with sizable admixtures of convicts and impressed seamen and foreign deserters (especially American), manned the ships. In 1828 sailors' pay came in "pay tickets," which were exchanged for less than one-sixth of face value.[78]

The history of the only battleship in the Mexican navy illustrated the problems. As part of the Spanish fleet in the Orient, the crew of the *Asia* mutinied in the Mariana Islands and surrendered in Monterrey. On June 11, 1825, the *Asia* entered Acapulco harbor, and Mexico was handed a seventy-four-gun battleship free. The War Department rechristened it the *Congreso Mejicano* and decided to send it around to Veracruz. The vessel was fifty years old, however, and had to put into Valparaiso for repairs, there to be detained since the repairs could not be paid for, and it finally arrived in Veracruz on January 9, 1828, minus part of its crew. The *Congreso Mejicano* had a dead-end future. It was used first as a command ship, then as a prison, and then, when the wood rotted, was towed out to sea and sunk.[79] As it turned out, the wisest course of action would have been to follow an earlier recommendation to disassemble the *Asia* and sell the wood as scrap.

The final duty of the navy was raiding Spanish shipping. When on August 12, 1828, the last raider came in from the base at Cayo Hueso in the Florida Keys, the War Department could claim several prizes, but Spanish raiders in their turn had done considerable damage off the Yucatán coast. During the raiding, a chance encounter of the *Guerrero* with the Spanish *Lealtad* offered opportunity for valor. When the *Guerrero,* damaged from an engagement with two Spanish brigs and captained by David H. Porter (the commodore's nephew), came upon the larger *Lealtad* on February 10, 1828, it could not escape. After a spirited two-and-a-half-hour contest and the death of Porter, the *Guerrero* was forced to strike its colors.[80]

The new administration in 1830 had no plans to revive the navy. Most of the seaworthy vessels had been lost when Yucatán defected in 1829. Facio's idea was to start up a type of auxiliary navy, cheaper than the real thing, but the idea stalled at the planning stage, and so the navy was left to die. In 1830, with the Veracruz fleet of five ships rotting in the harbor, port officials did not even have the means to force an American ship to pay its duties. When they sent out in pursuit their best ship, the *Luisiana,* it foundered.[81]

THE PRESS

The Yorkino-federalists had taken naturally to the rough and tumble of public debate. Most of them, after all, had to fight their way up, but the *hombres de bien* had an instinctive aversion to the raucous journalistic style of the 1820s. In his 1830 *Memoria* Alamán announced his displeasure with the legalities. Authors of criminal pamphlets usually turned out to be derelicts who sold their signatures, and since the publishers mailed out their papers before sending the mandatory copies to the authorities, even a conviction was of little use, for the damage was done.[82] The other side saw it differently. An 1832 pamphlet accused Alamán of filling the country with ministerial publications and of paying foreign newspapers to publicize the good side of the government, all the while making it impossible for the opposition press to say anything.[83] In fact, that was just what happened. From the administration's point of view, the new policy merely enforced rules of propriety and returned political debates to the high road of civilized discussion. What the policy meant in practice was that it became extremely hazardous to print more than mild criticisms of the national executive.

The administration was able to obtain some legislation. A law of May 14, 1831, allowed a plaintiff to appeal an adverse decision and gave him the alternative of prosecuting slander either through the press laws or the personal injury laws. It was intended that judges sitting on the personal injury cases would hand down sterner justice than the juries for press infractions.[84]

For the most part, the Bustamantistas did quite well in silencing abrasive commentators with the available judicial processes. The Cortes law had provided for jail sentences of several years, which had never been given out until now, but early on the government gave notice that critics would publish their views at their own risk. On February 1, 1830, Luis Heredia, responsible for *Con constitución y leyes nos quieren hacer esclavos,* was sentenced to six years' imprisonment.[85] Like sentencings followed, driving the point home. One printer was reportedly fined 500 pesos for not carrying a complete date on a pamphlet.[86] Printers learned soon enough whom to print for. Rocafuerte and Quintana Roo both complained that they could find no one to publish their writings.[87]

One of the beleaguered newspapers, *El Federalista Mexicano,* which appeared in January 1831, was edited by Andrés Quintana Roo (1787–1851), later to be judged one of Mexico's distinguished men of letters. Quintana Roo came from a revolutionary creole family. His father, José Matías Quintana (1767–1841) was a store owner, militia captain, and regent of Mérida—with an interest in literature. An associate of Zavala and the Sanjuanistas, Quintana senior wrote newspaper articles sympathetic to the insurgents until imprisoned by the Spaniards, and after independence served in the state and national congresses. Andrés was also linked with Zavala, studying with him under Pablo Moreno. They were his best students. In 1808 Andrés was sent to the university in Mexico City to study law, but left to join the Revolution in 1812, where he wrote proclamations and tracts for Ignacio Rayón and Morelos.[88]

Quintana Roo was not a facile writer. To call forth his creative talents he needed a proximate stimulus and it was sometimes necessary to resort to violence, "locking him up in his room so that he could produce some poetry, a tract, a manifesto, or some legal draft."[89] He derived great fortitude from his wife Leona Vicario (1788–1842), whom he courted in a celebrated romance while a young law student and finally married in 1813. Her revolutionary will possibly exceeded his. Following him in the insurgent camps, she gave birth to their first child while a fugitive, and on several occasions kept him from giving up the struggle. He finally did accept an amnesty from the royalists in 1818. Under Guadalupe Victoria he served on the Supreme Court, and was then elected to the 1827–1828 Chamber of Deputies from the state of Mexico.

During the Bustamante administration Quintana Roo defended the cause of Gómez Pedraza, whom he had supported in 1828. *El Federalista Mexicano,* which he founded on January 5, 1831, soon attracted the attention of the authorities, and once again Leona Vicario stepped in. On February 2 government agents went from the newspaper offices to the Quintana Roo home in search of him, and Leona Vicario, fearing for her husband's life, went to the national palace. When she was finally admitted to the vice-president's offices, Bustamante called for Federal District commander Felipe Codallos who stated that it was necessary "to answer these writers with clubs" because military men could not combat them literarily. She remonstrated and Bustamante replied, "What do you want? They are so insulting!" and finally vouched for Quintana Roo's safety only if he remained at home.[90] *El Federalista Mexicano* was crushed under the weight of fines in April 1831.[91]

A large part of the administration's propaganda effort went into positive channels. To symbolize the new order, a new government newspaper was established, the *Registro Oficial,* which circulated among a large captive audience of civil and military officials. In addition, *El Sol* could usually be counted on for editorial support, and newspapers and pamphlets subsidized by the Ministry of Relations' secret fund vehemently attacked administration enemies. Carlos María de Bustamante was on the government payroll until October 1831, when his *Voz de la patria* strayed too far from the government line. *El Gladiador* was probably subsidized too. It appeared on March 27, 1830, with the expressed intention of doing battle with the pro-Guerrero *El Atleta,* and ceased publication after *El Atleta* was fined out of existence. Then it reappeared January 10 to June 3, 1831, to combat Quintana Roo's *Federalista Mexicano.*[92]

Beyond Mexico City, various government dependents were employed to spread the official view. From the correspondence of the commanding generals there emerges the strong probability that they blanketed their areas with "ministerial" newspapers.[93] Rocafuerte charged that the Banco de Avío or Credit Bank officials were used for the same purposes.[94] In May 1832, Tepic commander Luis Correa suggested that the government organize a friendly newspaper in Guadalajara to serve as a "brake" on revolutionary publications.[95] Abroad, the diplomats Tomás Murphy and Manuel Eduardo Gorostiza were directed to place favorable announcements in New York and European newspapers.[96]

THE WAR OF THE SOUTH, 1830–1831

The men of the South took to war again in March 1830 under their old captain, Vicente Guerrero. This War of the South, as the insurrection came to be called, was centered in the Costa Grande (the coastal region around Acapulco), an unruly area that had produced not only Guerrero, but Juan Álvarez and Nicolás Bravo. Since 1810 these countrymen of Indian and African blood had been in a state of almost continuous rebellion against the constituted government: against the *gachupines* under Morelos and Guerrero and Álvarez, against Iturbide in 1823, against local Spaniards in 1827, and against the candidacy of Gómez Pedraza in 1828.

In early 1830 Guerrero was living at his Tierra Colorada hacienda. He took note of the March 11 declaration by Michoacán's former commanding general Codallos, which called for restoring the legislatures and officials deposed by the Jalapistas.[97] Letters arrived, and entire villages of Indians came seeking an audience with Guerrero, all with the obvious intent to urge resistance.[98] Then, as he explained it later at his trial, seeing his followers persecuted and troops moving closer to his hacienda, he made the decision to act. In a note to the ayuntamientos of southern Mexico he announced he would fight for Codallos' Plan.[99]

In April another leader of the South rode into the rebel camp. Juan Álvarez too had spent much of his life fighting in the hills of the South, first against the Spaniards and then against Iturbide. He then served as Acapulco commander. At the Jalapa pronouncement in December 1829 Álvarez had called upon his Indian followers to fight for their rights against the *gente de razón*. Although he accepted the Bustamante government on January 3, the new regime felt uncomfortable with him in command of a strategic fort and sent an officer of royalist precedents to replace him, General Francisco Berdejo. The replacement orders directed Álvarez to March against the invading Spaniards at Tecpan, on the western side of Mexico, and Álvarez was reputed to have asked the War Department if the invaders had come in balloons *(globos aerostáticos)*.[100]

On the government's side, an Army of the South, some 1,600 strong, was organized and entrusted to Nicolás Bravo. Coming in July as Bravo's second in command was Gabriel Armijo (d. 1830), who as a royalist had carried on a bloody war of pacification in these same villages. It seemed like a reenactment of the Revolution, and the 1830 rebellion gave signs of turning into a race war. Guerrero harangued his men against the whites in the Indian language, and the Acapulco prefect in January 1831 wrote the War Department that the Indians of Atoyac and San Jerónimo were bragging publicly that they were going to "finish off the whites."[101] Armijo, a man of aggressive military habits, did what he had done as a royalist: burn huts and shoot Indians found with a gun.[102]

Alamán belittled the Guerrero-led rebels, "a few pueblos of Indian rioters and bands of thieves," but the government could never track down and corner the main body.[103] As folk heroes, Guerrero and Álvarez could move freely through the mountains and fall upon Bravo's soldiers at places of their choosing. Since Guerrero's old wounds had never completely healed, Álvarez was the more active campaigner, but he preferred to stay on horseback since he himself had wounds dating back to the days of Morelos and could not move his legs below the knee.

The administration had difficulty limiting the outbreak. Although the Army of the South put the rebels to flight at Venta Vieja (April 24), the insurgents won at Manglar (June 6)—both battles in the Acapulco region—and by 1831 the insurrection was reaching into Oaxaca in the south and Jalisco in the north. Old revolutionaries emerged. Loreto Cataño operated around Cuautla just south of Mexico City, Gordiano Guzmán around Tacámbaro and Apatzingán, and Guadalupe Montenegro in the Jalisco cantons of Sayula and Etzatlán.[104]

To check these movements, the regular army made liberal use of the law of September 27, 1823, and continued punishing Guerrero's partisans.

With the military ignoring the debate over the law's validity, the distinction between civil and political crimes became blurred. Among the executed were Colonel Francisco Victoria, brother of the ex-president, and revolutionary hero Juan Nepomuceno Rosaíns. On December 5, 1830, Loreto Cataño died of a fever while in government custody, amid rumors of poisoning. The most pitiless commander was General Pedro Otero of Michoacán, whose own reports showed twenty-eight political prisoners executed between December 1830 and July 1831.[105]

In late 1830 the administration received several blows from friends as well as enemies. On November 17 Jalisco commander Miguel Barragán called for a general conference, with Guerrero invited, to consider ways to end the civil war.[106] There were renewed attacks on Facio in the Chamber of Deputies, blaming him for Otero's executions in Michoacán and for not letting Gómez Pedraza return home. Then in January Cañedo brought up the issue of the government's legitimacy.[107]

The administration's enemies had been given hope by events at the village of Texca, about a day's ride northeast of Acapulco. After Manglar, Armijo decided to follow Álvarez right to his mountainous stronghold. At dawn on September 30 Armijo and his men found themselves the hunted, surrounded in Texca. Armijo tried to escape on foot but was chased down and hacked to death with machetes, so mutilated that Álvarez turned away when he saw the cadaver. His remains were left on display and the Texca inhabitants, having lost friends and relatives on his account, came to excoriate the tall, husky, corpse. Álvarez had to sleep near the prisoners to prevent a slaughter.[108]

In a startling turn of events, however, the fortunes of war shifted in early 1831 and the War of the South was brought to an end. On the second day of the new year Bravo defeated the rebels decisively near Chilpancingo. As Manuel Zavala (no apparent relation to Lorenzo) described it from his vantage point in the rebel camp, Guerrero's men had thrown back the first government charge, but then busied themselves "stripping the dead of their clothing, watches, and money" when Bravo's troops regrouped, counterattacked, and took the field.[109]

Further good fortune came to the government when it was announced on January 31 that former President Guerrero had been taken prisoner.[110] Slowly the news trickled in that the former president had been handed over to government troops by a Genoese ship's captain, Francisco Picaluga, and then been court-martialed and executed in Oaxaca on February 14.

The last days of Vicente Guerrero can be reconstructed from a few archival pieces and the *Proceso Instructivo,* documents gathered when the Chamber of Deputies in 1833 prosecuted Guerrero's prosecutors. At Guerrero's court-martial, Picaluga testified he had arrived at Acapulco in June of 1830, and that after the Texca battle, which allowed Guerrero and Álvarez to occupy Acapulco, he journeyed to Mexico City to settle an account with the government.[111] In Mexico City he met with Facio, who wrote later from exile in France that Picaluga had agreed to hand over only his boat, the *Sardo Colombo,* and that the government, which could make good use of it to combat insurrection, promised to compensate him with 50,000 pesos. Alamán gave him a passport to return to Acapulco.[112]

After Picaluga left Mexico City, the military was set in motion along the southern coast, but not relative to receiving the *Sardo Colombo.* There are in the *Proceso Instructivo* three War Department orders, dated December 18, January 8, and January 23. In the first, Facio ordered Oaxaca's commanding general Francisco García Conde to invest the port of Huatulco (in Oaxaca) with personnel "of the greatest confidence," there to guard against a disembarkation by the enemy. In the second, García Conde delegated the job to Captain Miguel González, sending along also Captain José María Llanes who "for his preparation can be very useful in carrying out" the mission—Llanes later served as prosecutor *(fiscal)* at Guerrero's court-martial. In the third, García Conde wrote to Major Villarreal that, as Guerrero would soon flee Acapulco, suitable measures had been taken, mainly garrisoning Huatulco.[113]

Unaware of all this troop movement, Guerrero had finally accepted a repeated invitation to take a meal with Picaluga—on January 11—on board the *Sardo Colombo* in the Acapulco harbor. The treachery took place, as Guerrero recounted it, when he was saying goodbye to Picaluga whom he had spoken of as *"mi muy buen amigo."*[114] In the version of Manuel Zavala, who accompanied Guerrero, Picaluga had unsuccessfully tried to induce the party to drink alcoholic beverages, and then about 4:00 P.M. as Guerrero was taking his leave, several armed men approached in menacing fashion. Picaluga said they were only drunk and he would calm them down if Guerrero would go below deck. When Guerrero went down, Picaluga's men forced him to lie down, fettered him, and tied up his friends, including Zavala.[115] The *Sardo Colombo* then weighed anchor and made for the port of Huatulco, where Guerrero and the others were handed over to waiting government troops.

A military court tried Guerrero for a variety of crimes to the state, including an attempt to sell Texas, and unanimously found him guilty.[116] The historian Suárez y Navarro stated that he had seen a draft, in Facio's handwriting, listing the crimes that Guerrero was to be charged with. The Zacatecas legislature petitioned Congress on February 7 not to execute Guerrero,[117] but the decision had been made.

On February 14 Guerrero was taken from his confinement in Cuilapam to the place of execution. Although he had been depressed for the past several days—Manuel Zavala wrote he had acted as supplicant toward his captors[118]—he was calm now, putting the blindfold on by himself and sitting down to await the bullets. His body was buried immediately.[119]

Congress voted an annual pension of 3,000 pesos for Guerrero's widow, but the executive's leaders exhibited no remorse. Alamán said the execution had saved Mexico from dissolution. Necessarily, the government had sent "some important persons to the scaffold," he wrote Gorostiza, but the "rod of iron" was understandable when one considered the anarchy of January 1830.[120] Publicly, the Bustamante administration held to the explanation that Picaluga had taken Guerrero on his own, but only the naive believed that.

Whether the Bustamante men had truly inaugurated a reign of stability or merely terrified their opponents, Guerrero's death spelled peace. The rebels gave up Acapulco on March 23, and many of their leaders took advantage of an amnesty passed by Congress on March 2.[121] Álvarez came to terms on April 15 and even used his influence to calm the villages of the South.[122] Codallos, warring in Michoacán and pursued by government troops, refused amnesty entreaties sent by his brother Felipe, and Colonel Moctezuma finally caught up and executed him in Pátzcuaro on July 11.[123]

With the War of the South suffocated, there was no active resistance to the Bustamante administration. Congress was obedient, and there were murmurings but no violent opposition from the state governments. Even García of Zacatecas, while not friendly, was not stirring up trouble. For the latter two-thirds of 1831 the Republic had relative peace.

In the latter months of 1831 it seemed that Alamán had won in the long ideological struggle he had been waging with Zavala. It was tranquil enough that he took leave from June 6 to July 29 and spent the congressional recess at his hacienda near Celaya.[124]

Zavala was now making arrangements for his Texas lands in the United States where he would remain, with the exception of a brief trip to France, until mid-1832. He was still instigating newspaper attacks against the Bustamante administration, and writing self-justifying histories of Mexican politics, but since the 1828 election he had discredited himself even in the eyes of fellow federalists.[125]

There were few outward signs that he was being listened to. Perhaps Mexico could be governed only with a heavy hand.

« 9 »

Alamán's Program for Renewal
1830–1832

Alamán looked back politically, but he also looked ahead to a new Mexico. Peace and security were only the necessary backdrop to make way for Mexico's advancing civilization. Unlike his aristocratic brethren of the colony, his way was not merely a defensive conservatism. He was a builder. It was Alamán's intention to bring in such of the modern world as might be appropriate to a Republic with Hispanic traditions.

The driving motive of Alamán's policy was to reverse the 1820s drift toward fragmentation and weakness. He would bring to government finance a respectability it never had, and inject into the Mexican economy the latest European techniques. He would check the slide of the church, restoring its capability of providing succor to the Mexican people. Cultural and educational establishments would be reinvigorated and rationalized, and finally he would mexicanize the northern frontier and throw back the North American advance.

THE ECONOMY

First, of course, the national government had to be rescued from fiscal embarrassment. Defenders of the Bustamante administration always stressed the salvaging of the government's credit, and the historical record bears them out. The crises of 1829 had forced Zavala to turn to resident lenders—foreign borrowing was out of the question since 1827—which loans were normally backed up by customs house obligations. In early 1830, the government could hardly function: European legations were kept up only through the courtesy of Baring Brothers in London, and the customs revenues were so mortgaged that Mangino, in need of about 1 million pesos a month, could not count on more than 200,000 pesos, which was "barely sufficient for the pay of the Troops in actual service."[1]

Two years later, Mangino could triumphantly report that "never, in effect, have the revenues of the Federation given such copious amounts."[2] Until the 1832 rebellion altered the situation, net government revenues showed a marked upswing.[3]

1829–1830	12,200,000 pesos
1830–1831	17,256,882 pesos
1831–1832	16,375,960 pesos

(The economic year was from July 1 to June 30.)

One of the administration's most impressive feats was its progress in working out of the debt morass, where arrears had reached more than 4 million pesos since missing the October 1827 dividend. Alamán, who greatly valued international respectability, contacted Baring Brothers and succeeded in renegotiating the payment arrangements, granting the bondholders one-sixth of the Veracruz and Tampico customs house duties, less generous but more realistic than an 1828 scheme.[4] And the administration kept to the bargain.[5] Similarly, the local debt was restructured, with Mexican noteholders receiving 15 percent of customs house revenues. This compromise was satisfactory enough to the lending class that Mangino was soon able to obtain loans at 3 percent interest a month, where his predecessors had to promise twice the amount they borrowed.[6] Mangino had to borrow very little in 1831.

The government accomplished this revolution in public credit, brief as it was, without any real innovation in taxing. The old unprofitable tobacco monopoly, which Zavala had scheduled to abolish in 1831, was instead farmed out to a joint company that agreed to split earnings with the government—a system that turned out to be quite profitable.[7] The administration angered foreign importers but extracted greater revenues by shortening the time for paying import fees, requiring detailed manifests to limit smuggling, and levying a new "consumption" tax at the ports.[8] Mangino had learned well the virtues of strict accounting during his years in the royal treasury.

In matters of general economic policy Alamán aimed to leave behind the suppositions of the 1820s, particularly the reliance on mining. By 1830 the mining promoters were thoroughly disillusioned. Alamán had been through this himself with the United Mexican Mining Company. As he explained it, the London directors had complained about his choice of mines and had never given him his salary of 10,000 pesos a year, only a 30,000-peso loan. Alamán asked the directors to consider the loan, plus 20,000 pesos and a percentage on future company earnings, as payment for his services. The directors answered by embargoing any remittances to him.[9]

By 1830 the era of the British mining companies was over, although some of the firms were still in business. In Zacatecas, which along with Real del Monte and Bolaños led the nation in production, the state government took up the slack. After the Spanish expulsion law closed the Bolsas mine, 100,000 pesos were raised in 1829 between individuals and the state, and the First Company of Zacatecan mines was born. The state lost money in this, and in a second company that was also undercapitalized with 75,000 pesos; however, from 1829 to 1834 the governor of Zacatecas was Francisco García, who had worked in mining since before the Revolution and who knew the lodes and how to organize a mining concern. Despite these two false starts, the state went ahead with its biggest project yet, the Fresnillo Company, created in February 1831. Governor García personally supervised construction at the site (Fresnillo was about thirty-five miles northwest of the city of Zacatecas). Labor came from a new *presidio*, and capital from a treasury subsidy, a loan from the mint, and loans from Mexican investors. The Fresnillo *ayuntamiento* offered a building to house the convicts.

The Fresnillo Company was a novelty in postindependence mining—a large-scale, all-Mexican venture. Although the works had to be built from scratch, the first Fresnillo silver arrived at the Zacatecas mint in March 1832, and the company produced over 2 million pesos by the end of 1833. It was the most productive operation in Mexico at that time. As a revenue producer, the Fresnillo Company was only a modest success, and the national government took control of its operations in 1835, but the company provided employment and mined silver until the 1870s.[10]

The administration's economic policy centered on the need to bring Mexico out of economic backwardness. All types of encouragement and cajolery were employed to raise Mexicans' technical consciousness: patriotic societies offered prizes for new industrial and agricultural techniques, and experts were persuaded to write or translate treatises on techniques like silkworm raising and farming innovations.[11]

The unique contribution of the day was the Banco de Avío, or Credit Bank, a project of Alamán's that was designed to institutionalize economic modernization. The basic idea, which actually originated with Zavala in 1829, was to cure the shortage of capital by advancing credit to joint-stock companies which would then import the latest technology. Laws of April 6 and October 16, 1830, created a fund financed by the twentieth part from the cotton import duties—the cotton cloth exclusion law of May 22, 1829, was repealed in the same April 6 law—and created a Credit Bank with a maximum capital of 1 million pesos. It was to give preference to the production of cotton, wool, and silk cloth, but could promote other industries.[12]

Alamán, who oversaw the bank, looked to the development of a technology-conscious capitalist class, a class that existed in Mexico in embryonic form if it existed at all, and to hasten its growth he used his office to call in debts and apply pressure. Even as Congress was approving the April 6 law, he exhorted governors to promote companies and called capitalists to meetings. He prevailed upon his personal and official contacts to subscribe to stock and promote and run errands for the bank—from clerks to bishops, ambassadors, governors, and generals.[13]

The plan was to order machinery and place it in the hands of Mexican companies on the basis of five-year and six-year loans. After a year in operation the Banco de Avío appeared to be on the verge of success. It had circulated technical treatises and opened a school in Coyoacán to teach silk production. Machinery from the United States and France—cotton gins, cloth factories, paper mills, and silk looms—was en route, and foreign technicians had already arrived to inspect potential plant sites. The 1832 revolution, however, halted the momentum. With Veracruz and then Tampico in the revolutionaries' hands, the machinery remained impounded in port warehouses or rusted on the wharves, and the rebels commandeered Bank funds awaiting embarkation. When the Bustamante administration was replaced in December 1832, not a single textile mill was operating. After 1832 the Bank struggled on and achieved partial success—a total of fourteen of its companies went into production—until Santa Anna dissolved it in 1842.[14]

THE CHURCH

On May 3, 1830, Vicente Rocafuerte wrote Alamán about a request he had received from James Thompson, representative of the British and Foreign Bible Society. It concerned the release of eight boxes of Bibles the Veracruz customs officials had embargoed. There had been no trouble since 1827, so Thompson thought there must be some mistake. The help never came, however, and the Bibles stayed in Veracruz to the end of the Bustamante administration.[15]

Rocafuerte wrote to Alamán remembering him as a young, somewhat anticlerical, Cortes liberal of 1821–1822 who had been persecuted by the Inquisition. Those days were long past. By 1830 Alamán no longer looked upon the church as a barrier to enlightenment but as a stabilizing agent for a people who were adrift culturally. He saw a church with no bishops, where half of the parishes had no regular priest,[16] and so he saw it as the call of duty to turn back, in part, the movement he had helped initiate as a young man.

First attention went to winning the pope's consent for new bishops. Back in September 1829 President Guerrero had decided to make such an attempt, since the failure of the Spanish invasion should have convinced the

Vatican that Spain's cause in Mexico was hopeless. Under wartime authority a circular was sent (September 23) to the cathedral chapters asking them to list nominees for bishops, from which lists Guerrero would make a selection, with advice from the governors. Guerrero never had the chance to complete the process, but the Bustamante administration followed his plan. A middle path was chosen, one that would *ask* the pope for new bishops, but which would at the same time not surrender the right of patronage. The law of February 17, 1830, stated that "for one time" the patronage issue would be put aside and the list developed under Guerrero would be sent to Rome for approval.[17]

On March 5 Minister of Justice and Ecclesiastical Affairs Espinosa wrote to Vásquez to present the names for confirmation. Pope Pius VIII was still fearful of angering the Spanish and would name only "apostolic vicars" (not resident bishops). Vásquez rejected this, and the situation remained at an impasse until Pius died on November 30, 1830. His successor Gregory XVI decided that halting the decline of the church in Mexico was worth offending the Spaniards. He issued the appropriate bulls, confirmed Vásquez himself for the mitre of Puebla, and Vásquez returned home immediately and began confirming bishops as fast as possible. It was done with much haste since it was feared Vásquez might die and the bishops-elect would have to journey to Rome for confirmation. No appointments were made at this time for Oaxaca and the archbishopric, since the incumbents were still alive, if in Spain.[18]

The bishops' appointment did not arouse any noticeable opposition. But the renewal of the canons did. The May 16, 1831, law was the least popular move of the Bustamante administration—and was later annulled under Gómez Farías. The bishops being seen as a clique of doddering, reactionary *gachupines* who did nothing useful anyway, cathedral chapters declined with the blessing of many Mexicans. The unallotted salaries, in any event, accrued to needy state treasuries. A bill introduced in 1830 came up for serious discussion in early 1831 with the Chamber of Deputies sharply divided. Voting on the legislation in the Chamber was riotous, as the sixteen clerics fought for the right of the church to decide upon its own personnel, and others wanted the state governors to make the nominations: insults were exchanged, deputies stayed home for fear of violence, and when Yorkino deputies tried a walkout during the debate, they found the way barred by soldiers at the locked doors. In its final form, the law of May 16, 1831, "for one time" let the bishop (or the canons in his absence) select the chapter members, while the respective governors were given the veto *(exclusiva)*. One ironic result was that the passionate federalist of years gone by, Ramos Arizpe, joined this august company as dean of the Puebla cathedral.[19]

The fervent opponents of the cathedral chapter legislation had lost in

Congress, but Zacatecas Governor García had his own type of revenge. The Zacatecas legislature held an essay contest on the topic of the government's right to take over church property. José María Luis Mora's essay, which repeated the regalist argument of the 1820s, won the 2,000 pesos and the gold medal—an essay that became the guide of later anticlerical reformers.[20]

The negative side of the administration's policy was to call a halt to measures that would weaken the church. The Zacatecas plan to expropriate certain church properties for a land bank was halted after an editorial campaign by *El Sol* and a ruling of unconstitutionality by a Chamber of Deputies committee.[21] Congress returned four haciendas that Zavala as secretary of the treasury had confiscated from Dominican and Augustinian missionaries of the Philippines.[22] When Rocafuerte had the temerity to publish a pamphlet defending religious toleration in 1831, Espinosa exerted pressure to have him indicted for breach of the press laws. With Cañedo as his defense counsel, however, a jury voted eleven to one to exonerate him, and a crowd of well-wishers accompanied him home.[23]

While the Bustamante administration was prepared to give up some regalist faculties for the sake of rebuilding, it still felt the impulse to instill propriety in the church. For example, a circular of April 18, 1831, to be read in all religious communities, promised that the government would respond to the plea of any cloistered person claiming mistreatment by a superior. This inclination was also illustrated by the matter of monastery and convent reform, an issue left hanging when a Cortes decree for the reform of the regular clergy was not promulgated in New Spain. While Vásquez was in Rome, it was agreed that he should be empowered to carry out certain reforms. A papal brief to this effect, dated July 12, 1831, arrived and was presented to the Senate which voted it the *pase* (approval for circulation) without discussion. A public outcry thereupon ensued, motivated partially by opponents of the administration who objected because the Vatican had directed the brief to Vásquez personally, once again ignoring the fact of Mexico's independence. Additionally, reported Carlos María de Bustamante, several friars, fearing a tightening of their regimen, met with Facio secretly and won him to the opposition.[24] As a result of these attacks from both sides, the government did not circulate the brief.

The Bustamante administration, in two years, succeeded in putting the church back on its feet. But it also gave a prominence to ecclesiastics they did not have before. Ignacio Inclan wrote Alamán that when he became the military commander of Michoacán, he found that "theocracy reigns over everything," and made it a point to begin his duties by making calls on the clergy.[25] This did not sit well with many independence-minded Mexicans. They still remembered the church as an all too visible supporter of Spanish authority.

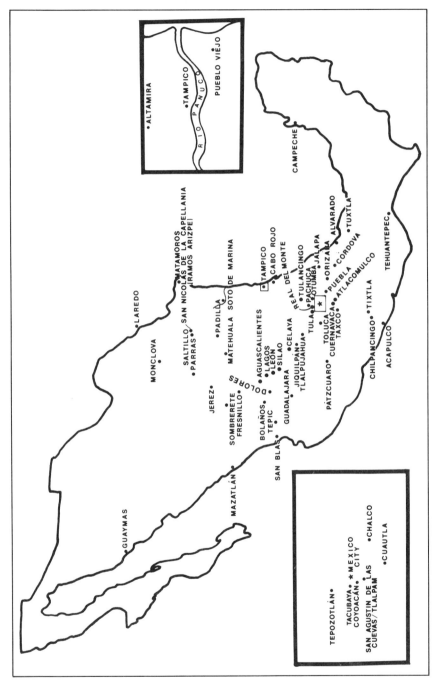

Places Cited in Text

CULTURE

The diversions of the Mexican masses were simple but addictive. Many of the pastimes were of a rustic nature, and as they required little institutional support, did not suffer greatly from the Revolution. Bull rings were to be found in most of the provincial capitals, even as far north as Santa Fe at one time. The Guanajuato governor's report of 1830 noted that almost every town had a cockpit, which also hosted plays, circuses, puppet shows, and acrobatic performances.[26] Mexicans were much given to music and dancing, and even in the smaller towns found the instrumental means—frequently guitars—to put on dances where they favored boleros, Spanish fandangos, indigenous *jarabes,* and a type of polonaise.[27] Up on the Rio Grande frontier a visitor remarked that the soldiers, after returning from the field, lapsed into a great somnolence, from which they could be roused only by "the monotonous shrilling of an ill-tuned violin, which will keep them dancing for several nights running."[28] Civic occasions provided entertainment, where enough fireworks were set off that the *cohetero* (rocket maker) had become a stock literary figure. Religious celebrants frequently marked the sacred calendar with pageants such as processional representations of biblical events and battles between Moslems, "Saxons," and Christians.[29]

The greatest religious celebration was Holy Week, but in the environs of Mexico City it had degenerated into an orgy of gambling. Officially gambling was something less than legal, frequently requiring licensing, but keeping the gambling houses closed was impossible, given the general fondness for games of chance. Poinsett remarked that Guadalupe Victoria was the only nongambler in his administration. At Easter time there was a mass migration from Mexico City to San Agustín de las Cuevas (or Tlalpam) for dances, cockfights, a mass in the plaza, and above all for the twenty monte houses where women wagered alongside men and where Vice-President Bustamante could enter and hardly be noticed.[30]

Elegant night life in the capital had revolved around the theater. The presentations were varied—chamber music, singing, dancing, prestidigitation, and scientific feats—but the heart of the theater was dramatic productions. The great historian of Mexican drama, Enrique de Olavarría y Ferrari, recorded the excitement of independence, shared by theater impresarios who planned spectacles and contracted for famous European artists, most of them Spaniards. Some of the players, native and imported, maintained a great repertoire, performing fifteen to twenty different works a year. They were highly regarded and paid accordingly, commanding 2,000–3,000 pesos a year—and up.[31] Generally the producers were criticized for relying overmuch on the old standard plays, but one theater group in 1824 was going to present a comedy based on the Virgin of Guadalupe and even put up advertisements depicting Bishop Zumárraga dancing the jarabe in joy over her appearance. The government tore down the placards.[32]

Olavarría y Ferrari saw aesthetic hopes straitened by declining budgets and an uncouth public. Stage lights might fail in mid-scene, or in any case were so weak that viewers from middle seats back had difficulty in distinguishing the personages. Scenery was rarely changed. "We are always in the same city, in the same building, in the same room."[33] Performers were distracted by conversations in the audience, and spectators in the loges were themselves discomfited by cigarette butts and spittle flying from the galleries. Then there was the general lack of security that affected all concerned. Homebound theatergoers feared being accosted by robbers, and when the famous Spanish tenor Manuel García was on his way out of the country, highwaymen not only dispossessed him of his baggage, but also obliged him to render some of their "favorite airs."[34]

To Alamán, the embodiment of creole sensibility and learning, such a situation was an affront. He observed that the theaters, the museums, and the colleges all seemed to have withered under the political heat of independence. The projects of the hopeful years—the societies to patronize the arts and worthy causes, the schools of political economy, the Philharmonic Society, the Academy of Engineers—had rarely progressed further than optimistic pronouncements. Alamán now proposed to breathe life into the agencies of culture. If men of his class were born to rule, they also inherited the obligation to lead their fellow men toward civilization. It thus became an integral part of administration policy to subsidize the arts and to bring education up to date.

Alamán immediately set about to restore the stage to its former elegance. The *Registro Oficial* devoted columns to the topic, and impresarios were contracted with to bring over European dancers, actors, and musicians to establish schools of music and verse. One proud accomplishment was to bring an opera company from Italy, which arrived in August 1831 and began offering two shows a week.[35]

To stimulate interest the *Registro Oficial* published a monthly supplement on the arts, science, and industry, and Alamán wrote to *ayuntamientos* recommending that they subscribe. He tried to further the "establishment of the sciences and the arts," a project he had initiated under Guadalupe Victoria, but whose collections never truly amounted to anything worthy of a museum. After five weeks in office, he proposed that Congress create a "scientific establishment" with three branches: antiquities, industrial products, and natural history, including a botanical garden. Congress answered the call with a law of November 21, 1831. To fill the museum Alamán sent out instructions to the governors on preparing and shipping plant specimens, and asked them to send historical curiosities and examples of their states' handicrafts for annual expositions—plus state maps from which to fashion an up-to-date map of the Republic. Diplomats and federal officials cooperated by sending plants, roots, seeds, paintings, and maps.[36]

The most ambitious scientific project was the Waldeck expedition. After an earlier visit as a mining engineer, Jean Frederic Waldeck became interested in Mexico lore, did a study on the Teotihuacán pyramids, and decided to examine Mayan remnants. He departed from Mexico City in early 1832 and spent fifteen months exploring and sketching the Petén and Palenque ruins, but the project dissolved in 1834 and 1835 among recriminations that Waldeck sold Indian relics.[37] It is possible that Alamán indirectly contributed to these developments. In March 1831, when he heard that foreigners were unearthing and removing historical objects in the Federal District, he wrote the governor to have the practice stopped. Then on March 14, 1832, Congress decreed that the government had priority in purchasing native works of art discovered on private property and could prevent them from being taken out of the country.[38]

Alamán's penchant for technology and rational order guided the administration's educational policy. In his 1830 *Memoria* he proposed an institutional division of labor for Mexico City's colleges: the Seminary would handle the ecclesiastical sciences; the Colegio de San Idelfonso the political and economic sciences, law, and classical literature; the Colegio de Minería the physical sciences; the Museum and Botanical Garden the natural sciences; and the Colegio de San Juan de Letrán medicine. A committee was created to explore the idea, but as Mora explained it, the project died because the college alumni feared the respective schools would lose their identity and influence in the process.[39] The idea did not die, though, for the succeeding government followed the concept in assigning each of six state "establishments"—formerly colleges—an academic specialty.[40]

It fell to Alamán in 1830 to report that the Republic's principal experiment in elementary education, the Lancasterian system, had not lived up to its promise.[41] The system had been put to an imperfect test. From the beginning there were money problems: members of the capital's Lancasterian Society did not pay their dues, and the *ayuntamiento* never carried through on its pledge. The society's two Mexico City schools came near to closing in 1826, and El Sol was closed in 1830. In 1831 the society decided to cancel dues and place all hopes in the national government. Congress gave the society 3,250 pesos in 1831 and donated the houses of the former Bethlehemite monastery (worth 1,215 pesos in 1832) but under the Gómez Farías government of 1833 the society had to dissolve temporarily.[42]

State Lancasterian societies traveled the same road. Oaxaca's declined from twenty-nine members to two.[43] The societies—and public education to some extent—fell under general suspicion since many French residents, reputedly freethinkers, were involved: the Morelia priests accused the Lancasterians of teaching heresy.[44] Affecting everything was the problem of finding trained teachers. As the societies looked to founding schools, there were numerous advertisements for bona fide Lancasterian teachers, and later, when the schools did not live up to expectations, there were comments about unqualified instructors. It should be noted that even in the best days the Lancasterian schools amounted to only 10 or 15 percent of the total, and many of the planned schools never went into operation. The Guanajuato governor noted in February 1830 that the Lancasterian schools were supposed to be everywhere but in fact were hardly anywhere.[45] Later the society would achieve a success in official circles at least. In 1842 its method was approved as the national system, and the society continued to be active in Mexico for several decades.[46]

The Bustamante officials never had time to carry out their plan of a government renovation of culture. Revolution cut short many of the projects, and the new government of 1833 was to take a dim view of culture for the leisured class. Culture would have to revive at its own pace.

TEXAS AND THE NORTH

For the first time, the national government realized that Texas was in peril. During the past decade North Americans had been steadily moving in, but Zavala and his federalist friends owed the United States too much ideologically and were blinded to the danger. Alamán, however, with his preference for the Hispanic, was already calling them "gringos" in distaste.[47]

In the 1820s Texas had remained a peripheral issue. While the number of Americans grew to about 20,000, five or six times the number of Mexicans living around San Antonio de Béxar, Nacogdoches, and the fort at La Bahía del Espíritu Santo, most Mexicans were preoccupied with other matters. Mier y Terán was sent up as boundary commissioner and commander of the Eastern Interior Provinces to examine the border area, but this was done as much to get him away from his centralist friends in Mexico City. Congress did not even bother to appropriate funds for his expedition until Haden Edwards's proclamation of the Fredonia Republic precipitated a flurry of activity in 1826. The War Department found troops and alerted them for Texas duty, and President Guadalupe Victoria was ready to lead them himself,[48] but the Fredonia Republic collapsed and attention fell again to problems nearer home. Ward lent his good offices in helping recruit non-American settlers and continued to warn Guadalupe Victoria of the danger.[49]

The Bustamante government had been in power for only two weeks when Lieutenant Colonel Constantino Tarnava arrived with a report from Mier y Terán detailing the American takeover of Texas.[50] Alamán acted immediately. In a February 8 secret session of Congress he reviewed the situation and offered Mier y Terán's plan for strengthening Mexico's hold: call in Texas affairs from state administration to federal jurisdiction, and build up military readiness, the Mexican population, and the coastal trade. To these Alamán added the recommendation that there should be an end to all North American immigration, "whatever be the cause." The government ought to cancel all unfulfilled impresario agreements. In a band along the Texas–United States frontier should be settled Europeans "whose religion, language, customs, and habits are in contradiction to those of the North Americans." At the end of his presentation he uttered an ominous prediction. If energetic steps were not taken, Texas would cease to belong to the United Mexican States.[51] These proposals resulted in the famous law of April 6, 1830. The next day Vice-President Bustamante named Mier y Terán federal commissioner to administer the law, and orders went out to Mexican agents in the United States to publicize the new rules.[52]

Earlier the policy was to make Texas safe through a diplomatic accord. Alamán in Mexico City and Mier y Terán in Matamoros now realized this was a terrible miscalculation, and that only a stronger Mexican presence could save Texas.

Attracting non-American colonists to Texas was not an easy task. Since the first days of independence, the prospect of European colonies had a singular fascination for Mexican officials, especially Tadeo Ortiz, who became a crusader for European immigration as a means to tame the wilds and spread progressive ideas among the citizenry. His main project was the Coatzacoalcos colony on the Isthmus of Tehuántepec. He first contracted with an English house (1825) to bring in 1,500 families, a venture canceled by the company's bankruptcy, and then brought in Indian colonists from the Oaxacan highlands to their new villages of Minatitlán, Hidalgotitlán, Morelostitlán, and Allendetitlán—none of which flourished. His main efforts, though, were directed at Europeans. After campaigns in Mexico and abroad, and after his appointment as Mexican consul at Bordeaux in 1829, the first French ship arrived in November 1829. There ensued a series of disagreeable experiences, involving a ship running aground, voracious mosquitoes, and inadequate preparations; eventually the colonists left for cities in Mexico or returned to France.[53] Nonetheless, it was a testament to the persistence of Ortiz—and the French—that between 1829 and 1834 a total of ten ships left French ports with 1,000 colonists.

In 1830 the attraction of colonization had not worn off, and since the essential goal in Texas was a counterweight to the Americans, there were several alternatives. Irish, German, and Swiss-Catholic peasants had been considered the best prospects, and Mexican diplomats abroad tried to recruit them through the newspapers. But Mier y Terán had reservations about their eventual sympathies. They might serve as a temporary measure, but he feared that eventually they would forsake the "uncultured" Mexicans and make common cause with the Americans. "Remember," he said, "what is the second-generation North American, a mixture of every known nation."[54] Although the government had to drop the original subsidy plan, the advertising campaign to attract Europeans went on, and a few did find their way to Texas.[55]

Populating Texas with Indians was another possibility, or rather almost an accomplished fact. Through 1830, Indians continued to arrive, notably the Cherokees.[56] In March 1830, Mier y Terán wrote he had received word that a commissioner from the Coahuila-Texas government was in Nacogdoches conducting land negotiations with the Savanna tribe. Alamán was not enthusiastic. He directed Mier y Terán to let them in on a family basis only, not by tribes, and their children were to be instructed in the Spanish language. Mier y Terán thought even less of these "savages," a greater evil than white North Americans whom he would admit only in an emergency.[57] But he could not stop them any more than he could stop North Americans.[58]

Black colonists were even less welcome. A Francisco Snaer (or Esnaer) presented himself to Mier y Terán as the agent of 50,000 black exiles from Havana living in New Orleans. Although Snaer stated that his clients were businessmen, artisans, and farmers, Mier y Terán was cool to the idea and the colony never materialized.[59]

As for Mexican colonists, they never appeared. With Mexico's northern frontier contracting, not expanding, Mier y Terán was skeptical about inducing families to leave their homes, and about their capacity to withstand the onslaught from the United States. He wrote that the Mexican population had just begun to flow down from "the high countries to Nuevo León and Tamaulipas . . . and a state as badly formed and as poor as Coahuila cannot have subjects of the class of the North Americans."[60] In August 1830, Mier y Terán wrote of dispatching about a hundred families, but this was as much as he could do. Even the garrison town founded in 1830 on the San Antonio–Nacogdoches road—and given the name Tenoxtitlán— had American residents by 1832.[61]

The government came closest to carrying out the purely military aspects of the April 6 law, although the additional soldiers deployed at San Antonio, La Bahía, and Nacogdoches were never sufficient for the purpose. The exact number of soldiers Mier y Terán had at his disposal, even after the buildup, only reached about 1,000 in Texas, plus 700 at Matamoros.[62] Underlying military logistics lay the treasury's limitations which, even in this relatively solvent period, turned the April 6 law into a half-measure. By June 1830, Mier y Terán's budget for the military and colonial expenses approached 100,000 pesos monthly.[63] His letters were taken up with incessant pleas for more supplies and more money.[64] The April 6 law had earmarked a portion of the duties on cotton cloth imports for a special fund to "maintain the integrity of the Mexican territory," but almost immediately the government began siphoning off the income.[65] The northern border problem was only one of several issues confronting the Bustamante administration, and in the list of priorities self-preservation came first, a distant province later.

Federalism and distrust of the Bustamante centralists compounded the problem. The state of Coahuila-Texas continued trafficking in Texas lands, only occasionally slowed by Mier y Terán.[66] And state officials were always reluctant to divert scarce local resources to federal projects. The War Department requested from the states 2,965 new soldiers for Texas, but very few turned up.[67] Governor García of Zacatecas, for example, offered a few token cavalrymen but turned down repeated requests to send part of his militia to Texas and Durango, claiming it was unconstitutional and that the men were needed in Zacatecas to pursue smugglers and bandits.[68] He might have added that to leave himself without militia protection would have been political suicide. San Luis Potosí officials intercepted one Texas-bound specie shipment and appropriated parts of it for their own use.[69]

Texas trade was not diverted to Matamoros, Tamaulipas, and Veracruz, but still followed its earlier channels to New Orleans and New York. In December 1831, Mier y Terán was thinking about placing a detachment on the Brazos River to prevent a "very active trade" between Austin's colony and New York, adding that Austin, whom Mier y Terán earlier courted, gave proof each day that he was a "solemn scoundrel, occupying himself in nothing more than conspiracies against Mexico."[70]

Mier y Terán's lack of soldiers meant that he could neither stop illegal trade nor afford to provoke a confrontation by turning back North Americans. Thus he let Austin admit settlers at his own discretion.[71] But this broke down, and the North Americans again began entering as they wished.

Curiously, Mier y Terán was looked to by many Mexicans—even by some of the federalists—as the next president for his moderately conservative philosophy now placed him at a midpoint between the contending factions. Yet the northern command would be his undoing in the fullest sense. As he saw Texas slipping away, his letters assumed a tone of increasing despondency. In May 1830 he wrote about the possibility of another Spanish invasion: "I believe that the Spaniards can only cause us temporary damages; the serious and permanent ones are reserved for our own hands, and those of the North American neighbors." A month after that he asked if he were the only one who had eyes for the tragedy in Texas. In March 1831 he foresaw "a disgrace in Texas without having the means to remedy it." Mier y Terán wrote his last letter to Alamán on July 2, 1832, from Padilla, Tamaulipas: he asked how Mexicans could expect to hold Texas when they could not even stop killing each other. "The revolution is about to break forth and Texas is lost." The next day he rose early, dressed, shaved, and left for a walk. When he did not return as expected, his servant went out to search for him and found him dead. He had thrown himself upon his own sword.[72]

Ironically, on April 5, 1832, while the government program in Texas crumbled, in Mexico City the United States made a formal acknowledgment that Mexico owned Texas. A treaty had actually been signed and approved by both sides in 1828, but ratified copies had not been formally exchanged until now.[73]

The treaty with the United States did not change the sympathies of the Americans in Texas, and the death blow to the administration's foundering Texas program came as a result of the revolution of 1832. The government was forced to divert yet more troops and resources that might have gone to Texas, and the Americans' declaration in favor of the revolutionaries forced Mexican troops to evacuate Nacogdoches and Tenoxtitlán. After this the North Americans in Texas were largely on their own.

Americans were not the main worry in the far north: the Indians were. These were years of violence, and almost no one escaped. In any section the resident Indians might be exceedingly gentle, but raiders could strike hundreds of miles from their home ground. The Comanches, roaring down from the high plains and pushing the Lipán Apaches ahead of them, depopulated stretches of Coahuila-Texas, Tamaulipas, and Nuevo León. In Coahuila raiding increased by the decade, until by the 1850s Indians would virtually "overrun the state."[74] Losses of cattle in northern Tamaulipas totaled 1.5 million head from 1813 to 1823.[75] Some forty-four ranches in Laredo's jurisdiction lay vacant in the early 1820s, and one of the regular activities there was gathering in stray sheep, horses, and cattle. At the other end of the frontier, the Apaches of Sonora and Chihuahua did the same. A Chihuahua official in 1834 said it had become so bad the inhabitants all wanted to leave and the state was "going to disappear."[76]

When the Yaquis took up arms in Sonora, the result was not the usual raiding, but full-scale war. About 30,000 Yaquis and Mayos lived along the rivers of the same name, in towns where the Jesuits had gathered them.[77] In 1825–1827 and then in 1832 they almost overran Sonora, led in both wars by the Yaqui chieftain Juan Ignacio Juzucanea, called Banderas because of his banner of Guadalupe. The 1825 uprising began after land evaluators from the tax office visited Yaqui towns. Banderas, who envisioned uniting all the Sonora Indians in an independent state, persuaded the Mayos to help by appealing to them as descendants of the Aztecs and reminding them of lost lands. The state government was forced to move from Fuerte to Cosalá, but on April 13, 1827, after an offer of amnesty and with troops coming in from Chihuahua, Banderas and 200 others agreed to lay down their arms. The 1825–1827 outbreak cost some 3,000 lives. The legislature passed several decrees designed to appease the Indians—schools, exemptions from the *alcabala*, return of lands—and appointed Banderas *alcalde mayor* of the River Yaqui. But he preferred to style himself general of the Yaquis, and called out his men again in 1832. This time it took the state militia nine months to quell the fighting. The Apaches took the opportunity to raid, and threatened Chihuahua City in 1833.[78]

Even the usually pacific California Indians rose in rebellion. Duhaut-Cilly, who visited in 1827–1828, described them as dressed in rabbit skins and feathers and having developed a kind of "hoof" from running barefoot. Relations with the white men led to a series of attacks by free Indians and revolts in the missions, where disease had raised the annual death rate to as high as 50–75 percent in some instances. Duhaut-Cilly also told the story of Pomponio, whose thirst for freedom was so great he escaped from his fetters by cutting off his heels while the guard slept.[79]

The violence in the North was a by-product of independence. As in the South, officials noted how little the Indians appreciated their new constitutional equality.[80] Some northern officials publicly yearned for the return of the Jesuits. In a sense, independence made the Indians free also, free from the missions, and virtually free of the soldiers. Independence even brought Indians prosperity in places, since they could now plunder with no great fear from the undermanned presidios, and then, as the Mexican officials complained, they could exchange their booty for weapons with the North Americans.[81]

The relationship was often something between peace and war. The Swiss botanist-zoologist Jean Louis Berlandier, who accompanied Mier y Terán's boundary commission, described a Lipán hymn to peace in 1828:

> During our first stay at the presidio of Laredo, the Lipáns roamed through the streets after sundown, singing their songs of peace. These songs consisted of prolonged low notes and sudden high ones, the former interspersed with brief silences. This was followed by a single voice that rose gradually, then by loud cries like the barking of dogs. The way they walk is most impressive. A great number of them I saw drawn up in single file, standing very close to one another, and walking so slowly that at first they did not appear to be moving at all. In the center of the main square of the presidio, they performed a most extra-ordinary dance, accompanied by songs. The individuals who were taking part in it were gathered about a buffalo hide which they held very taut and which they struck at random while singing songs of joy. At the same time their feet made a sound like that of a huge throng of people marching in the distance.[82]

With the frontier presidios and garrisons at part strength, it had become Mexican policy to conciliate. After a 1,500-man expedition led by New Mexico's Governor Vizcárraga against the Navajos in 1823, the northern military launched no major campaigns. In New Mexico, soldiers were under orders to avoid giving offense, and not to recover stolen goods unless authorized.[83] Apaches, after their 1832 stock raids in Chihuahua, received a brand to legitimize their booty.[84] Mexican officials now treated. In New Mexico rather temporary agreements were struck with the pueblos and "the nations of the north" (Comanches)—when a spokesman of the fragmented tribes could be found.[85] An 1822 treaty with the Lipán Apaches of Texas promised land and protection from the Lipán's enemies, the Comanches.[86] To demonstrate the value of friendliness, governments continued the Spanish practice of gifts—insofar as finances permitted. The northern forts passed out cloth, knives, buttons, mirrors, shirts, hats, medals, rings, and food.[87]

The initial impression one receives from studying the far North in these years is that here the white man and the Indian met on roughly equal terms. The Comanches and Yaquis best illustrate this. In documents they were mentioned, without affection, surely, but with a certain amount of respect. José Antonio Barreiro in New Mexico wrote that the Comanche was recognized for his "athletic and gallant presence, his frank, martial air," and when he attacked he disdained treacherous maneuvers.[88] And these years certainly showed that the Yaqui and Comanche civilizations were the military equal of the white man's civilization.

On second look, however, one can see here the same processes that were wearing down Indian life toward the south. A portion of these indigenous peoples were relatively primitive farmers or hunters and gatherers. These, pushed to marginal lands by both the white man and their Indian enemies, had become dispirited, prey to attrition and vice. Mexican reports are full of comments about local Indians dying out. In New Mexico, native women reputedly limited their families by drinking a potion called a *brebaje*.[89] Alcoholism had become common, an addiction looked upon approvingly by many Mexicans.

Also, Hispanic civilization had successfully established its political authority, a fact tacitly admitted even by many of the ethnocentric Comanches who would not be subdued for half a century. The Comanche chief Pancho Conuque asked the New Mexico commander in June 1828 that his "cane of authority" be exchanged for one of harder wood.[90] Although the Yaquis' government was in large measure independent, their pueblos had Spanish-style officials, *alcaldes mayores* and *regidores*.[91] The Yaquis, as well as the Comanches, sported the honorific title of general bestowed by the Mexicans.

Texas was a unique case in the 1820s, for owing to the enormous pressure of the American frontier it had become the home of many tribes or remnants of tribes that had lived elsewhere a generation before. Berlandier surveyed fifty-one tribes, almost all decimated by wars, epidemics, mission life, and the vices of civilization. He estimated a Texas population approaching 20,000, excluding the numerous bands of Coahuiltecans living around the lower Rio Grande, and the roving Comanches whom he counted at 10,000–12,000. Berlandier described a broad typology, from the Cherokee farmers, barely distinguishable from the whites, and the Cutchate (Coushatta) with their animals, larder, and log houses where the "traveler is as sure to find a welcome as he is in the cabin of an Anglo-American colonist," to the Tancahueses (Tonkawas), living wretchedly in their huts of green branches or skins. The Texas Indians were quite intelligent in their adaptation to the environment and invested with great fortitude. He noted that even the most backward could count up to a hundred. But their relative distance from civilization had not ennobled them. They perpetrated cruelties on opposing Indians far in excess of what they did to white people. Warriors treated females as "objects of scorn." Bought and sold as property, required on campaigns to satisfy their husbands' relatives and friends, women "could not approach their husbands except with great respect. They are forever barred from paradise, and no single circumstance in their daily lives fails to remind them of their inferiority."[92]

In discussing these customs Berlandier captured a moment soon to be lost. Many of the peoples he described would be extinct within about a generation. The tidal wave of North American settlers that Alamán and Mier y Terán could not stop was about to overwhelm all competing civilizations in the far North.

THE 1832 CIVIL WAR

At twelve noon on November 22, 1831, Jalisco's commanding general Ignacio Inclán went to the shop of Juan Brambila, who had printed a pamphlet accusing him of financial and sexual improprieties, had his aides tear up the establishment, and then personally arrested Brambila and gave him three hours to prepare for execution.[93]

Although Brambila was reprieved, many felt the administration's misfortunes dated from this Guadalajara incident. About this time a contingent of former moderate Escoceses and Yorkinos, including Quintana Roo, Rejón, Pacheco Leal, and Rodríguez Puebla, began meeting to engineer the return of Gómez Pedraza.[94] One of the first recruits was Vicente Rocafuerte, who in December began to publish *El Fénix de la Libertad,* a newspaper that harried the Bustamante government to the end. Rocafuerte authored a three-installment pamphlet diatribe against the ministers, in particular against Alamán.[95] Colonel Antonio Gaona filed suit against Rocafuerte on December 20 as proxy for the secretaries—according to *El Fénix* the authorities required a 20,000-peso bond when the maximum fine was only 187.5 pesos—but Alamán decided to drop the charges and responded through an anonymous pamphlet.[96]

At the beginning of 1832, the Bustamante administration appeared impregnable. If it was not conspicuously successful on all fronts, it was moving ahead in its programs for the economy, culture, and institutions. The stain of Vicente Guerrero's execution hung over the Bustamantistas, but his followers were quiet, and the comparison with the anarchy of 1829 was obvious.

In the pamphlet and newspaper war that went on in late 1831 and 1832, however, it became clear that while the Bustamante government had stifled opposition, it had not created a new political consensus. The issues that were prompted by independence were still alive in spite of the political imperfections of the 1820s. State politicians were kept quiet by the local commanders, but they were still not prepared to submit to Mexico City. Neither were Mexicans prepared to accept law and order at the price of summary executions by the military. The church had for too long been identified with the Spaniards, and with privileged classes in general, to be accepted now as a social and political arbiter. The press since the turn of the century had acquired followers who had come to feel it a basic right to criticize without restrictions. And the Bustamante government had touched upon one of Mexicans' deep-set prejudices when it tried to ease the situation of the Spaniards.[97] In time many of these contradictions between colonial traditions and republican patterns would be resolved—frequently to the loss of republicanism—but now it was too soon after independence.

When the revolution came, however, it was touched off not by the administration's political enemies, but by the impetuous sovereign of Veracruz, Santa Anna, whose politics were usually obscure but always personal. When the administration removed his ally Pedro Landero as Veracruz port commander, he issued a pronouncement of January 2 that called upon Vice-President Bustamante to remove his ministers for their attacks on federalism and civil rights.[98]

Santa Anna was given to rash acts, but this looked like a forlorn cause. The federalists did not trust him, and nobody answered his call. Alamán, Facio, Espinosa, and Mangino offered their resignations on January 10, but phrased in such a way that Bustamante could accept only by repudiating himself.[99] After attempts at negotiation and bribery, Veracruz was put under siege, but General Calderón was unable to force the issue. A foray by Santa Anna was turned back at the village of Tolomé on March 3, and a military stalemate held through the spring of 1832: Santa Anna unable to push inland and Calderón unwilling to storm the Veracruz walls.[100] It was Santa Anna's personal revolution. He had no program other than presumably substituting his own influence for that of the ministers, or possibly postponing the presidential election to a time when the legislatures might view his candidacy with favor. His emissaries to the states were not well received.[101]

But he could not be dislodged, and this ultimately spelled the government's doom. Administration enemies elsewhere were given heart, and the one-city mutiny widened into civil war. On May 13 Calderón, whose men were dying at the rate of fifteen a day from the fever, lifted the siege at Veracruz, and five days later Alamán, Facio, and Espinosa resigned.[102]

As might be expected, Santa Anna ignored the ministers' resignations and proceeded with the revolution. A turning point occurred in June when Santa Anna came to an agreement with Zacatecas Governor García that ultimately provided the balance of power. García, distrustful of the revolutionaries all along, finally had to come to terms with a man that had successfully held out against the vaunted Bustamante military. He agreed to throw Zacatecas' large militia in on the rebels' side and Santa Anna agreed to amend his original January proclamation, which he did on July 2, to include a call for the return of Gómez Pedraza. On July 10 the Zacatecas legislature recognized Gómez Pedraza as Mexico's legitimate president.[103]

Through the summer the list of states in rebellion grew. Vice-President Bustamante, who was one of the most effective campaigners in the army, took personal command in the field and the government regained some ground after his bloody victory on September 18 at Gallinero (a hacienda near San Miguel de Allende). But the government was being worn down. As Santa Anna marched toward Mexico City, panic spread. So many went to the convents for sanctuary that Arechederreta had to make a public statement that there was no more room. One of those seeking refuge—according to one report[104]—was Alamán, who also tried to have Anthony Butler transfer his official residence to the Alamán home.[105]

In December Bustamante finally realized it was all over and agreed to an armistice whose terms were finally approved by both armies' leaders on December 23 as the Pact of Zavaleta. This agreement made Gómez Pedraza, who had returned to Mexico, interim president until April 1, and ordered a presidential election for March, nullifying the September elections in which twelve states had participated. The new Congress was to grant amnesty for all political acts since September 1, 1828. On January 3, Santa Anna and Gómez Pedraza entered Mexico City in the same carriage.[106]

The result of 1832 was a victory for the traditional federalist states, especially Zacatecas—as opposed to the 1828 Acordada Revolution, which had been the doing of Zavala and Santa Anna. In a larger sense, the defeat of the *hombres de bien* in 1832 showed that there was no going back. As a reaction to the coercive politics of the Bustamante administration, the liberals, who were not able to succeed on a laissez-faire, volunteeristic, basis in the 1820s, were now prepared to use an activist state.

The 1832 civil war also cut short Alamán's programs to modernize and strengthen Mexico's institutions. His policies did have a clarity and sense of social reality about them. They were logical and even plausible, but they were anchored in an obsolete economic base. Alamán had in mind the building of a governing class composed of the remnants of the old aristocracy and new economic leaders. At a later date it would work, but in 1830–1831 the essential ingredient left out of the formula was the federalist leadership that had sprung up since independence—and this element could not accommodate Alamán's group.

Epilogue

Zavala's side won the civil war, but he was missing from the high councils of government in 1833. The state legislatures on March 1 elected Santa Anna as president and Gómez Farías as vice-president. With Santa Anna sounding out the ideological climate at his Veracruz estate—he said he was too ill to take office—Gómez Farías became chief of state on April 1. Gómez Farías planned to carry out the liberal reforms Zavala had only thought about in 1829, but Zavala was not invited. Zavala might have led the way to federalism and liberalism in the 1820s, but the 1833–1834 government represented the victors of the 1832 civil war—Santa Anna's military circle and the Zacatecas federalists—and Zavala did not fit in with either group. His closest ties had always been with Guerrero.

Zavala played a secondary role in 1833, in his old job in the state of Mexico. As governor there he presided over a series of reform laws, such as the regulation of the *cívicos*, the confiscation of certain ecclesiastical properties, and the exclusion of clerics from elementary education. By October he had taken a seat in the Chamber of Deputies where he led the attack on the church, but he was appointed minister to France and on December 18 boarded ship for the trip to the United States and Europe.[1]

Part of the program of the Gómez Farías party in 1833 was to emasculate the institutions that had given strength to the Anastacio Bustamante administration. Another part was to make an example of the Bustamante officials. The chief of these was Lucas Alamán, who must have sensed vengeance was in the making when Juan Álvarez issued a petition on February 10 calling upon the new government to punish those ministers who had executed Guerrero, the "victim of Cuilapam." Several states issued similar petitions and the Chamber of Deputies' grand jury opened an investigation on April 7. The central issue was Guerrero's execution, and a key witness was José Antonio Mejía, who testified that he had carried to Guerrero's widow a letter from Bustamante to Santa Anna in which Bustamante stated that the cabinet had met and voted three to one to execute Guerrero.[2]

On April 22 the grand jury instructed the War Department to detain Alamán, Facio, and Mangino, who were rumored to be contemplating flight. The former two had already gone into hiding. Facio reappeared in France, while Alamán remained out of sight for fifteen months. The Chamber of Deputies voted not to pursue judicial action against Mangino, since he was reputedly the one minister who voted in Guerrero's favor in the alleged cabinet meeting, but the deputies voted overwhelmingly against the others: against Alamán fifty-one to one, against Facio fifty to one, and against Espinosa forty-one to one. In his place of concealment Alamán wrote a defense—infused with righteous indignation—and offered it to the public at twelve reals (one and a half pesos) a copy on about July 23, 1834, a few days before he emerged from hiding.[3]

The key to Alamán's return was Santa Anna. While he had left Gómez Farías in charge, he avoided a commitment to the new legislation, finally acceded to the opposition in late April 1834, and reassumed the executive power. As part of his effort to overturn the Gómez Farías program he decided to take up Alamán's case.[4] Santa Anna's change of sides guaranteed the outcome. Carlos María de Bustamante, speaking as Alamán's defense lawyer, was emboldened to speak thus of Guerrero and the War of the South: "Ah! What masses of horror we would have seen if General Guerrero had penetrated as far as this capital leading those hordes of coastal barbarians, that barely have the form of men and all the ferocity of tigers."[5] On March 17, 1835, the Supreme Court finally pronounced the verdict, completely exonerating Alamán as well as Espinosa.[6]

A parenthetical note should be added about the alleged cabinet vote on Guerrero's execution. Statements by the principals over the years suggest that a cabinet meeting did take place. Aside from the letter borne by Mejía, Bustamante wrote on at least one other occasion that there was such a meeting, although he subsequently denied it. Twenty years later Alamán told Tornel about the cabinet meeting, that he and Mangino had voted for exile to South America, that Facio and Espinosa had voted for execution, and that Vice-President Bustamante's vote had broken the tie.[7]

Gómez Farías had been radicalized by the Bustamante years. After seeing what the military and the church did in power, he was determined to limit them. But Gómez Farías was no more able to impose a liberal pattern than Alamán a viceregal pattern. Mexico was caught between two worlds; where no one had the legitimacy to enforce stability in the manner of old, yet where the citizenry lacked the sophistication to operate by the rules of liberalism. The cultures of Mexico's diverse population did not fit into any one governmental model. Government by consensus had broken down because there was no cultural consensus.

By now, a decade after Iturbide's overthrow, there was no denying that Mexico had lost the sheen of independence. But the excitement of freedom had once gripped much of the populace, and while it lasted it gave to the 1820s the unique tone of that era. Institutions were vivified, however briefly, with a new purpose. The political process was to be opened to the people, even if there were no precedent for it. Schools were to prepare the citizens and carry the gospel of the Republic out to the villages. For the press it was a golden age of expression, the political-social pamphlets being one of the truly distinctive developments of the period. Wherever possible, social and racial distinctions were swept away. While Mexicans learned that self-government required skills they did not possess, it was a testament to their resilience and tenacity that the nation endured. Mexico could have gone the way of the United Provinces of Central America or of Gran Colombia.

If one looks at the first decade of the Republic with a broad vision, the panorama of nineteenth-century Mexico can be seen in the making. The basic forces of Mexico were clearly sorting themselves out in preparation for the War of the Reform—the final war between colony and Republic. The tragedy of 1846–1848 was building inevitably, which Mier y Terán and a few others saw with dismay. Foreign governments were already coming to look on Mexico as a source of enrichment as well as difficulty, and the Mexican view of foreigners was already characterized by a combination of admiration and resentment. The hunger for land and the stirrings toward land redistribution were already voiced even though the times were not ready for action. Another idea that was fermenting was the notion that the church's wealth should be controlled for social ends. And Mexicans were taking their first lessons in the economics of the colonial experience, namely, that when they dealt with the developed world, legal independence meant very little.

As for our two protagonists, Lorenzo de Zavala and Lucas Alamán, their lives after this period were anticlimatic. The Santa Anna turnabout that rescued Alamán had the reverse effect on Zavala. After resigning as minister to France in August 1834, Zavala learned that the Mexican authorities had orders to arrest him, and he decided to go to Texas. He signed the Texas Declaration of Independence on March 2, 1836, and fifteen days later—at 4 A.M.—took the oath of office as vice-president of the Republic of Texas. He had the upper hand in his last meeting with Santa Anna, in the discussions after the battle of San Jacinto. Then, after he and his son fell from a canoe into the Buffalo Bayou, he contracted pneumonia. On November 15, 1836, Zavala died.[8]

Alamán survived Zavala by seventeen years, and although he occasionally accepted a government commission, generally spent the time immersed in business pursuits and writing his multivolume history of Mexico. It was not until after the war with the United States, when the country was at another crossroads and Mexicans were receptive to ideologues, that he entered government service again. To the day he died in June 1853, Alamán never escaped the onus of Guerrero's execution. In 1849, when he was proposed for public office in Guadalajara, electors began shouting, "Down with the murderer of Guerrero, down with the monarchist." The man who made the nomination was beaten up in the plaza.[9]

Alamán and Zavala belong to the opening years of the Republic, when two systems were struggling for the Mexicans' allegiance. In the long run, Alamán's grip on the Mexican reality was to prove more sure. His prescription for an authoritarian government to maintain a facade of democracy and sponsor economic modernization has had a tried and true history ever since. Yet Zavala's liberal vision has been equally enduring among many Mexicans, and has served as a basis for the periodic outbursts that have convulsed the nation.

A final glance at the meaning of the first decade of the Republic would see it as a first step. A highly varied population—some literate sophisticates, some living a stone-age life, but most of a folk culture in between—had its first encounter with self-determination. Exulting in a sense of nationhood that masked the social and cultural differences, the former colonials resolved to shake off Hispanic forms and embrace new ones coming from Europe and the United States. But the imported institutions did not fit, and Hispanic traditions, however execrated, proved durable. The new citizens thus had to embark on a long trek—one that would take more than a century—toward a unique public system that would suit a unique society.

NOTES

GLOSSARY

BIBLIOGRAPHY

INDEX

Notes

Chapter 1
MEXICO AT INDEPENDENCE

1. Anna, *Fall of the Royal Government in Mexico City,* pp. 220–21; a discussion of peninsular developments and their relation to Mexican independence can be found in Rodríguez O., *Emergence of Spanish America,* chs. 1–2, and in Garza, "Spanish Origins of Mexican Constitutionalism," pp. 36–79.

2. Rodríguez O., *Emergence of Spanish America,* p. 10; on the Cortes and Mexico in general, *Mexico and the Spanish Cortes,* ed. Benson.

3. The triumph of the Plan of Iguala is discussed in Robertson, *Iturbide of Mexico,* chs. 4–6.

4. Ibid., ch. 9.

5. Valadés, *Alamán,* p. 2; Ortega y Pérez Gallardo, *Historia genealógica,* pp. 4–5 of section on the Marquesado de San Clemente; *Apuntes para la biografía del Exmo. Sr. D. Lucas Alamán,* pp. 4–6; "Autobiografía de D. Lucas Alamán," in Alamán, *Obras* 4:12–13.

6. Estep, "The Life of Lorenzo de Zavala," pp. 1–6.

7. Ibid., pp. 10–11.

8. "Autobiografía de D. Lucas Alamán," in Alamán, *Obras* 4:14.

9. Ibid., pp. 14–20.

10. Estep, "The Life of Lorenzo de Zavala," pp. 12–19.

11. *Suplemento á las semblanzas de los diputados á cortes,* p. 17.

12. *Apuntes para la biografía de Alamán,* p. 7; Alamán, *Canción patriótica.*

13. O'Gorman, *Historia de las divisiones territoriales,* pp. 13–14.

14. Ibid., pp. 40, 48.

15. Benson, "The Plan of Casa Mata," pp. 49–52.

16. Dublán and Lozano, eds., *Legislación mexicana* 1:632–33.

17. "Autobiografía de D. Lucas Alamán," in Alamán, *Obras* 4:22.

18. *Gaceta del Gobierno Supremo de México,* May 17, 1823, pp. 2–3.

19. Estep, "The Life of Lorenzo de Zavala," pp. 70–78.

20. Oaxaca, *Memoria,* 1827, p. 8; Oaxaca, *Memoria,* 1832, p. 24; Hamnet, *Politics*

and Trade in Southern Mexico, 1750–1821, pp. 48, 56–57, 143–44; "Noticia de las cantidades de grana," Appendix to reprint of "Estadística . . . de Guaxaca" of José María Murguía y Galardi, follows p. 267 in *Boletín de la Sociedad Mexicana de Geografía y estadística,* 1859.

21. Murguía y Galardi, "Extracto general . . . del Estado de Guaxaca," pt. 1, pp. 7, 58–60, pt. 2, pp. 28, 30–31.

22. Oaxaca, *Memoria,* 1832, pp. 26–27.

23. *El Sol,* September 2, 1824, pp. 2–3, September 6, 1824, p. 3, and September 7, 1824, p. 2; Bidwell, "The First Mexican Navy, 1821–1830," p. 184.

24. Ancona, *Historia de Yucatán* 3:258–59.

25. Yucatán, *Memoria de estadística,* 1826, pp. 2–3.

26. *El Sol,* January 11, 1824, pp. 2–3; Chiapas, *Memoria,* 1831, pp. 28–30.

27. Tabasco, *Estadística,* 1826, pp. 5–8, estado 3; Tabasco, *Memoria,* 1831, pp. 6–7, "Estado que manifiesta el número de las haciendas con distinción de sus claces [sic]."

28. México, *Memoria,* 1826, p. 10; ibid., 1828, pp. 6–11, estado 1.

29. Querétaro, *Nota estadística,* 1826, p. 1; Telmo Primo, *Querétaro en 1822,* pp. 40–41; Di Tella, "The Dangerous Classes in Early Nineteenth Century Mexico," pp. 91–92.

30. Puebla, *Memoria,* 1826, pp. 25–26; México, Congreso, *Crónicas* 1:71; Reyes Heroles, *El liberalismo mexicano* 1:171.

31. O'Gorman, *Historia de las divisiones territoriales,* p. 70.

32. *El Sol,* December 8, 1832, pp. 3–4, January 26, 1824, pp. 3–4.

33. Veracruz, *Nota estadística,* 1827, pp. 1–7; *Águila Mejicana,* April 3, 1827; p. 2; González de Cossío, *Xalapa,* p. 433; Leiby, "Report to the King," p. 60.

34. Ward to Canning, no. 27, Mexico City, February 5, 1827, FO 50/31A.

35. Jalisco, *Memoria,* 1826, pp. 22–24, estado 2; Jalisco, *Nota estadística,* 1826, pp. 3–7; Jalisco, *Memoria,* 1832, pp. 15–16; *El Tiempo,* October 20, 1834, p. 1; Ward to Canning, no. 27, Mexico City, February 5, 1827, FO 50/31A; Lindley, "Kinship and Credit in the Structure of Guadalajara's Oligarchy, 1800–1830," pp. 54–55; Van Young, *Hacienda and Market,* pp. 11, 25–27, table 1.

36. *Águila Mexicana,* February 1, 1824, p. 2; México, Congreso, *Crónicas* 1:578.

37. San Luis Potosí, *Memoria,* 1831, pp. 11–12, estado 5; *Gaceta del Gobierno Supremo de la Federación Mexicana,* 1824, p. 5; Ward to Canning, no. 27, Mexico City, February 5, 1827, FO 50/31A.

38. Zacatecas, *Memoria,* 1831, p. 18, estado 7; ibid., 1834, pp. 16–17, 26, 28; Ward to Canning, no. 27, Mexico City, February 5, 1827, FO 50/31A.

39. Guanajuato, *Memoria,* 1826, estado 5; Guanajuato, *Memoria,* 1827, p. 4; Guanajuato, *Memoria instructiva,* 1830, pp. 34, 41; Guanajuato, *Memoria,* 1832, p. 5; *Águila Mexicana,* May 3, 1824, pp. 1–2; Taylor, "Socioeconomic Instability," pp. 116–22, 536–37.

40. O'Gorman, *Historia de las divisiones territoriales,* pp. 17–18; Benson, "Spain's Contribution to Federalism in Mexico," p. 91.

41. Harris, *Sánchez Navarros,* pp. 186, 235.

42. McElhannon, "Imperial Mexico and Texas, 1821–1823," pp. 134–36.

43. Guice, ed., "Texas in 1804," pp. 53–55; Benson, ed. and trans., "A Governor's Report on Texas in 1809," p. 611; the 1821 report of governor Antonio Martínez is discussed in McElhannon, "Imperial Mexico and Texas, 1821–1823," pp. 119–21.

44. Morton, *Terán and Texas,* pp. 58–67.

45. Coahuila-Texas, *Nota estadística,* 1827, p. 8; general surveys of Mexican Texas are Downs, "The History of Mexicans in Texas, 1820–1845"; and Tijerina, "Tejanos and Texas: The Native Mexicans of Texas, 1820–1850."

46. Coahuila-Texas, *Nota estadística,* 1827, p. 7.

47. Nuevo México, *Ojeada,* 1832, pp. 17–20, 22–23, 25–26; *Noticias históricas y estadísticas de la antigua provincia de Nuevo-México,* p. 73; Tyler, "New Mexico in the 1820's," pp. 78–88.

48. Tyler, "New Mexico in the 1820's," pp. 45, 95, 107–25, 135–36, 153; *Noticias históricas y estadísticas de la antigua provincia de Nuevo México,* p. 73; Nuevo México, *Ojeada,* 1832, pp. 17–26; Weber, *The Taos Trappers,* pp. 9, 66–67, 134; Loyola, *The American Occupation of New Mexico,* pp. 10, 16, 17.

49. Poinsett, "The Republic of Mexico," p. 29.

50. Forbes, *California,* pp. 62–64, 71–75; Geary, *The Secularization of the California Missions (1810–1846),* p. 92; Barron to Pakenham, Confidential, Tepic, June 22, 1827, FO 50/39; Tays, "Revolutionary California During the Mexican Period, 1822–1846," p. 101.

51. Alta California, *Breve noticia,* 1833, p. 4, "Estado que manifiesta la población de los presidios, pueblos y misiones del territorio"; Richman, *California Under Spain and Mexico,* pp. 226, 230, 241, 246; Forbes, *California,* pp. 259–66.

52. Duhaut-Cilly, "Account of California in the Years 1827–28," pp. 152–53, 241.

53. Hornbeck, "Land Tenure and Rancho Expansion," pp. 379–84, 388.

54. Barron to His Majesty's Secretary of State, Tepic, January 1, 1825, FO 50/17; O'Gorman, *Historia de las divisiones territoriales,* p. 71; Sonora, *Rápida ojeada,* 1835, p. 18; Stevens, "Mexico's Forgotten Frontier: A History of Sonora, 1821–1846," pp. 27, 45–47; Bourne, "Notes on the State of Sonora and Cinaloa," pp. 559–66.

55. O'Gorman, *Historia de las divisiones territoriales,* p. 61; Durango, *Nota estadística,* 1826, estado 2; Durango, *Memoria,* 1827, pp. 4–5; Ward to Canning, no. 17, Mexico City, February 5, 1827, FO 50/31A.

56. Chihuahua, *Memoria,* 1831, pp. 26–27; Chihuahua, *Noticias estadísticas,* 1834, pp. 97–98, 109, 167–68, 171, 173.

57. Nuevo León, *Memoria,* 1828, p. 9; ibid., 1831, p. 6, estado 2; ibid., 1832, estado 3.

58. De la Torre et al., *Historia general de Tamaulipas,* pp. 108–09, 217; Saldívar, *Historia compendiada de Tamaulipas,* p. 118.

59. Bullock, *Six Months' Residence,* pp. 47–48.

60. Oaxaca, *Memoria,* 1827, p. 15.

61. González de Cossío, *Xalapa,* p. 175.

62. Bullock, *Six Months' Residence,* p. 79; Poinsett, *Notes on Mexico,* pp. 39–40.

63. *Águila Mexicana,* May 3, 1824, pp. 1–2.

64. Vizcaya Canales, "Monterrey, los primeros años después de la independencia," pp. 531–38; Potter, "First Impressions of Mexico, 1828, by Reuben Potter," pp. 66–67.

65. Lyon, *Journal of a Residence* 1:62, 2:221; Hall, *Extracts from a Journal* 2:296; Bullock, *Six Months' Residence,* pp. 26, 288; Rivera Cambas, *Historia antigua y moderna de Jalapa* 2:323–24.

66. Kicza, "Business and Society in Late Colonial Mexico City," p. 529.

67. This description is based essentially, except where otherwise indicated, on the following contemporary descriptions of Mexico City by foreigners: Berlandier, *Journey to Mexico;* Bullock, *Six Months' Residence;* Lyon, *Journal of a Residence;* Poinsett, *Notes on Mexico;* Tayloe, *Mexico 1825–1828;* Becher, *Cartas sobre Mexico.* An excellent overview of Mexico's capital, based on published descriptions and contemporary documents, is Shaw, "Poverty and Politics in Mexico City, 1824–1854," ch. 1.

68. Moreno Toscano and Aguirre Anaya, "Migrations to Mexico City in the Nineteenth Century," pp. 33–34.

69. Mora, *Memoria que para informar sobre . . . el desagüe,* Appendix 2.

70. México, *Memoria,* 1829, p. 24.
71. Shaw, "Poverty and Politics," p. 4.
72. Ibid., p. 15.
73. Ibid., pp. 53–55, 179; Moreno Toscano and Aguirre Anaya, "Migrations to Mexico City in the Nineteenth Century," p. 30; Mexico City, Ayuntamiento, *Memoria económica de . . . 1830,* pp. 28–45, 64–66; *El Atleta,* March 28, 1830, p. 3; Tornel y Mendívil, *Manifestación del C. José María Tornel,* pp. 15, 21.
74. Acuario, *Iniciativa al ayuntamiento sobre asuntos de policía.*

Chapter 2
FROM MONARCHY TO FEDERAL REPUBLIC
1823–1824

1. Bustamante, *Diario histórico,* p. 474.
2. *El Sol,* September 22, 1823, p. 1.
3. Alamán, *Historia de Méjico* 5:507.
4. *Suplemento á las semblanzas de los diputados á Cortes.*
5. Bidwell, "The First Mexican Navy, 1821–1830," p. 183; Chandler, "Jacobo de Villaurrutia and the Audiencia of Guatemala, 1794–1804," pp. 402–21; *Breve idea de los méritos del ziudadano Jacobo de Villa Urrutia;* Ladd, *The Mexican Nobility at Independence, 1780–1826,* p. 367; Anna, *The Fall of the Royal Government in Mexico City,* pp. 77, 119, 130.
6. Among the many biographical sketches of Michelena are those found in the following: *Águila Mexicana,* February 17, 1824, p. 4; *Semblanzas de los representantes que compusieron el congreso constituyente de 1836;* and *Jefes del ejército,* pp. 76–77.
7. Father Mier's life has been chronicled a number of times; for a contemporary sketch, see *El Observador de la República Mexicana,* 1827, 3:214–16.
8. Benson, "Servando Teresa de Mier, Federalist," p. 515; Bustamante, *Diario histórico,* p. 495.
9. The principal biography of Mier y Terán is Morton, *Terán and Texas;* for contemporary descriptions, see *Correo de la Federación Mexicana,* November 25, 1826, p. 4; and Tornel, *Breve reseña,* pp. 27–28.
10. *Suplemento á las semblanzas de los diputados á Cortes,* pp. 3–4.
11. Sosa, *Biografías de mexicanos distinguidos,* pp. 864–65; Benson, "The Provincial Deputation," pp. 7, 156.
12. The most detailed biography is Hutchinson, "Valentín Gómez Farías: a Biographical Study"; his early years are related on pp. 2–23.
13. *Suplemento á las semblanzas de los diputados á Cortes,* p. 5.
14. Sosa, *Biografías de mexicanos distinguidos,* pp. 199–200.
15. Ibid., pp. 390–91; Obituary in *Diario del Gobierno,* December 16, 1841, pp. 1–3.
16. Hale, *Mexican Liberalism in the Age of Mora 1821–1853,* pp. 61–68, 298–305.
17. Villaurrutia to Secretario de Relaciones, Veracruz, July 9, 1823, Hernández y Dávalos papers, UTLAC, 16–5–3362.
18. Dublán and Lozano, eds., *Legislación mexicana* 1:163.
19. Obituary of Domínguez in *Voz de la Patria,* April 24, 1830, p. 6.
20. *Colección de los decretos y órdenes del Soberano Congreso Mexicano, Desde su instalación en 24 de Febrero de 1822, hasta 30 de Octubre de 1823 en que cesó,* pp. 154–55.
21. Ibid., June 12, 1823, p. 3.
22. Obituaries in *El Fénix de la Libertad,* July 15, 1833, p. 3.
23. *Jefes del ejército,* pp. 22–25; Bidwell, "The First Mexican Navy, 1821–1830," p. 37.

24. Benson, "The Plan of Casa Mata," p. 53; Benson, "Spain's Contribution to Federalism in Mexico," p. 99; *Observaciones á la carta,* p. 90; Benson, "The Provincial Deputation," pp. 1, 15, 55, 56, 92, 101, 129.

25. *Observaciones á la carta,* pp. 56–57.

26. Bustamante, *Diario histórico,* p. 329.

27. Robertson, *Iturbide,* pp. 251–58; Bustamante, *Diario histórico,* p. 400.

28. Bustamante, *Diario histórico,* p. 367; *Diario de las sesiones del Congreso Constituyente de México* 4:262; *Colección de órdenes y decretos de la Soberana Junta Provisional Gubernativa* 2:91.

29. *Gaceta del Gobierno Supremo de México,* May 15, 1823, p. 3, May 17, 1823, p. 2.

30. Dublán and Lozano, eds., *Legislación mexicana* 1:649–50; Benson, "Servando Teresa de Mier, Federalist," pp. 516–18; *Águila Mexicana* for 1823: May 11, pp. 2–3, May 13, p. 2, May 14, p. 2, May 15, pp. 2–3, May 18, p. 3, May 19, pp. 1–2, May 20, p. 1.

31. The earliest dates of the eleven statements (all 1823) and sources, are: Puebla, April 4 (Benson, "Provincial Deputation," pp. 203–04); Yucatán, April 25 (Ancona, *Historia de Yucatán* 3:268–69); Guanajuato, April 30 (Benson, "Provincial Deputation," p. 230); Michoacán, May 7 (ibid., pp. 226–29); Guadalajara, May 9 and 12 (*Águila Mexicana,* May 22, 1823, pp. 1–2); San Luis Potosí, April or May (Benson, "Provincial Deputation," p. 235); Oaxaca, June 2 (*Águila Mexicana,* June 11, 1823, pp. 1–2; Benson, "Provincial Deputation," pp. 298–99); Coahuila, June 5 (*Águila Mexicana,* July 1, pp. 3–4, July 2, p. 3); Querétaro, June 12 (ibid., July 28, p. 3); Zacatecas, June 22 (ibid., July 3, p. 3, July 4, p. 2); in each case, the date given is for the declaration by provincial deputation, except in case of Puebla, where the declaration was made to a committee of Congress by a designated representative of the Puebla provincial deputation (along with, it should be noted, designated representatives for Oaxaca, Zacatecas, San Luis Potosí, Guanajuato, Michoacán, Guadalajara, and Querétaro).

32. *Observaciones á la carta,* p. 90; Bustamante, *Diario histórico,* p. 36.

33. *Águila Mexicana* for 1823: May 22, pp. 1–2, June 24, pp. 1–2, July 5, p. 2, July 6, p. 4, July 13, pp. 2–3; Banegas Galván, *Historia de México* 2:410, 414.

34. May 30 was the installation date of a provisional governing junta, which then conducted elections for a state legislature (*Águila Mexicana,* June 21, 1823, pp. 3–4).

35. June 2 was the date of presentation of the "Plan" of state government by the governing junta (Benson, "The Provincial Deputation," pp. 259–67).

36. June 18 was the date the provincial deputation issued a provisional plan of state government (*Águila Mexicana,* July 3, 1823, p. 3).

37. Benson, "The Provincial Deputation," pp. 259, 265–66, 272, 286, ch. 7.

38. Bustamante, *Diario histórico,* pp. 379–80; Tays, "Revolutionary California, 1822–1846," pp. 103–05; *Águila Mexicana* for 1823: July 12, p. 2, July 23, pp. 3–4, July 24, p. 2, August 1, p. 4, August 3, p. 2, August 15, pp. 1–2; Benson, "The Provincial Deputation," pp. 308, 323–24.

39. Olavarría y Ferrari, *México independiente 1821–1855,* p. 98.

40. Santa Anna delivered his version of the affair in *Manifiesto de Antonio López de Santana á sus conciudadanos;* other accounts are found in Benson, "The Provincial Deputation," pp. 236–37, 319–21; Fuentes Mares, *Santa Anna,* pp. 42–43, 48; Valadés, *México, Santa Anna, y la guerra de Texas,* pp. 63–66; Callcott, *Santa Anna,* pp. 48–49; and Díaz Díaz, *Caudillos y caciques,* pp. 70–71; also see *Águila Mexicana,* June 15, 1823, pp. 1–2, September 5, 1823, pp. 1–2; documents relating to Santa Anna's trial were printed in Suárez y Navarro, *Historia de México* 1:40–45.

41. *Águila Mexicana* for 1823: July 5, p. 2, July 6, pp. 3–4, August 22, pp. 2–3,

September 1, pp. 1–2, September 2, p. 1, September 3, pp. 1–2; *Observaciones á la carta,* p. 42; Benson, "The Provincial Deputation," pp. 281–83.

42. Benson, "The Provincial Deputation," p. 223; *Gaceta del Supremo Gobierno de México,* August 5, 1823, pp. 1–3; *Colección de órdenes y decretos de la Soberana Junta Provisional Gubernativa* 2:146.

43. Bustamante, *Diario histórico,* p. 545; Alamán, *Historia de Méjico* 5:484.

44. *La diplomacia mexicana* 1:279–83.

45. Bidwell, "The First Mexican Navy, 1821–1830," pp. 67–69, 89, 102, 143–47; Rivera Cambas, *Historia antigua y moderna de Jalapa* 2:373, 377.

46. Bidwell, "The First Mexican Navy, 1821–1830," pp. 143–57, 183; Rivera Cambas, *Historia antigua y moderna de Jalapa* 2:298.

47. Printed in *Águila Mexicana,* October 12, 1823, p. 2.

48. Ward, *Mexico in 1827* 2:174.

49. Mackenzie to Canning, no. 33, Xalapa, November 15, 1824, FO 50/7; Morier and Ward to Canning, no. 2, Mexico City, April 12, 1825, FO 50/12.

50. *Águila Mexicana,* September 20, 1823, pp. 1–2, August 2, 1824, p. 2; Alamán, *Historia de Méjico* 5:493–94; *El Sol,* June 29, 1824, p. 3, July 2, 1824, p. 4; Maxwell, "The 'Diario histórico' of Carlos María Bustamante for 1824," pp. 163, 225, 242, 273, 330, 338.

51. *Águila Mexicana,* September 20, 1823, pp. 1–2, April 7, 1824, pp. 1–2; Bustamante, *Diario histórico,* pp. 458, 505–06, 544, 568–69; De Tapia, *Apéndice al manual de práctica forense,* p. 73.

52. Bustamante, *Diario histórico,* pp. 616–17, 626–27.

53. México, Congreso, *Crónicas* 1:152, 199–200, 308–09.

54. Draft of Circular of Minister of Relations, December 16, 1823, AGN, Gobernación, legajo 139; México, Congreso, *Crónicas* 1:253–54.

55. Dublán and Lozano, eds., *Legislación mexicana* 1:693–97; Maxwell, "The 'Diario histórico' of Bustamante for 1824," p. 74.

56. Lyon, *Journal of a Residence* 1:206; Alamán, *Historia de Méjico* 5:490; a general account of Lobato's insurrection is given in *El Sol,* January 27, 1824, pp. 3–4, also January 28, 1824, pp. 1–2; Giménez, "Memorias del Coronel Manuel María Giménez," p. 290; *Águila Mexicana,* January 27, 1824, p. 4; Maxwell, "The 'Diario Histórico' of Bustamante for 1824," pp. 35–38; Suárez y Navarro, *Historia de México* 1:53.

57. *Águila Mexicana,* January 13, 1824, pp. 2–3, January 28, 1824, pp. 1–2; Banegas Galván, *Historia de México* 2:458–59; *El Sol,* January 18, 1824, p. 4, January 20, 1824, p. 2, January 27, 1824, pp. 2–3; Parrish, "The Life of Nicolás Bravo," pp. 133–34. A copy of the Plan of Cuernavaca is in UTLAC, Hernández y Dávalos Collection 17–1.3768.

58. *Jefes del ejército,* pp. 3–4.

59. *Águila Mexicana,* March 5, 1824, pp. 2–3, April 9, 1824, p. 4; Alamán, *Historia de Méjico* 5:492.

60. *El Sol,* August 10, 1824, p. 4; Alamán, *Historia de Méjico* 5:507.

61. Maxwell, "The 'Diario histórico' of Bustamante for 1824," pp. 219–20, 244; on reasons for need of a supreme director, see debates in sessions of early April in México, Congreso, *Crónicas,* vol. 2.

62. Maxwell, "The 'Diario histórico' of Bustamante for 1824," pp. 108, 140, 248; Robertson, *Iturbide,* p. 293.

63. Banegas Galván, *Historia de México* 2:477–78, 496, 502; *El Sol,* May 14, 1824, p. 4, June 21, 1824, pp. 2–3; Maxwell, "The 'Diario histórico' of Bustamante for 1824," p. 286; *Discursos pronunciados por los Ecsmos. Señores Ministros de Relaciones y de Guerra . . . Sobre las ocurrencias de Guadalajara;* also, *Gaceta Extraordinaria del Gobierno Supremo de la Federación Mexicana,* June 19, 1824, pp. 1–4, June 25, 1824, p. 1.

64. *Gaceta del Gobierno Supremo de la Federación Mexicana,* July 26, 1824, p. 2.
65. De la Garza to Alamán, August 13, 1824, reprinted in Suárez y Navarro, *Historia de México* 1:379–84.
66. Robertson, *Iturbide* 1:295–97.
67. *Jefes del ejército,* p. 185.
68. Suárez y Navarro, *Historia de México* 1:66.
69. *Gaceta del Gobierno Supremo de la Federación Mexicana,* July 20, 1824, pp. 2–3; *El Sol* for 1824: February 6, pp. 1–2, July 12, pp. 1–3, July 13, pp. 3–4, August 3, p. 4, August 7, p. 2; Victoria to Ministro de Guerra, August 17, 1824, printed in *Gaceta Extraordinaria del Gobierno Supremo de la Federación Mexicana,* August 19, 1824; Maxwell, "The 'Diario histórico' of Bustamante for 1824," pp. 441–43; Bustamante, *Continuación* 2:240–41.
70. *El Sol,* July 15, 1824, p. 4; Morier to Canning, no. 11, Xalapa, November 19, 1824, FO 50/6; *Suplemento á la Águila Mexicana* of January 2, 1824 (no. 263); Gil y Saenz, *Historia de Tabasco,* pp. 171–73.
71. *El Sol,* January 26, 1824, p. 1; Díaz Díaz, *Caudillos y caciques,* pp. 70–71; Fuentes Mares, *Santa Anna,* p. 48; Bidwell, "The First Mexican Navy, 1821–1830," pp. 184, 260–62; Banegas Galván, *Historia de México* 2:470–73; Ancona, *Historia de Yucatán* 3:284–91; *Águila Mexicana,* March 20, 1824, p. 1; Ortiz de la Tabla, *Comercio exterior,* pp. 128–31.
72. Ancona, *Historia de Yucatán* 3:299–300; Fuentes Mares, *Santa Anna,* pp. 50–53.
73. Fuentes Mares, *Santa Anna,* pp. 53–54; Bidwell, "The First Mexican Navy, 1821–1830," p. 278.
74. Bidwell, "The First Mexican Navy, 1821–1830," p. 271; Fuentes Mares, *Santa Anna,* pp. 55–56.
75. Reyes Heroles, *Liberalismo mexicano* 1:216; Dealey, "The Spanish Source of the Mexican Constitution of 1824," pp. 163–67.
76. Discussed in Benson, "The Provincial Deputation," pp. 346, 349–51.
77. Relaciones, *Memoria,* 1825, in Alamán, *Documentos Diversos* 1:157–58.
78. Poinsett to Clay, no. 7, July 18, 1825, and no. 9, July 27, 1825, Despatches from U.S. Ministers to Mexico, 1823–1906.
79. See Camp, "La cuestión chiapaneca"; Banegas Galván, *Historia de México* 2:380–82; O'Gorman, *Historia de las divisiones territoriales,* p. 59.
80. Trens, *Historia de Chiapas,* p. 309; Dublán and Lozano, eds., *Legislación mexicana* 1:713; O'Gorman, *Historia de las divisiones territoriales,* pp. 59, 60, 68–69, 86.
81. O'Gorman, *Historia de las divisiones territoriales,* pp. 70–71.
82. Bustamante, *Continuación* 2:245.
83. Maxwell, "The 'Diario histórico' of Bustamante for 1824," pp. 625–26.
84. The most detailed biography is Flaccus, "Guadalupe Victoria."
85. A detailed chronicle of Bravo's life is Parrish, "The Life of Nicolás Bravo."
86. *Correo de la Federación Mexicana,* December 7, 1826, p. 4.
87. Ward to Canning, October 22 and 25, 1826, FO 50/25; Poinsett to Secretary of State, no. 166, March 10, 1829, Despatches from U.S. Ministers to Mexico, 1823–1906; Rivera Cambas, *Historia antigua y moderna de Jalapa* 2:308–09; Harrell, "Vicente Guerrero," p. 77.
88. Cuevas, *Porvenir de México,* p. 198.
89. Parrish, "The Life of Nicolás Bravo," p. 150; election results are found in *Redactor Municipal,* October 1, 1824, p. 4, *Gaceta del Gobierno Supremo de la Federación Mexicana,* October 12, 1824, p. 3.
90. Macune, "A Test of Federalism," p. 306.
91. Mateos, *Historia parlamentaria* 2:871, 909, 964.

Chapter 3
THE MEXICANS AND MEXICAN INSTITUTIONS

1. Colonial censuses are discussed in Sierra, *Nacimiento de México*, pp. 104–11; for population breakdown by states and territories, see table 1.

2. Sierra, *Nacimiento de México*, p. 116, referring to the late colonial period.

3. Dublán and Lozano, eds., *Legislación mexicana* 1:628.

4. In *Historia de Méjico* 1:23, Alamán discussed opinions of his contemporaries on the caste breakdown; in his own estimate on the proportions, which were 40 percent Indian, 40 percent *casta*, and 20 percent white, Alamán was in close agreement with Von Humboldt, *Political Essay on the Kingdom of New Spain* 1:109, 131, 206, 243; for Navarro y Noriega's and other estimates on the same topic, see Sierra, *Nacimiento de México*, pp. 111–12; also, da Ponte Ribeiro, "Memoria sobre la República Mexicana," p. 366.

5. López Sarrelangue, "Población indígena de la Nueva España en el siglo XVIII," table 9; López Sarrelangue did not include the Intendancy of Mérida, but the general evidence suggests a large percentage of this area's population was Indian; on the uprooted Indians, see Cook and Borah, *Essays in Population History* 1:289–92.

6. Carroll, "Mexican Society in Transition," pp. 66–70, 193–96; also see Alamán, *Historia de Méjico* 1:25–27; Sierra, *Nacimiento de México*, p. 82; Brading and Wu, "Population Growth and Crisis: León, 1720–1860," pp. 9–10.

7. Taylor, "Socio-Economic Instability," pp. 154–55.

8. Ibid., pp. 144–46; Alamán, *Historia de Méjico* 5:28; Hamill, *The Hidalgo Revolt*, p. 43.

9. Guanajuato, *Memoria*, 1826, "Plan que manifiesta el censo general"; *Noticias históricas de Nuevo México*, pp. 56–57; Nuevo León, *Memoria*, 1831, estado 2; Oaxaca, *Memoria*, 1832, "Resumen general de la población que tiene este Estado. . ."; for León (Guanajuato), see *Águila Mexicana*, November 22, 1823, p. 4, for Dolores (Guanajuato), see *Águila Mexicana*, March 3, 1824, p. 4; Zacatecas figures were something of an exception, showing 6,773 artisans (Zacatecas, *Memoria*, 1831, "Plan que manifiesta el censo general del Estado"); Poinsett to Secretary of State, no. 166, Mexico City, March 10, 1829, Despatches from U.S. Ministers to Mexico, 1823–1906.

10. Lindley, "Kinship and Credit in the Structure of Guadalajara's Oligarchy, 1800–1830," pp. 69–70; Koppe, *Cartas á la patria*, pp. 108–09; Lyon, *Journal of a Residence* 2:233–34; for a current opinion in agreement with this, see Brading, "La estructura de la producción agrícola en el Bajío de 1700 a 1850," p. 136; for an example of a governor's report, see Guanajuato, *Memoria*, 1826, estado 5.

11. Lira-Gonzalez, "Indian Communities in Mexico City," pp. 3–70.

12. A table of Mexico City marriages, births, and deaths for the years 1790–1825 is found in *La Lima de Vulcano*, December 17, [1834?], p. 2, bound in Lafragua Collection, vol. 118.

13. Shaw, "Poverty and Politics," pp. xvi–xvii, 38–39, 49, 146, 374; Shaw's description of the upper class is based on an 1849 population sampling, and his figure of 80 percent for the laboring classes comes from 1841.

14. Poinsett, *Notes on Mexico*, pp. 49, 73; Scardaville, "Crime and the Urban Poor: Mexico City," pp. 20, 22, 67, 71.

15. Dublán and Lozano, eds., *Legislación mexicana* 2:61–62; Shaw, "Poverty and Politics," pp. iv, 45, 47, 286, 374–79.

16. México, Congreso, *Crónicas* 2:507–08; the principal population study in

recent years, Cook and Borah, *Essays in Population History* 1:179–83, has confirmed this.

17. Valdés, *Censo actual de la república mexicana*, p. 7; on the nobility, see Poinsett, *Notes on Mexico*, pp. 56–57; and Gutiérrez, "Marriage, Sex, and the Family," table 13, shows girls of the nobility marrying at about sixteen.

18. Brading and Wu, "Population Growth and Crisis; León, 1720–1860," pp. 6, 13–14; Gutiérrez, "Marriage, Sex, and the Family," tables 1, 2, 9.

19. Scardaville, "Crime and the Urban Poor: Mexico City," p. 185n; Nuevo México, *Ojeada*, 1832, p. 17.

20. For Carlos María de Bustamante's response to a foreigner's criticisms, see *Voz de la Patria*, February 1, 1831, pp. 4–5.

21. Alamán, *Historia de Méjico* 1:19.

22. Lindley, "Kinship and Credit in the Structure of Guadalajara's Oligarchy, 1800–1830," pp. 108–09.

23. Duhaut-Cilly, "Account of California in the Years 1827–28," p. 311; Shaw, "Poverty and Politics," pp. 220, 225.

24. *Voz de la Patria*, March 8, 1830, pp. 3–7; *El Sol* for 1826: May 20, p. 4, May 23, p. 3, May 28, p. 4, July 15, p. 4.

25. Staples, "La cola del diablo en la vida conventual," pp. 12, 15, 26, 29, 30.

26. Greenow, *Credit and Socioeconomic Change in Colonial Mexico*, pp. 122–28, 225; Morales, "Estructura urbana," p. 368.

27. Shaw, "Poverty and Politics," p. 119; Lecompte, "The Independent Women of Hispanic New Mexico, 1821–1846," pp. 20–21.

28. Ladd, *The Mexican Nobility at Independence, 1780–1826*, p. 367.

29. Ibid., pp. 296–98.

30. Maxwell, "The 'Diario histórico' of Bustamante for 1824," pp. 296–97.

31. Ladd, *The Mexican Nobility at Independence, 1780–1826*, pp. 248–49, 302.

32. Da Ponte Ribeiro, "Memoria sobre la República Mexicana," p. 382.

33. Zavala, *Umbral de la independencia*, pp. 23–24.

34. Koppe, *Cartas á la patria*, p. 109; Poinsett, "Mexico and the Mexicans," p. 167.

35. Koppe, *Cartas á la patria*, p. 121.

36. Poinsett, *Notes on Mexico*, p. 83.

37. Hervey to Canning, Mexico City, December 15, 1824, FO 50/16; the Mexico state lieutenant-governor stated in 1829 that 87.5 percent of the state's population was Indian (cited in Macune, "A Test of Federalism," p. 14).

38. López Sarrelangue, "Población indígena en el siglo XVIII," pp. 521–22, table 9, estimated Indian population at 2.5 million for 1800 (excluding the Intendancy of Mérida), based on tribute records.

39. México, *Memoria*, 1829, p. 12.

40. Guanajuato, *Memoria*, 1826, p. 30.

41. Taylor, *Landlord and Peasant in Colonial Oaxaca*, p. 201.

42. Hutchinson, "The Mexican Government and the Mission Indians of California," p. 348; Valdés, *Censo actual de la república mexicana*, p. 8; Barker, *The Life of Stephen F. Austin*, p. 282.

43. *Correo de la Federación Mexicana*, July 3, 1827, p. 1; Alamán, *Historia de Méjico* 1:26–27.

44. Oaxaca, *Memoria*, 1828, p. 15.

45. Chiapas, *Memoria*, 1831, p. 9.

46. The decrees are found in *Colección de decretos y órdenes de las Cortes de España, que se reputan vigentes*, pp. 54–55, 56–59, 105–06.

47. Rivera Cambas, *Historia antigua y moderna de Jalapa* 2:318.

48. Reyes Heroles, *El liberalismo mexicano* 1:281; Ancona, *Historia de Yucatán* 3:333–34.
49. México, *Memoria,* 1828, p. 63; Chihuahua, *Noticias estadísticas,* 1834, p. 34; Weber, "Mexico's Far Northern Frontier, 1821–1854," p. 291.
50. Guanajuato, *Memoria,* 1827, p. 17.
51. Poinsett, "Mexico and the Mexicans," p. 169.
52. Saldívar, *Historia compendiada de Tamaulipas,* p. 165; Michoacán, *Memoria,* 1829, p. 16; *Águila Mexicana,* January 24, 1827, pp. 2–3 (Veracruz), and March 12, 1827, p. 4 (San Luis Potosí); Ezell and Ezell, *The Aguiar Collection,* p. 35 (Sonora-Sinaloa); *Colección de acuerdos . . . de los indígenes . . . de Jalisco,* p. 131.
53. *Colección de acuerdos . . . de los indígenes . . . de Jalisco,* pp. 14, 131–32.
54. Poinsett, "Mexico and the Mexicans," p. 169.
55. Michoacán, *Memoria,* 1829, p. 16.
56. *Colección de acuerdos . . . de los indígenes . . . de Jalisco,* pp. 141–42.
57. Lindley, "Kinship and Credit in the Structure of Guadalajara's Oligarchy, 1800–1830," pp. 268–70.
58. Oaxaca, *Memoria,* 1827, p. 18.
59. Maxwell, "The 'Diario histórico' of Bustamante for 1824," p. 254.
60. *Correo de la Federación Mexicana* for 1828: April 14, p. 4, April 17, pp. 2–3, April 18, pp. 3–4, April 19, pp. 3–4; *Voz de la Patria,* January 17, 1831, pp. 7–8; México, *Memoria,* 1829, pp. 16–17.
61. Ward to Canning, no. 23, Mexico City, January 31, 1827, FO 50/31A.
62. Lyon, *Journal of a Residence* 2:115; Gilmore, "British Mining Ventures in Early National Mexico," pp. 108–09.
63. *Águila Mexicana,* March 13, 1825, pp. 2–3.
64. Barker, "The French Colony in Mexico, 1821–1861," pp. 597–99, 602.
65. Lyon, *Journal of a Residence* 2:146; *El Amigo del Pueblo,* vol. 4 (1828), p. 617.
66. Randall, *Real del Monte,* p. 126.
67. *Correo de la Federación Mexicana,* May 22, 1828, p. 4.
68. Valadés, *Orígenes de la República mexicana,* p. 239; *Águila Mexicana,* April 16, 1823, p. 4; Morier to Canning, unnumbered [ca. February 15, 1825], FO 50/11, pp. 66–70.
69. Valadés, *Orígenes de la República mexicana,* pp. 237, 252.
70. Deposition of Prisette in St. Clair's court martial, AGN, Archivo de Guerra, vol. 371, pp. 285, 289–90; *Águila Mexicana,* April 8, 1824, p. 4; Zavala, *Albores de la República,* pp. 25–36.
71. Jordan, *Serious Actual Dangers of Foreigners,* pp. 8, 9, 22.
72. Bustamante, *Diario histórico,* pp. 567–68; *Examen de las facultades del gobierno sobre el destierro de estrangeros,* p. 5.
73. Ward to Canning, no. 4, Mexico City, May 21, 1825, and no. 14, Mexico City, June 25, 1825, FO 50/13; Ward to Canning, no. 47, May 21, 1826, FO 50/21; Court of Inquiry Documents, AGN, Archivo de Guerra, vol. 371, pp. 112–26.
74. Ward to Canning, no. 11, Mexico City, March 10, 1826, FO 50/20.
75. Ward to Canning, no. 66, Mexico City, June 2, 1826, FO 50/21; decree of June 5, 1826, printed in Jordan, *Serious Actual Dangers of Foreigners,* pp. 40–49; law of March 12, 1828, in Dublán and Lozano, eds., *Legislación mexicana* 2:64–65.
76. Dublán and Lozano, eds., *Legislación mexicana* 1:712, 2:66–68.
77. Pakenham to Palmerston, no. 24, Mexico City, April 2, 1831, FO 50/65.
78. *Examen de las facultades del gobierno sobre el destierro de los estrangeros,* p. 4.
79. Morier to Canning, unnumbered [ca. February 15, 1825], FO 50/11, pp. 66–70; Ward to Canning, no. 11, Mexico City, March 10, 1826, FO 50/20; law of October 10, 1823, cited in Berninger, "Mexican Attitudes Towards Immigration, 1821–1857," p. 30;

law of December 23, 1824, in *Legislación mexicana,* ed. Dublán and Lozano 1:763; law of May 9, 1826, in *Examen de las facultades del gobierno sobre el destierro de los estrangeros,* p. 7; law of May 1, 1828, in *Legislación mexicana,* ed. Dublán and Lozano 2:69.

80. Ward to Canning, no. 34, Mexico City, September 19, 1825, FO 50/14, no. 50, Mexico City, October 30, 1825, FO 50/15, and no. 54, Mexico City, November 15, 1825, FO 50/15; Pakenham to Dudley, unnumbered, Separate and Confidential, Mexico City, December 20, 1827, FO 50/36; Dublán and Lozano, eds., *Legislación mexicana* 2:64–65.

81. Bourne, "Notes on the State of Sonora and Cinaloa," p. 586; Short to Pakenham, Mexico City, May 21, 1830, copy, FO 50/61; Pakenham to Palmerston, no. 63, Mexico City, October 11, 1832, and no. 64, October 14, 1832, FO 50/73; Becher, *Cartas sobre México,* pp. 134–35.

82. Arnold, "Bureaucracy and Bureaucrats in Mexico City, 1808–1824," pp. 26, 129; about 100 of Jalisco's employees were unsalaried, but it is probable that they received fees (Jalisco, *Memoria,* 1831, "Lista de los empleados del Estado, con espresión del sueldo que disfrutan los que lo tienen" [appendix]).

83. Published in *Colección de constituciones de los Estados Unidos Mexicanos.*

84. Ibid., 2:8.

85. Trens, *Historia de Chiapas,* pp. 356–57; Puebla, *Memoria,* 1830, p. 6.

86. Benson, ed., *Mexico and the Spanish Cortes,* pp. 65–76; Jalisco, *Memoria,* 1826, estado 3; México, *Memoria,* 1826, estado 1.

87. Hale, *Mexican Liberalism in the Age of Mora, 1821–1853,* p. 87.

88. Justicia, *Memoria,* 1826, p. 6; ibid., 1827, p. 9.

89. Dublán and Lozano, eds., *Legislación mexicana* 1:738.

90. Ibid., p. 795.

91. Justicia, *Memoria,* 1823, p. 13; ibid., 1825, p. 7; De Tapia, *Apéndice al manual de práctica forense,* pp. 25–26; Chihuahua, *Noticias estadísticas,* 1834, pp. 45–46; Hale, *Mexican Liberalism in the Age of Mora, 1821–1853,* p. 95.

92. Puebla, *Memoria,* 1826, p. 7; Rivera Cambas, *Historia antigua y moderna de Jalapa* 2:614.

93. Harris, *Sánchez Navarros,* pp. 199, 222; Guanajuato, *Memoria instructiva,* 1830, p. 17; San Luis Potosí, *Memoria,* 1831, p. 28; Alamán to Monteleone, November 5, 1830, and November 30, 1830, copies, AGN, Hospital de Jesús, legajo 440, expediente 6; Tornel, *Manifestación del C. José María Tornel,* p. 17.

94. Ibar, *Muerte política de la república mexicana,* no. 18, June 20, 1829; Maxwell, "The 'Diario histórico' of Bustamante for 1824," pp. 106–08, 265.

95. San Luis Potosí, *Memoria,* 1829, p. 16; Nuevo México, *Ojeada,* 1832, p. 39.

96. Puebla, *Memoria,* 1826, p. 18; Durango, *Memoria,* 1827, pp. 8–9; Nuevo León, *Memoria,* 1832, p. 6.

97. Jalisco, *Memoria,* 1832, pp. 4, 7, estado 2.

98. Koppe, *Cartas á la patria,* pp. 122–23.

99. Lyon, *Journal of a Residence* 1:192; Tayloe, *Mexico 1825–1828,* p. 112; Bustamante, *Continuación* 3:163; Poinsett, *Notes on Mexico,* p. 87; Becher, *Cartas sobre México,* pp. 85, 98–99, 122.

100. Ricker, "The Lower Secular Clergy," pp. 204–05.

101. *Gaceta del Gobierno Supremo de la Federación Mexicana,* October 7, 1824, pp. 1–4.

102. Ward to Canning, no. 20, Mexico City, July 12, 1825, no. 12, Mexico City, June 23, 1825, FO 50/13.

103. Benson, ed., *Mexico and the Spanish Cortes,* pp. 126–30; Farriss, *Crown and Clergy,* pp. 246–47; Staples, *La iglesia en la primera república federal mexicana (1824–1835),* p. 138.

104. Alcalá Alvarado, *Una pugna diplomática,* pp. 15–16; Pérez Memén, *El episcopado y la independencia de México 1810–1836,* pp. 221–26.

105. Farriss, *Crown and Clergy,* pp. 242–43; Staples, *La iglesia en la primera república federal mexicana (1824–1835),* p. 10.

106. Staples, *La iglesia en la primera república federal mexicana (1824–1835),* p. 21.

107. Brief biographical data on the bishops are found enclosed with Morier to Canning, no. 12, February 10, 1825, FO 50/11.

108. Ricker, "The Lower Secular Clergy," p. 188.

109. Justicia, *Memoria,* 1826, p. 13, estado 7; Justicia, *Memoria,* 1828, estado 6; Staples, *La iglesia en la primera república federal mexicana (1824–1835),* p. 23; Harris, *The Sánchez Navarros,* p. 220.

110. Staples, *La iglesia en la primera república federal mexicana (1824–1835),* pp. 23–24.

111. Justicia, *Memoria,* 1827, estado 10; ibid., 1828, estado 14; México, *Memoria,* 1827, estado 22; ibid., 1829, estado 18.

112. Farriss, *Crown and Clergy,* pp. 254–65.

113. Justicia, *Memoria,* 1826, estado 11.

114. Ibid., 1828, estado 14; for coverage of the nunneries in the archbishopric, see Staples, "La cola del diablo en la vida conventual."

115. Justicia, *Memoria,* 1828, estado 11; the minister of justice and ecclesiastical affairs in 1825 reported an 1822 figure of 3,050,578 pesos for *capitales impuestos* (capital obligations to the orders), but this figure may have included such unrecoverable claims as the 1804 Consolidation (ibid., 1825, "Estado de las provincias de religiosos, su ubicación, conventos, número de individuos, fincas, y capitales que les pertenecen hasta el año de 1822").

116. Staples, "La cola del diablo en la vida conventual," p. 5; Justicia, *Memoria,* 1828, estado 14.

117. Alamán, *Historia de Méjico* 1:151; Morales, "Estructura urbana," pp. 366–68, 378–79, 401.

118. Costeloe, "The Administration, Collection, and Distribution of Tithes in the Archbishopric of Mexico, 1800–1860," pp. 13–16.

119. Staples, *La iglesia en la primera república federal mexicana (1824–1835),* p. 100.

120. Ibid., pp. 101–03.

121. Ibid., pp. 119–24.

122. Ward to Canning, no. 42, Confidential, Mexico City, March 6, 1827, FO 50/31B.

123. Ward was given these figures by Ramos Arizpe, then minister of justice and ecclesiastical affairs, (*Mexico in 1827* 1:333–34).

124. Morier to Canning, no. 13, Mexico City, December 27, 1824, FO 50/6.

125. Costeloe, "The Administration, Collection, and Distribution of Tithes in the Archbishopric of Mexico, 1800–1860," p. 20.

126. Ward to Canning, no. 27, Mexico City, February 27, 1827, FO 50/31A; Jalisco, *Memoria,* 1832, estado 17.

127. Justicia, *Memoria,* 1826, p. 15.

128. Stevens, "Mexico's Forgotten Frontier," pp. 21, 81, 110, 210; Tyler, "New Mexico in the 1820's," pp. 65–74; *Noticias históricas y estadísticas de Nuevo México,* p. 15; Chihuahua, *Noticias Estadísticas,* 1834, p. 30; Justicia, *Memoria,* 1826, p. 17, estado 11; ibid., 1828, estado 12; ibid., 1831, p. 13; ibid., 1835, p. 30.

129. Beechey, *Narrative of a Voyage to the Pacific,* pp. 351–70.

130. Kroeber, *Handbook of the Indians of California,* p. 888; also see Heizer, *California,* pp. 6–13; and Cook, *The Population of the California Indians,* p. 43.

131. Hutchinson, "The Mexican Government and the Mission Indians of Upper California," pp. 338–39.

132. Reyes Heroles, *El liberalismo mexicano* 3:92–93; Justicia, *Memoria,* 1825, pp. 13–14; Staples, *La iglesia en la primera república federal mexicana (1824–1835),* pp. 74–75.

133. Ricker, "The Lower Secular Clergy," pp. 233, 260.

134. Reyes Heroles, *El liberalismo mexicano* 1:283–84; O'Gorman, ed., *Guía Bibliográfica de Carlos María de Bustamante,* pp. 69–71, cites several of these pamphlets.

135. Ladd, *The Mexican Nobility at Independence, 1780–1826,* p. 126.

136. Ward to Canning, no. 42, Confidential, Mexico City, March 6, 1827, FO 50/31B; a law of November 27, 1824, limited national religious holidays to four: Holy Thursday, Good Friday, Feast of Corpus Christi, and the Festival of Guadalupe (Dublán and Lozano, eds., *Legislación mexicana* 1:745); a law of January 28, 1826, added a fifth, for the Mexican San Felipe de Jesus (ibid. 1:772).

137. Dublán and Lozano, eds., Legislación mexicana 1:712–13.

138. Ibid. 1:662–64; Benson, ed., *Mexico and the Spanish Cortes,* pp. 124–31.

139. The main work on the Patronato is Costeloe, *Church and State;* see also Staples, *La iglesia en la primera república federal mexicana (1824–1835),* pp. 35–53; Pérez Memén, *El Episcopado y la independencia de México,* pp. 215–19.

140. *Colección de constituciones de los Estados Unidos Mexicanos* 3:336.

141. Ibid. 1:420, 2:169, 265.

142. Pérez Memén, *El episcopado y la independencia de México,* pp. 246–52; *Colección de documentos relativos á la conducta del cabildo eclesiástico de la diócesis de Guadalajara,* pp. 8–22, 120–21.

143. Pérez Memén, *El episcopado y la independencia de México,* p. 265.

144. *Colección de constituciones de los Estados Unidos Mexicanos* 1:419–20.

145. Ward to Canning, no. 88, Mexico City, August 4, 1826, FO 50/22.

146. Berninger, "Immigration and Religious Toleration," p. 552.

147. Ward to Canning, no. 42, Confidential, Mexico City, March 6, 1827, FO 50/31B.

148. Ward to Canning, no. 87, Mexico City, August 3, 1826, FO 50/22, and no. 150, Aguas Calientes [sic], December 29, 1826, FO 50/25.

149. *El Sol,* August 31, 1824, p. 4; *Gaceta del Gobierno Supremo de la Federación Mexicana,* September 7, 1824, p. 1; Hervey to Canning, no. 41, Mexico City, September 9, 1824, FO 50/5; Ward to Canning, no. 42, Confidential, Mexico City, March 6, 1827, FO 50/31B.

150. Ward to Canning, no. 25, August 12, 1825, FO 50/14.

151. Archer, *The Army in Bourbon Mexico, 1760–1810,* pp. 228–34; the amalgamation process was discussed by General Arthur Wavell in Morier to Canning, no. 13, Mexico City, February 10, 1825, FO 50/11; Wavell's figure for incoming Spanish soldiers was 10,000; Sims, in *Descolonización,* gives the figure of 8,000 (p. 11).

152. A history of the army's organization in this period is given in Guerra, *Memoria,* 1835, pp. 9–13, and in Treviño, "Attempts at Organizing and Reforming the Mexican National Army, 1821–1824"; the best general survey of the army of the Republic is Samponaro, "The Political Role of the Army in Mexico, 1821–1848."

153. Guerra, *Memoria,* 1823, p. 24; ibid., 1826, p. 5.

154. Ibid., 1826, p. 9.

155. Morier to Canning, no. 13, Mexico City, February 10, 1825, FO 50/11; Archer, *The Army in Bourbon Mexico, 1760–1810,* p. 23, indicates the various militias had about 40,000 men on their rolls in the mid-1780s, but Revillagigedo disbanded many of

the militia units in the 1790s (pp. 28–32); for a general discussion of the size of New Spain's army at the end of the colonial period, see Benson, ed., *Mexico and the Spanish Cortes,* pp. 135–36.

156. Guerra, *Memoria,* 1827, p. 10, estados 1, 2; ibid., 1828, estados 1, 2; ibid., 1829, estados 1, 2.

157. Poinsett to Van Buren, no. 181, Mexico City, September 2, 1829, Despatches from U.S. Ministers to Mexico, 1823–1906.

158. Treviño, "Attempts at Organizing and Reforming the National Army, 1821–1824," pp. 13–14, 23–24; Alamán, *Historia de Méjico* 5:237–38.

159. Dublán and Lozano, eds., *Legislación mexicana* 1:685–86.

160. México, Congreso, *Crónicas* 1:346–47.

161. Sosa, *Biografías de mexicanos distinguidos,* pp. 51–54.

162. *Diccionario Porrúa,* p. 2146; *Jefes del ejército,* pp. 40–44.

163. *Jefes del ejército,* pp. 59–60; Sosa, *Biografías de mexicanos distinguidos,* p. 712.

164. *Jefes del ejército,* p. 11; Sosa, *Biografías de mexicanos distinguidos,* pp. 686–87; Tornel, *Breve reseña,* p. 84.

165. *Jefes del ejército,* pp. 61–62; Sosa, *Biografías de mexicanos distinguidos,* pp. 424–26; Tornel, *Breve reseña,* pp. 34–35.

166. Saldívar, *Historia compendiada de Tamaulipas,* pp. 301–03; *Diccionario Porrúa,* p. 836.

167. Archer, "Pardos, Indians, and the Army of New Spain," pp. 231–55.

168. Treviño, "Attempts at Organizing and Reforming the National Army, 1821–1824," pp. 29–30.

169. Oaxaca, *Memoria,* 1827, p. 25; *Voz de la Patria,* March 16, 1831, pp. 1–2.

170. Guerra, *Memoria,* 1826, pp. 10–11; Yucatán, *Memoria,* 1827, estado 3.

171. Guerra, *Memoria,* 1826, p. 8.

172. Benson, ed., *Mexico and the Spanish Cortes,* pp. 135–36, 148–50; *Águila Mexicana,* September 12, 1823, p. 1; Guerra, *Memoria,* 1826, p. 13.

173. De Tapia, *Apéndice al manual de práctica forense,* pp. 30–31.

174. Rocafuerte, *Bosquejo de la revolución,* p. 161; Dublán and Lozano, eds., *Legislación mexicana* 1:801; México, *Memoria,* 1826, p. 16; Nuevo León, *Memoria,* 1832, pp. 2–3.

175. Guerra, *Memoria,* 1823, pp. 35, 37, 38; ibid., 1827, p. 11; Valadés, *Orígenes de la República mexicana,* p. 132; Bidwell, "The First Mexican Navy, 1821–1830," p. 338; Rincón, *El General Manuel Rincón justificado,* pp. 18–19, 40.

176. *Colección de órdenes y decretos de la soberana junta provisional gubernativa y soberanos congresos generales de la nación mexicana* 2:94–95; *Gaceta del Gobierno Supremo de México,* May 10, 1823, p. 3; Rocafuerte, *Bosquejo de la revolución,* p. 184.

177. Brungardt, "The Civic Militia in Mexico, 1820–1835," pp. 6–7.

Chapter 4
THE YORKINOS AND MASS POLITICS
1825–1826

1. Printed in *Águila Mexicana,* January 2, 1826, pp. 1–4.

2. "Politics of Mexico," p. 129.

3. Tornel, *Breve reseña,* p. 33.

4. Alamán, *Historia de Méjico* 5:516; Ward to Canning, no. 63, December 4, 1825, FO 50/15.

5. On Camacho see Sosa, *Biografías de mexicanos distinguidos,* p. 185; and Lerdo de Tejada, *Apuntes de la heróica ciudad de Veracruz* 3:114–17; on Alamán's political problems and resignation, see Ward to Canning, no. 21, July 14, 1825, FO 50/13, and

Ward to Canning, no. 26, August 16, 1825, FO 50/14; Rocafuerte to Michelena, London, July 18, 1825, Hernández y Dávalos Collection, UTLAC; Poinsett to Clay, October 12, 1825, Despatches from U.S. Ministers to Mexico, 1823–1906; Cañedo, *Acusación contra El Ecs-Ministro de Relaciones Don Lucas Alamán;* "Autobiografía de D. Lucas Alamán," in Alamán, *Obras* 4:23.

6. Barragán was elected governor on May 29, 1824 (Bidwell, "The First Mexican Navy, 1821–1830," p. 193) and was appointed state commander on June 20, 1824 (Barbabosa, *Memorias para la historia megicana ó los últimos días del castillo de San Juan de Ulúa,* pp. 1–2); a January date for his appointment as commander-general was given in *El Sol,* January 2, 1824, p. 4; for a biography, see Sosa, *Biografías de mexicanos distinguidos,* pp. 118–19; and Rivera Cambas, *Historia antigua y moderna de Jalapa* 2:460.

7. Bidwell, "The First Mexican Navy, 1821–1830," p. 366.

8. Ibid., pp. 366–69; Rivera Cambas, *Historia antigua y moderna de Jalapa* 2:372.

9. Bidwell, "The First Mexican Navy, 1821–1830," pp. 370–72; Rivera Cambas, *Historia antigua y moderna de Jalapa* 2:373, 377; *Águila Mexicana,* November 25, 1825, p. 1; Barbabosa, *Memorias para la historia megicana,* document 24.

10. Mateos, *Historia de la masonería en México* p. 8; Navarrete, *La masonería en la historia y en las leyes de Méjico,* pp. 30–31.

11. Hruneni, "Palmetto Yankee," pp. 115–16, 121.

12. Ambassador Poinsett discussed this in a number of places, including Poinsett to Clay, July 8, 1827, and in Poinsett to Secretary of State, no. 166, March 10, 1829, Despatches from U.S. Ministers to Mexico, 1823–1906; Poinsett, *Esposición de la conducta política de los Estados-Unidos para con las nuevas repúblicas de América;* the same story of the Yorkino origin is given in Zavala, *Juicio imparcial,* p. 10.

13. Hruneni, "Palmetto Yankee," pp. 122–23, 128; Estep, *Lorenzo de Zavala,* p. 111; *Correo de la Federación Mexicana,* July 6, 1827, pp. 2–3.

14. Ward to Canning, unnumbered, Secret and most Confidential, October 22 and 25, 1826, FO 50/25, no. 128, Mexico City, October 25, 1826, FO 50/25, and no. 46, Mexico City, March 31, 1827, FO 50/31B.

15. Ibar, *Muerte política de la República Mexicana,* no. 17, June 17, 1829, p. 3.

16. Pakenham to Vaughan, January 13, 1829, copy enclosed in Pakenham to Aberdeen, no. 6, Mexico City, January 14, 1829, FO 50/53.

17. Rincón, *El General M. Rincón justificado,* pp. 4–6.

18. Estep, *Lorenzo de Zavala,* p. 113.

19. Estep, "The Life of Lorenzo de Zavala," p. 123.

20. Morier to Canning, no. 10, February 10, 1825, FO 50/10; on Esteva, also see Bustamante, *Continuación* 3:411; Alamán, *Historia de Méjico* 5:507; and *Rasgo analítico de J.Y.E.*

21. Alamán, *Historia de Méjico* 5:525.

22. Costeloe, *La primera república de México (1824–1835),* p. 51; Mateos, *Historia de la masonería en México,* p. 29; Tornel, *Breve reseña,* p. 45; Manning, "Poinsett's Mission to Mexico," p. 799.

23. Ancona, *Historia de Yucatán* 3:312; Tays, "Revolutionary California, 1822–1846," p. 117; Stevens, "Mexico's Forgotten Frontier," p. 87; Hale, "Masonry in the Early Days of Texas," p. 374; Chihuahua, *Memoria,* 1830, p. 5.

24. The strange union of Iturbidists and York rite Masons was commented on by Tornel, *Breve reseña,* p. 289; and on pp. 9, 13–14 of *Manifiesto del Congreso de Veracruz á la nación mexicana* (dated June 19, 1827). The estimate of the number of Masons in the capital is found in Ward to Canning, unnumbered, Secret and most Confidential, October 22 and 25, 1826, FO 50/25.

25. Printed in Ibar, *Regeneración política de la República Mexicana,* no. 14, February 13, 1830; Lorenzo de Zavala's calculation is found in *Juicio imparcial,* p. 10.

26. Pakenham to Vaughan, January 13, 1829, copy enclosed in Pakenham to Aberdeen, no. 6, Mexico City, January 14, 1829, FO 50/53.

27. Gómez Pedraza, *Manifiesto,* pp. 30–31, 36–37; Poinsett to Clay, no. 60, October 21, 1826, Despatches from U.S. Ministers to Mexico, 1823–1906.

28. Letters to Johnston are quoted in Harrell, "Vicente Guerrero," pp. 96–97.

29. Ward to Canning, no. 24, March 30, 1826, FO 50/26.

30. Flaccus, "Guadalupe Victoria," pp. 544, 548; Poinsett, *Esposición de la conducta política de los Estados-Unidos para con las nuevas repúblicas de América,* pp. 13–14.

31. Manning, "Poinsett's Mission to Mexico," p. 802; Flaccus, "Guadalupe Victoria," p. 571; Poinsett's defense, his *Esposición de la conducta,* was also carried in *El Sol,* July 7, 1827, pp. 1–2.

32. *Águila Mexicana,* April 4, 1827, p. 4; *Voz de la Patria,* March 15, 1830, p. 4; Costeloe, *La primera república federal de México (1824–1835),* pp. 73, 76–78; Lizardi, *Conversaciones del Payo y el Sacristán* vol. 1, no. 10.

33. Tornel, *Breve reseña,* p. 82.

34. *Correo de la Federación Mexicana,* November 7, 1826, p. 4; another version is that Zavala bought the house from the former countess of Miravalle and then sold it for 20,000 pesos to Mexico state for a mint (*El Sol,* July 17, 1827, p. 4).

35. *Documentos importantes tomados del espediente instruído a consecuencia de . . . las elecciones verificadas en Toluca,* pp. 63–67.

36. Ibid., pp. 74–77; the controversy is discussed in Macune, "A Test of Federalism," pp. 309–17.

37. Ibid., p. 87; *Correo de la Federación Mexicana,* December 8, 1826, p. 4; *Águila Mexicana,* January 19, 1827, p. 4.

38. Ward to Canning, no. 19, Mexico City, January 29, 1827, FO 50/31A.

39. Ibar, *Regeneración política de la República Mexicana,* no. 14, February 13, 1830; Zalce y Rodríguez, *Apuntes para la historia de la masonería en México* 1:57, 73–74.

40. Valadés, *Orígenes,* pp. 236–37.

41. Alamán, *Historia de Méjico* 1:83–84; Spell, *The Life and Works of José Joaquín Fernández de Lizardi,* p. 92.

42. Benson, ed., *Mexico and the Spanish Cortes,* pp. 87–106.

43. Bustamante, *Diario histórico,* p. 502.

44. Trens, *Historia de Chiapas,* p. 329; Gil y Saenz, *Historia de Tabasco,* p. 175.

45. Hale, *Mexican Liberalism in the Age of Mora, 1821–1853,* p. 75.

46. Mexico City's newspapers of the 1820s are discussed in Tornel, *Breve reseña,* p. 80.

47. *Águila Mexicana,* July 10, 1823, p. 3, June 14, 1825, p. 4.

48. Ibid., June 15, 1827, p. 4, June 18, 1827, pp. 3–4.

49. *El Sol,* October 28, 1823, p. 4; Poinsett, *Notes on Mexico,* p. 83; Spielman, "Mexican pamphleteering and the rise of the Mexican nation, 1808–1830," pp. 7, 17, 41.

50. [Secretario de Estado] to EE. SS. vocales Srios. de la Cámara de Representantes, February 4, 1825, draft, AGN, Gobernación, legajo 20.

51. Maxwell, "The 'Diario Histórico' of Carlos María Bustamante for 1824," pp. 157–58.

52. Spell, *The Life and Works of José Joaquín Fernández de Lizardi,* p. 45.

53. Contemporary sketches of Bustamante can be found in the *Correo de la Federación Mexicana,* March 10, 1828, p. 4; and in *Semblanzas de los representantes que compusieron el congreso constituyente de 1836,* pp. 8–9; also see Sosa, *Biografías de mexicanos distinguidos,* pp. 161–62.

54. Spielman, "Mexican Pamphleteering and the Rise of the Mexican Nation,

1808–1830," pp. 141–43, 206; *Gaceta del Gobierno Supremo de la Federación Mexicana,* October 7, 1824, pp. 1–3; *Águila Mexicana,* January 8, 1824, pp. 3–4; for Lizardi's life, see Spell, *The Life and Works of José Joaquín Fernández de Lizardi,* pp. 9–53; and Radin, "An Annotated Bibliography," pp. 287–88.

55. Lizardi's ideology is discussed in Spell, *The Life and Works of José Joaquín Fernández de Lizardi,* pp. 48–53; and can be studied through his Payo-Sacristán conversations, the originals of which are in the Lafragua Collection, vol. 107 bis, and which were reprinted in Lizardi, *Obras.*

56. McKegney, *The Political Pamphlets of Pablo Villavicencio, "el Payo del Rosario,"* pp. i–vi; Fernández de Córdoba, *Pablo de Villavicencio,* pp. 7–18.

57. [Secretario de Estado] to Gobernador del Distrito Federal, January 14, 1825, draft, AGN, Gobernación, legajo 20; Ward to Canning, no. 60, Mexico City, November 23, 1825, FO 50/15; Fernández de Córdoba, *Pablo de Villavicencio,* p. 12.

58. Fernández de Córdoba, *Pablo de Villavicencio,* p. 18.

59. Spielman, "Mexican Pamphleteering and the Rise of the Mexican nation 1808–1830," pp. 88, 111, 178, 188, 197, 204; *Voz de la Patria,* January 17, 1831, pp. 3–4.

60. [Secretario de Estado] to Gobernador del Distrito Federal, January 14, 1825, draft, AGN, Gobernación, legajo 20; México, Congreso, *Crónicas* 1:126; Spielman, "Mexican Pamphleteering and the Rise of the Mexican Nation, 1808–1830," pp. 145–46.

61. Flaccus, "Guadalupe Victoria," p. 383.

62. *Gaceta del Gobierno Supremo de México,* June 5, 1823, pp. 2–3.

63. Espinosa de los Monteros to Exmos. SS. Secretarios de la cámara de senadores, November 28, 1826, enclosing copy of governors' reports on lodges, printed copy in Lafragua Collection, vol. 192; also printed in *Águila Mexicana,* January 2–18, 1827; Gómez Pedraza, *Manifiesto,* pp. 36–37.

64. Tornel, *Breve reseña,* pp. 132–33; Costeloe, *La primera república federal de México (1824–1835),* pp. 117–18; possibly the origin of the Novenarios can be found in fall 1826, for Poinsett mentioned a third party began when Ramos Arizpe left the Yorkinos out of pique and took others with him, Poinsett to Clay, no. 60, October 21, 1826, Despatches from U.S. Ministers to Mexico, 1823–1906.

65. México, *Memoria,* 1828, p. 28.

66. Estep, *Zavala,* pp. 131–32.

67. The by-laws of the Institute are in *Águila Mejicana,* June 13, 1825, pp. 1–2; Alamán's circular was entitled "Proyecto de Reglamento general de Instrucción Pública," dated December 1823, AGN, Gobernación, legajo 18.

68. Ramos Escandón, "Planes educativos en México independiente 1821–1833," p. 41, mentions the 1826 plan; the 1827 plan was entitled "Plan de educación para el Distrito y Territorios," AGN, Gobernación, legajo 18, expediente "Ynstr publ 1827," pp. 28–38.

69. Zavala, *Umbral,* pp. 44–45.

70. Tanck Estrada, *La educación ilustrada (1786–1836),* pp. 128, 244.

71. Echeverría, "Mexican Education in the Press and Spanish Cortes: 1810–1821," pp. 56–58, 110–13, Appendices A, B.

72. Lee, "Nationalism and education in Mexico 1821–1861," pp. 51–52; Tanck Estrada, "Las Cortes de Cádiz y el desarrollo de la educación en Mexico," p. 5.

73. Blair, "Educational Movements in Mexico: 1821 to 1836," p. 137; Tanck Estrada, *La educación ilustrada (1786–1836),* pp. 176, 178.

74. Lee, "Nationalism and Education in Mexico, 1821–1861," pp. 50, 56, 57, 64, 65; Tanck Estrada, *La educación ilustrada (1786–1836),* pp. 176, 178.

75. Tanck Estrada, *La educación ilustrada (1786–1836),* pp. 188, 197, 200, Appendix 4; Lee, "Nationalism and Education in Mexico, 1821–1861," pp. 18, 63; Lee writes that Mexico City had (in 1830) about 3,000 pupils in approximately 100 elementary

schools, two-thirds of them private (pp. 25, 30); an 1820 report by Juan Espinosa de los Monteros (maestro mayor) showed less than 5,000 pupils in Mexico City schools (cited in Anna, *Fall of the Royal Government,* pp. 176–78).

76. Summary of documents entitled "Primera Secretaría. Sección de fomento. año de 1825. Libro 1, Político No. p°.," AGN, Gobernación, legajo 18; Vizcaya Canales, "Monterrey, los primeros años después de la independencia," pp. 534–35; Narbona to Alamán, May 30, 1823, AGN, Gobernación, legajo 18; northern education is surveyed in Tyler, "The Mexican Teacher," pp. 207–21.

77. Childers, "Education in California under Spain and Mexico, and under American rule in 1851," pp. 93, 101–02, 108.

78. For general discussions of Mexico's Lancasterian experiment, see Blair, "Educational movements in Mexico: 1821–1836," ch. 6; Tanck Estrada, "Las escuelas Lancasterianas en la ciudad de México; 1822–1844"; and Marshall, "History of the Lancasterian Educational Movement in Mexico."

79. J. I. Esteva and Manuel Castro [to Secretario de Estado, ca. April 23, 1826], AGN, Instrucción Pública, vol. 31, expediente 1, pp. 2–4; José Yáñez to Alamán, April 19, 1831, AGN, Instrucción Pública, vol. 31, expediente 10; Marshall, "History of the Lancasterian Educational Movement in Mexico," pp. 51–59; Blair, "Educational Movements in Mexico: 1821 to 1836," pp. 210–18.

80. Blair, "Educational Movements in Mexico: 1821 to 1836," pp. 231–32, 252–53, 266; Marshall, "History of the Lancasterian Educational Movement in Mexico," ch. 4.

81. Tanck Estrada, *La educación ilustrada (1786–1836),* pp. 232–36.

82. Ibid., pp. 87–109.

83. Tyler, "New Mexico in the 1820's," p. 61.

84. Tanck Estrada, *La educación ilustrada (1786–1836),* p. 140.

85. Ibid., pp. 216–17, 220.

86. Ibid., pp. 220, 230–31; Echeverría, "Mexican Education in the Press and Spanish Cortes: 1810–1821," pp. 18–23, 66.

87. Justicia, *Memoria,* 1825, pp. 23–24; Lee, "Nationalism and Education in Mexico, 1821–1861," pp. 33, 54, 67; Dewton, "Public Primary Education in Mexico," pp. 26–27.

88. Lee, "Nationalism and Education in Mexico, 1821–1861," p. 30.

89. Poinsett, *Notes,* p. 190; for similar comments about methodology, see Lyon, *Journal of a Residence* 1:145–46, 2:87–88; and Tyler, "The Mexican Teacher," p. 219.

90. Tanck Estrada, *La educación ilustrada (1786–1836),* p. 242.

91. Zacatecas, *Memoria,* 1831, estado 3; Zacatecas, *Memoria,* 1833, Estado "Plan que manifiesta el censo general"; Lee, "Nationalism and education in Mexico, 1821–1861," pp. 62–63; poor school attendance is noted in Tanck Estrada, "Las escuelas Lancasterianas," pp. 509–10.

92. Tanck Estrada, *La educación ilustrada (1786–1836),* p. 211.

93. Shaw, "Poverty and Politics," p. 118.

94. Esparza, *Informe,* p. 50; Segura, *Apuntes para la estadística del departamento de Orizava,* p. 138.

95. Blair, "Educational movements in Mexico: 1821 to 1836," pp. 275–76.

96. *Estatutos del Nacional Colegio de Abogados de México,* pp. 5, 15–16.

97. Blair, "Educational Movements in Mexico: 1821–1836," pp. 278–79; Febles, *Esposición . . . á los profesores de medicina, cirugía, farmacia, y flebotomía,* pp. 1, 3, 5.

98. *Semblanza de los individuos de la cámara de diputados de los años de 1825 y 1826,* p. 6.

99. Ramos Escandón, "Planes educativos en México independiente 1821–1833," pp. 12–13; Lee, "Nationalism and Education in Mexico, 1821–1861," pp. 114–18.

100. "Estado de las Fincas y censos que tiene la Nacional y Pontificia Universidad," AGN, Instrucción Pública, vol. 28, expediente 2, pp. 15–17; also see "Estado gral que demuestra los fondos con que cuentan los establecimientos científicos de esta capital," AGN, Gobernación, legajo 18, pp. 141–49; and "Estado que manifiesta el origen de las Rentas de la Nacional y Pontificia Universidad de México," AGN, Gobernación, legajo 18, expediente "Ynstr. publ. no. 1," p. 14.

101. Ramos Escandón, "Planes educativos en México independiente," pp. 50, 51, 57; Relaciones, *Memoria*, 1830, in Alamán, *Documentos diversos* 1:224.

102. A general history of the Mexico City colleges is given in Osores, "Historia de todos los colegios de la ciudad de México."

103. "Ynstrucción que El Rector del Colegio de San Juan de Letrán da," AGN, Gobernación, legajo 18, expediente "Año de 1828. Ynstrucción pública," pp. 4–5; Arechederreta, Cuevas, and Fernández to Ministro del Despacho de Relaciones Interiores y Exteriores, March 19, 1833, AGN, Instrucción Pública, vol. 25, expediente 4, pp. 35–46.

104. Guzmán to Ministro de estado y del despacho de relaciones, January 10, 1833, AGN, Gobernación, legajo 18, expediente "Año de 1832/Ynstrucción pública," and "Estado q. manifiesta el origen de las Rentas del Colegio de San Yldefonso," AGN, Gobernación, legajo 18, expediente "Ynstr. publ. no. 1," p. 16.

105. Gómez Calderón to Secretario de Estado y del Despacho de Relaciones, November 29, 1828, AGN, Gobernación, legajo 18, expediente "Año de 1828. Ynstrucción pública," pp. 7–8; "Estado que manifiesta el origen de las Rentas del Colegio de Santos," AGN, Gobernación, legajo 18, expediente "Ynstr. publ. no. 1," p. 15; "Fundamento en que puede apoyarse la estinción del Colegio," and draft of Mangino dated February 22, 1831, AGN, Instrucción Pública, vol. 34, expediente 2, pp. 7–8, 10; the college of Santos was opened again from 1831–1833 and 1836 until 1843, when it closed for good (Osores, "Historia de todos los colegios de la ciudad de México," p. 921).

106. Cervantes to Ministro de Relaciones, January 23, 1829, AGN, Gobernación, legajo 18; "Reglamento dado por el Supremo Gobierno", February 21, 1826, AGN, Instrucción Pública, vol. 1, expediente 44, pp. 306–09; Rodríguez [to Secretario de Relaciones?], March 13, 1830, AGN, Instrucción Pública, vol. 20, expediente 8, pp. 41–42.

107. Blair, "Educational Movements in Mexico: 1821 to 1836," pp. 37, 272–74.

108. "Colegio de San Juan de Letrán y Comendadores Juristas de San Ramón," by José María de Iturralde, March 12, 1829, AGN, Gobernación, legajo 18, expediente "Ynstr. públ. no. 1," pp. 7–9; Cervantes to Ministro de Relaciones, March 11, 1829, ibid., pp. 4–5; colleges' properties and income for 1823 are listed in "Estado gral que demuestra los fondos con que cuentan los establecimientos científicos de esta capital," AGN, Gobernación, legajo 18, pp. 141–49; similar documents for the early 1830s are in AGN, Instrucción Pública, vol. 34, expediente 11, and vol. 25, expediente 4.

109. Mora to Garcia Ylueca, April 24, 1823, enclosing Plan, AGN, Gobernación, legajo 18, expediente 2.

110. Fees for the San Juan de Letrán school are noted in Iturralde to Bocanegra, June 23, 1829, AGN, Gobernación, legajo 18, expediente "Instr. publ/1829"; San Ildefonso's uniforms are described in Guzmán to Ministro de Estado y del Despacho de Relaciones, January 10, 1833, AGN, Gobernación, expediente "Año de 1832/Ynstrucción pública"; clothing worn at Santos is described in Diez de Bonilla, Flores Alatorre, and Castillo Quintero [to Ministro de Estado], May 14, 1825, AGN, Instrucción Pública, vol. 86, pp. 36–37; descriptions of the food service at San Juan de Letrán are found in Arechederreta, Cuevas, and Fernández to Ministro del

Despacho de Relaciones Interiores y Exteriores, March 19, 1833, AGN, Instrucción Pública, vol. 25, expediente 4, pp. 35–46.

111. Mora to Garcia Ylueca, April 24, 1823, enclosing plan, AGN, Gobernación, legajo 18, expediente 2.

112. Simón Elías [to Ministro de lo interior], December 30, 1837, AGN, Instrucción Pública, vol. 92, pp. 142–43; Guanajuato, *Memoria,* 1826, p. 7; ibid., 1832, estado 12; Estep, *Zavala,* p. 138; Oaxaca, *Memoria,* 1827, p. 22; ibid., 1829, p. 9; San Luis Potosí, *Memoria,* 1831, p. 15; Tabasco, *Memoria,* 1831, p. 4; Rivera Cambas, *Historia antigua y moderna de Jalapa* 2:336; Velásquez, *Historia de San Luis Potosí* 3:149.

113. Puebla, *Memoria,* 1826, pp. 22–23, estado 10.

114. Jalisco, *Memoria,* 1832, estado 11; *El Tiempo,* October 19, 1834, p. 1, October 22, 1834, p. 1; Lee, "Nationalism and Education in Mexico, 1821–1861," p. 133; contemporary detail on Sánchez's life can be found in Tornel, *Breve reseña,* pp. 182–83, and in *Elogio fúnebre dedicado á la memoria del ciudadano Prisciliano Sánchez;* and see Pérez Verdía, *Biografía del Exmo. Sr. Don Prisciliano Sánchez.*

115. Lee, "Nationalism and Education in Mexico, 1821–1861," p. 149.

116. Tanck Estrada, *La educación ilustrada (1786–1836),* pp. 160, 193.

117. For example, see Guanajuato, *Memoria,* 1832 (February), estado 4; México, *Memoria,* 1828, p. 26, estado 4.

118. "Plan de Educación para el Distrito y Territorios," AGN, Gobernación, legajo 18, expediente "Ynstrucción pública 1827," pp. 28–38.

119. Yturralde to Ministro de Relaciones, January 12, 1833, AGN, Gobernación, legajo 18, expediente "Año de 1832/Ynstr publ."

120. Mora to Garcia Ylueca, April 24, 1823, AGN, Gobernación, legajo 18, expediente 2.

121. Lee, "Nationalism and education in Mexico, 1821–1861," p. 245; Blair, "Educational Movements in Mexico: 1821 to 1836," p. 288.

122. *El Sol,* October 18, 1824, pp. 1–2.

123. A considerable mass of documents was generated by the appointments, in a three-way flow among Indians, the board, and the government. Much of it is in the AGN, Instrucción Pública, vol. 1; expediente 43 of this volume contains a number of printed petitions by the Indians.

124. La Llave to Alamán, March 29, 1830, AGN, Instrucción Pública, vol. 1, expediente 45, pp. 365–69.

125. Summary of communications in AGN, Instrucción Pública, vol. 1, expediente 45, pp. 323–26; Lee, "Nationalism and Education in Mexico, 1821–1861," p. 249.

126. Sosa, *Biografías de mexicanos distinguidos,* pp. 907–09.

127. *Ya les pesa a ciertos hombres el que se ilustren los indios,* dated February 20, 1828, pamphlet in AGN, Instrucción Pública, vol. 1, expediente 43.

128. *Representación al Escmo. Señor Presidente Don Vicente Guerrero, en favor de la educación de los indios,* pamphlet in ibid.

129. Lee, "Nationalism and Education in Mexico, 1821–1861," p. 64.

Chapter 5

EARNING A LIVING

1. Quirós, *Memoria de Estatuto: Idea de la riqueza,* pp. 127–132 (in copy consulted, pagination began on p. 97).

2. Sierra, *El Nacimiento de México,* pp. 173–75, compares various authorities on production.

3. Quirós estimated the annual value of agriculture had declined (from a pre-1810 level of 138,850,120 pesos) by about 60 million pesos (or 70 million pesos, as there may be a typographical error) due to the Revolution (*Memoria de estatuto. Idea de la riqueza*, pp. 119–21); Quirós discussed the economic effect of the foreign and domestic warring in another pamphlet, *Memoria de Estatuto. Causas*, pp. 2–5, 28.

4. Estep, *Zavala*, pp. 68–69; Valadés, *Orígenes de la república mexicana*, p. 66; *Águila Mexicana*, September 15, 1825, p. 4; *Dictamen de la comisión de industria de la Cámara de Diputados sobre el nuevo arbitrio para dar . . . ocupación y medios de subsistir á la clase de gentes pobres de la república mexicana*, p. 8.

5. Tanck Estrada, *La educación ilustrada (1786–1836)*, pp. 23, 115–16.

6. Dublán and Lozano, eds., *Legislación mexicana* 1:738; Smith and Flores, *Los consulados de comerciantes*, pp. 36–38, 54–63, 151; see also Hamnet, "Mercantile Rivalry and Peninsular Division."

7. Dublán and Lozano, eds., *La educación mexicana* 1:795.

8. *Águila Mexicana*, October 29, 1823, pp. 1–2.

9. Costeloe, *Church Wealth in Mexico*, pp. 61–62.

10. Petition in Mexico City Ayuntamiento Archives, cited in Shaw, "Poverty and Politics," pp. 22–23.

11. Ibid., pp. 209–10; *Águila Mexicana*, September 2, 1823, pp. 2–3.

12. *Águila Mexicana*, December 8, 1824, p. 1; Harrell, "Vicente Guerrero," p. 115.

13. *Águila Mexicana*, September 19, 1827, p. 3, July 1, 1828, pp. 2–4.

14. Lindley, "Kinship and Credit in the Structure of Guadalajara's Oligarchy, 1800–1830," pp. 248–52.

15. Ibid., pp. 132–34.

16. There are numerous sources on this, for example, O'Gorman to Bidwell, no. 6, Mexico City, January 24, 1827, FO 50/37; Alamán to Monteleone, July 13, 1830, copy, AGN, Hospital de Jesús, legajo 440, expediente 6; *Dos años en Méjico*, p. 67.

17. Morier to Canning, no. 12, Xalapa, November 19, 1824, FO 50/6; Ward to Canning, no. 57, November 18, 1825, FO 50/15; Kelley, *River of Lost Dreams*.

18. Ward to Canning, no. 122, Mexico City, October 20, 1826, FO 50/24; Dublán and Lozano, eds., *Legislación mexicana* 1:800–01.

19. Lionel Hervey, in his report of December 24, 1824, listed seven main roads, not all leading out of Mexico City (FO 50/16, pp. 45–49); Mackenzie to Canning, no. 14, Xalapa, July 24, 1824, FO 50/7; Probert, "Mules, Men, and Mining Machinery," pp. 106–11.

20. Poinsett, *Notes on Mexico*, p. 29; Guanajuato, *Memoria instructiva*, 1830, estado 3.

21. Yucatán, *Memoria de estadística*, 1826, p. 2.

22. Agricultural methods are discussed in Poinsett, "Republic of Mexico," pp. 23, 29; Lyon, *Journal of a Residence* 2:249–54; and Forbes, *California*, pp. 246–80.

23. Poinsett, "Mexico and the Mexicans," pp. 173–74.

24. Forbes, *California*, p. 276.

25. Ibid., pp. 279–80.

26. *Águila Mexicana*, August 7, 1824, p. 1; Alamán to Monteleone, January 29, 1827, AGN, Hospital de Jesús, legajo 440, expediente 3.

27. Shaw, "Poverty and Politics," p. 84; *El Amigo del Pueblo*, August 6, 1828, p. 624.

28. Shaw, "Poverty and Politics," pp. 86–87.

29. Poinsett, *Notes on Mexico*, p. 139.

30. Shaw, "Poverty and Politics," p. 85; on late colonial textiles, see Miñó Grijalva, "Espacio económico e industria textil."

31. Shaw, "Poverty and Politics," pp. 70–79.

32. Ward to Canning, no. 27, Mexico City, February 5, 1827, FO 50/31A; Stevens, "A History of Sonora, 1821–1846," pp. 30–31; Ward to Canning, no. 13, Mexico City, March 13, 1826, FO 50/20; Taylor, "Socioeconomic Instability," p. 70; Brading, *Haciendas and Ranchos in the Mexican Bajío,* p. 37.

33. Chiapas, *Memoria,* 1831, p. 10.

34. Murguía, "Extracto de Guaxaca," pt. 1, p. 59.

35. Harris, *Sánchez Navarros,* pp. 207, 212, 215–16; concerning wage levels, see ibid., p. 213; Barron to His Majesty's Secretary of State, Tepic, January 1, 1825, FO 50/17; Chihuahua, *Noticias Estadísticas,* 1834, pp. 115–16; Segura, *Apuntes para la estadística de Orizava,* p. 138; and Gilmore, "The Condition of the Poor in Mexico, 1834," p. 224; concerning payment in kind, see Tyler, "New Mexico in the 1820's," pp. 79, 82; and Ward to Canning, no. 27, Mexico City, February 5, 1827, FO 50/31A.

36. *Correo de la Federación Mexicana,* April 14, 1828, p. 4.

37. Puebla, *Memoria,* 1826, p. 5.

38. Oaxaca, *Memoria,* 1827, pp. 7–8.

39. *Águila Mexicana,* October 8, 1827, p. 3.

40. Harris, *Sánchez Navarros,* p. 223; *Dos años en Méjico,* pp. 91–92.

41. Harris, *Sánchez Navarros,* p. 230.

42. Brading, *Haciendas and Ranchos in the Mexican Bajío,* p. 110.

43. Humboldt, *Political Essay on the Kingdom of New Spain* 1:236.

44. Maxwell, "The 'Diario histórico' of Bustamante for 1824," p. 4.

45. O'Gorman to Bidwell, no. 31, Mexico City, September 17, 1829, FO 50/56; Ward to Canning, no. 13, Mexico City, March 13, 1826, FO 50/20.

46. Amador, *Bosquejo histórico de Zacatecas* 2:332; Creer, "Spanish-American Slave Trade in the Great Basin, 1800–1853," pp. 175–79.

47. *Águila Mexicana,* September 14, 1825, p. 1; O'Gorman to Bidwell, no. 31, Mexico City, September 17, 1829, FO 50/56; Arrillaga, ed., *Recopilación de leyes,* vol. 1829, p. 213.

48. Alessio Robles, *Coahuila y Texas* 1:242; Schwartz, *Across the Rio to Freedom,* p. 23.

49. Cross, "The Mining Economy of Zacatecas," ch. 8; pp. 312–13 discuss peonage revisionism.

50. Taylor, "Socioeconomic Instability and the Revolution for Mexican Independence in the Province of Guanajuato," pp. 49–51, 70; also see the following governors' reports: Chihuahua, *Noticias Estadísticas,* 1834, p. 101; San Luis Potosí, *Memoria,* 1829, estado 2; Durango, *Nota estadística,* 1826, estado 2; Guanajuato, *Memoria instructiva,* 1830, estado 6; Oaxaca, *Memoria,* 1832, estado "Resumen general de la población que actualmente tiene este Estado. . . ."

51. Brading, *Haciendas and Ranchos in the Mexican Bajío,* pp. 149–73.

52. Ward to Canning, no. 27, Mexico City, February 5, 1827, FO 50/31A; Guanajuato, *Memoria,* 1830, estado 9; Auld and Buchan, *Notice of the Silver Mines of Fresnillo in the State of Zacatecas,* pp. 43–44 (copy of this pamphlet enclosed in Auld to Palmerston, London, August 22, 1834, FO 50/88).

53. Bazant, *Cinco haciendas mexicanas,* pp. 41, 74, 94; Ladd, *The Mexican Nobility at Independence 1780–1826,* pp. 153–55.

54. *Águila Mexicana,* October 17, 1825, p. 2; also see Harris, *Sánchez Navarros,* p. 162; and Brading, *Haciendas and Ranchos in the Mexican Bajío,* pp. 83–85, 89.

55. Ward, *Mexico in 1827* 1:334.

56. Murguía, "Extracto de Guaxaca," pt. 1, p. 59.

57. Tabasco, *Estadística,* 1826, p. 7.

58. Guanajuato, *Memoria,* 1827, p. 2; Bazant, *Cinco haciendas mexicanas,* pp. 41–42, 66, 86; Harris, *Sánchez Navarros,* p. 27; Chihuahua, *Noticias Estadísticas,* 1834, p. 86.

59. From provisional decree of December 11, 1829, copy in Lafragua Collection, vol. 1441 (title page missing).

60. *Diario de las sesiones del Congreso Constituyente de México* [March 7–May 13, 1823], 4:252–53; Guanajuato, *Memoria instructiva,* 1830, pp. 33–34.

61. Bazant, *Cinco haciendas mexicanas,* pp. 93–94; Lindley, "Kinship and Credit in the Structure of Guadalajara's Oligarchy, 1800–1830," pp. 156–57.

62. Brading, *Haciendas and Ranchos in the Mexican Bajío,* p. 118.

63. Brading, "Government and Elite in Late Colonial Mexico," p. 390.

64. Ward to Canning, no. 27, Mexico City, February 5, 1827, FO 50/31A; a *sitio* was 4,338 acres; a league varied at the time—for example, given as 4 miles in Mendarte, *Guía ó Nociones útiles,* p. 20, although the more common equivalent was 2.6 miles, as given in Carrera Stampa, "The Evolution of Weights and Measures in New Spain," p. 10.

65. Harris, *Sánchez Navarros,* pp. 6–9, 162–67; Alessio Robles, *Coahuila y Texas* 1:49–50; Altman, "The Marqueses de Aguayo: A Family and Estate History," pp. 80–82; Ward to Canning no. 160, September 19, 1825, FO 50/14; for the 1825 bill on foreigners, see Harrell, "Vicente Guerrero," pp. 123–24; the March 12, 1828, law is in *Legislación mexicana,* ed. Dublán and Lozano 2:64–65.

66. Harris, *Sánchez Navarros,* pp. 3–8, 23–27, 30–31, 162, 185–89, 206–29, 231.

67. Ward to Canning, no. 27, Mexico City, February 5, 1827, FO 50/31A; Murguía, "Extracto de Guaxaca," pt. 1, p. 58.

68. Lindley, "Kinship and Credit in the Structure of Guadalajara's Oligarchy, 1800–1830," pp. 63–68, 193.

69. Ibid., pp. 60–63.

70. Benson, ed., *Mexico and the Spanish Cortes,* p. 160; *Colección de decretos y órdenes de las Cortes de España,* pp. 56–59.

71. Decree of June 4, 1823, in *Colección de decretos y órdenes del Soberano Congreso Mexicano,* pp. 143–44; Ward to Canning, no. 66, Mexico City, December 13, 1825, FO 50/15.

72. Tabasco, *Memoria,* 1831, p. 6; Trens, *Historia de Chiapas,* pp. 331, 340–41; Chiapas, *Memoria,* 1829, p. 10; ibid., 1830, p. 6.

73. Jalisco, *Memoria,* 1832, p. 14.

74. Chihuahua, *Noticias Estadísticas,* 1834, p. 167.

75. Valadés, *Orígenes de la república mexicana,* p. 264; Reyes Heroles, *El liberalismo mexicano* 1:145; Nuevo León, *Memoria,* 1827, pp. 3–4.

76. Copy of provisional decree of December 11, 1829, is in Lafragua Collection, vol. 1441 (title page missing); Amador, *Bosquejo histórico de Zacatecas* 2:360–61, 387; Reyes Heroles, *El liberalismo mexicano* 3:563–66; Zacatecas, *Memoria,* 1833, p. 19; *Colección eclesiástica mexicana* 4:88–91.

77. Reyes Heroles, *El liberalismo mexicano* 1:138–39, 3:550–52; Lindley, "Kinship and Credit in the Structure of Guadalajara's Oligarchy, 1800–1830," pp. 264–66.

78. Durango, *Memoria,* 1827, p. 4.

79. *Voz de la Patria,* January 17, 1831, pp. 7–8; Alamán to Monteleone, August 22, 1827, and October 3, 1827, AGN, Hospital de Jesús, legajo 440, expediente 3.

80. *Voz de la Patria,* January 17, 1831, p. 7.

81. Costeloe, *Church Wealth,* pp. 68–69.

82. Harrell, "Vicente Guerrero," pp. 72–73, 142–43, 231–32; *Correo de la Federación Mexicana,* February 6, 1828, p. 2.

83. Estep, "The Life of Lorenzo de Zavala," pp. 216–29.

84. Ibid., pp. 229–37.

85. "Autobiografía de D. Lucas Alamán," in Alamán, *Obras* 4:24.

86. Alamán to Monteleone, November 24, 1824, copy, AGN, Hospital de Jesús, legajo 374, expediente 37. (Alamán made copies of his correspondence with Monte-

leone by placing a type of onion skin sheet over the original, a damp cloth on top of that, and then pressing down with a block so that a passable, if blurry, copy was left on the onion skin.)

87. "Razón que manifiesta los ramos productivos" [1823], legajo 298, expediente 81 bis; "Censos de Tehuantepec," legajo 448, expediente 7; "Censos de Oaxaca, 1835," ibid.; "Censos de Toluca," dated November 12, 1829, copy, legajo 303, expediente 4; "Cuenta General de las rentas del Excelentísimo Señor Duque de Terranova y Monteleone," legajo 216, expediente 2; "Ynventario de la entrega de los bienes del Señor Duque y Hospital de Jesús," legajo 216, expediente 1, all in AGN, Hospital de Jesús. Measured by wealth, as opposed to income, Doris Ladd found Monteleone to be one of the half-dozen richest (but not *the* richest) noblemen of the post-1810 decades, calculating his wealth at 1.4 million pesos in 1821 (*The Mexican Nobility at Independence, 1780–1826,* Appendix E).

88. "Plan provisional de los empleados," dated August 27, 1826, legajo 374, expediente 37, "Administración de las rentas pertenecientes al Señor Duque de Terranova y de Monteleone," legajo 337, expediente 22, Alamán to Monteleone, December 20, 1827, copy, legajo 440, expediente 3, all in AGN, Hospital de Jesús.

89. "Razón que manifiesta las ramos productivos" [1823], AGN, Hospital de Jesús, legajo 303, expediente 1.

90. Zacatecas law of August 16, 1827, in Garviso, *Exposición,* Lafragua Collection, vol. 314; Veracruz law of May 27, 1825, in *El Sol,* June 3, 1827, p. 3; Alamán, *Esposición que hace á la cámara;* Alamán to Monteleone, June 27, 1827, and March 3, 1828, AGN, Hospital de Jesús, legajo 440, expediente 3.

91. Alamán to Monteleone, August 22, 1827, copy, AGN, Hospital de Jesús, legajo 440, expediente 3.

92. Alamán to Monteleone, October 3, 1827, copy, AGN, Hospital de Jesús, legajo 440, expediente 3.

93. Alamán to Monteleone, April 6, 1829, copy, legajo 440, expediente 4; Alamán to Honorable Congreso del Estado de México, March 27, 1829, copy, legajo 424, expediente 12; Zavala to Diputados Secretarios del Congreso del Estado, March 31, 1829, copy, legajo 303, expediente 1; Alamán to Monteleone, June 5, 1829, copy, legajo 440, expediente 5; state of Mexico law of May 16, 1829, clarifying law of May 7, 1829, copy in legajo 303, expediente 4, all in AGN, Hospital de Jesús.

94. Dublán and Lozano, eds., *Legislación mexicana* 2:110–12, 116.

95. Alamán to Monteleone, August 22, 1829, copy, AGN, Hospital de Jesús, legajo 440, expediente 5; Arrillaga, ed., *Recopilación de leyes,* vol. 1829, pp. 214–23, 332–33, 341–42, vol. 1831, pp. 24–36, vol. 1836, p. 512; proclamation *(bando)* of September 4, 1829, by Tornel (Federal District governor), copy in AGN, Hospital de Jesús, legajo 303, expediente 2 (copy of this law in *Recopilación de leyes,* ed. Arrillaga, vol. 1831, p. 53, does not have a preface that contains reference to "enemies"); Alamán to Monteleone, September 17, 1829, copy, AGN, Hospital de Jesús, legajo 440, expediente 5.

96. Elhuyar, *Memoria sobre el Influjo de la Minería,* pp. 85–94, discussed the revolutionary breakdown.

97. Randall, *Real del Monte,* pp. 28, 183; *Memoria acerca de los medios que se estiman justos para el fomento y pronto restablecimiento de la minería,* pp. 39–41.

98. On Alamán's arguments in favor of foreign investment, see *Águila Mexicana,* September 6, 1823, p. 4, September 7, 1823, pp. 1–2; Valadés, *Alamán,* pp. 163–72; *Colección de los decretos y órdenes del Soberano Congreso Mexicano,* pp. 188–89.

99. *Proposición, informe, y dictámenes presentados al Supremo Congreso General Constituyente sobre la ley de denuncio de minas.*

100. Morier to Canning, no. 18, Mexico City, February 28, 1825, FO 50/11.

101. Anonymous, *An Inquiry,* pp. 59–66.
102. See section 4 of Ward's December 30, 1827, "Report on Mining," FO 50/32, pp. 99–244.
103. Discussions of the companies are found in Gilmore, "British Mining Ventures in Early National Mexico," pp. 63–116, 161–90; in Ward to Canning, no. 124, Mexico City, October 21, 1826, FO 50/24; and in Pakenham to Aberdeen, No. 42, June 3, 1831, FO 50/66.
104. United Mexican Mining Association, *Report* (1825), pp. xv, xvi, 5, 53.
105. Hruneni, "Palmetto Yankee," p. 151; Becher, *Cartas sobre México,* pp. 156, 161, 234; Ward, *Mexico in 1827* 2:67–68, 111, 188, 378–79.
106. Guanajuato, *Memoria,* 1826, "Razón en que se manifiesta el estado actual de Guanajuato con respecto al laborío de sus Minas."
107. Gilmore, "British Mining Ventures in Early National Mexico," pp. 80–83.
108. Ward to Canning, no. 27, Mexico City, February 5, 1827, FO 50/31A.
109. Randall, *Real del Monte,* pp. 188, 191; Pakenham to Palmerston, no. 38, Mexico City, June 9, 1832, FO 50/72; table of taxes on silver coin and silver bars enclosed in O'Gorman to Bidwell, no. 39, Mexico City, July 22, 1828, FO 50/48.
110. "No. 4. Statement of the Total Exportation of Gold and Silver from the several Ports of the Mexican Federation from the 1st of January 1790 to the 31st of December 1829," enclosed in Pakenham to Palmerston, no. 19, Mexico City, March 1, 1831, FO 50/65; the figures given in this table exceed somewhat the official Mexican government figures published in the annual *Balanza general de comercio;* Lafragua Collection, vol. 23, has these for the years 1825, 1826, 1827, and 1828, plus the *Suplemento de comercio marítimo . . . de 1825,* although the title pages of some are missing.
111. Randall, *Real del Monte,* pp. 138–39; Gilmore, "British Mining Ventures in Early National Mexico," pp. 134–35.
112. Gilmore, "British Mining Ventures in Early National Mexico," p. 99.
113. Hacienda, *Memoria,* 1828, p. 13; see also "Abstract of the Coinage of Gold and Silver in all the Mints of the Mexican Republic, between the 1st of January 1821 and the 31st of December 1829—Taken from the General Returns," FO 50/65, p. 154.
114. Gilmore, "British Mining Ventures in Early National Mexico," pp. 107, 109, 115.
115. Randall, *Real del Monte,* p. 73.
116. Alamán, *Historia de Mejico,* vol. 5, document 25; English, *A General Guide,* pp. 30–34.
117. English, *A General Guide,* pp. 67–70; *El Sol,* May 12, 1824, p. 3; Gilmore, "British Mining Ventures in Early National Mexico," p. 87; United Mexican Mining Association, *Report* (1827), p. 3.
118. Pakenham to Dudley, no. 60, May 28, 1828, FO 50/43; Valadés, *Alamán,* pp. 229–30.
119. W. A. Symond to Alamán, January 13, 1829, Agassiz and Glennie to Pakenham, January 24, 1829, enclosed in Pakenham to Aberdeen, no. 16, January 31, 1829, FO 50/53.
120. United Mexican Mining Association, *Report* (1825), p. 54.
121. *The Times* (London), July 26, 1827, p. 3; "Translation. Inclosure No. 5. Report of the United Mexican Mining Company. In Mr. Ward's Dispatch no. 124 of 21st October 1826," written for Ward, signed by Alamán and Agassiz, dated October 2, 1826, FO 50/24, pp. 94–145.
122. Guanajuato, *Memoria Instructiva,* 1830, p. 40.
123. Mackenzie to Canning, no. 14, Xalapa, July 24, 1824, FO 50/7.
124. Barron to His Majesty's Secretary of State, Tepic, January 1, 1825, FO 50/17.

125. Baur, "The Evolution of a Mexican Foreign Trade Policy, 1821–1828," p. 227.

126. "Recapitulación general . . .," copy enclosed in Mackenzie to Canning, Xalapa, no. 14, July 24, 1824, FO 50/7.

127. Welsh [to Bidwell], December 31, 1826, FO 50/28; *Balanza general de comercio* (1825), estado 2; *Suplemento del comercio marítimo* (1825), "Resumen general"; *Balanza general de comercio* (1826), estado 2; ibid. (1827), "Resumen de los buques . . ."; ibid. (1828), estado 2.

128. *Órdenes y circulares espedidas por el Supremo Gobierno desde el año de 1825 hasta la fecha, para el arreglo y legitimidad del comercio marítimo nacional,* pp. 1–7; Pakenham to Palmerston, no. 27, Mexico City, April 2, 1831, FO 50/65; Pakenham to Palmerston, no. 39, June 3, 1831, FO 50/66; Arrillaga, ed., *Recopilación de leyes,* vol. 1831, pp. 311–12.

129. Barron to His Majesty's Secretary of State, Tepic, January 1, 1825, FO 50/17; Barron to O'Gorman, Tepic, July 27, 1827, FO 50/39; Booker, "The Merchants of Veracruz," pp. 135–36, 202; Smith, "Shipping in the Port of Veracruz, 1790–1821," pp. 11–14.

130. Benson, ed., *Mexico and the Spanish Cortes,* p. 171.

131. The 1821 tariff schedule is in *Legislacion mexicana,* ed. Dublán and Lozano 1:567–87.

132. Ibid., 706–08.

133. Baur, "The Evolution of a Mexican Foreign Trade Policy, 1821–1828", pp. 239, 248; Dublán and Lozano, eds., *Legislacion mexicana* 1:594 (February 16, 1822, decree), 1:602 (March 22, 1822, decree).

134. The original *avería* or convoy tax (2½ percent) and internation (15 percent) percentages were based on a special valuation made by the *alcabala* office, which was one-fourth more than the 1821 import valuation; adjusted to this 1821 import valuation, they became 3⅛ percent and 18¾ percent, respectively; workings of the tariff discussed in Barron to His Majesty's Secretary of State, Tepic, January 1, 1825, and Barron to Bidwell, Tepic, July 5, 1825, FO 50/17; and in John Welsh [to Bidwell], December 31, 1826, FO 50/28; total import charges come from "Remarks upon the Tariff of 1821 which was brought into operation in January 1822 through-out the Mexican Empire," signed Charles T. O'Gorman, January 17, 1829, FO 50/54B, pp. 140–43.

135. Dublán and Lozano, eds., *Legislación mexicana* 2:109–10.

136. Mackenzie to Canning, no. 14, Xalapa, July 24, 1824, FO 50/7.

137. *Balanza general de comercio* (1825), estado 1; ibid. (1826), estado 1; ibid. (1827), estado 1; ibid. (1827), estado 1; ibid. (1828), "Notas," pp. 147, 152, estado 1; for 1824–1825, also see O'Gorman to Bidwell, no. 40, Mexico City, December 26, 1825, FO 50/17.

138. *Balanza general de comercio* (1826), "Notas"; ibid. (1827), "Notas"; ibid. (1828), "Notas."

139. Welsh [to Bidwell], Veracruz, December 31, 1826, FO 50/28; Dashwood to Canning, no. 4, Xalapa, August 20, 1826, FO 50/28.

140. *Balanza general de comercio* (1826), "Notas"; ibid. (1827), "Notas"; ibid. (1828), "Notas," pp. 148–49; Pakenham to Canning, no. 17, Mexico City, May 22, 1827, FO 50/34.

141. Dashwood to Planta, Private, Xalapa, August 8, 1826, FO 50/28; O'Gorman to Bidwell, no. 19, Mexico City, July 30, 1830, FO 50/62.

142. Baur, "The Evolution of a Mexican Foreign Trade Policy, 1821–1828," p. 234.

143. Ward to Canning, no. 66, Mexico City, December 13, 1825, FO 50/12; Bidwell, "The First Mexican Navy, 1821–1830," p. 527.

144. Oaxaca, *Memoria,* 1832, p. 28; Reyes Heroles, *El liberalismo mexicano* 1:113–14.

145. Beaufoy, *Mexican Illustrations,* pp. 113–14.

146. Ward to Canning, no. 116, Mexico City, October 11, 1826, FO 50/23.

147. "General Statement of the Total amounts of Custom House Values . . . 1825 to . . . 1829," FO 50/65, p. 163.

148. Pakenham to Palmerston, no. 33, May 3, 1831, FO 50/65.

149. Ward to Canning, no. 9, Tlalpujahua, January 19, 1827, FO 50/31A.

150. Dashwood to Canning, no. 4, Xalapa, August 20, 1826, FO 50/28.

151. Ward to Canning, no. 27, Mexico City, February 5, 1827, FO 50/31A.

152. Dashwood to Canning, no. 4, Xalapa, August 20, 1826, FO 50/28.

153. Pakenham to Aberdeen, no. 83, Mexico City, September 18, 1829, FO 50/55.

154. Lindley, "Kinship and Credit in the Structure of Guadalajara's Oligarchy, 1800–1830," pp. 239–47.

155. O'Gorman to Bidwell, Mexico City, April 21, 1829, FO 50/56.

156. On the French, see Barker, "The French Colony in Mexico, 1821–1861," pp. 610–14; O'Gorman to Bidwell, no. 3, Mexico City, January 12, 1827, FO 50/37; O'Gorman to Bidwell, no. 11, Mexico City, April 30, 1829, FO 50/56.

157. Potter, "First Impressions of Mexico, 1828," pp. 62, 64, 67.

158. Jalisco, *Memoria,* 1827, estado 5; ibid., 1829, estado 1; Puebla, *Memoria,* 1826, estado 5; Michoacán, *Memoria,* 1829, estado 4; Guanajuato, *Memoria instructiva,* 1830, estado 5; San Luis Potosí, *Memoria,* 1831, estado 6.

159. Dashwood to Canning, no. 4, Xalapa, August 20, 1826, FO 50/28.

160. Hall, *Extracts from a Journal* 2:193.

161. Quirós, *Memoria de Estatuto. Causas de que ha procedido,* pp. 22, 24.

162. Reyes Heroles, *El liberalismo mexicano* 1:164–65, 169–171; *Águila Mexicana,* January 21, 1824, pp. 3–4; *Diario de las sesiones del Congreso Constituyente de México,* vol. 4 [sessions March 7–May 13, 1823], p. 291 (April 17, 1823, session); Pakenham to Aberdeen, no. 18, Mexico City, January 31, 1829, FO 50/53.

163. See Spielman, "Mexican Pamphleteering and the Rise of the Mexican Nation, 1808–1830," pp. 165–69.

164. Oaxaca, *Memoria,* 1827, p. 8; México, *Memoria,* 1828, p. 10.

165. Pakenham to Dudley, no. 51, Mexico City, April 18, 1828, FO 50/43; Pakenham to Aberdeen, no. 117, September 26, 1828, FO 50/45; Pakenham to Aberdeen, no. 11, Mexico City, February 15, 1831, FO 50/65; Pakenham to Palmerston, no. 31, May 3, 1831, FO 50/65.

166. O'Gorman to Bidwell, no. 16, April 21, 1828, FO 50/46; Pakenham to Palmerston, no. 12, Mexico City, January 31, 1829, FO 50/53.

167. Pakenham to Aberdeen, no. 102, Mexico City, November 16, 1829, FO 50/55.

168. Pakenham to Canning, no. 17, Mexico City, May 22, 1827, FO 50/34; Pakenham to Aberdeen, no. 15, Mexico City, January 31, 1829, FO 50/53.

169. Taylor to Van Buren, Veracruz, July 1, 1829, Despatches from U.S. Consuls in Veracruz.

170. See the report of O'Gorman to Pakenham, June 17, 1829, FO 50/54B.

171. Pakenham to Aberdeen, no. 31, Mexico City, March 4, 1829, FO 50/53; Pakenham to Palmerston, no. 41, Mexico City, June 3, 1831, FO 50/66; O'Gorman to Bidwell, no. 24, April 2, 1831, and no. 32, May 3, 1831, FO 50/65; Pakenham to Aberdeen, no. 33, May 7, 1830, FO 50/60; Pakenham to Aberdeen, no. 72, October 5, 1830, FO 50/61; Pakenham to Palmerston, no. 51, August 2, 1831, FO 50/66; *Voz de la Patria,* February 11, 1830, p. 7.

172. *Gaceta del Gobierno Supremo de Zacatecas,* June 28, 1831, enclosed in Pakenham to Palmerston, no. 51, August 2, 1831, FO 50/66; Pakenham to Palmerston, no. 49, July 1, 1831, FO 50/66; Ezell and Ezell, *The Aguiar Collection,* p. 14.

173. Quoted in Shaw, "Poverty and Politics," p. 37.

Chapter 6
THE YORKINOS TRIUMPHANT
1827–1828

1. The liberal creed is discussed in Reyes Heroles, *El liberalismo mexicano* 2:xiv.
2. On this latter activity, see Archivo de Notarías, Protocolo Calapiz 1828, pp. 1041–46.
3. Alamán, *Historia de Méjico* 1:15; Sims, *Descolonización*, p. 11.
4. *Redactor Municipal,* June 9, 1824, pp. 3–4.
5. Sims, "Expulsion of the Spaniards from Mexico, 1827–1828," p. 342.
6. Ibid., p. 14.
7. Bullock, *Six Months' Residence,* p. 160.
8. Veracruz Vice-Consul Charles Mackenzie, however, offered the more conservative estimate of 36.5 million pesos (Baur, "The Evolution of a Mexican Foreign Trade Policy 1821–1828," pp. 228, 250); Mackenzie also passed on a report of 140 million pesos leaving the country since 1810 (Mackenzie to Canning, no. 14, Xalapa, July 24, 1824, FO 50/7); U.S. Consul General Wilcocks was informed by a man whose "veracity and probity" were well known to him that 36 million pesos had left the country in the first seven months of 1822 (Wilcocks to Adams, unnumbered, Pueblo Viejo de Tamaulipas, July 30, 1822, Despatches from U.S. Consuls in Mexico City).
9. Sims, "Expulsion of the Spaniards from Mexico, 1827–1828," pp. 14–15, 155; Sims, *Descolonización*, pp. 11, 193–94.
10. On Arenas's life, see *Águila Mexicana,* June 2, 1827, pp. 3–4; Alamán, *Historia de Méjico* 5:518–19; and Tornel, *Breve reseña,* p. 86.
11. *Jefes del Ejército,* p. 21.
12. Tornel, *Breve reseña,* pp. 87–88; *Causas que se han seguido y terminado contra los comprendidos en la conspiración llamada del padre Arenas,* pp. 9–12, 18–19.
13. *Águila Mexicana,* June 2, 1827, pp. 3–4; *Pedimento fiscal del señor coronel José Antonio Facio,* p. 7.
14. The dossier is cited in Costeloe, *La primera república federal de México (1824–1835),* pp. 93–94.
15. Sims, "Expulsion of the Spaniards from Mexico, 1827–1828," p. 177.
16. Costeloe, *La primera república federal de México (1824–1835),* pp. 95–97; Ward to Canning, no. 46, Mexico City, March 31, 1827, FO 50/31A.
17. Alamán, *Historia de Méjico* 5:522–23.
18. Sims, "Expulsion of the Spaniards from Mexico, 1827–1828," p. 176; Tornel, *Breve reseña,* p. 92.
19. *Causas que se han seguido y terminado contra los comprendidos en la conspiración llamada del padre Arenas,* pp. 12–14, 91–109; Bustamante, *Continuación del cuadro histórico* 3:86.
20. Tornel, *Breve reseña,* p. 113; for recent research that questions the theory that Aviraneta was the royal agent, see Sims, "Expulsion of the Spaniards from Mexico, 1827–1828," p. 195, n.
21. Ward to Canning, no. 15, Mexico City, January 29, 1827, FO 50/31A, and no. 46, Mexico City, March 31, 1827, FO 50/31B; Costeloe, *La primera república federal de México (1824–1835),* pp. 95–96.
22. One of numerous sources for this is Taylor to Clay, Veracruz, June 21, 1826, Despatches from U.S. Consuls in Veracruz.
23. *Jefes del ejército,* pp. 29–33, 89; Bidwell, "The First Mexican Navy, 1821–1830," p. 40; a birthdate of 1776 for José Rincón is given in *Diccionario Porrúa* (1970 ed.), p. 1762.

24. Rivera Cambas, *Historia antigua y moderna de Jalapa* 2:427; Trens, *Historia de Veracruz* 3:571; *Correo de la Federación Mexicana,* April 27, 1827, pp. 2–3; Esteva, *Esposición de las ocurrencias que motivaron la salida de Veracruz.*

25. Pakenham to Canning, no. 24, June 17, 1827, FO 50/34; *Águila Mexicana,* June 8, 1827, p. 4, and June 16, 1827, pp. 2–4; *El Sol,* June 2, 1827, p. 4, and June 7, 1827, p. 4.

26. *Correo de la Federación Mexicana,* July 3, 1827, p. 2, July 30, 1827, p. 4, August 4, 1827, pp. 3–4, and August 5, 1827, p. 4; *Repertorio Mexicano,* August 9, 1827, p. 2; the sedition of the Veracruz Escoceses is discussed in Tornel, *Breve reseña,* pp. 130–31; and in Bidwell, "The First Mexican Navy, 1821–1830," pp. 458–60; Guerrero's sojourn in Veracruz is discussed in Harrell, "Vicente Guerrero," pp. 162–67.

27. Costeloe, *La primera república federal de México (1824–1835),* p. 103; Flores Caballero, *La contrarevolución,* p. 108.

28. Costeloe, *La primera república federal de México (1824–1835),* p. 103; Dublán and Lozano, eds., *Legislación mexicana* 2:12.

29. Sims, "Expulsion of the Spaniards from Mexico, 1827–1828," pp. 209, 243, 258–71; Costeloe, *La primera república federal de México (1824–1835),* p. 104; Harrell, "Vicente Guerrero," p. 173; Barron to O'Gorman, unnumbered, Tepic, September 7, 1827, FO 50/38.

30. Sims, "Expulsion of the Spaniards from Mexico, 1827–1828," pp. 294–98, 342–43.

31. Ibid., pp. 243–46, 250–52; Pakenham to Dudley, no. 61, Mexico City, September 20, 1827, FO 50/35, no. 69, Mexico City, October 10, 1827, FO 50/35, and no. 84, Mexico City, December 3, 1827, FO 50/36.

32. Sims, "Expulsion of the Spaniards from Mexico, 1827–1828," pp. 211, 246; Tornel, *Breve reseña,* p. 164; Gómez Pedraza, *Manifiesto,* p. 47; Pakenham to Dudley, no. 84, Mexico City, December 3, 1827, FO 50/36, and no. 90, Mexico City, December 22, 1827, FO 50/36.

33. Sims, "Expulsion of the Spaniards from Mexico, 1827–1828," pp. 307–10; Dublán and Lozano, eds., *Legislación mexicana* 2:47.

34. Sims, "Expulsion of the Spaniards from Mexico, 1827–1828," pp. 332, 334, 355–56, 408–15.

35. Ibid., p. 344.

36. O'Gorman to Bidwell, no. 3, Mexico City, January 25, 1828, FO 50/46.

37. Pakenham to Dudley, no. 35, Mexico City, March 12, 1828, FO 50/42.

38. Sims, "Expulsion of the Spaniards from Mexico, 1827–1828," pp. 402–05, 424; Gómez Pedraza, *Manifiesto,* p. 29; Barron to Pakenham, Tepic, June 22, 1827, FO 50/39; Bidwell, "The First Mexican Navy, 1821–1830," p. 461.

39. Poinsett to Clay, no. 128, June 4, 1828, Despatches from U.S. Ministers to Mexico, 1823–1906.

40. Sims, "Expulsion of the Spaniards from Mexico, 1827–1828," pp. 408–13.

41. See México, *Memoria,* 1828, esp. pp. 18–33.

42. Poinsett [to Guerrero], October 20, 1827, University of Texas, Barker Collection, Poinsett Papers, Box 2R 153 (typescript).

43. Alamán to Monteleone, January 12, 1827, copy, AGN, Hospital de Jesús, legajo 424, expediente 12; Alamán to Monteleone, December 20, 1827, copy, AGN, Hospital de Jesús, legajo 440, expediente 3.

44. *Voz de la Patria,* February 18, 1830, pp. 1–2.

45. Deposition of Manuel Montaño, printed in Castillo Negrete, *México en el siglo XIX* 18:88–94.

46. Ibid.

47. Printed in Olavarría y Ferrari, *México independiente 1821–1855,* p. 160.

48. Parrish, "Nicolás Bravo," pp. 188–94.

49. Deposition of Manuel Montaño, printed in Castillo Negrete, *México en el siglo XIX* 18:88–94; *Correo de la Federación Mexicana,* January 20, 1828, p. 1; Facio, *Memoria que sobre los sucesos del tiempo de su ministerio,* p. 204.

50. Flaccus, "Guadalupe Victoria," p. 580.

51. Cited in Costeloe, *La primera república federal de México (1824–1835),* p. 145; *Suplemento al Águila Mexicana No. 14,* January 14, 1828; deposition of Manuel Montaño, printed in Castillo Negrete, *México en el siglo XIX* 18:88–94; Sobrearias, *Defensa legal,* p. 13.

52. *Águila Mexicana,* February 3, 1828, p. 3.

53. *Correo de la Federación Mexicana,* January 23, 1828, p. 4, February 24, 1828, p. 4, and February 27, 1828, pp. 3–4; an account of the trial proceedings, based on original documents, is in Costeloe, *La primera república federal de México (1824–1835),* pp. 147–51; Pakenham to Dudley, no. 35, Mexico City, March 12, 1828, FO 50/42; Arrillaga, ed., *Recopilación de leyes,* vol. 1828, pp. 86–87; the trial documents were printed in Tornel, *Breve reseña,* pp. 212–15.

54. Pakenham to Dudley, no. 54, Mexico City, April 23, 1828, FO 50/43.

55. *Manifiesto del Exmo. Señor D. Nicolás Bravo* (1828).

56. Pakenham to Dudley, no. 64, Mexico City, May 28, 1828, FO 50/53; *Correo de la Federación Mexicana,* June 20, 1828, p. 1.

56. The Real hacienda is discussed in Alamán, *Historia de Méjico* 1:65–76; and in Sierra, *El Nacimiento de México,* pp. 183–93.

58. Dublán and Lozano, eds., *Legislación mexicana* 1:710–12, 715–17.

59. Hacienda, *Memoria provisional,* 1823, p. 9; Medina, *Exposición al soberano congreso mexicano,* p. 37; Esteva, *Manifiesto de la . . . hacienda federal mexicana desde Agosto de 24 á Diciembre de 26,* p. 5.

60. Hacienda, *Memoria,* 1823, pp. 25–26; México, Congreso, *Crónicas* 2:137–39, 281, 295; the debt law was formalized on June 28, 1824 (Arrillaga, ed., *Recopilación de leyes,* vol. 1831, p. 307).

61. Hacienda, *Memoria,* 1823, estado 7; ibid., 1826, estado 43; Medina, *Apéndice á la exposición al soberano congreso,* p. 22.

62. See the "Estado General" of the *Memorias* of Hacienda for 1827, 1828, and 1829.

63. Hacienda, *Memoria,* "Estado General," for 1826, 1827, and 1828; ibid., 1828, estado 5; ibid., 1829, "Estado General", estado 5; ibid., 1830, "Estado General", estado 6; the workings of the *alcabala* were discussed in *Correo de la Federación Mexicana,* May 19, 1828, p. 4.

64. Hacienda, *Memoria provisional,* 1823, p. 6; Hacienda, *Memoria,* 1823, p. 11; ibid., 1825, p. 39; ibid., 1827, p. 1; Dublán and Lozano, eds., *Legislación mexicana* 1:698–99.

65. Tayloe, *Mexico, 1825–1828,* pp. 59–60.

66. Esteva, *Manifiesto de la . . . hacienda federal mexicana desde Agosto de 24 á Diciembre de 26,* p. 106; Pakenham to Dudley, no. 42, March 27, 1828, FO 50/43; Poinsett to Clay, no. 144, July 16, 1828, Despatches from U.S. Ministers to Mexico, 1823–1906; Macune, "A Test of Federalism," p. 215.

67. Pakenham to Dudley, No. 42, March 27, 1828, and no. 71, May 28, 1828, FO 50/43; Macune, "A Test of Federalism," pp. 215, 221–23; the law of May 23, 1829, is in *Legislación mexicana,* ed. Dublán and Lozano 2:112–15.

68. *Leyes, decretos, y convenios relativos á la deuda estrangera,* pp. iii–vi.

69. Main sources for negotiations and terms of the loans are Hacienda, *Memoria,* 1825, pp. 25–27, 35–36; ibid., 1826, pp. 35–38; Esteva, *Manifiesto de la . . . hacienda*

federal mexicana desde Agosto de 24 á Diciembre de 26, pp. 87–95; and Alamán, *Liquidación General de la Deuda esterior,* in Alamán, *Documentos diversos* 2:321–472.

70. For use of proceeds of foreign loans, see Esteva, *Manifiesto de la . . . hacienda federal mexicana desde Agosto de 24 á Diciembre de 26,* pp. 91–96; Rodríguez O., *Emergence of Spanish America,* pp. 109–11, 118, 126–27; Borja Migoni gave his account of the negotiation in a secret report, which Tornel later published in his *El Amigo del Pueblo,* September 12, 1827, pp. 1–34, and then reprinted in *Breve reseña,* pp. 117–28.

71. Hacienda, *Memoria,* 1825, pp. 25–26; ibid., 1826, pp. 36, 38, "Estado que manifiesta el líquido producto del préstamo de 3,200,000 libras esterlinas"; ibid., 1827, p. 20; *Dictamen de la comisión de crédito público de la Cámara de Diputados sobre el arreglo de la deuda inglesa,* p. 6; this latter committee report of 1850 has a useful compendium of the two major loans, utilizing other debt studies of the 1840s.

72. *The Times* (London), February 11, 1825, p. 4; Esteva, *Manifiesto de la . . . hacienda federal mexicana desde Agosto de 24 á Diciembre de 26,* p. 89.

73. Ward to Canning, no. 121, Mexico City, October 18, 1826, FO 50/24.

74. Pakenham to Dudley, no. 47, Mexico City, August 15, 1827, and no. 73, Mexico City, October 13, 1827, FO 50/35.

75. Hacienda, *Memoria,* 1827, p. 6; ibid., 1828, "Estado General"; summary of hacienda figures 1824 to 1842 is given in Wyllie [Willie], *México: Noticia sobre su hacienda pública.*

76. Hacienda, *Memoria,* 1827, p. 20.

77. Zavala, *Esposición del secretario del despacho de hacienda,* p. 6.

78. See the "Estado General" in the Hacienda *Memoria* for 1826, 1827, 1828, 1829.

79. O'Gorman to Bidwell, no. 3, Mexico City, January 25, 1828, FO 50/46.

80. Pakenham to Aberdeen, no. 9, Mexico City, January 13, 1828, FO 50/42.

81. Zavala, *Esposición del secretario del despacho de hacienda,* pp. 6, 9; *Razón de los préstamos que ha negociado el Supremo Gobierno de la Federación;* the figure of 3,797,065 pesos includes manuscript additions made in the copy of this latter document in Lafragua Colection, vol. 773; also see Platt, "Finanzas Británicas en México," p. 229.

82. Dublán and Lozano, eds., *Legislación mexicana* 1:710–12; the law of December 22, 1824, allowed the states the 3 percent tax on consumption of foreign goods (ibid. 1:748–49).

83. Trens, *Historia de Chiapas,* p. 335; Oaxaca, *Memoria,* 1828, p. 28; Tabasco, *Estadística,* 1826, estado 1; Yucatán, *Memoria de estadística,* 1826, "Demostración de los ingresos y egresos de la Tesorería . . . "; Puebla, *Memoria,* 1826, p. 31.

84. México, *Memoria,* 1829, estado 8.

85. Michoacán, *Memoria,* 1829, p. 29; ibid., 1830, pp. 14–15.

86. For example, see Guanajuato, *Memoria,* 1827, p. 29; Jalisco, *Memoria,* 1831, pp. 12–13; Michoacán, *Memoria,* 1830, pp. 14–15; México, *Memoria,* 1826, p. 44; Puebla, *Memoria,* 1827, p. 28; Rivera Cambas, *Historia antigua y moderna de Jalapa* 2:387.

87. Guanajuato, *Memoria instructiva,* 1830, p. 46.

88. Tabasco, *Estadística,* 1826, estado 1; Yucatán, *Memoria,* 1826, "Demostración de los ingresos y egresos de la Tesorería de este estado"; Guanajuato, *Memoria,* 1830, estado 1; Michoacán, *Memoria,* 1829, estado 4; Jalisco, *Memoria,* 1831, estado 1.

89. Nuevo León, *Memoria,* 1827, estado 3; Puebla, *Memoria,* 1827, estado 1.

90. Lavrín, "Problems and Policies," p. 72.

91. Tornel, *Breve reseña,* p. 311.

92. Harrell, "Vicente Guerrero," p. 240.

93. Guerrero's life and career are surveyed in two biographies: Harrell,

"Vicente Guerrero"; and Sprague, *Vicente Guerrero;* a contemporary account of his revolutionary exploits is in *Correo de la Federación Mexicana,* August 16, 1828, pp. 1–2.

94. For a physical description of Guerrero, see *Correo de la Federación Mexicana,* November 17, 1826, p. 4; Tayloe, *Mexico 1825–1828,* p. 159; and Prieto, *Memorias de mis tiempos,* p. 73.

95. For Gómez Pedraza's background, see Sosa, *Biografías de mexicanos distinguidos,* pp. 424–26; *Jefes del ejército,* pp. 61–62; Tornel, *Breve reseña,* pp. 34–35; *Suplemento á las semblanzas de los diputados á Cortes,* p. 13; Tornel, *Notas al manifiesto publicado en Nueva-Orleans por el General D. Manuel Gómez Pedraza,* p. 35; Bidwell, "The First Mexican Navy, 1821–1830," p. 290; Gómez Pedraza, *Manifiesto* (1831), p. 23; on charges concerning 1824 assault, see *Gaceta del Gobierno Supremo de la Federación Mexicana,* September 25, 1824, pp. 1–2.

96. Alamán, *Historia de Méjico* 5:527.

97. *Correo de la Federación Mexicana,* July 4, 1828, p. 4, and July 23, 1828, pp. 2–3; Tornel, *Breve reseña,* p. 236.

98. Sources for these cabinet changes are *Correo de la Federación Mexicana,* March 1, 1828, p. 4, March 2, 1828, p. 4, and March 8, 1828, p. 4; *Águila Mexicana,* January 17, 1827, p. 4, February 15, 1827, p. 4, March 6, 1827, p. 4, November 2, 1827, p. 4, January 18, 1828, p. 4, March 7, 1828, p. 4, and March 8, 1828, p. 4; Tornel, *Breve reseña,* pp. 175–76.

99. Pakenham to Aberdeen, no. 110, Mexico City, August 23, 1828, FO 50/44; *Correo de la Federación Mexicana,* January 20, 1828, p. 4, and March 27, 1828, pp. 1–2.

100. Zavala listed seven governors in *Albores de la república,* pp. 199–200.

101. *Jefes del ejército,* p. 15.

102. Santa Anna is described in *Correo de la Federación Mexicana,* December 2, 1826, p. 4; and in Cameron to Jackson, February 14, 1831, Despatches from U.S. Consuls in Veracruz.

103. *Repertorio Mexicano,* September 11, 1827, pp. 1–2; *Correo de la Federación Mexicana,* September 11, 1827, pp. 1–2.

104. Alamán, *Historia de Méjico* 5:527.

105. For a discussion of the presidential campaign, see Harrell, "Vicente Guerrero," ch. 7.

106. *Pronunciamiento de Perote,* pp. 8–9.

107. *Correo de la Federación Mexicana,* August 25, 1828, p. 3, and September 2, 1828, pp. 2–3; *El Sol,* September 9, 1828, pp. 2–4; the drafts of this Zavala correspondence are at the University of Texas, Barker Collection, Adina de Zavala Papers, box 2N 145, folder 3.

108. *Correo de la Federación Mexicana,* September 19, 1828, p. 3.

109. Election results were published in *Águila Mexicana,* October 13, 1828, p. 3; Tabasco and Michoacán, whose legislatures were almost evenly divided in preference, counted for both candidates; Durango, its government derecognized by Congress after a long dispute between the two state houses, did not vote; Durango events are discussed in Harrell, "Vicente Guerrero," pp. 235–36.

110. *Segundo Congreso Constitucional del estado libre y soberano de Veracruz,* pp. 3–20.

111. *Águila Mexicana,* September 24, 1828, p. 2.

112. Díaz Díaz, *Caudillos y caciques,* p. 79; Harrell, "Vicente Guerrero," p. 263; Dublán and Lozano, eds., *Legislación mexicana* 2:79; for letters of adhesion, see *Águila Mexicana* for September 1828.

113. *Pronunciamiento de Perote,* pp. 21–91; *El General Manuel Rincón justificado,* pp. 16–80; Valadés, *México, Santa Anna, y la guerra de Texas,* pp. 84–87.

114. Suárez y Navarro, *Historia de México* 1:105; *Correo de la Federación Mexicana,* September 14, 1828, p. 3, and September 17, 1828, p. 1.

115. *Águila Mexicana,* September 30, 1828, p. 2, and October 6, 1828, p. 4; *Correo de la Federación Mexicana,* October 5, 1828, pp. 2–3 (Zavala's defense), October 6, 1828, p. 1, and October 8, 1828, pp. 1–3.

116. Dublán and Lozano, eds., *Legislación mexicana* 2:86.

117. Gómez Pedraza, *Manifiesto,* p. 86; Paz, *Estupendo grito de la Acordada,* pp. 20–21.

118. The main sources on the Acordada Revolution are Poinsett to Clay, no. 57, Mexico City, December 10, 1828, Despatches from U.S. Ministers to Mexico, 1823–1906; Paz, *Estupendo grito de la Acordada;* Ibar, *Muerte política de la república mexicana,* no. 1, January 30, 1829; Tornel, *Manifestación* (1833); and "Extracto del diario," enclosed in O'Gorman to Backhouse, unnumbered, December 19, 1828, FO 50/49.

119. Bustamante, *Continuación del cuadro* 3:203; "Extracto del diario"; Cuevas, *Porvenir de Mexico,* pp. 300–02.

120. Gómez Pedraza, *Manifiesto,* pp. 87–92.

121. Tornel, *Manifestación* (1833), pp. 8–9.

122. "Extracto del diario."

123. O'Gorman to Backhouse, unnumbered, Mexico City, December 19, 1828, FO 50/49.

124. [Santa Anna] to Zavala, Oajaca, December 30, 1828, University of Texas, Barker Collection, Adina de Zavala Papers, box 2N 145, folder 2; accounts of these incidents are in Suárez y Navarro, *Historia de México* 1:95–97; and in Pakenham to Aberdeen, no. 153, Mexico City, December 19, 1828, FO 50/45; Zavala gave a defense of his actions in *Manifiesto del Gobernador del Estado de México, Ciudadano Lorenzo de Zavala,* pp. 21, 38–39.

125. Zavala to Santa Anna, Tlalpam, December 24, 1828, draft, University of Texas, Barker Collection, Adina de Zavala Papers, box 2N 145, folder 3; Harrell, "Vicente Guerrero," pp. 280–82; *Pronunciamiento de Perote,* pp. 112–22; *Suplemento al Número 33 de la Minerva del día 16 de Diciembre de 1828,* Lafragua Collection, vol. 313; Pakenham to Aberdeen, no. 3, Mexico City, January 8, 1829, FO 50/53; Jalisco, *Memoria,* 1829, p. 4.

126. Alamán to Monteleone, January 22, 1828, copy, AGN, Hospital de Jesús, legajo 440, expediente 3.

127. Alamán to Monteleone, March 3, 1828, draft, AGN, Hospital de Jesús, legajo 440, expediente 3.

128. Alamán to Monteleone, September 24, 1828, and October [31], 1828, drafts, AGN, Hospital de Jesús, legajo 440, expediente 4; Alamán to Huth and Company, November 27, 1828, copy, AGN, Hospital de Jesús, legajo 424, expediente 1.

Chapter 7
ZAVALA AND THE POPULIST INTERLUDE
1829

1. Arrillaga, ed., *Recopilación de leyes,* vol. 1829, pp. 5–6; *Correo de la Federación Mexicana,* January 10, 1829, pp. 3–4.

2. Arrillaga, ed., *Recopilación de leyes,* vol. 1829, pp. 6, 9; Harrell, "Vicente Guerrero," p. 280.

3. Bustamante, *Continuación* 3:81, 229; *Voz de la Patria,* September 7, 1830, p. 2, and November 24, 1830, p. 1.

4. Tornel, *Manifestación* (1833), p. 26.

5. *Voz de la Patria,* September 7, 1830, p. 7.

6. Zavala to Santa Anna, Tlalpam, March 4, 1829, draft, University of Texas, Barker Collection, Adina de Zavala Papers, box 2N 145, folder 3.

7. Zavala to Santa Anna, Mexico City, June 2, 1829, draft, ibid.

8. This collection is also in ibid.

9. Pakenham to Dudley, no. 89, Mexico City, July 2, 1828, FO 50/44.

10. Copies of this newspaper, with the title varying somewhat, are found in the Lafragua Collection, vol. 153; Harrell, "Vicente Guerrero," p. 299; Pakenham to Aberdeen, no. 32, Mexico City, March 4, 1829, FO 50/53.

11. *Voz de la Patria,* September 13, 1830, p. 1, September 29, 1830, pp. 1–2, and October 27, 1830, p. 1; Sims, *Descolonización,* pp. 170–73.

12. Sims, *Descolonización,* p. 183.

13. Ibid., p. 196.

14. Ibid., p. 231; Sims, "Los exiliados," pp. 393–96, 410.

15. Sims, *Descolonización,* pp. 218–19, 230.

16. Arrillaga, ed., *Recopilación de leyes,* vol. 1829, pp. 78, 86; Harrell, "Vicente Guerrero," p. 317.

17. Dublán and Lozano, eds., *Legislación mexicana* 2:110–12, 116.

18. *Muerte Política de la República Mexicana,* no. 16, June 13, 1829, pp. 2, 6, and no. 17, June 17, 1829, p. 7.

19. Poinsett to Van Buren, no. 173, Mexico City, July 15, 1829, Despatches from U.S. Ministers to Mexico, 1823–1906.

20. *El Sol,* August 8, 1829, p. 4.

21. *Voz de la Patria,* March 23, 1831, p. 4; Pakenham to Aberdeen, no. 73, Mexico City, August 26, 1829, FO 50/54A; Pakenham to Aberdeen, no. 98, Mexico City, October 30, 1829, FO 50/55; Manning, "Poinsett's Mission to Mexico," pp. 813–15.

22. Manning, "Poinsett's Mission to Mexico," pp. 817–21.

23. Sánchez Lamego, *La invasión española de 1829,* pp. 26–27, 52.

24. Discussed in Delgado, *España y México en el siglo XIX* 1:429, 471.

25. Rivera Cambas, *Historia antigua y moderna de Jalapa* 2:527–28; Suárez y Navarro, *Historia de México* 1:144.

26. *Voz de la Patria,* January 29, 1830, p. 1, and January 10, 1831, pp. 1–2; Estep, *Zavala,* p. 184; Pakenham to Aberdeen, no. 77, Mexico City, August 26, 1829, FO 50/55; Harrell, "Vicente Guerrero," pp. 329–30; the August 25, 1829, decree is in *Recopilación de leyes,* ed. Arrillaga, vol. 1829, p. 188.

27. Dublán and Lozano, eds., *Legislación mexicana* 2:147–50, 154–55, 163–67.

28. Sánchez Lamego, *La invasión española de 1829,* pp. 24–26; Rivera Cambas, *Historia antigua y moderna de Jalapa* 2:524–26.

29. Taylor to Van Buren, Veracruz, August 11, 1829, Despatches from U.S. Consuls in Veracruz, vol. 2; Welsh to Pakenham, Veracruz, August 4, 1829, FO 50/55.

30. Rivera Cambas, *Historia antigua y moderna de Jalapa* 2:530–31; Valadés, *Orígenes de la república mexicana,* pp. 90–91, 175; Sánchez Lamego, *La invasión española de 1829,* pp. 59–66, 106–09; Crawford to Bidwell, Tampico, August 29, 1829, FO 50/58.

31. *Conversaciones del Payo y el Sacristán,* vol. 1, no. 4.

32. Sánchez Lamego, *La invasión española de 1829,* pp. 66–80; Saldívar, *Historia compendiada de Tamaulipas,* p. 169.

33. Dios Peza, *Recuerdos de mi vida,* pp. 51–52.

34. *El Sol,* September 23, 1829, p. 2; Tornel, *Manifestación* (1833), p. 33.

35. Sánchez Lamego, *La invasión española de 1829,* pp. 94–95; Rivera Cambas, *Historia antigua y moderna de Jalapa* 2:545–46; Valadés, *Orígenes de la república mexicana,* p. 93; Díaz Díaz, *Caudillos y caciques,* p. 84.

36. Sánchez Lamego, *La invasión española de 1829,* p. 85; Crawford to O'Gorman, Tampico, September 17, 1829, FO 50/57.

37. Sánchez Lamego, *La invasión española de 1829,* pp. 96–97; Rivera Cambas, *Historia antigua y moderna de Jalapa* 2:544.

38. *El Sol,* September 13, 1829, p. 1.

39. Harrell, "Vicente Guerrero," pp. 335–36; Sims, *Descolonización,* p. 177.

40. [Santa Anna] to Zavala, Veracruz, October 7, 1829, University of Texas, Barker Collection, Adina de Zavala Papers, box 2N 145, folder 2; in folder 2 are other Santa Anna letters of this period; for Carlos María de Bustamante's version of Zavala's pursuit of Tornel's relative, see *Voz de la Patria,* March 30, 1831, pp. 1–2.

41. Pakenham to Aberdeen, no. 99, Mexico City, October 30, 1829, FO 50/55; [Zavala] to José María Gallegos, January 3, 1830, draft, University of Texas, Barker Collection, Adina de Zavala Papers, box 2N 145, folder 3.

42. Macune, "A Test of Federalism," p. 330; Pakenham to Aberdeen, no. 98, Mexico City, October 30, 1829, FO 50/55; Pakenham to Aberdeen, no. 99, Mexico City, October 30, 1829, FO 50/55; *Correo de la Federación Mexicana,* October 9, 1829, p. 3; *El Sol,* October 17, 1829, pp. 1–2.

43. Pakenham to Aberdeen, no. 90, Mexico City, September 30, 1829, FO 50/55; Pakenham to Aberdeen, no. 108, Mexico City, November 16, 1829, FO 50/55; Tornel, *Manifestación* (1833), pp. 36–37.

44. Dublán and Lozano, eds., *Legislación mexicana* 2: 156, 163; Amador, *Bosquejo de Zacatecas* 2:355–56.

45. Harrell, "Vicente Guerrero," pp. 341–43.

46. *Correo de la Federación Mexicana,* November 11, 1829, pp. 1–2.

47. Ancona, *Historia de Yucatán* 3:317–19; the *Acta* of November 6, 1829, was reprinted in Suárez y Navarro, *Historia de México* 1:170–71.

48. Rivera Cambas, *Historia antigua y moderna de Jalapa* 2:574.

49. Ibid., pp. 556–65; Poinsett to Van Buren, no. 191, Mexico City, November 20, 1829, Despatches from U.S. Ministers to Mexico, 1823–1906; Facio, *Memoria sobre el tiempo de su ministerio,* pp. 109–11; *El Correo de la Federación Mexicana,* October 5, 1829, p. 1.

50. Arrillaga, ed., *Recopilación de leyes,* vol. 1830, pp. 40–42.

51. Furlong to Guerrero, December 8, 1829, AGN, Gobernación, legajo 72, letter no. 82; Suárez y Navarro, *Historia de México* 1:425, stated the leaders were Facio, Sebastián Camacho, and Juan Grambi, a Guanajuato friend of Alamán's.

52. Andrés María Nieto to Guerrero, Mexico City, December 10, 1829, AGN, Gobernación, legajo 72, letter no. 59.

53. Macune, "Test of Federalism," p. 331; Valadés, *Alamán,* p. 239.

54. Pakenham to Aberdeen, no. 8, Mexico City, January 9, 1830, FO 50/60; *El Sol,* January 8, 1830, pp. 2–3.

55. *Diccionario Porrúa* (1970 ed.), pp. 271–72; Zavala, *Venganza,* pp. 12–13.

56. Pakenham to Aberdeen, no. 8, Mexico City, January 9, 1830, FO 50/60; *El Sol,* January 8, 1830, pp. 2–3; Poinsett to Van Buren, no. 197, Mexico City, December 23, 1829, Despatches from U.S. Ministers to Mexico, 1823–1906; *Voz de la Patria,* June 15, 1831, pp. 1–3.

57. Alamán, *Historia de Méjico,* vol. 5, document 26; Dublán and Lozano, eds., *Legislación mexicana* 2:210.

58. Trens, *Historia de Veracruz* 3:682, 685–90; Rivera Cambas, *Historia antigua y moderna de Jalapa* 2:569; *El Atleta,* January 2, 1830, p. 1, and January 3, 1830, pp. 1–4; Suárez y Navarro, *Historia de México* 1:175–76.

59. *Voz de la Patria,* January 21, 1831, p. 4; Alamán, *Historia de Méjico,* vol. 5, document 26.

60. Alamán circular of January 2, 1830, and Santa Anna to Secretario de Estado

y Relaciones, January 3, 1830 (with enclosures), AGN, Gobernación, legajo 90, expediente 8; Santa Anna to Alamán, January 15, 1830, Noriega Archive.

61. Brading, "Government and Elite in Late Colonial Mexico," pp. 399–400, 403.

62. See ch. 3, note 82.

63. México, *Memoria*, 1833, p. 4.

64. Alamán, *Historia de Méjico* 3:226; on signed lists see *Suplemento á la Águila Mexicana: Número 310*, February 18, 1824.

65. Bustamante, *Diario histórico*, p. 503.

66. Tornel, *Breve reseña*, p. 83.

67. For description of professions, see Bustamante, *Diario histórico*, p. 538; Morier to Canning, no. 10, Xalapa, November 19, 1824, FO 50/6; *El Sol*, July 26, 1830, p. 2; *Registro Oficial*, October 4, 1830, p. 4; Rivera Cambas, *Historia antigua y moderna de Jalapa* 2:460.

68. Macune, "Test of Federalism," pp. 42–75, 103, 113, 307, 362.

69. See, for example, Rincón, *Vindicación*, pp. 30–31.

70. Estado "Despacho criminal. Espedientes promovidos contra alcaldes por los motivos que se expresan"; also see Durango, *Memoria*, 1827, p. 2.

71. Chihuahua, *Noticias Estadísticas*, 1834, p. 207; Durango, *Memoria*, 1827, p. 3.

72. Guanajuato, *Memoria*, 1827, p. 9; Guanajuato, *Memoria instructiva*, 1830, p. 6; San Luis Potosí, *Memoria*, 1831, p. 5; Michoacán, *Memoria*, 1830, p. 5; Puebla, *Memoria*, 1830, pp. 9–10; Mexico State, Legislature, *Dictamen de la comisión de análisis de las memorias . . . de 26 y 27*, p. 4.

73. Described in Rodríguez O., *Emergence of Spanish America*, p. 204.

74. *Correo de la Federación Mexicana*, October 12, 1828, pp. 2–3; law of October 14, 1828, is in *Legislación mexicana*, ed. Dublán and Lozano 2:81–86.

75. Tornel, *Manifestación* (1833), pp. 34–35; México, *Memoria*, 1833, p. 55.

76. Justicia, *Memoria*, 1828, estado 5.

77. Staples, "La cola del diablo en la vida conventual," p. 10; Sims, "The Expulsion of the Spaniards from Mexico, 1827–1828," pp. 403–06, summarizes the drop in personnel (based on the Justicia *Memorias*).

78. Sosa, *Biografías de mexicanos distinguidos*, p. 1047; Tornel, *Breve reseña*, pp. 59–60.

79. These reports are printed in *Colección eclesiástica mejicana* 2:4–61, 274–78; and discussed in Staples, *La iglesia en la primera república federal mexicana (1824–1835)*, pp. 41–53; in Pérez Memén, *El episcopado y la independencia de México 1810–1836*, pp. 233–43, 272; and in Costeloe, *Church and State*, pp. 87–91.

80. Rodríguez O., *Emergence of Spanish America*, pp. 169–77; also discussed in Gómez Ciriza, *México ante la diplomacia vaticana*, pp. 139–52, 225–78.

81. Alcalá Alvarado, *Una pugna diplomática*, p. 80; Justicia, *Memoria*, 1833, pp. 11–12.

82. Pérez Memén, *El episcopado y la independencia de México 1810–1836*, pp. 265–67; Arrillaga, ed., *Recopilación de leyes*, vol. 1829, p. 86.

83. Ward to Canning, no. 42, Confidential, Mexico City, March 6, 1827, FO 50/31B; Ward to Canning, no. 15, Mexico City, January 29, 1827, FO 50/31A; Pérez Memén, *El episcopado y la independencia de México 1810–1836*, p. 235; México, Archivo de la Cámara de Diputados, "Sesiones Secretas," vol. 11, sessions of January 20 and 25, 1825, and vol. 16, sessions of January 19 and 23, 1826.

84. Ward to Canning, no. 42, Confidential, Mexico City, March 6, 1827, FO 50/31B; Justicia, *Memoria*, 1825, p. 23, Estado "Razón de las capellanías y sus capitales"; Justicia, *Memoria*, 1827, p. 15.

85. *Águila Mejicana*, April 7, 1827, p. 3.

86. Staples, *La iglesia en la primera república federal mexicana (1824–1835)*, p. 50.
87. Reyes Heroles, *El liberalismo mexicano* 2:35, 3:77–78, 112.
88. Staples, *La iglesia en la primera república federal mexicana (1824–1835)*, pp. 59–61.
89. Ibid., p. 144; Pérez Memén, *El episcopado y la independencia de México*, p. 258; Ancona, *Historia de Yucatán*, 3:333.
90. *Colección de acuerdos . . . de los indígenes . . . de Jalisco*, pp. 15–16, 131–32, 135.
91. Velásquez, *Historia de San Luis Potosí* 3:152–53.
92. Guanajuato, Jalisco, Nuevo León, San Luis Potosí, Michoacán, and Zacatecas, in Staples, *La iglesia en la primera república federal mexicana (1824–1835)*, pp. 106–13.
93. Ward, *Mexico in 1827* 2:669; Guanajuato, *Memoria*, 1826, p. 29; Harris, *Sánchez Navarros*, p. 219.
94. Staples, *La iglesia en la primera república federal mexicana (1824–1835)*, pp. 127–32.
95. Reyes Heroles, *El liberalismo mexicano* 3:80.
96. Ibid., p. 76; Staples, *La iglesia en la primera república federal de Mexico (1824–1835)*, pp. 123–34; the other states were Jalisco, México, Michoacán, Veracruz, and Zacatecas.
97. *Águila Mejicana*, June 24, 1827, pp. 3–4.
98. Ricker, "The Lower Secular Clergy," pp. 184–89.
99. Jalisco, *Memoria*, 1826, p. 17.
100. Stevens, "Mexico's Forgotten Frontier: A History of Sonora, 1821–1846," pp. 110–11; *Bancroft's Works* 16:650–51; Kessel, "Friars versus Bureaucrats," p. 160.
101. Chihuahua, *Memoria*, 1834, pp. 30–31.
102. Nuevo México, *Ojeada*, 1832, pp. 15–16.
103. Downs, "History of Mexicans in Texas 1820–1835," p. 92; Walters, "Secularization of the La Bahía Missions," p. 289.
104. De la Torre, et al., *Historia general de Tamaulipas*, p. 199.
105. Downs, "History of Mexicans in Texas, 1820–1835", pp. 93–94; Habig, "Mission San José y San Miguel de Aguayo 1720–1824," pp. 513–14.
106. Kessel, "Friars vs. Bureaucrats," pp. 160–61.
107. Geary, *The Secularization of the California Missions (1810–1846)*, pp. 84, 98–102, 151–57; the August 17, 1833, secularization law is in *Legislación mexicana*, ed. Dublán and Lozano 2:548–49.
108. Dublán and Lozano, eds., *Legislación mexicana* 1:776; Pynes, "The Mexican National Army, 1824–1829," pp. 35–38.
109. Guerra, *Memoria*, 1827, p. 17.
110. *El Sol*, August 14, 1823, p. 3.
111. Rivera Cambas, *Historia antigua y moderna de Jalapa* 2:341.
112. Crawford to Bidwell, Tampico, August 29, 1829, FO 50/58.
113. *Dos años en Méjico*, p. 71.
114. Gómez Pedraza, *Manifiesto*, p. 32; Guerra, *Memoria*, 1826, p. 14; ibid., 1827, p. 10, estado 3; ibid., 1828, estado 3.
115. Guerra, *Memoria*, 1826, p. 9.
116. México, *Memoria*, 1826, pp. 58–59; Guanajuato, *Memoria*, 1827, p. 13; Guerra, *Memoria*, 1827, p. 9.
117. Oaxaca, *Memoria*, 1829, p. 6; Barton, "Anglo-Americans under the Militia," p. 65; Lyon, *Journal of a Residence* 1:57–58; Pynes, "The Mexican National Army . . . 1824–1829," p. 48; Shaw, "Poverty and Politics," p. 188.
118. Pynes, "The Mexican National Army . . . 1824–1829," pp. 41, 48–51; Guerra, *Memoria*, 1827, p. 16.

119. Hervey to Canning, unnumbered, December 15, 1824, FO 50/16, see pp. 88–91; Guerra, *Memoria,* 1826, estado 1.
120. Crawford to O'Gorman, Confidential, Tampico, October 11, 1828, FO 50/49.
121. Rivera Cambas, *Historia antigua y moderna de Jalapa* 2:514.
122. *Gaceta del Gobierno Supremo de la Federación Mexicana,* July 6, 1824, p. 4.
123. Bermúdez, *Verdadera causa de la revolución del Sur,* p. 19.
124. *Correo de la Federación Mexicana,* May 21, 1828, p. 4.
125. *Águila Mejicana,* May 25, 1827, p. 1.
126. Beechey, *Narrative of a Voyage to the Pacific,* p. 349.
127. Tyler, "New Mexico in the 1820's," p. 16.
128. Sánchez, "A Trip to Texas in 1828," p. 258.
129. Guerra, *Memoria,* 1828, p. 4.
130. Tyler, "New Mexico in the 1820's," p. 191.
131. Beechey, *Narrative of a Voyage to the Pacific,* pp. 350–51.
132. Tyler, "New Mexico in the 1820's," pp. 164, 177–78, 181, 185–87, 192, 203.
133. Tijerina, "Tejanos and Texas," p. 176.
134. Brungardt, "The Civic Militia in Mexico 1820–1835," pp. 9–11, 20–22, 24–25; a copy of the *Reglamento de la milicia activa,* containing the December 29, 1827, law can be found in Lafragua Collection, vol. 341.
135. México, *Memoria,* 1827, estado 2; Amador, *Bosquejo de Zacatecas* 2:347–48; Tyler, "New Mexico in the 1820's," p. 221; Stevens, "Mexico's Forgotten Frontier: A History of Sonora, 1821–1846," p. 70.
136. Tabasco, *Memoria,* 1831, p. 3.
137. Jalisco, *Informe,* 1828, tabla 1; Yucatán, *Memoria,* 1827, estado 4.
138. Zacatecas, *Memoria,* 1831, pp. 6–7, estado 1.

Chapter 8
THE POLITICS OF CONTROL
1830–1831

1. Arrillaga, ed., *Recopilación de leyes,* vol. 1830, pp. 1, 4, 34; *El Sol,* January 9, 1830, pp. 1–2; *Registro Oficial,* January 22, 1830, p. 2.
2. On Facio's career, see Rivera Cambas, *Historia antigua y moderna de Jalapa* 2:405, 565–66; Facio, *Memoria que sobre los sucesos del tiempo de su ministerio . . . ,* pp. 196–202; Maxwell, "The 'Diario histórico' of Bustamante for 1824," pp. 105, 147, 224; Rocafuerte, *Consideraciones generales,* pt. 1, pp. 10–11.
3. Alamán to Monteleone, January 22, 1828, AGN, Hospital de Jesús, legajo 440, expediente 3.
4. Bustamante, *Diario histórico,* p. 641; Mangino's life is summarized in Arnold, "Bureaucracy and Bureaucrats in Mexico City: 1808–1824," pp. 105–06.
5. Hamnet, "Anastacio Bustamante y la independencia"; Becher, *Cartas sobre México,* pp. 99–100; Rivera Cambas, *Historia antigua y moderna de Jalapa* 2:578–82; *Jefes del ejército,* pp. 6–9; Sosa, *Biografías de mexicanos distinguidos,* pp. 163–66; Prieto, *Memorias de mis tiempos,* p. 296.
6. Printed copy of Bustamante's speech at June 28, 1830, opening of Congress' special sessions, with note, "This one and all of the following I wrote. Lucas Alamán" (Noriega Archives).
7. "Autobiografía de D. Lucas Alamán," in Alamán, *Obras* 4:22.
8. See AGN, Hospital de Jesús, legajos 416 and 460.
9. *Registro Oficial,* January 23, 1830, pp. 1–2, January 31, 1830, p. 1, February 24, 1830, pp. 1–2; *Voz de la Patria,* February 22, 1830, p. 7.

10. Printed in *Voz de la Patria*, April 20, 1831, pp. 7–8; Sims, *Descolonización*, pp. 208–16, 230; also see Cameron to Jackson, February 2, 1832, Despatches from U.S. Consuls in Veracruz, vol. 2; circular of minister of relations, September 11, 1830 (citing a similar circular of February 23, 1830), Arrillaga, ed., *Recopilación de leyes*, vol. 1830, pp. 434–36, and circular of March 24, 1831, ibid., vol. 1831, pp. 223–24; Olavarría y Ferrari, *Reseña histórica del teatro en México* 1:272–73.

11. Butler to Van Buren, no. 3, March 9, 1830, Despatches from U.S. Ministers to Mexico, 1823–1906.

12. Hale, *Mexican Liberalism in the Age of Mora, 1821–1853*, pp. 95–96.

13. Arrillaga, ed., *Recopilación de leyes*, vol. 1830, pp. 353–89.

14. Costeloe, *La primera república federal de México (1824–1835)*, p. 283; Macune, "Test of Federalism," p. 338.

15. The other two professions were unknown (*Registro Oficial*, October 4, 1830, p. 4).

16. For commandancy appointments, see *Registro Oficial*, March 3, 1830, pp. 2–3.

17. Bermúdez, *Verdadera causa de la revolución del Sur*, pp. 2, 7; Costeloe, *La primera república federal de México (1824–1835)*, pp. 245, 255.

18. [Zavala] to José María Gallegos, January 3, 1830, draft, University of Texas, Barker Collection, Adina de Zavala Papers, box 2N 145, folder 3.

19. Estep, *Zavala*, pp. 181–87; *Segundo Suplemento al Registro Oficial (Num. 42)*, March 3, 1830.

20. *Voz de la Patria*, June 22, 1831, pp. 3, 7; Pakenham to Aberdeen, no. 17, Mexico City, January 30, 1830, FO 50/60; a December 29, 1829, manifesto of the dissident deputies is in the Lafragua Collection, vol. 393.

21. *Voz de la Patria*, July 2, 1831, p. 2, July 6, 1831, p. 2; *Dos años en Méjico*, p. 36; *Proceso instructivo*, p. 234; Alamán, *Defensa*, pp. 116–17.

22. Costeloe, *La primera república federal de México (1824–1835)*, p. 264.

23. Pakenham to Aberdeen, no. 77, Mexico City, October 5, 1830, FO 50/61; *Voz de la Patria, Suplemento Num. 2*, October 9, 1830, p. 11; *Dos años en Méjico*, p. 69.

24. [Alamán], *Este sí está más picante que él del Senor Bustamante* (copy in Noriega Archives includes Alamán's note stating that he wrote it).

25. Arrillaga, ed., *Recopilación de leyes*, vol. 1830, pp. 40–42.

26. *El Sol*, January 16, 1830, p. 3.

27. Ibid., January 8, 1830, p. 4.

28. Ibid., January 15, 1830, pp. 1–3; *Registro Oficial*, February 2, 1830, pp. 1–2; Arrillaga, ed., *Recopilación de leyes*, vol. 1830, p. 72.

29. Gomez Pedraza, *Manifiesto*, pp. 95, 100; Alamán to Gorostiza, Reservado, No. 27, August 30, 1830, AREM, L-E 2071; Rivera Cambas, *Historia antigua y moderna de Jalapa* 2:605–06.

30. *El Toro*, January 23, 1830, pp. 2–3.

31. *Registro Oficial*, April 2, 1830, p. 4; Valadés, *México, Santa Anna, y la guerra de Texas*, pp. 97–98; *El Sol*, August 13, 1830, p. 2; Alamán to Santa Anna, April, 1830 [*sic*], and Alamán to Landero, May 8, 1830, in Alamán, *Obras* 4:169–70; Santa Anna to Alamán, July 25, 1830, Noriega Archive.

32. Rivera Cambas, *Historia antigua y moderna de Jalapa* 2:546.

33. *Registro Oficial*, March 8, 1830, p. 4, March 10, 1830, pp. 2–4; *El Atleta*, March 9, 1830, p. 4; *El Gladiador*, April 10–17, 1830, carried documents and news concerning Alpuche's case.

34. *El Gladiador*, March 30, 1830, p. 4.

35. *El Atleta*, March 25, 1830, p. 4; *Registro Oficial*, June 23, 1830, p. 4, June 25, 1830, p. 4, November 19, 1830, pp. 1–2.

36. Bustamante, *Continuación* 4:26; Olavarría y Ferrari, *México independiente, 1821–1855,* p. 288; Rejón, *Correspondencia inédita de Manuel Crescencio Rejón,* pp. 27–29.

37. Circular of minister of relations to governors of México, Puebla, Michoacán, Querétaro, Veracruz, the Federal District, and the political chief of Tlaxcala, June 12, 1830, in *Recopilación de leyes,* ed. Arrillaga, vol. 1830, pp. 291–92; also, proclamation of September 11, 1830, ibid., pp. 436–37, and proclamation of October 29, 1831, ibid., vol. April–July 1833, pp. 209–14.

38. Wilcocks to Poinsett, June 27, 1831, Poinsett Papers, Pennsylvania Historical Society.

39. Butler to Van Buren, unnumbered, August 26, 1830, Despatches from U.S. Ministers to Mexico, 1823–1906; also see *The Times* (London), April 1, 1831, p. 2.

40. Costeloe, *Primera república federal de México (1824–1835),* p. 279.

41. Alamán to Michelena, January 19, 1830, UTLAC, Hernández y Dávalos Collection.

42. Alamán, *Historia de Méjico* 5:850.

43. Background on congressional review of state laws is in Harrell, "Vicente Guerrero," pp. 234–35, 283–84.

44. On political intimidation by commanding generals, see *El Atleta,* March 1, 1830, p. 3.

45. Bravo Ugarte, *Historia sucinta de Michoacán* 3:75–76.

46. Ibid., pp. 79–80; *Jefes del ejército,* pp. 32–33.

47. Salgado to Sr. encargado del Ministerio de Relaciones, January 5, 1830, and Salgado to Ministerio del Relaciones, January 8, 1830, and January 9, 1830, AGN, Gobernación, legajo 90.

48. Salgado to Ministro de Relaciones interiores y exteriores, January 18, 1830, and [Alamán to Salgado] draft, AGN, Gobernación, legajo 90.

49. Arrillaga, ed., *Recopilación de leyes,* vol. 1830, p. 117; Bravo Ugarte, *Historia sucinta de Michoacán* 3:77–79.

50. Velásquez, *Historia de San Luis Potosí* 3:158, 169.

51. *Registro Oficial,* February 19, 1830, pp. 1–2; *El Atleta,* March 21, 1830, pp. 1–2, and March 28, 1830, pp. 2–3; *El Gladiador,* March 31, 1830, pp. 1–2, and April 1, 1830, p. 4; San Luis Potosí, *Memoria,* 1831, pp. 17–18.

52. *El Atleta,* April 14, 1830, p. 2; Velásquez, *Historia de San Luis Potosí* 3:163–65; San Luis Potosí, *Memoria,* 1831, pp. 17–19.

53. *Registro Oficial,* March 2, 1830, p. 2; Macune, "A Test of Federalism," pp. 333–37.

54. Arrillaga, ed., *Recopilación de leyes,* vol. 1830, p. 83; *El Atleta,* February 10, 1830, pp. 1–2; Pérez Verdía, *Historia particular del estado de Jalisco* 2:325–28.

55. *El Atleta,* March 20, 1830, p. 2.

56. Arrillaga, ed., *Recopilación de leyes,* vol. 1830, p. 111; Trens, *Historia de Veracruz* 3:698, 703–08; Rivera Cambas, *Historia antigua y moderna de Jalapa* 2:586.

57. *Alcance al número 2 del Oajaqueño Constitucional,* in Hemeroteca Nacional de México, has the February 6 decree; *Registro Oficial,* February 10, 1830, p. 3, and February 23, 1830, p. 2.

58. Trens, *Historia de Chiapas,* pp. 347–55.

59. Gil y Saenz, *Historia de Tabasco,* p. 178.

60. *El Atleta,* February 10, 1830, pp. 2–3; Relations, *Memoria,* 1830, in Alamán, *Obras* 1:181.

61. *El Atleta,* March 1, 1830, pp. 1–2, and April 15, 1830, pp. 1–2.

62. Ibid., February 27, 1830, pp. 1–2, and March 24, 1830, pp. 1–2; González Flores, *Chihuahua de la independencia á la revolución,* pp. 47–48.

63. Saldívar, *Historia compendiada de Tamaulipas,* p. 306; Relations, *Memoria,* 1830, in Alamán, *Obras* 1:181.

64. Cortazar to Alamán, December 24, 1830, AGN, Hospital de Jesús, legajo 416, expediente 2.

65. Ancona, *Historia de Yucatán* 3:328–34; Baranda, *Recordaciones históricas,* p. 191; Toro to Santa Anna, August 17, 1831, copy, and Santa Anna to Alamán, June 19, 1831, Noriega Archive; Gil y Saenz, *Historia de Tabasco,* pp. 176–77.

66. *El Atleta,* April 15, 1830, pp. 2–3.

67. Alamán, *Obras* 1:186–87, 352–53.

68. Francisco Moctezuma to Alamán, April 24, 1832, AGN, Hospital de Jesús, legajo 416, expediente 9; Cortazar to Alamán, December 20, 1830, September 26, 1831, and April 16, 1832, AGN, Hospital de Jesús, legajo 416, expediente 2; Ramírez y Sesma to Alamán, November 27, 1831, AGN, Hospital de Jesús, legajo 416, expediente 5.

69. *Registro Oficial,* January 23, 1830, p. 2.

70. Ibid., February 8, 1830, pp. 1–2, February 21, 1830, pp. 2–3, February 22, 1830, p. 2, May 28, 1830, p. 1, and June 21, 1830, p. 1.

71. *El Fénix de la Libertad,* August 13, 1832, p. 4.

72. The following sources are all found in AGN, Hospital de Jesús, legajo 416: Ramírez y Sesma to Alamán, December 20, 1831, expediente 5; Domínguez to Alamán, May 19, 1830, expediente 3; Mier y Terán to Alamán, June 14, 1830, expediente 1; Cortazar to Alamán, March 22, 1832, October 14, 1831, and September 26, 1831, expediente 2.

73. Ladd, *The Mexican Nobility at Independence, 1780–1826,* p. 207; Suárez y Navarro, *Historia de México* 2:75.

74. *Dos años en Méjico,* p. 41.

75. *Conversaciones del Payo y el Sacristán,* vol. 1, no. 5; also see Hale, *Mexican Liberalism in the Age of Mora 1821–1853,* p. 143, n.

76. Mier y Terán to Alamán, May 14, 1830, AGN, Hospital de Jesús, legajo 416, expediente 1; *El Telégrafo,* February 7, 1833, pp. 3–4, February 18, 1833, p. 1, February 19, 1833, pp. 1–3; *El Atleta,* March 25, 1830, p. 1; Michoacán, *Memoria,* 1830, p. 24; México, *Memoria,* 1833, p. 23.

77. Relations, *Memoria,* 1830, in Alamán, *Obras* 1:193.

78. Bidwell, "The First Mexican Navy, 1821–1830," pp. 225–34, 246–50, 403–35, 502–07, 544; Welsh to Pakenham, Private, Veracruz, August 13, 1828, FO 50/44.

79. Bidwell, "The First Mexican Navy, 1821–1830," pp. 291–316, 324.

80. Ibid., pp. 397–403, 470, 480, 487–90.

81. Ibid., pp. 497–567; Pakenham to Aberdeen, no. 91, Mexico City, September 30, 1829, FO 50/55.

82. Alamán, *Obras* 1:197–198.

83. Anonymous, *Memorial ajustado á la causa de la administración usurpadora,* pp. 10–11.

84. Arrillaga, ed., *Recopilación de leyes,* vol. 1831, pp. 257–58; this change had been suggested in 1827, *Águila Mexicana,* April 13, 1827, p. 4.

85. *Registro Oficial,* February 6, 1830, p. 2; for the Cortes law, see Arrillaga, ed., *Recopilación de leyes,* vol. 1831, pp. 258–77.

86. *Registro Oficial,* April 7, 1830, p. 2; *El Sol,* June 20, 1830, p. 2, May 2, 1831, p. 4, and April 1, 1832, pp. 3–4; Rivera Cambas, *Historia antigua y moderna de Jalapa* 2:591.

87. Butler to Poinsett, November 30, 1830, Poinsett Papers, Pennsylvania Historical Society.

88. The lives of the Quintana family are chronicled in Sosa, *Biografías de mexicanos distinguidos,* pp. 841–45; *Encyclopedia Yucatenense* 7:9–32;, and Suárez y Navarro, *Historia de México* 2:59.

89. Suárez y Navarro, *Historia de México* 2:59.

90. *Encyclopedia Yucatenense* 7:31–32.

91. *El Sol,* April 24, 1831, p. 4.

92. The January 1830 contract between the government and printer is in AGN, Gobernación, legajo 139; [Alamán] to José Jimeno, August 21, 1830, ibid.; *Proceso instructivo,* pp. 42–45; Alamán, *Defensa,* pp. 190–91; *Voz de la Patria,* October 18, 1831, pp. 5–6.

93. See the following in AGN, Hospital de Jesús, legajo 416: José María Jarero to Alamán, May 23, 1830, expediente 8; Luis Correa to Alamán, March 16, 1832, expediente 7; Mier y Terán to Alamán, September 19, 1831, expediente 6; Francisco Moctezuma to Alamán, April 24, 1832, expediente 9.

94. Rocafuerte, *Consideraciones generales sobre la bondad de un gobierno,* pt. 3, p. 7.

95. Luis Correa to Alamán, May 11, 1832, AGN, Hospital de Jesús, legajo 416, expediente 7.

96. [Alamán] to Murphy, August 29, 1831, copy, UTLAC, Hernández y Dávalos Collection; also see Alamán to Ministro Plenipotenciario de los Estados Unidos Mexicanos cerca de S.M.B., Confidential no. 12, August 29, 1831, AREM, L-E-2075, and Murphy to Gorostiza, September 5, 1831, AREM, L-E-2118; Alamán to Encargado de Negocios de la República cerca de S.M.B., Confidential no. 10, March 5, 1830, AREM, L-E-2070; Alamán to Ministro Plenipotenciario de los Estados Unidos Mexicanos cerca de S.M.B., no. 209, October 6, 1831, AREM, L-E-2074.

97. Printed in *Proceso instructivo,* pp. 120–21.

98. Bermúdez, *Verdadera causa de la revolución del Sur,* p. 6.

99. *Proceso instructivo,* p. 103; Guerrero note to *ayuntamientos,* printed in Olavarría y Ferrari, *México independiente 1821–1855,* p. 239; the plan had originally been issued by Col. Francisco Victoria, *El Atleta,* March 14, 1830, pp. 1–2, March 17, 1830, p. 4.

100. Díaz Díaz, *Caudillos y caciques,* p. 105; Bermúdez, *Verdadera causa,* pp. 2, 4–5.

101. *Registro Oficial,* May 4, 1830, pp. 1–2; *El Atleta,* May 8, 1830, pp. 1–3; Bermúdez, *Verdadera causa,* p. 6; Bustamante, *Continuación* 3:405, 433; Díaz Díaz, *Caudillos y caciques,* p. 106.

102. Díaz Díaz, *Caudillos y caciques,* p. 107; Bustamante, *Continuación* 3:384; Pakenham to Aberdeen, no. 48, Mexico City June 10, 1830, FO 50/61.

103. Alamán to Borja Migoni, June 10, 1830, AGN, Hospital de Jesús, legajo 424, expediente 2.

104. Bermúdez, *Verdadera causa,* p. 14; Bustamante, *Continuación* 3:402; Jalisco, *Memoria,* 1832, pp. 3–4; Suárez y Navarro, *Historia de México* 1:209–10.

105. *Registro Oficial,* September 4, 1830, p. 2, October 20, 1830, p. 4, October 18, 1830, pp. 1–3; *El Sol,* December 9, 1830, p. 4; Suárez y Navarro, *Historia de México* 1:236–37; *El Federalista Mexicano,* January 5, 1831.

106. A copy of the proclamation is in Lafragua Collection, vol. 395, no. 82.

107. Costeloe, *La primera república federal de México (1824–1835),* pp. 312–13; Suárez y Navarro, *Historia de México* 1:260; *Voz de la Patria,* December 9, 1830, pp. 1–8.

108. Bustamante, *Continuación* 3:424–28; Díaz Díaz, *Caudillos y caciques,* p. 108; *Registro Oficial,* October 18, 1830, pp. 1–3.

109. Manuel Zavala, "Viage de Guadalajara al Sur, año de 1830," pp. 73–74; *El Sol,* January 13, 1831, pp. 2–4.

110. *El Sol,* January 31, 1831, p. 4.

111. *Proceso instructivo,* pp. 94–95.

112. Facio, *Memoria que sobre los sucesos del tiempo de su ministerio,* pp. 32–33; "Documentos relativos á Francisco Picaluga, 1830," p. 397.

113. *Proceso instructivo,* pp. 73–74, 79.

114. Ibid., pp. 102–03.
115. Manuel Zavala, "Viaje de Guadalajara al Sur, año de 1830," pp. 78–80.
116. *Proceso instructivo,* pp. 165–67; in connection with perhaps the least credible of the charges, Carlos María de Bustamante published a letter allegedly captured after the battle of Chilpancingo wherein Guerrero stated to Zavala that he would comply with the promise made to Poinsett to sell Texas (*Voz de la Patria,* February 9, 1831, p. 8).
117. Suárez y Navarro, *Historia de México* 1:230.
118. Manuel Zavala, "Viaje de Guadalajara al Sur, año de 1830," pp. 84–85.
119. Bustamante, *Continuación* 3:449.
120. [Alamán to Gorostiza], April 2, 1831, UTLAC, Hernández y Dávalos Collection.
121. Arrillaga, ed., *Recopilación de leyes,* vol. 1831, pp. 218–21.
122. Alamán to Borja Migoni, May 3, 1831, AGN, Hospital de Jesús, legajo 440, expediente 2.
123. *El Sol,* July 16, 1831, p. 4.
124. Circulars of Ministers of Relations, June 6, 1831, and July 29, 1831, AGN, Gobernación, legajo 112, expediente 439; Alamán to Borja Migoni, June 1, 1831, AGN, Hospital de Jesús, legajo 440, expediente 2.
125. Zavala described this trip in *Journey to the United States of North America.*

Chapter 9
ALAMÁN'S PROGRAM FOR RENEWAL
1830–1832

1. Pakenham to Aberdeen, no. 17, Mexico City, January 30, 1830, FO 50/60.
2. Mangino was speaking of the 1830–1831 economic year (Hacienda, *Memoria,* 1832, p. 1).
3. See the Estado General of the Hacienda *Memorias* for 1831, 1832, and 1833.
4. Hacienda, *Memoria,* 1830, pp. 12–14, estados 62 and 63; Alamán to Baring Brothers and Company, March 5, 1830, Baring Brothers Archives (London); John Marshall to Pakenham, June 19, 1830, enclosed in Pakenham to Aberdeen, no. 66, August 30, 1830, FO 50/61; Arrillaga, ed., *Recopilación de leyes,* vol. 1830, pp. 448–50.
5. Alamán to Gorostiza, no. 6, January 21, 1832, AREM, L-E-2077; Hacienda, *Memoria,* 1832, p. 12, estado 4; also described in True, "British Loans to the Mexican Government, 1822–1832," pp. 359–60.
6. Hacienda, *Memoria,* 1831, pp. 4–5; *Dos años en Méjico,* p. 67.
7. Harrell, "Vicente Guerrero," p. 316; Dublán and Lozano, eds., *Legislación mexicana* 2:236–37; see the Estado General of the Hacienda *Memorias* for 1832 and 1833.
8. Pakenham to Aberdeen, no. 29, Mexico City, March 25, 1830, FO 50/60; Dublán and Lozano, eds., *Legislación mexicana* 2:319; Hacienda, *Memoria,* 1831, p. 26; I. P. Penny and Co. et al. to O'Gorman, Mexico City, August 25, 1830, FO 50/61.
9. Alamán to Borja Migoni, October 5, 1830, AGN, Hospital de Jesús, legajo 440, expediente 2; "Autobiografía de D. Lucas Alamán," in Alamán, *Obras* 4:26; United Mexican Mining Association, *Report* (1827), appendix; Alamán to Borja Migoni, August 27, 1831, and February 15, 1832, and Huth and Company to Alamán, December 14, 1831, AGN, Hospital de Jesús, legajo 440, expediente 2.
10. Zacatecas, *Memoria,* 1831, pp. 18–21, 1833, pp. 20–23, estados 5, 6, and ibid., 1834, pp. 44–51; Auld, *Notice of the Silver Mines of Fresnillo,* pp. 11–16; Cross, "The Mining Economy of Zacatecas," pp. 210, 220–28.

11. *El Sol*, September 17, 1830, p. 3; circular of minister of relations, April 7, 1832, in *Recopilación de leyes*, ed. Arrillaga, vol. January 1832–March 1833, pp. 50–54; see introduction in Yllanes, *Cartilla sobre cría de gusanos de seda*; and title page of Hordas y Balbuena, *Dictamen sobre la chóleramorbus*.

12. Potash, *El Banco de Avío*, pp. 70–71; *Dictamen de la comisión de industria de la Cámara de Diputados sobre el nuevo arbitrio para dar ocupación y medios de subsistir á la clase de gentes pobres* (1829); Arrillaga, ed., *Recopilación de leyes*, vol. 1835, pp. 510–13, 520–23.

13. Alamán's efforts to promote a capitalist class are seen in numerous citations found throughout Alamán's correspondence.

14. Potash, *El Banco de Avío*, pp. 90, 92–93, 113–18, 180–85.

15. Rodríguez O., *Emergence of Spanish America*, pp. 195–96.

16. Justicia, *Memoria*, 1830, estado 3.

17. Alcalá Alvarado, *Una pugna diplomática*, pp. 145–46; Staples, *La iglesia en la primera república federal mexicana (1824–1835)*, pp. 76–77; Arrillaga, ed., *Recopilación de leyes*, vol. 1830, pp. 94–96.

18. Alcalá Alvarado, *Una pugna diplomática*, pp. 147–48, 183–208, 216–29; Justicia, *Memoria*, 1835, pp. 26–27; Staples, *La iglesia en la primera república federal mexicana (1824–1835)*, pp. 78–84; a listing of the first bishops of independent Mexico is in appendix 8 of Gómez Ciriza, *México ante la diplomacia vaticana*.

19. Staples, *La iglesia en la primera república federal mexicana (1824–1835)*, pp. 64–66; Bustamante, *Continuación* 4:11–16; Arrillaga, ed., *Recopilación de leyes*, vol. 1831, pp. 296, 480; *Dictamen de la comisión de negocios eclesiásticos de la Cámara de Diputados, proponiendo se declaren nulas las canongías de última provisión*, pp. 3, 6, 8.

20. Costeloe, *Church and State in Independent Mexico*, pp. 120–26.

21. *El Sol*, February 4, 1830, pp. 1–4, March 2, 1830, pp. 1–4, and supplements of February 7, February 10, and March 3, 1830.

22. Macune, "A Test of Federalism," pp. 290–93.

23. Rodríguez O., *Emergence of Spanish America*, pp. 200–07.

24. Arrillaga, ed., *Recopilación de leyes*, vol. 1831, p. 241; Bustamante, *Continuación* 4:30–32; Cuevas, *Porvenir*, p. 372; also see Tornel, *Breve reseña*, pp. 61–62.

25. Costeloe, *Church and State*, pp. 126–27.

26. *Old Santa Fe*, vol. 1, no. 2, p. 168; Guanajuato, *Memoria instructiva*, 1830, p. 25.

27. Koppe, *Cartas á la patria*, p. 139.

28. Berlandier, *The Indians of Texas in 1830*, p. 29.

29. Shaw, "Poverty and Politics," p. 256.

30. Becher, *Cartas sobre México*, pp. 109–11.

31. Olavarría y Ferrari, *Reseña histórica del teatro* 1:228, 253.

32. Maxwell, "The 'Diario histórico' of Bustamante for 1824," pp. 28–29.

33. Olavarría y Ferrari, *Reseña histórica del teatro* 1:181–82.

34. Ibid., pp. 183, 205, 248–49, 260–61, 276, 282.

35. Ibid., pp. 262–80.

36. Alamán to Ministro de Hacienda, August 24, 1825, copy in Jose C. Valadés Archives; *Voz de la Patria*, March 12, 1830, p. 3; the 1830 proposal is appended to the Relations *Memoria*, 1830, in Alamán, *Obras* 1:240–41; Arrillaga, ed., *Recopilación de leyes*, vol. 1831, pp. 496–98; Alamán's efforts to fill the museum are documented in AGN, Gobernación, legajo 102.

37. Waldeck to Alamán, November 16, 1831, Noriega Archives; Waldeck to Alamán, December 17, 1831, December 24, 1831, Manuel Diez de Bonilla to Gobernador de Chiapas, Guatemala City, April 18, 1832, Waldeck to Juan Cayetano Portugal, September 30, 1834, Juan Corroy [to Minister of Relations, summer 1835], and

Francisco Toro to Secretario de Estado, February 3, 1836, all in AGN, Gobernación, legajo 102; also see Waldeck, *Viaje pintoresco y arqueológico á la provincia de Yucatán.*

38. [Alamán] to Gobernador del Distrito, March 5, 1831, AGN, Gobernación, legajo 102; Arrillaga, ed., *Recopilación de leyes,* vol. January 1832–March 1833, pp. 31–32.

39. Blair, "Educational Movements in Mexico: 1821 to 1836," p. 204; the 1827 plan is in AGN, Gobernación, legajo 18, expediente "Ynstr. publ. 1827," pp. 28–38; Relations, *Memoria,* 1830, in Alamán, *Obras* 1:222–25; [Alamán] to Rectores de la Universidad, San Yldefonso, and San Juan de Letrán, Director del Cuerpo de Sanidad militar, and Manuel Tejada, March 1, 1830, AGN, Gobernación, legajo 18; Mora, *Obras sueltas,* pp. 114–15.

40. Hale, *Mexican Liberalism in the Age of Mora, 1821–1853,* p. 171.

41. Relations, *Memoria,* 1830, in Alamán, *Obras* 1:221.

42. José Yáñez to Alamán, April 15, 1830, AGN, Instrucción Pública, vol. 33, expediente 30, pp. 169–70; "Satisfacción q. da el q. subscribe," signed by Juan Antonio de Unzueta (society treasurer), December 7, 1831, AGN, Ramo de Compañía Lancasteriana, vol. 1; José Yáñez to Alamán, April 19, 1831, AGN, Instrucción Pública, vol. 31, expediente 10, pp. 46–47; "Compañía Lancasteriana de México. Estado que manifiesta los ingresos y egresos que ha tenido la tesorería de dicho establecimiento desde 1º de enero á 31 de diciembre de 1830," AGN, Ramo de Compañía Lancasteriana, vol. 1; "Estado general que demuestra los ingresos, egresos, y existencias de la Compañía Lanc. de México" (dated December 31, 1831), AGN, Ramo de Compañía Lancasteriana, vol. 1; "Razón de los individuos arrendatarios de las viviendas del antiguo Convento de los Belemitos" (dated December 31, 1832), AGN, Ramo de Compañía Lancasteriana, vol. 1; J. M. Terán and V. Gracidas [to Secretario de Relaciones], September 2, 1834, AGN, Instrucción Pública, vol. 33, expediente 16, pp. 104–05.

43. Oaxaca, *Esposición,* 1835, p. 10.

44. [Secretary of Relations] to Ministro de Justicia, April 16, 1825, draft, AGN, Instrucción Pública, vol. 33, p. 206.

45. Guanajuato, *Memoria,* 1830, p. 12.

46. Blair, "Educational Movements in Mexico: 1821 to 1836," p. 267.

47. Zavala to Mier y Terán, June 24, 1829, draft, University of Texas, Barker Collection, Adina de Zavala Papers, box 2N 145, folder 3; Mier y Terán to Alamán, February 23, 1832, AGN, Hospital de Jesús, legajo 416, expediente 6.

48. Ward to Canning, no. 34, Confidential, Mexico City, February 21, 1827, FO 50/31B.

49. Ward to Canning, no. 54, Mexico City, November 15, 1825, FO 50/15; Ward to Canning, no. 20, March 19, 1826, FO 50/20.

50. Tarnava to Secretario de Estado del despacho de Relaciones, January 14, 1830, UT Archives Transcripts, vol. 312.

51. Alamán's February 8, 1830, speech was printed in Alamán, *Obras* 2:523–43; Filisola, *Memorias para la historia de la guerra de Tejas,* vol. 1, pt. 2, pp. 590–612.

52. Alamán to Mier y Terán, April 7, 1830, UT Archives Transcripts, vol. 327; [Alamán] to vice-consuls, April 7, 1830, ibid., vol. 312; [Alamán] to Viesca, April 7, 1830, *The Austin Papers* 2:365–66.

53. Berninger, "Mexican Attitudes Towards Immigration, 1821–1857," pp. 58–63; Timmons, *Tadeo Ortiz,* pp. 16–35; Thompson, "La colonización en el Departamento de Acayucán," pp. 268–69.

54. Mier y Terán to Alamán, March 31, 1830, AGN, Hospital de Jesús, legajo 416, expediente 1.

55. [Alamán] to Tomás Murphy, June 1, 1831, draft, UTLAC, Hernández y Dávalos Collection; Spell, "Gorostiza and Texas," pp. 436–37.

56. Alamán to Gorostiza, Confidential, No. 20, July 10, 1830, AREM, vol. L-E-2071.

57. [Mier y Terán] to Secretario de Relaciones, March 15, 1830, UT Archives Transcripts, vol. 327; [Alamán] to Mier y Terán, June 16, 1830, ibid., vol. 314; Mier y Terán to Alamán, June 23, 1831, AGN, Hospital de Jesús, legajo 416, expediente 6.

58. Relaciones, *Memoria*, 1833, p. 6.

59. Mier y Terán to Alamán, November 11, 1830, November 25, 1830, October 31, 1831, AGN, Hospital de Jesús, legajo 416, expediente 6; Mier y Terán to Secretario de Relaciones interiores y exteriores, November 25, 1830, UT Archives Transcripts, vol. 314; Bustamante, *Continuación* 4:34.

60. Mier y Terán to Alamán, April 28, 1831, AGN, Hospital de Jesús, legajo 460, expediente 6.

61. McLean, "Tenoxtitlán, Dream Capital of Texas," p. 33.

62. Barker, *The Life of Stephen F. Austin*, p. 331.

63. Mier y Terán to Ministro de Relaciones, June 11, 1830, UT Archives Transcripts, vol. 312.

64. Mier y Terán to Secretario de Relaciones interiores y exteriores, March 6, 1831, UT Archives Transcripts, vol. 315; Mier y Terán to Alamán, January 20, 1832, AGN, Hospital de Jesús, legajo 416, expediente 6.

65. Arrillaga, ed., *Recopilación de leyes*, vol. 1831, p. 14; Mier y Terán to Alamán, January 25, 1823 [in error for 1832], AGN, Hospital de Jesús, legajo 416, expediente 1.

66. Mier y Terán to Alamán, January 3, 1831, AGN, Hospital de Jesús, legajo 416, expediente 6.

67. Morton, *Terán and Texas*, p. 106.

68. Alamán to Gobernador del Estado de Zacatecas, February 6, 1830, UT Archives Transcripts, vol. 327; Alamán to Secretario del Despacho de la Guerra, February 24, 1830, ibid., vol. 329.

69. Howren, "Causes and Origin of the Decree of April 6, 1830," p. 405.

70. Mier y Terán to Alamán, December 22, 1831, AGN, Hospital de Jesús, legajo 416, expediente 1.

71. Mier y Terán to Secretario de Relaciones Interiores y Exteriores, July 31, 1830, UT Archives Transcripts, vol. 312; *The Austin Papers* 2:412; Barker, *The life of Stephen F. Austin*, pp. 270–71, 275–76.

72. The following references are found in AGN, Hospital de Jesús, legajo 416: Mier y Terán to Alamán, April 19, 1830, expediente 1; Mier y Terán to Alamán, May 20, 1830, expediente 6; Mier y Terán to Alamán, June 1830 [sic], expediente 1; Mier y Terán to Alamán, January 3, 1831, May 12, 1831, expediente 6; the July 2, 1832, letter was not located in the AGN, but was reprinted, in part, in Morton, *Terán and Texas*, pp. 182–83.

73. Manning, *Early Diplomatic Relations Between the United States and Mexico*, p. 347.

74. Harris, *Sánchez Navarros*, pp. 187–89.

75. Saldívar, *Historia compendiada de Tamaulipas*, p. 164.

76. Chihuahua, *Noticias Estadísticas*, 1834, p. 125.

77. Stevens, "Mexico's Forgotten Frontier," pp. 13–22, 117–18.

78. Ibid., pp. 68–77, 113–15; Sonora, *Rápida ojeada*, 1835, p. 9; *The Works of Hubert Howe Bancroft* 16:652.

79. Duhaut-Cilly, "Account of California in the Years 1827–28," pp. 215, 314–15; Tays, "Revolutionary California," pp. 40–42, 51–58.

80. Chihuahua, *Memoria*, 1831, pp. 16–17; Sonora, *Rápida ojeada*, 1835, p. 52.

81. Nuevo México, *Ojeada,* 1832, p. 10; Chihuahua, *Noticias Estadísticas,* 1834, p. 245.
82. Berlandier, *The Indians of Texas in 1830,* pp. 65–66.
83. Stevens, "Mexico's Forgotten Frontier," pp. vi, xiii; Tyler, "New Mexico in the 1820's," pp. 206–07.
84. Chihuahua, *Noticias Estadísticas,* 1834, p. 121.
85. Tyler, "New Mexico in the 1820's," pp. 223–27.
86. Wilkinson, *Laredo and the Rio Grande Frontier,* p. 106.
87. Tyler, "New Mexico in the 1820's," p. 228.
88. Nuevo México, *Ojeada,* 1832, pp. 2–10, 15–17; also see *Old Santa Fe,* vol. 1, no. 1, pp. 24–26, no. 2, p. 131, no. 3, p. 240.
89. *Noticias históricas y estadísticas de Nuevo México,* pp. 16–17; Nuevo México, *Ojeada,* 1832, p. 17.
90. Tyler, "New Mexico in the 1820's," p. 230.
91. Sonora, *Rápida ojeada,* 1835, p. 42; *The Works of Hubert Howe Bancroft* 16:652.
92. Quotes are from Berlandier, *The Indians of Texas in 1830,* pp. 32, 34, 36, 146–47; Mier y Terán's account was published as "Documentos para la Historia. Año de 1828. Noticia de las tribus de salvajes conocidos que habitan en el Departamento de Tejas."
93. *El Fénix de la Libertad,* December 10, 1831, pp. 1–3, December 21, 1831, pp. 2–3, and January 18, 1832, p. 3; *El Sol,* December 4, 1831, p. 4, and December 22, 1831, pp. 2–3; Olavarría y Ferrari, *México independiente, 1821–1855,* p. 289; Amador, *Zacatecas* 2:377; Alamán to Ministro Plenipotenciario de la República cerca de S.M.B., January 18, 1832, AREM, L-E-2077; Suarez y Navarro, *Historia de México* 1:233–34.
94. Rodríguez O., *Emergence of Spanish America,* p. 214.
95. Rocafuerte, *Consideraciones generales sobre la bondad de un gobierno.*
96. *El Fénix de la Libertad,* December 24, 1831, p. 4, and December 28, 1831, pp. 1–3; Rodríguez O., *Emergence of Spanish America,* p. 215; [Alamán], *Un regalo de año nuevo para el Sr. Rocafuerte.*
97. For pamphlet critiques, see the following Lafragua Collection items: Anonymous, *El cañon de á treinta y seis que el pueblo se levante;* Un Mexicano, *El Monitor; Un impreso de más;* Anonymous, *Memorial ajustado á la causa de la administración usurpadora;* Anonymous, *Al Excmo. Sr. General de División D. Anastacio Bustamante.*
98. Olavarría y Ferrari, *México independiente, 1821–1855,* p. 292; Bustamante, *Continuación* 4:23–24, 40; *Dos años en Méjico,* p. 85; *El Fénix de la Libertad,* January 11, 1832, pp. 1–3.
99. *El Sol,* January 12, 1832, pp. 1–2.
100. Suárez y Navarro, *Historia de México* 1:274–75; Valadés, *Orígenes de la república mexicana,* p. 216; Valadés, *México, Santa Anna, y la guerra de Texas,* pp. 101–02.
101. On this see Costeloe, *La primera república federal de México (1824–1835),* pp. 328–29, 336.
102. *Noticia extraordinaria; exposición de la honorable legislatura de Zacatecas,* p. 4 (in Lafragua Collection, vol. 395); *Alcance al Fénix de la Libertad No. 42,* April 28, 1832; Cuevas, *El porvenir de México,* p. 378; Olavarría y Ferrari, *México independiente, 1821–1855,* p. 294; *El Fénix de la Libertad,* May 19, 1832, p. 4.
103. Valadés, *Orígenes de la república mexicana,* pp. 219–20; *El Guanajuatense,* July 19, 1832, pp. 3–4.
104. *El Fénix de la Libertad,* June 23, 1832, p. 3, October 10, 1832, p. 4; Costeloe, *La primera república federal de México (1824–1835),* p. 345; Alamán to Huth and Company, October 6, 1832, AGN, Hospital de Jesús, legajo 424, expediente 1.

105. Alamán to Butler, n.d., UT Archives, Anthony Butler Papers; Butler to Jackson, October 10, 1832, *Correspondence of Andrew Jackson* 4:479–80; Narcisa Castrillo de Alamán to Butler, October 12, 1832, October 18, 1832, ibid.

106. Costeloe, *La primera república federal de México (1824–1835)*, pp. 342–43; Fuentes Mares, *Santa Anna*, p. 77; Pact of Zavaleta printed in *Registro Oficial*, December 15, 1832, pp. 1–2.

EPILOGUE

1. *El Fénix de la Libertad*, February 23, 1833, p. 4; Estep, "Life of Lorenzo de Zavala," pp. 283–307.

2. *Proceso Instructivo*, pp. 1–3, 28–30.

3. Ibid., pp. 56–57, 64–65, 254–55; *La Lima de Vulcano*, July 23, 1834, p. 4; Alamán, *Defensa*, passim.

4. *El Telégrafo*, July 25, 1834, p. 1.

5. Bustamante's defense, dated December 27, 1834, MS copy, Noriega Archives.

6. *La Lima de Vulcano*, March 19, 1835, pp. 3–4.

7. Olavarría y Ferrari, *México independiente, 1821–1855*, pp. 278–79; Gallo, ed., *Hombres ilustres mexicanos* 4:369.

8. Estep, "Life of Lorenzo de Zavala," pp. 341–83.

9. Gregorio Dávila to Gómez Farías, October 9, 1849, UTLAC, Gómez Farías Papers; for Alamán's later career, see Valadés, *Alamán*, chs. 9–13.

Glossary

aguardiente	a spiritous liquor, brandy or rum
alcabala	sales tax
alcalde	head of city council and magistrate
alcalde mayor	district governor
Anáhuac	Valley of Mexico
arancel	schedule of fees, tariff
arroba	unit of weight, about 25 pounds
atole	drink made of corn flour
audiencia	royal high court; at times provincial or state high court
aviador	provider of credit or goods for an enterprise
ayuntamiento	city council or *cabildo*
Bajío	the Lerma River basin
barrio	district of a city
caballería	unit of land measurement, 105.8 acres
cabildo	city council or *ayuntamiento;* also governing body of a diocese
campesino	farm laborer
canalla	rabble, mob
capitulado	Spanish soldier who remained in Mexico after the Revolution
carga	a load, about 200 pounds
casta	person of mixed blood
caudillo	"strong man" leader
cédula	government decree
censo	perpetual lien
cívicos	civic militia
clavería	treasury of a cathedral
colonia	colony, neighborhood
consulado	merchant guild and its court
contingente	annual levy paid by states to the Federation
convento	convent or monastery
creole	person of Spanish blood born in America

285

diezmo	tithe
ejido	communal lands
expediente	file, dossier
expendio	retail store, often government-owned
fanega	unit of dry measure, about 1.5 bushels
fiscal	court prosecutor or city attorney
fuero	exemption from civil jurisdiction, right to trial by members of the same profession
gachupín	Spaniard born in Europe (derogatory)
ganado mayor	cattle and horses
ganado menor	sheep and goats
gente sensata	people of judgment and wisdom
gremio	teachers' union
hacendado	owners of a rural estate or hacienda
hacienda	large landed estate
hombres de bien	reputable, solid citizens
jornalero	day laborer
junta	board or committee
labor	grain farm
ladrón	thief
labrador	farm laborer
league	unit of linear measurement, about 2.6 miles
legajo	bundle of papers
lépero	street pauper
malacate	water-hoisting machine
mayorazgo	entailed estate
mestizo	person of mixed European and Indian blood
mulato	person of mixed European and Negro blood
obraje	workshop or factory, generally for textiles
parcialidad	party, faction
pardo	person of mixed ancestry with Negro blood, frequently synonymous with *mulato*
partido	district or subdivision of a state; also the share of ore of the mineworkers
patronato	privilege of nominating (in effect, appointing) the higher church officials
peninsular	Spaniard born in the Iberian Peninsula
peón	laborer, technically one indebted to his employer
peso	the Mexican peso had the same value as the American dollar and one-fifth the pound sterling in these years
petate	sleeping mat
piloncillo	loaf or cone of brown sugar
Plan	pronouncement or petition, often signifying armed defiance
populacho	vulgar masses, rabble
presidio	garrison or fortress
ranchero	owner or renter of a *rancho*
rancho	medium-sized farm, usually with crops and livestock
real	unit of money equal to an eighth of a peso; also a mining camp
regidor	city councilman
ronda	night patrol
secularization (of a mission)	transfer from control by the regular clergy to the secular clergy; mission lands would be sold

sitio de ganado mayor	unit of land measure (for grazing cattle and horses) equivalent to 4338.2 acres
sitio de ganado menor	unit of land measure (for grazing sheep and goats) equivalent to 864.9 acres
sorteo	lottery or raffle
trapiche	small workship, a mill
vaquero	cowboy
vara	unit of linear measure, about 33 inches
zambo	person of Indian and African blood

Bibliography

ARCHIVAL MATERIALS

Mexico City

AGN: Archivo General de la Nación
  Archivo de Guerra
  Archivo de Guerrero
  Hospital de Jesús
  Instrucción Pública
  Justicia
  Ramo de Gobernación
Archivo de Notarías
AREM: Archivo de Relaciones Exteriores de México
Cámara de Diputados Archives
Lafragua Collection. Biblioteca Nacional
Memorias (national): annual reports of the four ministries, by date of publication
    [sometimes *Memorias* appeared under the title *Nota Estadística* or *Resumen*]
  Secretaría de Relaciones Interiores y Exteriores
  Secretaría de Hacienda
  Secretaría de Guerra y Marina
  Secretaría de Justicia y Asuntos Eclesiásticos
Memorias (state): annual reports of the governors, by date of publication
Noriega Archives. Salvador Noriega Personal Library
Valadés Archives. José C. Valades Personal Library

Washington, D.C.

U.S. Department of State. Despatches from U.S. Consuls in Mexico City, 1822–1830
U.S. Department of State. Despatches from U.S. Consuls in Veracruz
U.S. Department of State. United States Embassy [Mexico City]. Despatches from
    U.S. Ministers to Mexico, 1823–1906

London

FO: Foreign Office of Great Britain. Diplomatic Correspondence
Baring Brothers. Manuscripts

MANUSCRIPT COLLECTIONS

Lucas Alamán Papers. University of Texas Latin American Collection (UTLAC)
Anthony Butler Papers. University of Texas Archives (UT)
Valentin Gómez Farías Papers. UTLAC
Hernandez y Dávalos Papers. UTLAC
Joel Roberts Poinsett Papers. Barker Collection, University of Texas; Pennsylvania
    Historical Society, Philadelphia
Adina de Zavala Papers. Barker Collection, University of Texas
Transcripts. UT

NEWSPAPERS

London

The Times

Mexico City

El Águila Mexicana (Title was *El Águila Mejicana* at certain times.)
El Amigo del Pueblo
El Atleta
Correo de la Federación Mexicana
Diario del Gobierno
El Federalista Mexicano
El Fénix de la Libertad
Gaceta del Gobierno Supremo de la Federación Mexicana
El Gladiador
La Lima de Vulcano
El Noticioso General
El Observador de la República Mexicana
Redactor Municipal
Registro Official
Repertorio Mexicano
El Sol
El Telégrafo
El Toro
Voz de la Patria

Zacatecas

Gaceta del Gobierno Supremo de Zacatecas

PRINTED MATERIALS: PRIMARY SOURCES

Acuario, *Iniciativa al ayuntamiento sobre asuntos de policía*. [Mexico City]: Imprenta á cargo de Martín Rivera [1827], in vol. II of *Actas* of secret sessions, Cámara de Diputados Archives, Mexico City.

Alamán, Lucas. *Canción patriótica en celebridad de los días de nuestro augusto y deseado monarca*. Mexico City: Oficina de Ontiveros, 1812.

———. *Defensa del ex-ministro de relaciones D. Lucas Alamán, en la causa formada contra él y contra los ex-ministros de guerra y justicia del vice-presidente D. Anastacio Bustamante, con unas noticias preliminares que dan idea del origen de esta. Escrita por el mismo ex-ministro, que la dirige á la nación*. Mexico City: Imprenta de Galván á cargo de M. Arévalo, 1834.

———. *Dictamen de la comisión especial nombrada para informar sobre el importante ramo de minería*. Madrid: En la imprenta especial de las Cortes, 1821. (Copy in Noriega Archive has Alamán's note that he wrote it.)

———. *Este sí está más picante que él del Señor Bustamante*. 5 pts. Mexico City: Imprenta á cargo del C. Tomás Uribe y Alcalde, 1830. Copy in Noriega Archives has Alamán's note that he wrote it.

———. *Esposición que hace á la Cámara de diputados del Congreso general el apoderado del duque de Terranova y Monteleone*. Mexico City: Imprenta á cargo de J. Fernández, 1828.

———. *Obras de D. Lucas Alamán: Documentos diversos (inéditos y muy raros)*. Ed. Rafael Aguayo Spencer. 4 vols. Mexico City: Editorial Jus, 1945–1947.

———. *Un regalo de año nuevo para el Sr. Rocafuerte*. Mexico City: Imprenta de Alejandro Valdés, 1832. Published anonymously, but copy in Noriega Archive has Alamán note that he wrote it.

Amigos de la igualdad ante la ley. *Roben á los estrangeros y verán como hay garrote*. Mexico City [1825]. Copy in Lafragua Collection, vols. 160, 633.

Anonymous. *Al Excmo. Sr. General de división D. Anastacio Bustamante*. México: Imprenta de las Escalerillas, 1832.

———. *Dos palabras al Exmo. Sr. Bravo*. Guadalajara and México: Oficina liberal á cargo del ciudadano Juan Cabrera, 1823.

———. *El cañon de á treinta y seis que el pueblo se levante, y que al tirano su clamor espante*. Mexico City: Impreso en Lagos y reimpreso en al Imprenta Liberal, 1832.

———. *Memorial ajustado á la causa de la administración usurpadora, ó dos palabras al Monitor*. Mexico City: Oficina Liberal, 1832.

Arrillaga, Basilio José, ed. *Recopilación de leyes, decretos, bandos, reglamentos, circulares, y providencias de los supremos poderes y otras autoridades de la república mexicana*. Vols. 1–5. Mexico City: Imprenta de J. M. Fernández de Lara, 1835–1838.

The Austin Papers, vol. 2. Ed. Eugene C. Barker. Washington, D.C.: Government Printing Office, 1928.

Balanza general de comercio marítimo. 1825, 1826, 1827. In Lafragua Collection, vol. 23 (title pages missing).

Balanza general del comercio marítimo por los puertos de la República Mexicana en el año de 1828. Mexico City: Imprenta del Aguila, 1831. In Lafragua Collection, vol. 23.

Beaufoy, Mark. *Mexican Illustrations*. London: Carpenter and Son, 1828.

Becher, Carl Christian. *Cartas sobre México: La República Mexicana durante los años decisivos de 1832 y 1833*. Trans. Juan A. Ortega y Medina. Mexico City: Universidad Nacional Autónoma de México, 1959.

Beechey, Frederick William. *Narrative of a voyage to the Pacific and Beering's strait . . . in the years 1825, 26, 27, 28.* London: H. Colburn and R. Bentley, 1831.

Berlandier, Jean Louis. *Journey to Mexico During the Years 1826 to 1834.* 2 vols. Austin: Texas State Historical Association, 1980.

Bourne, Colonel. "Notes on the State of Sonora and Cinaloa." Appendix to H. G. Ward, *Mexico in 1827.* London: Henry Colburn, 1828.

Bullock, William. *Six Months' Residence and Travels in Mexico.* Port Washington, N.Y., and London: Kennikat Press, 1971.

Bustamante, Carlos María de. *Diario histórico de México* [for 1823]. Ed. Elías Amador. Zacatecas: J. Ortega, 1896.

Cañedo, Juan de Dios. *Acusación contra el Ecs. Ministro de Relaciones Don Lucas Alamán, ante el Senado, por notorias infracciones de la Constitución Federal.* Mexico City: Imprenta de la Águila, 1825.

Castillo Negrete, Emilio del. *México en el siglo XIX.* 26 vols. Mexico City: Imprenta del Editor, 1875–1892.

Causas que se han seguido y terminado contra los comprendidos en la conspiración llamada del padre Arenas. Mexico City, 1828.

Colección de acuerdos, órdenes, y decretos, sobre tierras, casas, y solares, de los indígenes, bienes de sus comunidades y fundos legales de los pueblos del estado de Jalisco. Guadalajara: Imprenta del gobierno del Estado, 1849.

Colección de constituciones de los Estados Unidos Mexicanos. 3 vols. Mexico City: Imprenta de Galván á cargo de Mariano Arévalo, 1828.

Colección de decretos y órdenes de las Cortes de España, que se reputan vigentes en la República de los Estados Unidos Mexicanos. Mexico City: Imprenta de Galván, 1829.

Colección de documentos relativos á la conducta del cabildo eclesiástico de la diócesis de Guadalajara y del clero secular y regular de la misma, en cuanto á reusar el juramento de la segunda parte del artículo sétimo de la constitución del estado libre de Jalisco. Mexico City: Imprenta del C. Mariano Rodríguez, 1825.

Colección de los decretos y órdenes del Soberano Congreso Mexicano, Desde su instalación en 24 de Febrero de 1822, hasta 30 de Octubre de 1823 en que cesó. Mexico City: Imprenta de los Estados Unidos Mexicanos, 1825.

Colección de órdenes y decretos de la Soberana Junta Provisional Gubernativa y soberanos congresos generales de la nación mexicana. Mexico City, 1829.

Colección eclesiástica mejicana. 4 vols. Mexico City: Imprenta de Galván, 1834.

Da Ponte Ribeiro, Duarte. "Memoria sobre la República Mexicana" (1835). In México, Secretaría de Relaciones Exteriores. *Relaciones diplomáticas entre México y Brasil (1822–1867):* 364–89. Mexico City, 1964.

De Esparza, Marcos. *Informe presentado al Gobierno Supremo del Estado.* Zacatecas: Imprenta de gobierno á cargo de Pedro Piña, 1830.

De la Peña y Peña, Manuel. *Voto fundado por Manuel de la Peña y Peña, Ministro de la Suprema Corte de Justicia, en la causa formada contra los Señores D. Lucas Alamán, D. Ignacio Espinosa y D. José Antonio Facio.* Mexico City: Impreso por Ignacio Cumplido, 1835.

De Tapia, Eugenio. *Apéndice al manual de práctica forense de d. Eugenio de Tapia.* Mexico City: Imprenta del Águila, 1830.

Diario de las sesiones del Congreso Constituyente de México. Vol. 4. Mexico City: En la Oficina de Valdés, 1823.

Diccionario Porrúa. 2d ed. Mexico City: Editorial Porrúa, 1970.

Dictamen de la comisión de crédito público de la Cámara de Diputados sobre el arreglo de la deuda inglesa. Mexico City: Imprenta de Ignacio Cumplido, 1850.

Dictamen de la comisión de industria de la Cámara de Diputados sobre el nuevo arbitrio para dar . . . ocupación y medios de subsistir á la clase de gentes pobres de la república mexicana. Mexico City: Imprenta de Galván, 1829.

Dictamen de la comisión de negocios eclesiásticos de la Cámara de Diputados, proponiendo se declaren nulas las canongías de ultima provisión. Mexico City: Impreso por Ignacio Cumplido, 1833.

Discursos pronunciados por los Ecsmos. Señores Ministros de Relaciones y de Guerra, en la sesión del dia 8 de junio, del Congreso General de la Federación Mexicana. Sobre las ocurrencias de Guadalajara. Mexico City: Imprenta del Supremo Gobierno, 1824.

Documentos importantes tomados del espediente instruído á consecuencia de . . . las elecciones verificadas en Toluca. Mexico City: Imprenta y Librería á cargo de Martín Rivera, 1826.

"Documentos relativos á Francisco Picaluga, 1830." *Boletín del Archivo General de la Nación* 16:3 (July–September 1945).

Dos años en Mejico, ó Memorias críticas sobre los principales sucesos de la República de los Estados-Unidos Mejicanos, desde la invasión de Barradas hasta la declaración del Puerto de Tampico contra el Gobierno del General Bustamante. Escritas por un Español. Valencia: Imprenta de Cabrerizo, 1838.

Dublán, Manuel, and José María Lozano, eds. *Legislación Mexicana; ó colección completa de las disposiciones legislativas expedidas desde la independencia de la República.* 22 vols. Mexico City: Imprenta del Comercio, 1876–1893.

Duhaut-Cilly, Auguste. "Account of California in the Years 1827–28." *California Historical Society Quarterly* (June–September 1929): 131–66, 214–50, 306–36.

El Desengañado. *Un desengañado desengaña á muchos.* Mexico City: Imprenta del C. Alejandro Valdés, 1832.

Elogio fúnebre dedicado á la memoria del ciudadano Prisciliano Sánchez. Mexico City: En la imprenta del Águila, 1827.

Espediente instructivo, formado por la sección del gran jurado de la Cámara de Representantes, Sobre la acusación que los sres. Aburto y Tames hicieron contra el vicepresidente de la república D. Nicolás Bravo. Mexico City: Imprenta de las Escalerillas, 1828.

Espinosa de los Monteros, [Juan José]. Report to Senate on lodges, November 28, 1826. In Lafragua Collection, vol. 192 (title page possibly missing). Also printed in *Águila Mejicana,* January 2–18, 1827.

Estatutos del Nacional Colegio de Abogados de México. Dated March 22, 1829. Mexico City: Imprenta del Águila, 1830.

Esteva, José Ignacio. *Esposición de las ocurrencias que motivaron la salida de Veracruz del ciudadano.* Puebla: Imprenta del Gobierno, 1827.

———. *Manifiesto de la administración y progresos de los ramos de la hacienda federal mexicana desde Agosto de 24 á Diciembre de 26.* Mexico City: Imprenta del Supremo Gobierno en Palacio, 1827.

Examen de las facultades del gobierno sobre el destierro de estrangeros. Mexico City: Imprenta del Águila, 1826.

"Extracto del diario de las ocurrencias de esta ciudad desde el dia 1 de Diciembre hasta la mañana del 5." Enclosed in O'Gorman to Backhouse, unnumbered, December 19, 1828, FO 50/49.

Facio, José Antonio. *Memoria que sobre los sucesos del tiempo de su ministerio.* Paris: Moquet et Cie., 1835.

Febles, Manuel de Jesus. *Esposición que el Doctor y Maestro Manuel de Jesus Febles dirijió a los profesores de medicina, cirujía, farmacia, y flebotomía, al extinguirse el Proto-Medicato.* Mexico City: En la imprenta del ciudadano Alejandro Valdés, 1831.

Filisola, Vicente. *Memorias para la historia de la guerra de Tejas.* 2 vols. Mexico City: Tipografía de R. Rafael, 1849.

Garviso, Vicente. *Exposición al Augusto Congreso del Estado de Zacatecas.* Mexico City: Imprenta de Galván, 1832.

Gilmore, N. Ray. "The Condition of the Poor in Mexico, 1834." *Hispanic American Historical Review* 37:2 (May 1957): 213–26.

Giménez, Manuel María. "Memorias del Coronel Manuel María Giménez, Ayudante de Campo del General Santa Anna, 1798–1878." In *Documentos inéditos ó muy raros para la historia de México.* Vol. 59. Ed. Genaro García. Mexico City: Editorial Porrúa, 1974.

Gómez Pedraza, Manuel. *Manifiesto que Manuel Gómez Pedraza, Ciudadano de la República de Méjico, dedica á sus compatriotas, ó sea una reseña de su vida pública.* Impreso en Nueva Orleans y reimpreso en Guadalajara en la oficina de Brambila, 1831.

Guice, C. Norman, ed. "Texas in 1804." *Southwestern Historical Quarterly* 59:1 (July 1955): 46–56.

Hall, Basil. *Extracts from a Journal, Written on the Coasts of Chili, Peru, and Mexico, in the Years 1820, 1821, 1822.* 2 vols. Upper Saddle River, N.J.: Gregg Press, 1968.

Hardy, Robert William. *Travels in the Interior of México, in 1825, 1826.* Austin, Texas: Rio Grande Press, 1977.

Hordas y Balbuena, B. *Dictamen sobre la chólera-morbus.* Mexico City: Imprenta de Galván [1832].

Ibar, Francisco. *Muerte política de la República Mexicana ó Cuadro histórico de los sucesos políticos acaecidos en la República desde el 4 de diciembre de 1828 hasta el 23 de agosto de 1829.* Mexico City: Imprenta á cargo del Sr. Tomás Uribe y Alcalde, 1829 (pamphlet series).

———. *Regeneración política de la República Mexicana ó Cuadro Histórico de los sucesos políticos acaecidos en ella desde el 23 de diciembre de 829 hasta el 19 de junio de 830.* Mexico City: Imprenta de la Calle Cerrada de Jesús, 1830 (pamphlet series).

Jackson, Andrew. *Correspondence of Andrew Jackson.* Ed. John Spencer Bassett. 7 vols. Washington, D.C.: Carnegie Institution of Washington, 1926–35.

Jefes del ejército mexicano en 1847: Biografías de generales de división y de brigada y de coroneles del ejército mexicano por fines del año de 1847. Prol. by Alberto M. Carreño. Mexico City: Imprenta y Fototipia de la Secretaría de Fomento, 1914.

Jordan, John. *Serious Actual Dangers of Foreigners and Foreign Commerce in the Mexican States.* Philadelphia: Printed by P. M. Lafourcade, 1826.

Koppe, Carlos Guillermo. *Cartas á la patria: Dos cartas alemanas sobre el México de 1830.* Mexico City: Universidad Nacional Autónoma de Letras, 1955.

Leiby, John S. "Report to the King: Colonel Juan Camargo y Cavallero's historical account of New Spain, 1815." Ph.D. diss., Northern Arizona University, 1978.

Leyes, decretos, y convenios relativos á la deuda estrangera, que se reunen para la fácil inteligencia del Dictamen de la comisión de crédito público de la Cámara de Diputados. Mexico City: 1848.

Lizardi, José Joaquín Fernández de (El Pensador Mexicano). *Advertencias á las calaveras de los Señores diputados para el futuro congreso.* Dated October 30, 1823. Mexico City: Imprenta de D. Mariano Ontiveros, 1823.

———. *Obras.* Ed. María Rosa Palazón Mayoral. Vol. 5. Mexico City: Universidad Nacional Autónoma de México, 1973.

Lyon, George F. *Journal of a Residence and Tour in the Republic of Mexico in the year 1826.* 2 vols. Port Washington, N.Y., and London: Kennikat Press, 1971.

Manifiesto del Congreso de Veracruz á la nación mexicana. [June 19, 1827]. Veracruz, 1827.

Manifiesto del Exmo. Señor D. Nicolás Bravo. Mexico City: Imprenta de Galván, 1828.

Mateos, Juan A. *Historia parlamentaria de los congresos mexicanos.* Mexico City: Imprenta de J.V. Villada, 1877–.

Maxwell, Vera R. "The 'Diario histórico' of Carlos María Bustamante for 1824: Edited with Notes, Annotations, and a Complete Life of the Author." Ph.D. diss., University of Texas, 1947.

Medina, Antonio. *Apéndice á la Exposición al soberano congreso sobre el estado de la hacienda pública.* Mexico City: Imprenta de la Águila, 1824.

———. *Exposición al soberano congreso mexicano sobre el estado de la hacienda pública.* Mexico City: Imprenta de la Águila, 1823.

Memoria acerca de los medios que se estiman justos para el fomento y pronto restablecimiento de la minería. Mexico City: Imprenta á cargo de Martín Rivera, 1824.

México. Congreso. *Crónicas.* 3 vols. Vol. 1: *Acta Constitutiva de la Federación.* Vols. 2 and 3: *Constitución Federal de 1824.* Mexico City: 1974.

México. Secretaría de Relaciones Exteriores. *La diplomacia mexicana.* 3 vols. Mexico City: 1910, 1912, 1913.

Mexico City. Ayuntamiento. *Memoria económica de la municipalidad de México, formada de orden del Exmo. Ayuntamiento por una comisión de su seno en 1830.* Mexico City: Imprenta de Martín Rivera, 1830.

Mexico, State of. Legislature. *Dictamen de la comisión de análisis de las memorias que en los años de 26 y 27 presentó el ciudadano ex-gobernador Melchor Múzquiz; . . . del estado libre y soberano de México.* Tlalpam: Imprenta del Gobierno, 1828.

Mier y Terán, Manuel de. "Documentos para la Historia. Año de 1828. Noticia de las tribus de salvajes conocidos que habitan en el Departamento de Tejas." *Boletín de la Sociedad Mexicana de Geografía y Estadística.* 2d ser., vol. 2 (1870): 264–69.

Müller, Gene A. "The Status of the Clergy and the Condition of Church Wealth in Mexico: 1800–1850," M.A. thesis, University of Kansas, 1969.

Murguía y Galardi, José María. "Extracto general que abraza la Estadística toda en su 1a y 2a parte del Estado de Guaxaca." Manuscript. Microfilm copy in University of Texas Latin American Collection. [Published in *Boletín de la Sociedad Mexicana de Geografía y Estadística* 7 (1859).]

Noticia extraordinaria; Exposición de la honorable legislatura de Zacatecas. Mexico City: Imprenta Libre, 1832.

Noticias históricas y estadísticas de la antigua provincia de Nuevo-México, presentadas por su diputado en Cortes D. Pedro Bautista Pino, en Cádiz el año de 1812. Adicionadas por el Lic. Antonio Barreiro en 1839; y últimamente anotadas por el Lic. Don José Agustín de Escudero. Mexico City: Imprenta de Lara, 1849.

Observaciones á la carta que en 25 del último julio dirigió el Ecxmo. Sr. D. Pedro Celestino Negrete al Ciudadano Gobernador del estado libre de Xalisco, Luis Quintanar. Guadalajara: Imprenta del ciudadano Urbano Sanromán, 1823.

Órdenes y circulares espedidas por el Supremo Gobierno desde el año de 1825 hasta la fecha, para el arreglo y legitimidad del comercio marítimo nacional. Mexico City: Imprenta del Águila, 1830.

Ortega y Pérez Gallardo, Ricardo. *Historia genealógica de las familias mas antiguas de México.* 3d ed. Mexico City: Imprenta de A. Carranza y Compañía, 1908.

Paz, José Ignacio. *Estupendo grito de la Acordada.* Mexico City: Imprenta del Correo, 1829.

Pedimento fiscal del Señor coronel José Antonio Facio en la causa formada al religioso dieguino fray Joaquín de Arenas. Mexico City: Imprenta de la testamentaría de Ontiveros, 1827.

Poinsett, Joel R. *Esposición de la conducta política de los Estados Unidos para con las*

nuevas repúblicas de América. Mexico City: Imprenta en la Ex-inquisición, á
cargo de Manuel Ximeno, 1827.

———. "Mexico and the Mexicans." *Commercial Review of the South and the West* 2:2
(September 1846): 27–42.

———. *Notes on Mexico, Made in the Autumn of 1822. Accompanied by an Historical
Sketch of the Revolution.* New York: Praeger, 1969.

———. "The Republic of Mexico." *The Commercial Review of the South and West* 2
(July 1846): 27–42.

"Politics of Mexico." *North American Review* 31 (July 1830): 110–54.

Potter, Reuben. "First Impressions of Mexico, 1828, by Reuben Potter." Ed. Bill
Karras. *Southwestern Historical Quarterly* 79:1 (July 1975): 55–68.

Prieto, Guillermo. *Memorias de mis tiempos*. Puebla: Editorial José M. Cajica, Jr.,
1970.

Primo, Pedro Telmo. *Querétaro en 1822: Informe de Pedro Telmo Primo*. Mexico City:
Editorial Vargas Rea, 1944.

*Proceso instructivo formado por la sección del Gran jurado de la Cámara de diputados del
Congreso general, en averiguación de los delitos de que fueron acusados los ex-ministros
d. Lucas Alamán, d. Rafael Mangino, d. José Antonio Facio y d. José Ignacio Espinosa.*
Mexico City: Impreso por I. Cumplido, 1833.

*Pronunciamiento de Perote por el General Antonio López de Sta. Anna, y sucesos de su
campaña hasta la derogación de la ley que lo proscribió.* Mexico City: Imprenta del
Aguila, 1829.

*Proposición, informe, y dictámenes presentados al Supremo Congreso General Consti-
tuyente sobre la ley de denuncio de minas.* Mexico City: Imprenta del Supremo
Gobierno, 1824.

Quirós, José María. *Memoria de Estatuto. Causas de que ha procedido que la agricultura, industria y minería de Nueva España no hayan adquirido el gran fomento de
que son susceptibles.* Mexico City: En la oficina de Juan Bautista de Arizpe, 1818.

———. *Memoria de Estatuto. Idea de la riqueza que daban á la masa circulante de
Nueva España sus naturales producciones en los años de tranquilidad, y su abatimi-
ento en las presentes conmociones.* Veracruz, 1817.

*Razón de los préstamos que ha negociado el Supremo Gobierno de la Federación, en virtud
de la autorización concedida por los decretos del Congreso General de 21 de noviembre
y 24 de diciembre del año de 1827, 3 de octubre y 20 de noviembre de 1828.* Mexico
City: Imprenta del Correo, 1829.

*Reglamento de la milicia activa, y general de la cívica de la República Mejicana, con el
particular de la segunda en el Distrito Federal.* Mexico City: Imprenta de Galván,
1833.

Rejón, Manuel Crescencio. *Correspondencia inédita de Manuel Crescencio Rejón.* Ed.
Carlos A. Echánove Trujillo. Mexico City: Secretaría de Relaciones Exteriores,
1948.

Rincón, José Antonio. *Vindicación del ciudadano coronel de ingenieros José Antonio
Rincón, sobre la revolución del estado libre de Tabasco, promovida por los individuos
que en ella se espresan.* Mexico City: Imprenta á cargo de Martín Rivera, 1825.

Rincón, Manuel. *El General Manuel Rincón justificado á los ojos de los mexicanos
imparciales, de las imputaciones calumniosas y gratuitas que el Escelentísimo Señor
General Don Manuel Gómez Pedraza le hace en su manifiesto publicado en Nueva-
Orleans el 17 de marzo de 1831.* Mexico City: Impreso en la oficina del ciudadano
Alejandro Valdés, 1831.

Rocafuerte, Vicente. *Consideraciones generales sobre la bondad de un gobierno, aplica-
das a las actuales circunstancias de la República de México.* 3 pts. Mexico City:
Imprenta de la Calle de las Escalerillas, 1831.

————. *Bosquejo ligerísimo de la revolución de Méjico, desde el plan de Iguala hasta la proclamación de Iturbide*. Philadelphia: Imprenta de Teracrouef y Naroajeb (in error for Havana: Imprenta de Palmer—according to Jaime Rodríguez O., biographer of Rocafuerte), 1822.

Santa Anna, Antonio López de. *Manifiesto de Antonio López de Santana á sus conciudadanos*. Mexico City: Imprenta á cargo de Martín Rivera, 1823.

Segundo Congreso Constitucional del estado libre y soberano de Veracruz, Presidencia de C. Cowley. Cámaras Reunidas. Sesión permanente de los días 4, 5, y 6 de setiembre de 1828. Jalapa: Impreso en la oficina del gobierno, 1828.

Segura, Vicente. *Apuntes para la estadística del departamento de Orizava, formados por su gefe ciudadano Vicente Segura*. Jalapa: En la Oficina del Gobierno por Aburto y Blanco, 1831.

Semblanzas de los individuos de la Cámara de diputados de los años de 1825 y 26. Mexico City: Imprenta de la calle de Ortega num. 23, 1827.

Semblanzas de los representantes que compusieron el congreso constituyente de 1836. Mexico City: Imprenta de Manuel R. Gallo, 1837.

Sobrearias, Ignacio. *Defensa legal del Coronel D. Antonio Castro, del Teniente Coronel Graduado D. José María Moreno, y del Ayudante D. Francisco Moreno*. Mexico City: En la Imprenta de Galván, 1828.

Suplemento á las semblanzas de los diputados á cortes. Madrid: Imprenta de Albán y Compañía, y reimpreso en la imperial de México, 1822.

Suplemento del comercio marítimo que se hizo por algunos puertos de la república, en el año de 1825. In Lafragua Collection, vol. 23 (title page missing).

Tayloe, Edward Thornton, *Mexico 1825–1828: The Journals & Correspondence of Edward Thornton Tayloe*. Ed. C. Harvey Gardiner. Chapel Hill: University of North Carolina Press, 1959.

Tornel y Mendívil, José María. *Manifestación del C. José María Tornel*. Mexico City: 1833.

————. *Notas al manifiesto publicado en Nueva-Orleans por el General D. Manuel Gómez Pedraza*. México: Imprenta de Galván, 1831.

United Mexican Mining Association. *Report of the Court of Directors*. Dated June 13, 1827. London: Printed by the Philanthropic Society, 1827.

————. *Report of the Court of Directors, Addressed to the Share-Holders (1825)*. London: Printed by the Philanthropic Society, 1825.

Un Mexicano. *El Monitor: Un impreso de más con algunas reflexiones modestas sobre el estado presente de los negocios públicos*. Mexico City: Imprenta de Martín Rivera, 1832.

Valdés, Antonio José. *Censo actual de la república mexicana*. Jalapa: Impreso por Blanco y Aburto, 1831.

Waldeck, Jean Frederic. *Viaje pintoresco y arqueológico á la provincia de Yucatán (América Central) durante los años 1834 y 1836*. Mérida: Cía. Tipográfica Yucateca, 1930.

Ward, H. G. *Mexico in 1827*. 2 vols. London: Henry Colburn, 1828.

Yllanes, Tomás. *Cartilla sobre cría de gusanos de seda*. Mexico City: Imprenta del Águila, 1831.

Zavala, Lorenzo de. *Albores de la República*. Mexico City: Empresas Editoriales, 1949.

————. *Esposición del secretario del despacho de hacienda D. Lorenzo de Zavala, á las Cámaras de la unión, á su ingreso al despacho del ramo*. Mexico City: Imprenta del Águila, dirigida por José Ximeno, 1829.

————. *Journey to the United States of North America*. Trans. Wallace Woolsey. Austin, Texas: Shoal Creek Publishers, 1980.

————. *Juicio imparcial sobre los acontecimentos de México en 1828 y 1829*. Mexico City, 1830.

————. *Manifiesto del Gobernador del Estado de Mexico, Ciudadano Lorenzo de Zavala.* Tlalpam: Imprenta del Gobierno, 1829.
————. *Umbral de la independencia.* Mexico City: Empresas Editoriales, 1949.
Zavala, Manuel. "Viaje de Guadalajara al Sur, año de 1830." In *Anales del museo nacional, vol. 2.* Segunda Epoca.

SECONDARY SOURCES

Alamán, Lucas. *Historia de Méjico.* 5 vols. Mexico City: Editorial Jus, 1942.
————. *Liquidación general de la deuda esterior de la República Mexicana hasta fin de diciembre de 1841.* Mexico City: Impreso por I. Cumplido, 1845.
Alcalá Alvarado, Alfonso. *Una pugna diplomática ante la Santa Sede; el restablecimiento del episcopado en México 1825–1831.* Mexico City: Editorial Porrúa, 1967.
Alessio Robles, Vito. *Coahuila y Texas, desde la consumación de la independencia, hasta el tratado de paz de Guadalupe Hidalgo.* 2 vols. Mexico City, 1945–1946.
Altman, Ida Louise. "The Marqueses de Aguayo: A Family and Estate History." M.A. thesis, University of Texas, 1972.
Amador, Elías. *Bosquejo histórico de Zacatecas.* Vol. 2. Zacatecas: Talleres Tipográficos "Pedroza" Ags., 1943.
Ancona, Eligio, *Historia de Yucatán.* 3 vols. Barcelona: Imprenta de Jaime Jepus Roviralta, 1889.
Anna, Timothy E. *The Fall of the Royal Government in Mexico City.* Lincoln: University of Nebraska Press, 1978.
Anonymous. *Apuntes para la biografía del Exmo. Sr. D. Lucas Alamán, Secretario de Estado y del Despacho de Relaciones Exteriores.* Mexico City: Imprenta de José M. Lara, 1854.
Anonymous. *An Inquiry into the Plans, Progress, and Policy of the American Mining Companies.* London: John Murray, 1825.
Archer, Christon. *The Army in Bourbon Mexico, 1760–1810.* Albuquerque: University of New Mexico Press, 1977.
————. "Pardos, Indians, and the Army of New Spain: Inter-Relationships and Conflicts, 1780–1810." *Journal of Latin American Studies* 6:2 (November 1974): 231–55.
Arnold, Linda Jo. "Bureaucracy and Bureaucrats in Mexico City: 1808–1824." M.A. thesis, University of Texas, 1975.
Arreola, Daniel David. "Landscape Images of Eastern Mexico: A Historical Geography of Travel, 1822–1875." Ph.D. diss., University of California at Los Angeles, 1980.
Arrom, Silvia M. *La mujer mexicana ante el divorcio eclesiástico (1800–1857).* Mexico City: Ed. SepSetentas, 1976.
Auld, Robert O., and John H. Buchan. *Notice of the silver mines of Fresnillo in the state of Zacatecas, Mexico, now working for account of that state, and of their present condition, production, and prospects.* London: Cochrane and McRone, 1834.
Bancroft, Hubert H. *The Works of Hubert Howe Bancroft.* Vol. 16. New York: Arno Press, 196–(?).
Banegas Galván, Francisco. *Historia de México.* Vol. 2. Morelia: Tipografía Comercial, 1923.
Baranda, Joaquín. *Recordaciones históricas.* Mexico City: Tip. y Lit. "La Europea," [1907].

Barbabosa, M. *Memorias para la historia megicana ó los últimos días del castillo de San Juan de Ulúa.* Jalapa: Imprenta del Gobierno, 1826.

Barker, Eugene C. *The Life of Stephen F. Austin.* Austin: University of Texas Press, 1969.

———. *Mexico and Texas, 1821–1835.* New York: Russell & Russell, 1965.

Barker, Nancy Nichols. "The French Colony in Mexico, 1821–1861: Generator of Intervention." *French Historical Studies* 9:4 (1976): 596–618.

Baur, John E. "The Evolution of a Mexican Foreign Trade Policy, 1821–1828." *The Americas* 19 (January 1963): 225–61.

Bazant, Jan. *Cinco haciendas mexicanas; tres siglos de vida rural en San Luis Potosí (1600–1910).* Mexico City: El Colegio de México, 1975.

———. "La Familia Alamán y los descendientes del Conquistador." *Historia Mexicana* 101 (July–September 1976): 48–69.

———. "Los bienes de la familia de Hernán Cortés y su venta por Lucas Alamán." *Historia Mexicana* 74 (October–December 1969): 228–47.

Benson, Nettie Lee. "The Plan of Casa Mata." *Hispanic American Historical Review* 25:1 (February 1945): 45–56.

———. "The Provincial Deputation in Mexico, Precursor of the Mexican Federal State." Ph.D. diss., University of Texas, 1949.

———. "Servando Teresa de Mier, Federalist". *Hispanic American Historical Review* 28:4 (November 1948): 514–25.

———. "Spain's Contribution to Federalism in Mexico." In *Essays in Mexican History,* ed. Thomas E. Cotner and Carlos E. Castañeda. Westport, Conn.: Greenwood Press, 1972.

Benson, Nettie Lee, ed. and trans. "A Governor's Report on Texas in 1809." *Southwestern Historical Quarterly* 71:4 (April 1968): 603–15.

Benson, Nettie Lee, ed. *Mexico and the Spanish Cortes.* Austin: University of Texas Press, 1966.

Berlandier, Jean Louis. *The Indians of Texas in 1830.* Ed. John C. Ewers. Washington, D.C.: Smithsonian Institution Press, 1969.

Bermúdez, José María. *Verdadera causa de la revolución del Sur justificándose el que la suscribe con documentos que ecsisten en la Secretaría del Supremo Gobierno del estado de México que los certifica.* Toluca: Imprenta del Gobierno del Estado, 1831.

Berninger, Dieter G. "Immigration and Religious Toleration: A Mexican Dilemma 1821–1860." *The Americas* 32:4 (April 1976): 549–65.

———. "Mexican Attitudes Towards Immigration, 1821–1857." Ph.D. diss., University of Wisconsin, 1972.

Bidwell, Robert L. "The First Mexican Navy, 1821–1830." Ph.D. diss., University of Virginia, 1960.

Blair, Evelyn. "Educational Movements in Mexico: 1821–1836." Ph.D. diss., University of Texas, 1941.

Booker, Jackie Robinson. "The Merchants of Veracruz, Mexico: A Socioeconomic History, 1790–1829." Ph.D. diss., University of California, Irvine, 1984.

Brading, David A. "Government and Elite in Late Colonial Mexico." *Hispanic American Historical Review* 53:3 (August 1973): 389–414.

———. "La estructura de la producción agrícola en el Bajío de 1700 á 1850." *Historia Mexicana* 90 (October–December 1973): 197–237.

———. *Haciendas and Ranchos in the Mexican Bajío: León, 1700–1860.* Cambridge: Cambridge University Press, 1978.

Brading, David A., and Celia Wu. "Population Growth and Crisis: León, 1720–1860." *Journal of Latin American Studies* 5:1 (May 1973): 1–36.

Bravo Ugarte, José. *Historia sucinta de Michoacán.* 3 vols. Mexico City: Editorial Jus, 1962–64.

Brennan, Mary Caroline Estes. "American and British Travelers in Mexico, 1822–1846." Ph.D. diss., University of Texas, 1973.

Breve idea de los méritos del ziudadano Jacobo de Villa Urrutia. [Mexico City: 1827].

Brungardt, Maurice. "The Civic Militia in Mexico, 1820–1835." Unpublished, University of Texas, n.d.

Bustamante, Carlos Maria de. *Continuación del cuadro histórico de la revolución mexicana.* Vols. 1–3. Mexico City: Biblioteca Nacional, 1953, 1954. Vol. 4. Instituto Nacional de Antropología e Historia, 1963.

Callcott, Wilfrid Hardy. *Santa Anna. The Story of an Enigma That Once Was Mexico.* Hamden, Conn.: Archon Books, 1964.

Camp, Roderic A. "La cuestión Chiapaneca; Revisión de una polémica territorial." *Historia Mexicana* 96 (April–June 1975): 579–606.

Carrera Stampa, Manuel. "La ciudad de Mexico á principios del siglo XIX." *Memorias de la Academia Mexicana de la Historia* 26 (1967): 1–37.

———. "The Evolution of Weights and Measures in New Spain." *Hispanic American Historical Review* 29 (February 1949): 2–24.

Carroll, Patrick James. "Mexican Society in Transition: The Blacks in Veracruz, 1750–1830." Ph.D. diss., University of Texas, 1975.

Chandler, Dewitt S. "Jacobo de Villaurrutia and the Audiencia of Guatemala, 1794–1804." *The Americas* 32:3 (January 1976): 402–21.

Childers, Laurence Murrell. "Education in California under Spain and Mexico, and under American Rule to 1851." M.A. thesis, University of California, 1930.

Chism, Richard E. *Una contribución á la historia masónica de México.* Mexico City: Imprenta de el Minero Mexicano, 1899.

Cook, Sherburne F. *The Population of the California Indians.* Berkeley and Los Angeles: University of California Press, 1976.

Cook, Sherburne F., and Woodrow Borah. *Essays in Population History: Mexico and the Carribean.* 2 vols. Berkeley and Los Angeles: University of California Press, 1971–1974.

Costeloe, Michael P. "The Administration, Collection, and Distribution of Tithes in the Archbishopric of Mexico, 1800–1860." *The Americas* 23:1 (July 1966): 3–27.

———. *Church and State in Independent Mexico. A Study of the Patronage Debate 1821–1857.* London: Royal Historical Society, 1978.

———. *Church Wealth in Mexico: A Study of the "Juzgado de Capellanías" in the Archbishopric of Mexico, 1800–1856.* Cambridge: Cambridge University Press, 1967.

———. "Guadalupe Victoria and a Personal Loan from the Church in Independent Mexico." *The Americas* 25 (January 1969): 233–46.

———. *La primera república federal de México (1824–1835).* Mexico City: Fondo de Cultura Económica, 1975.

Creer, Leland Hargrave. "Spanish-American Slave Trade in the Great Basin, 1800–1853." *New Mexico Historical Review* 24:3 (July 1949): 171–83.

Cross, Harry Edward. "The Mining Economy of Zacatecas, Mexico, in the Nineteenth Century." Ph.D. diss., University of California, Berkeley, 1976.

Cuevas, Luis G. *El Porvenir de México, ó juicio sobre su estado político en 1821 y 1851.* Mexico City: Editorial Jus, 1954.

Dealey, James Q. "The Spanish Source of the Mexican Constitution of 1824." *Quarterly of the Texas State Historical Association* 3 (January 1900): 161–69.

De la Torre, Toribio, et al. *Historia general de Tamaulipas.* Ciudad Victoria: Universidad Autónoma de Tamaulipas, 1975.

Delgado, Jaime. *España y México en el siglo XIX*. 2 vols. Madrid: Instituto Gonzalo Fernández de Oviedo, 1950.

Dewton, Doris J. "Public Primary Education in Mexico During the Guadalupe Victoria Period: 1824–1829, and Students as a Political Pressure Group in Argentina, 1960–1970." M.A. Reports, University of Texas, 1970.

Díaz Díaz, Fernando. *Caudillos y caciques*. Mexico City: El Colegio de México, 1972.

Di Tella, Torcuato S. "The Dangerous Classes in Early Nineteenth Century Mexico." *Journal of Latin American Studies* 5:1 (May 1973): 79–105.

Downs, Fane. "The History of Mexicans in Texas, 1820–1845." Ph.D. diss., Texas Tech University, 1970.

Echeverría, Patricia. "Mexican Education in the Press and Spanish Cortes: 1810–1821." M.A. thesis, University of Texas, 1969.

Elhuyar, Fausto de. *Memoria sobre el Influjo de la Minería en la Agricultura, Industria, Población y Civilización de la Nueva España en sus diferentes épocas. . . .* Mexico City: Tipografía Literaria de Filomeno Mata, 1883.

Encyclopedia Yucatenense. Mexico City: 1944–1945.

English, Henry. *A General Guide to the Companies Formed for Working Foreign Mines*. London: Boosey & Sons, 1825.

Estep, Raymond. "The Life of Lorenzo de Zavala." Ph.D. diss., University of Texas, 1942.

———. *Lorenzo de Zavala; Profeta del liberalismo mexicano*. Trans. Carlos A. Echánove Trujillo. Mexico City: Librería de Manuel Porrúa, 1952.

Ezell, Paul, and Greta Ezell. *The Aguiar Collection in the Arizona Pioneers' Historical Society*. San Diego: San Diego State College Press, 1964.

Farriss, Nancy M. *Crown and Clergy in Colonial Mexico, 1759–1821: The Crisis of Ecclesiastical Privilege*. London: The Athlone Press, University of London, 1968.

Fernández de Córdoba, Joaquín. *Pablo de Villavicencio, el Payo del Rosario, escritor sinaloense, precursor de la reforma en México*. Mexico City: El Libro Perfecto, 1949.

Flaccus, Elmer William. "Commodore David Porter and the Mexican Navy." *Hispanic American Historical Review* 34 (August 1954): 365–73.

———. "Guadalupe Victoria: Mexican Revolutionary Patriot and First President, 1786–1843." Ph.D. diss., University of Texas, 1951.

Flores Caballero, Romeo. *La contra-revolución en la independencia; Los españoles en la vida política, social, y económica de México (1804–1838)*. Mexico City: El Colegio de México, 1969.

Forbes, Alexander. *California: A History of Upper and Lower California from Their First Discovery to the Present Time. . . .* London: Smith, Elder, & Co., 1839.

Francis, Jesse. "Economic and Social History of Mexican California, 1822–1846." Ph.D. diss., University of California, 1935.

Fuentes Mares, José. *Santa Anna: aurora y ocaso de un comediante*. 3d ed. Mexico City: Editorial Jus, 1967.

Gallo, Eduardo L., ed. *Hombres ilustres mexicanos*. Vol. 4. Mexico City: Imprenta de I. Cumplido, 1874.

García Martínez, Bernardo. *El Marquesado del Valle: Tres siglos de régimen Señorial en Nueva España*. Mexico City: El Colegio de México, 1969.

Garner, Richard L. "Zacatecas, 1750–1821: A Study of a Late Colonial Mexican City." Ph.D. diss., University of Michigan, 1970.

Garr, Daniel J. "A Rare and Desolate Land: Population and Race in Hispanic California." *Western Historical Quarterly* 6:2 (April 1975): 133–48.

Garza, David T. "Spanish Origins of Mexican Constitutionalism: An Analysis of

Constitutional Development in New Spain, 1808 to Independence." M.A. thesis, University of Texas, 1965.

Geary, Gerald J. *The Secularization of the California missions (1810–1846)*. Washington, D.C.: Catholic University of America, 1934.

Gil y Saenz, Manuel. *Historia de Tabasco*. San Juan Bautista, 1892.

Gilmore, Newton R. "British Mining Ventures in Early National Mexico." Ph.D. diss., University of California, 1956.

Gómez Ciriza, Roberto. *México ante la diplomacia vaticana: el período triangular, 1821–1836*. Mexico City: Fondo de Cultura Económica, 1977.

González de Cossío, Francisco. *Xalapa: Breve reseña histórica*. Mexico City: Talleres Gráficos de la Nación, 1957.

González Flores, Enrique. *Chihuahua de la independencia á la revolución*. Mexico City, Ediciones Bota, 1949.

Greenleaf, Richard E. "The Mexican Inquisition and the Masonic Movement: 1751–1820." *New Mexico Historical Review* 44:2 (April 1969): 93–118.

Greenow, Linda E. *Credit and Socioeconomic Change in Colonial Mexico: Loans and Mortages in Guadalajara, 1720–1820*. Boulder, Colo.: Westview Press, 1983.

Guía para el conocimiento de monedas y medidas de los principales mercados de Europa, en las operaciones del comercio. Mexico City: Oficina de Ontiveros, 1825.

Gutiérrez, Ramón Arturo. "Marriage, Sex and the Family: Social Change in Colonial New Mexico, 1690–1846." Ph.D. diss., University of Wisconsin, Madison, 1980.

Habig, Marion A., O.F.M. "Mission San José y San Miguel de Aguayo 1720–1824." *Southwestern Historical Quarterly* 21:4 (April 1968): 496–516.

Hale, Charles. *Mexican Liberalism in the Age of Mora 1821–1853*. New Haven, Conn.: Yale University Press, 1968.

Hale, Joseph W. "Masonry in the Early Days of Texas." *Southwestern Historical Quarterly* 49 (January 1946): 374–83.

Hamill, Hugh M. *The Hidalgo Revolt*. Gainesville: University of Florida Press, 1966.

Hamnet, Brian R. "Anastacio Bustamante y la guerra de independencia—1810–1821." *Historia Mexicana* 112 (April–June 1979): 515–45.

———. "Mexico's Royalist Coalition: The Response to Revolution 1808–1821." *Journal of Latin American Studies* 12 (May 1980): 55–86.

———. "Mercantile Rivalry and Peninsular Division: The Consulados of New Spain and the Impact of the Bourbon Reforms, 1789–1824." *Ibero-Amerikanisches Archiv* 2 (1976): 273–305.

———. *Politics and Trade in Southern Mexico, 1750–1821*. Cambridge: Cambridge University Press, 1971.

Harrell, Eugene Wilson. "Vicente Guerrero and the Birth of Modern Mexico, 1821–1831." Ph.D. diss., Tulane University, 1976.

Harris, Charles H. *A Mexican Family Empire: The Latifundio of the Sánchez Navarros, 1765–1867*. Austin: University of Texas Press, 1975.

Heiser, Robert F., ed. *California*. Vol. 8 of *Handbook of North American Indians*. Edited by William C. Sturtevant. Washington, D.C., 1978.

Herrera, Inés. *El comercio exterior de México—1821–1875*. Mexico City: El Colegio de México, 1978.

Hornbeck, David. "Land Tenure and Rancho Expansion in Alta California, 1784–1846." *Journal of Historical Geography* 4:4 (1978): 371–90.

Howren, Alleine. "Causes and Origin of the Decree of April 6, 1830." *Southwestern Historical Quarterly* 16 (April 1913): 378–422.

Hruneni, George Anthony, Jr. "Palmetto Yankee: The Public Life and Times of

Joel Roberts Poinsett: 1824–1851." Ph.D. diss., University of California, Santa Barbara, 1972.

Humboldt, Alexander Von. *Political Essay on the Kingdom of New Spain.* 4 vols. New York: AMS Press, 1966.

Hutchinson, C. Alan. "The Mexican Government and the Mission Indians of Upper California, 1821–1835." *The Americas* 21 (April 1965): 335–62.

———. "Valentín Gómez Farías: A Biographical Study." Ph.D. diss., University of Texas, 1948.

Kelley, Pat. *River of Lost Dreams: Navigation on the Rio Grande.* Lincoln: University of Nebraska Press, forthcoming.

Kessel, John L. "Friars versus Bureaucrats: The Mission as a Threatened Institution on the Arizona-Sonora Frontier, 1767–1842." *Western Historical Quarterly* 5:2 (April 1974): 151–62.

Kicza, John Edward. "Business and Society in Late Colonial Mexico City." Ph.D. diss., University of California, Los Angeles, 1979.

Kroeber, A. L. *Handbook of the Indians of California.* New York: Dover, 1976.

Ladd, Doris M. *The Mexican Nobility at Independence, 1780–1826.* Austin: University of Texas, 1976.

Lancaster-Jones, Ricardo. *Haciendas de Jalisco y Aledaños—1506–1821* Guadalajara: Financiera Aceptaciones, 1974.

Lavrín, Asunción. "Problems and Policies in the Administration of Nunneries in Mexico, 1800–1835." *The Americas* 28:1 (1971): 57–77.

———. "Women in Convents: Their Economic and Social Role in Mexico." In *Liberating Women's History, Theoretical and Critical Essays,* ed. Berenice A. Carroll, 250–77. Urbana: University of Illinois Press, 1976.

Lecompte, Janet. "The Independent Women of Hispanic New Mexico, 1821–1846." *Western Historical Quarterly* 12:1 (January 1981): 17–35.

Lee, James H. "Nationalism and Education in Mexico, 1821–1861." Ph.D. diss., Ohio State University, 1974.

Lerdo de Tejada, Miguel M. *Apuntes de la heróica ciudad de Veracruz.* Vol. 2. Mexico City: Oficina de Máquinas de la Secretaría de Educación Pública, 1940.

Lindley, Richard. "Kinship and Credit in the Structure of Guadalajara's Oligarchy, 1800–1830." Ph.D. diss., University of Texas, 1976.

Lira-González, Andrés. "Indian communities in Mexico City: the parcialidades of Tenochtitlán and Tlatelolco (1812–1919)." Ph.D. diss., State University of New York, Stony Brook, 1981.

López Sarrelangue, Delfina E. "Población indígena de la Nueva España en el siglo XVIII." *Historia Mexicana* 48 (April–June 1963): 515–29.

Loyola, Sister Mary. *The American Occupation of New Mexico.* New York: Arno Press, 1976.

Macune, Charles W., Jr. "A Test of Federalism: Political, Economic, and Ecclesiastical Relations between the State of Mexico and the Mexican Nation, 1823–1835." Ph.D. diss., University of Texas, 1970.

Manning, William R. *Early Diplomatic Relations Between the United States and Mexico.* Westport, Conn.: Greenwood Press, 1968.

———. Poinsett's Mission to Mexico: A Discussion of his Interference in Internal Affairs." *American Journal of International Law* 7 (1913): 781–822.

Marshall, Eleanor Jackson. "History of the Lancasterian Educational Movement in Mexico." M.A. thesis, University of Texas, 1951.

Mateos, José María. *Historia de la masonería en México desde 1806 hasta 1884.* Mexico City: 1884.

Matson, Robert W. "Church Wealth in Nineteenth Century Mexico: A Review of Literature." *Catholic Historical Review* 65:4 (1979): 600–09.

McElhannon, Joseph C. "Imperial Mexico and Texas, 1821–1823." *Southwestern Historical Quarterly* 63:2 (October 1949): 117–50.

McKegney, James C. *The Political Pamphlets of Pablo Villavicencio, "el Payo del Rosario."* Amsterdam: Rodopi, 1975.

McLean, Malcolm. "Tenoxtitlán, Dream Capital of Texas." *Southwestern Historical Quarterly* 70:1 (July 1966): 23–43.

Mendarte, Felis. *Guía ó Nociones útiles y curiosas para toda clase de personas, y más particularmente para comerciantes e individuos del Estado Veracruzano.* Veracruz: Imprenta del Autor, 1828.

Miñó Grijalva, Manuel. "Espacio económico e industria textil: Los trabajadores de Nueva España, 1780–1810." *Historia Mexicana* 128 (April–June 1983): 524–53.

Mora, José María Luis. *Memoria que para informar sobre el origen y estado actual de las obras emprendidas para el deságüe de las lagunas del Valle de México.* Mexico City: Imprenta de la Águila, 1823.

———. *Obras sueltas de José María Luis Mora.* Mexico City: Editorial Porrúa, 1963.

Morales, María Dolores. "Estructura urbana y distribución de la propiedad en la ciudad de México en 1813." *Historia Mexicana* 99 (January–March 1976): 363–402.

Moreno Toscano, Alejandra, and Carlos Aguirre Anaya. "Migrations to Mexico City in the Nineteenth Century." *Journal of Interamerican Studies* 17:1 (February 1975): 27–42.

Moreno Valle, Lucina. *Catálogo de la Colección Lafragua 1821–1853.* Mexico City: Instituto de Investigaciones Bibliográficas (UNAM), 1975.

Morton, Ohland. *Teran and Texas: A Chapter in Texas-Mexican Relations.* Austin: Texas State Historical Association, 1948.

Navarrete, Felix. *La masonería en la historia y en las leyes de Méjico.* Mexico City: Editorial Jus, 1957.

O'Gorman, Edmundo. *Historia de las divisiones territoriales de México.* Mexico City: Editorial Porrúa, 1968.

———. *Guía Bibliográfica de Carlos María de Bustamante.* Mexico City: Centro de Estudios de Historia de México (UNAM), 1967.

Olavarría y Ferrari, Enrique. *México independiente 1821–1855.* Vol. 4 of *México á través de los siglos.* Ed. Vicente Riva Palacio. Mexico City: Ballescá y Compañía, and Barcelona: Espasa y Compañía, 1888–1889.

———. *Reseña histórica del teatro en México.* 5 vols. Mexico City: Editorial Porrúa, 1961.

Ortiz de la Tabla, Javier. *Comercio Exterior de Veracruz—1778–1821—Crisis de dependencia.* Seville: Escuela de Estudios Hispano-Americanos, 1978.

Osores, Félix. "Historia de todos los colegios de la ciudad de México desde la conquista hasta 1780, por el Dr. Félix Osores." In *Documentos inéditos ó muy raros para la historia de México,* ed. Genaro García. Mexico City: Editorial Porrúa, 1975.

Parrish, Leonard. "The Life of Nicolás Bravo, Mexican Patriot (1786–1854)." Ph.D. diss., University of Texas, 1951.

Pérez Memén, Fernando. *El espiscopado y la independencia de México 1810–1836.* México: Editorial Jus, 1977.

Pérez Verdía, Luis. *Biografía del Exmo. Sr. don Prisciliano Sánchez. Primer Gobernador Constitucional de Jalisco.* Guadalajara: Tip. de Banda, 1881.

———. *Historia particular del estado de Jalisco.* Vol 2. Guadalajara: Gráfica, 1952.

Platt, D.C.M. "Finanzas Británicas en México (1821–1867)." *Historia Mexicana* 126 (October–December 1982): 226–61.

Potash, Robert A. *El Banco de Avío de México. El fomento de la industria, 1821–1846.* México: Fondo de Cultura Económica, 1959.

Probert, Alan. "Mules, Men and Mining Machinery: Transport on the Veracruz Road." *Journal of the West* 14:2 (1975): 104–13.

Pynes, Russell G. "The Mexican National Army: A Federalist Concept, 1824–1829." M.A. thesis, University of Texas, 1970.

Radin, Paul. "An Annotated Bibliography of the Poems and Pamphlets of Fernández de Lizardi (1824–1827)." *Hispanic American Historical Review* 26 (May 1945): 284–91.

Ramos Escandón, Carmen. "Planes educativos en México independiente 1821–1833." M.A. thesis, University of Texas, 1972.

Randall, Robert W. *Real del Monte. A British Mining Venture in Mexico.* Austin: University of Texas, 1972.

Rasgo analítico de J. Y. E. [José Ygnacio Esteva]. Mexico City: Imprenta del Águila, 1827.

Rawls, James J. *Indians of California: The Changing Image.* Norman: University of Oklahoma Press, 1984.

Rees, Peter W. "Origins of Colonial Transportation in Mexico." *Geographical Review* 65:2 (1975): 323–34.

Reyes Heroles, Jesus. *El liberalismo mexicano.* 3 vols. Mexico City: Universidad Nacional Autónoma de México, 1957–1961.

Richman, Irving Berdine. *California under Spain and Mexico 1535–1847.* New York: Cooper Square Publishers, Inc., 1965.

Ricker, Dennis P. "The Lower Secular Clergy of Central Mexico: 1821–1857." Ph.D. diss., University of Texas, 1982.

Rippy, J. Fred. "Latin America and the British Investment Boom of the 1820's." *Journal of Modern History* 19:2 (June 1947): 122–28.

Rivera Cambas, Manuel. *Historia antigua y moderna de Jalapa y de las revoluciones del estado de Veracruz.* Vols. 2, 3. Mexico City: Imprenta de I. Cumplido, 1869–1870.

Robertson, William Spence. *Iturbide of Mexico.* Durham, N.C.: Duke University Press, 1952.

Rodríguez O., Jaime E. *The Emergence of Spanish America: Vicente Rocafuerte and Spanish Americanism, 1808–1832.* Berkeley and Los Angeles: University of California Press, 1975.

Saldívar, Gabriel. *Historia compendiada de Tamaulipas.* Mexico City: Editorial Beatriz de Silva, 1945.

Samponaro, Frank N. "The Political Role of the Army in Mexico, 1821–1848." Ph.D. diss., University of New York at Stony Brook, 1974.

Sánchez, José María. "A Trip to Texas, 1828. . . ." *Southwestern Historical Quarterly* 30 (April 1926): 249–88.

Sánchez Lamego, Miguel A. *La invasión española de 1829.* Mexico City: Editorial Jus, 1971.

Scardaville, Michael C. "Crime and the Urban Poor: Mexico City in the Late Colonial Period." Ph.D. diss., University of Florida, 1977.

Schwartz, Rosalie. *Across the Rio to Freedom: U.S. Negroes in Mexico.* El Paso: Texas Western Press, 1975.

Shaw, Frederick John, Jr. "Poverty and Politics in Mexico City, 1824–1854." Ph.D. diss., University of Florida, 1975.

Shiels, W. Eugene. "Church and state in the First Decade of Mexican Independence." *Catholic Historical Review* 27 (April 1942–April 1943): 206–28.

Sierra, Catalina. *El nacimiento de México.* Mexico City: Universidad Autónoma de México, 1960.

Sims, Harold. *Descolonización en México; El Conflicto entre mexicanos y españoles (1821– 1831).* Mexico City: Fondo de Cultura Económica, 1982.

———. "The Expulsion of the Spaniards from Mexico, 1827–1828." Ph.D. diss., University of Florida, 1968.

———. "Los exiliados españoles de México en 1829." *Historia Mexicana* 119 (January–March 1981): 390–414.

Smith, Robert S. "The Puebla Consulado, 1821–1824." *Revista de Historia de América* 21:1 (1946): 19–28.

———. "Shipping in the Port of Veracruz, 1790–1821." *Hispanic American Historical Review* 23:1 (August 1943): 5–20.

Smith, Robert S., and José Ramirez Flores. *Los consulados de comerciantes de Nueva España.* Mexico City: Instituto Mexicano de Comercio Exterior, 1976.

Sosa, Francisco. *Biografías de mexicanos distinguidos.* Mexico City: Oficina tipográfica de la Secretaría de Fomento, 1884.

Spell, Jefferson R. *The Life and Works of José Joaquín Fernández de Lizardi.* Philadelphia, 1931.

Spell, Lota M. "Gorostiza and Texas." *Hispanic American Historical Review* 37 (November 1957): 415–62.

Spielman, Lynda Carol. "Mexican Pamphleteering and the Rise of the Mexican Nation, 1808–1830." Ph.D. diss., Indiana University, 1975.

Sprague, William Forrest. *Vicente Guerrero, Mexican liberator; A study in patriotism.* Chicago: Printed by R. R. Donnelley & Sons, 1939.

Staples, Anne F. "La cola del diablo en la vida conventual (Los conventos de monjas del arzobispado de México, 1823–1835)." Ph.D. diss., El Colegio de México, 1970.

———. *La iglesia en la primera república federal mexicana (1824–1835).* Mexico City: Editorial SepSetentas, 1976.

Stevens, Robert. "Mexico's Forgotten Frontier: A History of Sonora, 1821–1846." Ph.D. diss., University of California, Berkeley, 1963.

Suárez y Navarro, Juan. *Historia de México y del General Antonio López de Santa Anna.* 2 vols. Mexico City: Imprenta de Ignacio Cumplido, 1850–1851.

Tanck Estrada, Dorothy. *La educación ilustrada (1786–1836).* Mexico City: El Colegio de México, 1977.

———. "Las Cortes de Cádiz y el desarrollo de la educación en México." *Historia Mexicana* 113 (July–September 1979): 3–34.

———. "Las escuelas Lancasterianas en la ciudad de México: 1822–1844." *Historia Mexicana* 88 (April–June 1973): 494–514.

Tandrón, Humberto. "The Commerce of New Spain and the Free Trade Controversy." M.A. thesis, University of Texas, 1961.

Taylor, James William. "Socio-economic Instability and the Revolution for Mexican Independence in the Province of Guanajuato." Ph.D. diss., University of New Mexico, 1976.

Tays, George. "Revolutionary California: The Political History of California during the Mexican period, 1822–1846." Ph.D. diss., University of California, 1932.

Thomson, Guy P. C. "La colonización en el Departamento de Acayucán 1824–1834." *Historia Mexicana* 94 (October–December 1974): 253–98.

Tijerina, Andrew Anthony. "Tejanos and Texas: The Native Mexicans of Texas, 1820–1850." Ph.D. diss., University of Texas, 1977.

Timmons, Wilbert H. *Tadeo Ortiz*. El Paso: Texas Western Press, 1974.

Tornel y Mendívil, José María. *Breve reseña histórica de los acontecimientos más notables de la nación mexicana, desde el año de 1821 hasta nuestros días.* . . . Mexico City: Imprenta de Cumplido, 1852.

Trens, Manuel Bartolomé Marentes. *Historia de Chiapas; Desde los tiempos más remotos hasta la caída del Segundo Imperio.* Vol. 1. 2d ed. Mexico City: Talleres Gráficos de la Nación, 1957.

———. *Historia de Veracruz*. 3 vols. Jalapa: Jalapa-Enríquez, 1948.

Treviño, Jesus, Jr., "Attempts at Organizing and Reforming the Mexican National Army, 1821–1824." M.A. thesis, University of Texas, 1969.

True, C. Allen. "British Loans to the Mexican Government 1822–1832." *Southwestern Social Science Quarterly* 17 (1937): 353–62.

Tyler, Daniel. "The Mexican Teacher." *Red River Valley Historical Review* 1 (Autumn 1974): 207–21.

———. "New Mexico in the 1820's: The First Administration of Manuel Armijo." Ph.D. diss., University of New Mexico, 1970.

Valadés, José C. *Alamán, estadista e historiador*. Mexico City: Antigua Librería Robredo, J. Porrúa e hijos, 1938.

———. *México, Santa Anna, y la guerra de Texas*. 3d ed. Mexico City: Editores Mexicanos Unidos, 1965.

———. *Orígenes de la república mexicana*. Mexico City: Editores Mexicanos Unidos, 1972.

Van Young, Eric. *Hacienda and Market in Eighteenth-Century Mexico: The Rural Economy of the Guadalajara Region, 1675–1820*. Berkeley and Los Angeles: University of California Press, 1981.

Velasquez, Primo Feliciano. *Historia de San Luis Potosí*. Vol. 3. Mexico City: Sociedad Mexicana de Geografía y Estadística, 1947.

Vizcaya Canales, Isidro. "Monterrey, los primeros años después de la independencia." *Humanitás* (University of Nuevo León) 11 (1970): 531–38.

Walters, Paul H. "Secularization of the La Bahía missions." *Southwestern Historical Quarterly* 54:3 (January 1951): 287–300.

Weber, David J. "Failure of a Frontier Institution: The Secular Church in the Borderlands under Independent Mexico, 1821–1846." *The Western Historical Quarterly* 12:2 (April 1981): 125–43.

———. "Mexico's Far Northern Frontier, 1821–1854: Historiography Askew." *The Western Historical Quarterly* 7:3 (July 1976): 279–93.

———. *The Taos Trappers: The Fur Trade in the Far Southwest, 1540–1846*. Norman: University of Oklahoma Press, 1971.

Wilkinson, Joseph B. *Laredo and the Rio Grande Frontier*. Austin: Jenkins Publishing Co., 1975.

Wrangel, F. P. *De Sitka á San Petersburgo á través de Mexico*. México: SepSetentas, 1975.

Wyllie [Willie], Robert C. *Mexico City—Noticia sobre su hacienda pública bajo el gobierno español y después de la independencia*. Mexico City: Imprenta de Ignacio Cumplido, 1845.

Zalce y Rodríguez, L. J. *Apuntes para la historia de la masonería en México* 2 vols. Mexico City: 1950.

Index

Pitt Latin American Series
Cole Blasier, Editor

ARGENTINA

Argentina in the Twentieth Century
David Rock, Editor

Discreet Partners: Argentina and the USSR Since 1917
Aldo César Vacs

Juan Perón and the Reshaping of Argentina
Frederick C. Turner and José Enrique Miguens, Editors

The Life, Music, and Times of Carlos Gardel
Simon Collier

BRAZIL

The Politics of Social Security in Brazil
James M. Malloy

Urban Politics in Brazil: The Rise of Populism, 1925–1945
Michael L. Conniff

COLOMBIA

Gaitán of Colombia: A Political Biography
Richard E. Sharpless

Roads to Reason: Transportation, Administration, and Rationality in Colombia
Richard E. Hartwig

CUBA

Army Politics in Cuba, 1898–1958
Louis A. Pérez, Jr.

Cuba Under the Platt Amendment, 1902–1934
Louis A. Pérez, Jr.

Cuba Between Empires, 1878–1902
Louis A. Pérez, Jr.

Cuba, Castro, and the United States
Philip W. Bonsal

Cuba in the World
Cole Blasier and Carmelo Mesa-Lago, Editors

Cuban Studies, Vol. 16
Carmelo Mesa-Lago, Editor

Intervention, Revolution, and Politics in Cuba, 1913–1921
Louis A. Pérez, Jr.